The Making of a Hinterland

The Making of a Hinterland

State, Society, and Economy in Inland North China, 1853–1937

Kenneth Pomeranz

UNIVERSITY OF CALIFORNIA PRESS
Berkeley • Los Angeles • Oxford

This book is a print-on-demand volume. It is manufactured using toner in place of ink. Type and images may be less sharp than the same material seen in traditionally printed University of California Press editions.

University of California Press
Berkeley and Los Angeles, California

University of California Press, Ltd.
Oxford, England

© 1993 by
The Regents of the University of California

Library of Congress Cataloging-in-Publication Data

Pomeranz, Kenneth.
   The making of a hinterland : state, society, and economy in inland
North China, 1853–1937 / Kenneth Pomeranz.
        p.   cm.
   Includes bibliographical references and index.
   ISBN 0-520-08051-3 (alk. paper)
   1. Shantung Province (China)—Economic policy.   2. Shantung
Province (China)—Economic conditions.   I. Title.
HC428.S52P66   1993
338.951'14—dc20   92-17008
                                                                   CIP

Printed in the United States of America

To my parents, who rarely told me what to do,
but nonetheless showed me how; and to
Benjamin, who helped more than he knows.

Contents

Illustrations

Photographs following page 152

Tables

Acknowledgments

It is hard to say when this book began. One answer would be autumn 1979, when, as a college senior, I wandered into Sherman Cochran's Chinese history course. By the end of the term, I wanted to make a career of Chinese history; and Sherm has been an invaluable teacher, critic, adviser, and friend ever since. In graduate school, I was lucky enough to find mentors willing to tolerate an eccentric latecomer to Chinese studies and to help me through the many obstacles that lay ahead. Jonathan Spence and Beatrice Bartlett did everything one could ask from advisers, and more; and both have remained friends and teachers since I left Yale. Two other people I studied with at Yale—John Merriman and James Scott—have also been particularly helpful; though neither works on China, the influence of both should be evident throughout the book.

As a proposal turned slowly into a dissertation and then a book, many other people added helpful comments. Foremost among these scholars is R. Bin Wong, who read and discussed what must have seemed to be endless versions of the text; if there are better colleagues than he, I am unaware of them. Many others—Emily Honig, James Lee, Peter Lindert, Don McCloskey, Tom Rawski, James Scott, and the participants in an April 1989 workshop of the Southern California China Colloquium—commented helpfully on draft chapters, papers that were later incorporated into the work, and other fragments. As a manuscript reader for the University of California Press, Joseph Esherick provided comments that led to a much stronger final version of the book; the other, anonymous, reader was also extremely helpful.

At the research stage, I benefited from access to a number of libraries and archives and from contact with helpful staff members. In the United States, I found rare materials at Sterling Library (Yale), Starr East Asian Library (Columbia), the Harvard-Yenching Library, Library of Congress, Charles W. Wason Collection (Cornell), Bentley Historical Library (University of Michigan), UCLA, and the New York Public Library. In China, I was welcomed at the libraries of Shandong University, Shandong Normal University, People's University, Beijing University, and Nanjing University, and at the Shandong Provincial Library, the Beijing Library, the Capital (Shoudu) Library, the Library of the Chinese Academy of Social Sciences, and the First and Second Historical Archives of China. Special thanks are due to Wei Qingyuan and Ju Deyuan for the help they provided at the First Historical Archives. I am also grateful to the Bentley Historical Library for making it possible to use in this book several photographs from the Clifton O'Neal Carey papers.

Along the way, this project has received an ample share of institutional and financial support. The Yale Council on East Asian Studies provided fellowship support during most of the research and writing; the Committee on Scholarly Communication with the People's Republic of China made essential arrangements for a year's research in China; and final touches have been added during a research leave (mostly devoted to a new project) supported by the ACLS-SSRC Joint Committee on Chinese Studies and the University of California President's Research Fellowship. My editors at the University of California Press, Sheila Levine and Amy Klatzkin, have been as helpful and pleasant to work with as any author could wish. As copyeditor, Joanne Sandstrom ironed out numerous infelicities and found creative solutions to problems I had never noticed.

Thanks are also due to various people who fall into none of the above categories. David Pattinson provided a new copy of a crucial document that I somehow lost after leaving Jinan. Alan MacDonald and Jeni Umble each took a turn at rescuing me from word-processing disasters; Hod Finklestein made possible a legible version of figure 1.

Finally, Maureen Graves has done more than anyone—as sounding board, reader, and most of all, companion—to make this book possible; I cannot imagine it, or the years during which it took shape, without her.

A Note on Place Names

The Chinese words for jurisdictional units have been translated in the conventional manner: *fu* is rendered as "prefecture" and *xian* as "county." The term *xian* is appended to place names only when the name would otherwise be monosyllabic or ambiguous. The term *zhili zhou* (literally, "independent district"), has been translated as "county" when it refers to a district encompassing a single county and "prefecture" when it refers to a district encompassing multiple counties (e.g., the four-county units centered on Linqing and Jining). The province north of Shandong, which was Zhili until 1927 and Hebei afterward, is identified by the usage of the period discussed in a given passage, or occasionally by Zhili/Hebei. The city of Liaocheng, once known as Dongchangfu, has been rendered as Liaocheng throughout, reserving the name Dongchangfu for the prefecture of which it was the capital.

Abbreviations and Technical Notes on Selected Sources

AH   *anjuan hao.* Subdivider for files in Second Historical Archives, Nanjing.

CZGB   *Shandong caizheng gongbao.*

DFZZ   *Dongfang zazhi.*

Dissertation   Pomeranz, Kenneth. "The Making of a Hinterland: State, Society, and Economy in Inland North China, 1900–1937." Ph.D. dissertation, Yale University, 1988.

GCIC   Freeman, John Ripley. *Grand Canal Investigations.* Typescript, 1921; version held at library of Cornell University.

GCIM   Freeman, John Ripley. *Grand Canal Investigations.* Typescript, 1921; version held at library of University of Michigan.

GX   Guangxu reign (1875–1908).

HBMCLB   *Hebei mianchan lu bao.* Readers may be puzzled to see a number of points concerning events in Shandong supported by references to this Hebei journal; these pages come from the magazine's "cotton news from other provinces" section, which emphasized Shandong events.

HH	Shulibu, Huang He shuili weiyuanhui. *Huang He shuili shi shuyao* (Outline of the history of Yellow River water conservancy). Beijing: Shuili dianli chubanshe, 1984.
HWJB	*Hewu jibao.* This magazine also had a slightly irregular publishing schedule, and not all the issues I read had their covers; individual government orders reprinted in the magazine are usually dated, but the longer reports sometimes are not.
HWTK	*Shandong hewu tekan.*
JD	*jiguan daihao.* Reference number for files in Second Historical Archives, Nanjing.
JSGB	*Shandong jianshe gongbao.*
JSYK	*Shandong jianshe yuekan.*
LFZZ	Junjichu lufu zouzhe. Grand Council archival collection at First Historical Archives, Beijing.
NCH	*North China Herald.*
NSGB	*Nong shang gongbao.*
NYHH	Shandong Nan Yun Hu He su jun shiyi zhoubanchu. *Diyijie baogao* (Shandong Canal and Lake Dredging and Restoration Board, first report). Jinan(?), 1915.
OEI	Shandong Office to Encourage Industry (Quanyesuo).
QYHK	*Shandong quanye huikan.* This magazine had a slightly irregular publishing schedule, and covers were missing from many of the issues used, but in almost all cases, the exact publication date was verifiable; where this was not the case, publication dates could at least be fixed within one month.
QZ	*quanzong hao.* Reference number for files in Second Historical Archives, Nanjing.

RO   Shandong Reconstruction Office (Jiansheju).

SDXZJSSYQGB   *Shandong sheng xian zheng jianshe shiyanqu gongbao.*

SDZZ   *Shandong zazhi.*

SS   Tōa Dobunkai, *Shina Shōbetsu Zenshi* (The provinces of China). Vol. 4: *Shandong.* Tokyo: Tōa Dobunkai 1918.

SSYZ   Zhongguo shiyebu, guoji maoyiju. *Zhongguo shiye zhi, Shandong sheng* (Industrial gazetteer of China, Shandong province). 1934.

THS   Chintao Shubigun Minseibu Tetsudōbu. *Tōhoku Santō (Bokkai Santō Engan Shokō Iken Chīfū Kan Toshi)* (Northeast Shandong [all ports on Shandong's Bohai coast, and cities between Wei Xian and Yantai]). Chōsa Hōkoku Sho (Chōsa Shiryō 17) (Research report [research materials no. 17]). Qingdao: Chintao Shubigan Minseibu Tetsudōbu, 1919.

XCJSXK   *Xiangcun jianshe xunkan/Xiangcun jianshe banyuekan.* Magazine changed from every ten days to every two weeks in 1935, and name changed accordingly, but numbering remained consecutive. Because of missing covers of many issues of *XCJSXK* and the magazine's slightly irregular publication schedule, the exact day of publication for issues was often impossible to fix; however, the month of publication usually could be easily confirmed.

XT   Xuantong reign (1909–12).

YRO   Shandong Yellow River Office (Hewuju).

Introduction

The modern world is unimaginable without the nation-state and national and international markets, and the "integration" of localities into these huge structures is often taken as a crucial measure of "modernization." But that does not mean that earlier societies were made up of discrete and isolated communities. Late imperial China, for instance, had its own large-scale economic networks, which created integrated macroregions larger than most countries.[1] And although the empire could not match the modern nation-state's power to override local particularities, it did direct important flows of people, resources, and ideas across its entire territory. Nor were these earlier networks just clumsy precursors of modern states and markets; they linked a world that was knit together for different reasons and by a different logic.

Creating a modern state and national economy in post-1850 China involved the disruption of these older networks in the process of building new, even larger, and often stronger ones. Both activities were carried out largely by Chinese, though in the context of Western imperialism. Within that context, the state's new networks and its interventions in the economy were increasingly oriented toward new goals. Officials sought to produce and mobilize wealth for the inter-

1. See G. William Skinner, "Cities and the Hierarchy of Local Systems," in *The City in Late Imperial China*, ed. G. William Skinner (Stanford, 1977), 273–351, esp. 275–88.

national competition into which China had been forced by imperialism rather than to reproduce a Confucian society, as their predecessors
had. This new statecraft changed both the tasks the state cared about
and the places it considered most important. As China's position
changed, so did positions within China: both the geographic boundaries of regional cores and peripheries and the political and economic
implications for a community of being in a core or periphery.

This is the story of one Chinese region's wrenching transition from
a vital position in these older networks to a peripheral position in new,
stronger ones. The region—which I call Huang-Yun and define in
more detail below—is a large inland portion of the North China plain.
Its transition is symbolized by a technological change: the replacement
of the Grand Canal, which this region straddled, by railroads and
steamships, which ran near but not through the area. However, both
the causes and the results of this transition went much deeper.

Huang-Yun was for centuries part of the core of the North China
macroregion.[2] However, the decline of the canal and the increased
importance of coastal trade—particularly Manchurian and foreign
trade—created new core areas on the Shandong peninsula and turned
most of Huang-Yun into part of the periphery. This was the largest
displacement of any macroregion's core by the rise of the coastal

2. Joseph Esherick argues that the Shandong part of South Huang-Yun was in fact
part of the lower Yangzi (*Origins of the Boxer Uprising* [Berkeley, 1987], 5–7), but his
argument seems to me flawed, at least for the twentieth century. The area's high population density and high yields per acre suggest a core, and the fact that they are higher
than those for Huaibei, which is closer to the Lower Yangzi core, would create an anomalous pattern if the area were part of that macroregion. And while he notes periodic
flows of disaster victims from this area toward the Lower Yangzi core, my impression of
the twentieth-century data is that such people were more inclined to head for Manchuria. Moreover, other kinds of migrants from this area were definitely inclined to head for
other parts of the North China macroregion. The area's numerous sectarians did their
evangelizing in northwest Shandong and Zhili and targeted Linqing in their uprisings
throughout the eighteenth to twentieth centuries. At least in the twentieth century, most
of the area's most prominent people pursued careers and invested their money in Jinan,
Beijing, and Tianjin rather than, say, Shanghai.

While some problems arise either way, it still seems to me reasonable to retain Skinner's delineation of the North China macroregion and its core. As Esherick notes (p. 6)
the canal made macroregional boundaries in this area unusually fuzzy and permeable;
were a few counties at the edges of South Huang-Yun to be added to the Lower Yangzi,
this would not affect the central thrust of my argument. G. William Skinner, who first
developed the model of Chinese macroregions, is now reconsidering the shape of the
North China region based on twentieth-century data; however, it seems to me likely
that something like his original formulation should hold up well for the Ming and early
Qing, before North China's links to Manchuria assumed their present importance. That
such a model does not fit more recent data well underscores the fundamental nature of
the changes described in this volume.

economy.[3] This abstract-sounding process seriously disturbed people's lives. For instance, Huang-Yun's residents began to have trouble obtaining stone and wood, which were badly needed for flood control and fuel. As a long-time core, Huang-Yun had a population density that precluded self-sufficiency in these vital commodities; but as a newly peripheral area, no longer well-served by water transport, it could not import them.

The new political economy both helped and hurt Huang-Yun. In terms of trade, Huang-Yun benefited from becoming the hinterland of a more dynamic core; it might have benefited even more if local elites in South Huang-Yun had not obstructed incorporation into wider markets for credit and other resources. But if we look at resources distributed through nonmarket means—such as flood-control services, the building of infrastructure, or reforestation programs—Huang-Yun had been far better off before the new foreign trade, technologies, and threats of the late 1800s drew the state's attention to the coast and away from Huang-Yun.

The foreign onslaught destroyed basic principles of Ming-Qing statecraft, particularly a commitment to social reproduction that had often required rich areas to subsidize the infrastructure of poorer ones. Instead, foreign pressures helped impart a quasi-mercantilist logic to the actions of a state that was struggling to survive. Resources had to be used where they did the most to protect China's threatened autonomy from direct intervention or the consequences of foreign debt or both. By this logic, maintaining basic services in Huang-Yun became unimportant; alleviating the problems of such a low-priority area by sending it goods (such as timber) or services (such as hydraulic engineering) from abroad was actually harmful. In retrospect, we can see that this reorientation had enormous welfare costs; and since the Chinese Revolution eventually grew from hinterland bases, it also

3. Shanghai and Hong Kong did indeed spring up from a small town and a wasteland, respectively, but they were both very close to long-established core areas. Qingdao was at least close to the edge of what Skinner considers to have been the North China core even before the arrival of the West, but it was roughly ten days from Jinan before the building of the railroad, and even further from other important cities of the "core." Yantai, which boomed (at least temporarily) as a result of the foreign impact, was even further from pre-1850 core cities and was in fact more closely tied to Manchuria; Weihaiwei had been almost completely isolated. Conversely, certain riverine towns in other coastal macroregions, such as Yangzhou, may have been increasingly overshadowed by other Yangzi Valley cities after the Opium War, but they never became nearly as isolated as Huang-Yun's once-booming Linqing, Liaocheng, or Huaxian.

seems dubious as a state-building strategy. Amidst the crises of the time, however, the new course probably seemed obvious or inevitable or both; few voices were heard advocating anything else.

One cannot assess even the economic impact of imperialism without considering this fundamental change in statecraft. For many parts of China, the post-1850 switch to a mercantilist orientation was a more important regime change than those of 1911 or 1928, one with profound economic implications. Instead of comparing gains from trade only to direct economic losses, such as Huang-Yun's Boxer Indemnity payments or its spending on imported opium, we will also try to measure what Huang-Yun lost when a hard-pressed state stopped underwriting the area's infrastructure.

This sketch of the new political economy introduces three of the major themes of this study. The first is Huang-Yun's increasing, though very uneven, integration into markets focused on the treaty ports. The second is the disintegration of some of the area's older economic ties based on the Grand Canal, which had served as a subsidized channel for ecologically vital imports (for example, timber), and the failure of new networks to replace those imports. The third is the national government's abandonment of the area's hydraulic system— not only the Grand Canal, but also the Yellow River.

A fourth theme springs from an obvious but often neglected point: Huang-Yun was not a blank slate for state and market makers to write on. The sundering of old networks was largely the work of outsiders, but some localities were better equipped than others to resist it. Furthermore, the destruction of old networks did not guarantee incorporation into new ones. Struggles developed between supporters and opponents of greater participation in new markets and other networks. The outcome of these battles depended on local social structures, which differed sharply between North and South Huang-Yun; thus, so did the extent and experience of incorporation into supraregional markets and into the modern state that provincial and national governments were fitfully building.

THE TERRITORY

The region studied here had no official name, but by 1900 it had at least fifteen million people. I call it Huang-Yun, after the two waterways (the Yellow River and the Grand Canal) that intersect in the middle of it and shaped its ecology, economy, and politics. Most of it consists of western Shandong plus adjacent parts of Zhili (renamed Hebei in 1928) and Henan (map 1). China's two north-south railways, both built in the early twentieth century, help mark its boundaries: it runs from the Tianjin-Pukou railway in the east to the Beijing-Hankou railway in the west and from Shandong's southern border to slightly beyond its northern one. (One could, in fact, also include the northernmost part of Jiangsu; I have not done so, for reasons of both space and source limitations.) Using later, east-west railways, the region lies between the Dezhou-Shijiazhuang line, planned in 1898 but not built until after 1949, and the Long-Hai railway (which was begun in 1915, reached the coast in 1924, and was extended to Xi'an in 1934).[4]

A much older north-south link—the Grand Canal—also defined the region: not by bounding it, but by running through the middle of it. Thus, in the heyday of the canal, Huang-Yun had surrounded "the throat (*yanhou*) of China." As the canal declined, railroads and steamships that skirted Huang-Yun connected North and South China; they allowed Huang-Yun to interact with a larger world than ever, but from an increasingly marginal position.

Thus, while it is convenient for this discussion that railroads surround Huang-Yun, they did not help create it the way the canal did. In some places, rail lines ran alongside natural features that help define Huang-Yun (for example, the Yi-Meng mountains just beyond the Tianjin-Pukou railway or the Taihang mountains just west of the Beijing-Hankou line). In other cases they provide convenient but coincidental proxies for socioeconomic divisions. For instance, the Beijing-Hankou line ran just to the west of Huaxian; as the westernmost city to rise and fall with the Grand Canal (to which it was linked by the Wei River), Huaxian is also an outer limit of Huang-Yun.[5] In still other cases, the rail lines help to mark the new networks to which Huang-Yun was marginal. The Tianjin-Pukou line just east of Huang-Yun ran through Jinan, Shandong's capital; Jinan was also the western terminus of a railroad to the booming new port of Qingdao. Because Shandong narrows to a peninsula not far east of Jinan, almost every-

4. See Ralph Huenemann, *The Dragon and the Iron Horse* (Cambridge, Mass., 1984), 86–88, and the map at the front of Liu Jinyi, *Zhongguo tielu chuangjian bai nian shi* (Taibei, 1981).

5. On Huaxian, see Odoric Y. K. Wou, "Development, Underdevelopment and Degeneration: The Introduction of Rail Transport into Honan," *Asian Profile* 12:3 (June 1984), 215–30.

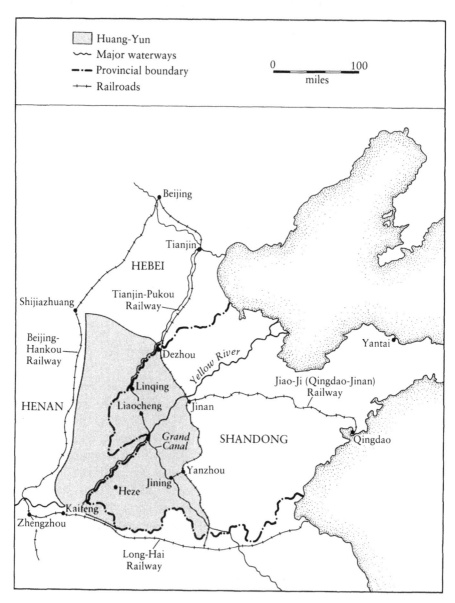

Map 1.   Huang-Yun (using largest possible boundaries) in North China

thing further east was near either the coast or the railway. Thus, these areas were strongly linked to the dynamic and contested areas of coastal North China and Manchuria, while Huang-Yun is in part defined by its weak links to coastal boom areas.

On a contemporary map, then, the region may look peculiar, since it is *bounded* by railroads and by important central places like Jinan and Shijiazhuang. But that is part of the point. Before the railroads, when Shijiazhuang was a village and Jining, Linqing, Liaocheng, and Huaxian were cities rivaling Jinan,[6] Huang-Yun was part of the North China core[7] and had dense internal networks. As transport lines emerged, were redrawn, or disappeared, the area fragmented; North Huang-Yun became oriented toward Tianjin, Qingdao, and other growing cities beyond its edges, and South Huang-Yun became an isolated backwater. The area as a whole came to share only a common experience based on some dubious distinctions: a particularly dramatic abandonment by the Chinese state and exceptionally widespread poverty.[8]

The Grand Canal was the centerpiece of an enormous hydraulic system, other parts of which also help define Huang-Yun. Of the many rivers the canal crossed, the hardest to control was the Yellow River. After that river shifted course in 1852–55, it ran through the center of this region; Huang-Yun extends roughly one hundred miles north and one hundred miles south from where these two waterways meet. The northern and southern borders of Huang-Yun defined above are also rough boundaries of the belt in which the Yellow River was the

6. See, for instance, the ranking of North China urban places circa 1843 in Skinner, "Regional Urbanization in Nineteenth-Century China," in *The City in Late Imperial China*, ed. G. William Skinner, 238; rankings circa 1800 in Gilbert Rozman, *Urban Networks in Qing China and Tokugawa Japan* (Princeton, 1973), 204, 214; and David Buck, *Urban Change in China* (Madison, 1978), pp. 21–23.

7. Compare, for instance, the map on pp. 214–15 of Skinner, "Regional Urbanization." Also note the discussion of Daming merchants in Skinner, "Cities and the Hierarchy of Local Systems," 343, where Skinner argues that the state deliberately drew boundaries to diffuse the influence of these merchants, whose networks spanned Huang-Yun.

8. Huang-Yun's exceptional poverty persists to this day, except in a small area (near Puyang) where oil was found in the 1980s. See, for instance, the map on 26–27 of E. B. Vermeer, "Income Differentials in Rural China," *China Quarterly* 89 (March 1982), 26–27, which uses dots to mark the counties in which per capita income from agricultural collectives fell below ¥50 in 1977, 1978, and 1979; about one-fifth of all the dots for China proper are in Huang-Yun, and several more are in counties immediately south and east of the region.

principal flood problem. Although some Yellow River floods did touch northern Jiangsu and people there sometimes worried that the river would return to that province (where it had been between 1188 and 1852), the Huai River was a greater threat. People north of Huang-Yun also worried about the Yellow River jumping its banks, but they too were more often victimized by other rivers. But in Huang-Yun itself, all of the many flood dangers were in some way part of the Yellow River problem.

The most flood-prone part of the Yellow River was its delta. Geologically, this began four hundred miles from the ocean, near Kaifeng, the Beijing-Hankou railway, and the western boundary of Huang-Yun.[9] The first two hundred miles of that delta lie in Huang-Yun. That stretch differs from the river's final two hundred miles largely because it lacks the convenient riverside quarries that exist further downstream. This difference need not have been a critical one, but human decisions made it so: institutional changes inaugurated in 1891 effectively denied Huang-Yun stone imports for its dikes and in various ways made this the most neglected and dangerous part of the Yellow River.

Huang-Yun can also be placed on a sociological and historiographical map. It begins at the northern fringe of the Huaibei region studied by Elizabeth Perry and runs north to overlap the southwestern portion of the areas explored by Philip Huang, Ramon Myers, Prasenjit Duara, and others (map 2). It bridges these areas thematically, too. Our emphases on central government neglect, chronic instability, and environmental crisis recall Perry's account of Huaibei, while we also note the ongoing commercialization and twentieth-century local state making described by Myers, Huang, and Duara.

This rich historiography on areas that overlap parts of Huang-Yun helps clarify the significance of differences within the region. The different social structures in North and South Huang-Yun—roughly divided by the Yellow River—decisively shaped their responses to the new threats and opportunities of the late Qing and the Republic. North Huang-Yun had a sparser population, less intensive (but more commercialized) farming, a relatively even distribution of wealth, weak rural elites, weak village communities, and very few residents with

---

9. John Ripley Freeman, "Flood Problems in China," *Proceedings of the American Society of Civil Engineers*, May 1922, p. 1122.

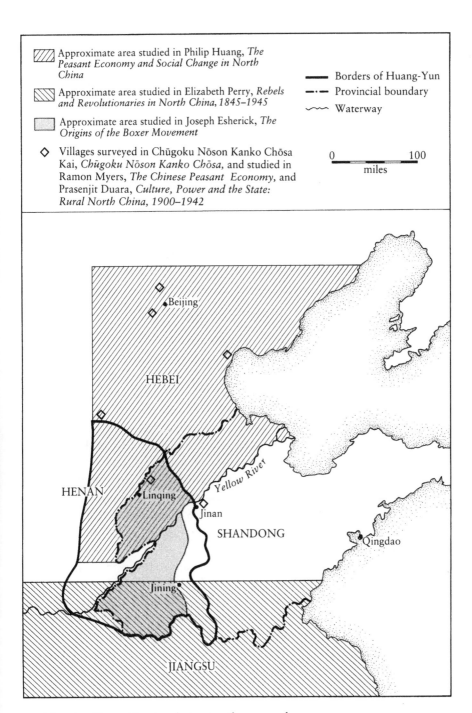

Map 2.   Huang-Yun in relation to other research

influence beyond the region. South Huang-Yun had a higher population density and higher crop yields per *mu* (one-sixth of an acre) but lower output per person. Wealth was more unevenly distributed, and rural elites were very strong; villages often resembled independent kingdoms. South Huang-Yun, particularly Jining, produced quite a few urban gentry and merchants with provincial or national influence; often, however, these same urban elites could not influence the strong rural elites in their own immediate hinterlands. Consequently, South Huang-Yun did slightly better than North Huang-Yun in tapping older networks for resources to support such traditional activities as water control; but it proved far more resistant to incorporation into new networks and to administrative and economic rationalization.

Some of the social differences between North and South Huang-Yun are discussed in the book whose territory most resembles Huang-Yun: Joseph Esherick's study of the Boxer movement (1895–1900), which argues that these areas produced two very different kinds of "Boxers."[10] I build on his analysis in at least two ways. First, I add an account of urban differences between these areas and look at how these urban differences refracted influences from the wider world. Then I argue that after 1900, the same rural differences that Esherick notes shaped the local responses to a number of important trends and urban-sponsored initiatives—from the introduction of new crop varieties to provincial water projects—in ways that were consistent across many cases and so generated two distinct patterns of development. Thus, Huang-Yun allows us to contrast the effects of similar events on relatively "permeable" (North Huang-Yun) and "impermeable" (South Huang-Yun) communities. (The usual terminology of "open" and "closed" communities strikes me as not fully adequate for Huang-Yun or for the twentieth century; the reasons will be discussed in chapter 2.)

Studying this region also demands a new approach to the effects of imperialism on North China. Huang-Yun's experience of imperialism differed from the experiences of two types of areas that have received far more attention. On the one hand are those areas for which we have foreign, especially Japanese, surveys; these places were usually close to modern transport. Studies based on those surveys tend to emphasize the penetration of villages by the state and the international market,

10. Esherick, *Boxer Uprising*.

even if these efforts proved abortive.[11] On the other hand, Perry's Huaibei and the Taihang mountain area studied by Ralph Thaxton were barely touched by the treaty-port economy; the main impact of imperialism in such remote areas was probably to further distract a national government that had never paid them much attention anyway. In Huang-Yun, however, the economic stimulus of coastal developments and the costs of becoming an underruled region were experienced together.

Consequently, Huang-Yun's story can also contribute to the continuing debate about the nature and significance of regional units in China. Two hypotheses now enjoy wide currency. One, pioneered by G. William Skinner, argues that for centuries China was composed of eight physiographic macroregions (plus Manchuria), each largely self-sufficient, with its own internal division of labor between core and periphery.[12] These regions were loosely bound together by a common culture and a national state; the latter was particularly weak after 1916. Other scholars, however, have suggested the existence of a national market and economy, even in many bulky, hard-to-transport staple goods. Wu Chengming, Peng Zeyi, and William Rowe argue that the outlines of such an economy are visible by the eighteenth century. Thomas Rawski, Loren Brandt, and others focus on the twentieth century and argue that despite political disunity, China was tied together by national and international markets that transcended macroregions. Moreover, improved communication and transportation allowed workers, traders, and investors to go where they perceived opportunities, reshuffling regional divisions of labor.[13]

11. Ramon H. Myers, *The Chinese Peasant Economy* (Cambridge, Mass., 1970); Prasenjit Duara, *Culture, Power, and the State: Rural North China, 1900–1942* (Stanford, 1988); Philip Huang, *The Peasant Economy and Social Change in North China* (Stanford, 1985), are among the many important works based on the South Manchuria Railroad studies that will be referred to repeatedly in this essay. For a study based on a different set of very accessible villages, but showing similar trends, see Sidney Gamble, *North China Villages* (Berkeley, 1963).

12. For Skinner's original statement of his hypothesis, see "Marketing and Social Structure in Rural China," *Journal of Asian Studies* 24:1–3 (Nov. 1964–May 1965), 3–44, 195–228, 363–99. The subsequent article most relevant to our discussion is Skinner, "Cities and the Hierarchy," 275–351.

13. See Wu Chengming, *Zhongguo zibenzhuyi de mengya* (Beijing, 1985) and "Woguo banzhimindi ban fengjian guonei shichang," *Lishi yanjiu*, no. 168 (April 1984), 110–21; Peng Zeyi, "Qingdai qianqi shougongye de fazhan," *Zhongguo shi yanjiu* no. 1 (1981), 43–60; William Rowe, *Hankow: Commerce and Society in a Chinese City* (Stanford, 1984); on the twentieth century, see Loren Brandt, "Chinese Agriculture and the International Economy, 1870s–1930s: A Reassessment," *Explorations in Economic*

This debate cannot, of course, be decided by one more regional study, particularly one entirely contained within one Skinnerian macroregion. Nor is Huang-Yun a spatial unit in Skinner's sense: an interdependent, largely self-contained area whose natural boundaries provide an invariant unit of analysis for most social phenomena over a very long time. Instead it is an area defined by shared infrastructural, ecological, and social problems. These problems did not all begin, end, or peak in precisely the same places. The problems also changed significantly over time; the intersection of the Yellow River and Grand Canal was itself outside the region until the 1850s. The boundaries of an area described by such a shared experience are inherently less exact and permanent than those of either a physiographic macroregion or a nation-state. But precisely because this approach highlights one area's changing relations with larger units, it can shed light on both the macroregional and national market analyses of late Qing and Republican China.

Because Huang-Yun relied on long-distance, canal-borne trade before 1850 and lost much of that trade thereafter, it fits neither the model of self-sufficient macroregions nor that of increasing national integration. The new markets that touched twentieth-century Huang-Yun may have been becoming nationwide or even worldwide, but they still had far to go; and while the notion of a division of labor between macroregional cores and peripheries clarifies many aspects of Huang-Yun's position in the larger political economy, it also leads to a puzzle: different areas appear to have been more "core-like" depending on what criteria we emphasize. Some possible modifications of the core-periphery model and our ways of defining spatial units are suggested in the Conclusion.

THE TIME FRAME

Japan's 1937 invasion of North China provides a logical end for this study; when to begin was less clear. Much of our story began in the

---

History 22:2 (April 1985), 168–93; Thomas Gottschaung, "Migration from North China to Manchuria: An Economic History, 1891–1942" (Ph.D. dissertation, University of Michigan, 1982); Thomas G. Rawski, *Economic Growth in Prewar China* (Berkeley, 1989); and numerous other studies. For a criticism of Skinner's model from this perspective, see Ramon H. Myers and Barbara N. Sands, "The Spatial Approach to Chinese History," *Journal of Asian Studies* 45:4 (Aug. 1986), 721–44.

1850s with the Yellow River shift, the opening of the treaty ports, the relaxation of curbs on Manchurian settlement, and the Taiping Rebellion, which changed the state's relationship to the revenue-surplus Lower Yangzi region. For subjects such as ecological decay, a still longer time frame has advantages; brief discussions of earlier periods are included where they seem essential. All the trends discussed here accelerated greatly after 1890, however, and even more after 1900. Thus, faced with an ungainly subject threatening to grow larger, I have stressed events after 1890 and treat earlier ones as background.

A quick list of events suggests many ways in which Huang-Yun entered a new era after 1890. In 1891 the Qing reformed the Yellow River control system, placing most of the burden in this area on localities. In 1901–2 the Qing abandoned grain tribute via the Grand Canal and left that waterway, too, in local hands. German soldiers came to Shandong in 1897; railroads followed soon thereafter. In 1896 the Shandong provincial government began reforming banking and currency; about 1900 it introduced the new cotton varieties that eventually dominated North Huang-Yun and began reforestation programs. Meanwhile, the Sino-Japanese (1895) and Boxer (1900) indemnities reduced Beijing's willingness to address expensive local problems. However, these events also intensified the fear of China's being "carved up" and thus gave a new impetus to "modernization" and state-building efforts.

STATE, MARKET, AND INTEGRATION IN HUANG-YUN

Much of this book concerns "integration": in the most general sense, links between one place and another. The first part of this book emphasizes economic ties between places in Huang-Yun and outside economic centers; the second half stresses political networks. The entire book emphasizes the relationships—reinforcing and conflicting—between these two types of integration and between integration within Huang-Yun and of Huang-Yun into larger networks. Though these relationships varied, they were not infinitely diverse or contingent. As the book moves through cases that typify various relationships between local and supralocal networks, between political and economic integration, and between old and new networks, it will clarify the regional effects of state making, market making, and imperialism in North China.

The first two chapters concern the integration of Huang-Yun into new economic networks. Chapter 1 analyzes the extent and (especially) limits of the area's participation in credit and currency markets centered in coastal cities. Chapter 2 discusses the spread (and, again, the limits) of new, imported cotton varieties; this crop offered higher profits for Huang-Yun peasants largely because it fit the needs of mechanized mills in Tianjin, Qingdao, Shanghai, and Osaka. In both cases, North Huang-Yun was incorporated into these larger markets far more than South Huang-Yun, and most of its residents were better off for that. These differences in incorporation owe much less to such geographic factors as soil types or distance from navigable rivers than to contrasts in political and social structure. While North Huang-Yun's weak communities were easily penetrated by outsiders, the strong villages and rural elites of South Huang-Yun put up more resistance; they even prevented the area's own urban elites from implementing changes that could upset the rural power structure. These differences in local society help explain why a wide variety of agents of change fared better in North than in South Huang-Yun.

In these first two chapters the story is driven by increasing, though uneven, market integration. However, imperialism, which stimulated much of this development, also accelerated another trend: political disintegration. Like market integration, this was not a linear trend: many signs of growing integration appear amid the collapse of the imperial Chinese state. In keeping with this book's focus on social and economic history, I ignore what some have called "nation building"— attempts to create a sense of shared citizenship, common beliefs and symbols, and commitment to an abstract national entity—and focus instead on "state making," particularly the creation of systems that extract and deploy resources in order to pursue the government's goals.

The literature on Chinese state making includes two sharply opposed accounts of the early twentieth century. Some writers emphasize the decay of China's old political system, others the creation of "modern" institutions that strengthened some of the state's capabilities.[14] An analysis of Huang-Yun's experience clarifies these

---

14. Prominent examples of the "decay" school include Chuzo Ichiko, "The Role of the Gentry: An Hypothesis," in *China in Revolution*, ed. Mary C. Wright (New Haven,

issues by highlighting changes in the state's goals, the vastly different impact these changes had on different regions, and relationships between the state's successes and failures. In particular, it shows how the state's new focus on international competition influenced its retreat from one of its crucial traditional tasks: subsidizing and/or supervising the management of ecological problems, particularly in areas (including Huang-Yun) where the ecological basis for subsistence and social reproduction was fragile.

In chapters 3 through 5, ecology, the state, and the collapse of formerly state-supported networks take center stage. Chapter 3, on deforestation and Huang-Yun's twentieth-century fuel crisis, provides a hinge, linking these problems with those of the first two chapters. It first discusses deforestation, and ecological degradation generally, as a case of market failure exacerbated by population growth. It then describes how imports of wood carried on the government-maintained Grand Canal helped stabilize Huang-Yun's fragile ecology. When this trade dried up, Huang-Yun's fuel shortage grew much worse. The chapter then turns to the state's twentieth-century reforestation programs; though these efforts were vigorous, they did not help relatively isolated areas, like Huang-Yun, which had the most severe problems. Instead, they were directed at more accessible areas that were addressing local shortages by "wasting" hard currency on Manchurian and foreign timber.

Thus, deforestation provides our first case in which the destruction of old networks and capabilities had a greater impact on Huang-Yun than the creation of new ones. It also highlights the goverment's newly mercantilistic priorities, in which substituting domestic supplies for wood imports was more important than increasing the fuel supplies of areas too isolated to have imports. This analysis begins to unravel the relationships among the state's new projects, its abandonment of old ones, and the regional "triage" implicit in its new priorities. These themes are further developed in the last part of the chapter, which dis-

1968), 297–317, and John K. Fairbank, "Introduction: The Old Order," in *The Cambridge History of China*, ed. John K. Fairbank, vol. 10, pt. 1, pp. 1–34. The burgeoning "state-making" literature includes Susan Mann, *Local Merchants and the Chinese Bureaucracy, 1750–1950* (Stanford, 1987), and Steven MacKinnon, *Power and Politics in Late Imperial China* (Berkeley, 1980). Other examples, including important variations on these basic positions, will be discussed throughout the text where they are most relevant.

cusses Huang-Yun's attempts to remain part of North China's core—
and retain access to vital resources—by getting the state to build a
railroad through the area.

The regional effects of the new statecraft are further developed in
chapters 4 and 5. Here market making largely disappears, and we
analyze the collapse of the state effort that had affected Huang-Yun
most: water control. Chapter 4 traces the state's abandonment of
inland Yellow River control and the Grand Canal, especially after
1891. It emphasizes that this abandonment was not a result of gen-
eralized government "collapse." Rather, a vigorous but hard-pressed
state shifted its resources to other projects and regions.

Some of the state's new commitments are well known: coastal
arsenals, New Armies, and indemnity payments to foreigners. They
also included improving river control near railroad crossings, major
cities, and certain coastal areas (including the mouth of the Yellow
River) where major floods seemed likely to provide excuses for further
foreign encroachment. The state spent large sums in these areas and
introduced technical innovations that greatly reduced flooding. Meanwhile, Huang-Yun water control regressed. The state withdrew funds
and supervision. The small-scale, cash-poor, and largely uncoordinated groups upon which responsibility fell reverted to techniques that
used exclusively local materials—and were thus often profitable for
the unsupervised organizers of the work—but cost far more and
achieved far less than the methods used in the high Qing. In short, the
late Qing reforms and spending cuts neither created nor solved North
China's water-control problems: instead they relocated them, making
Huang-Yun the most flooded part of North China.

Chapter 5 continues the story from a more local viewpoint. First it
examines the economic cost of hydraulic decay to Huang-Yun. By
1920 those costs were at least 9 percent (perhaps more than 20 percent) of the region's output. Thus, in this perhaps exceptional case, the
indirect impact of imperialism and the new statecraft on Huang-Yun
far exceeded the area's gains from joining the world economy. Calculating this measurement also continues a project begun with the
book's earlier descriptions of gleaning and fuel gathering: bringing
nonmarketized (and often nonmonetized) goods and services into our
analysis in a way that captures their relationships with the rest of the
political economy and that provides enough measurement of them to

see how they alter calculations of trends in rural living standards based solely on wages, prices, output, and consumption mediated by the market.[15]

The chapter then turns to three Republican-era attempts to repair Huang-Yun's hydraulic system, focusing on two recurring themes. The first is how the larger political economy limited Huang-Yun's access to badly needed outside resources. The second is the absence of a rural gentry that combined a large stake in what the state thought of them, extensive networks, and enough grass-roots influence to manage the needed work. While South Huang-Yun had a well-organized urban elite that was deeply involved in public projects, rural land, water, and labor were controlled by more parochial leaders, who opposed any measures that might compromise their local control. The state could penetrate North Huang-Yun's weak villages fairly easily but found few influential people to work with; and almost nobody in the region could effectively pressure the state to commit more resources. Consequently, these two areas spawned different types of water-control efforts, different kinds of abuses, and different patterns of popular resistance.

The Conclusion, which follows chapter 5, summarizes the book's major findings about Huang-Yun and suggests some implications for our understanding of the Chinese state, imperialism, and economic development. It also suggests some refinements in the way we look at cores, peripheries, and regional systems in China.

---

15. For instance, Loren Brandt, *Commercialization and Agricultural Development: Central and Eastern China, 1870–1937* (Cambridge, Eng., 1989), 106–37, and Rawski, *Economic Growth*, 285–329, base their inferences of improving living standards largely on wage data and (in Rawski's case) increased consumption of cotton goods. Philip Huang, while sharply critical of this approach, makes no attempt to analyze directly what peasants consumed, simply asserting that compared to the dramatic changes in the West, changes in rural Chinese living standards were so insignificant that for his purposes they can be said to have remained at subsistence from 1350 through the 1970s (Huang, *The Peasant Family and Rural Development in the Yangzi Delta, 1350–1988* [Stanford, 1990], esp. 137–43). It is also worth noting that while Huang devotes a great deal of attention to unpaid family labor, arguing that such labor was often compensated at rates far below those for wage labor, he considers only unpaid labor that was producing goods for the market (e.g., cotton and silk). My own attempts at direct measurements of how much of certain nonmarket goods (fuel) and services (flood control) peasants had access to is of course nowhere near a complete account of noncommercial economic activities; but it is enough, I think, to show that neither Huang's nor Rawski's picture of the early-twentieth-century economy apply to Huang-Yun.

POLITICAL ECONOMY
AND CHINESE DEVELOPMENT

Essentially, then, this is a work of political economy, a genre that has been largely absent from the recent English-language China literature. Much of the earlier literature on the emergence of China's modern sector focused on important state-sponsored firms and so necessarily focused on state policy, but it did not attempt a systematic account of the overall political economy.[16] Early works on China's rural sector (by Chen Hanseng and R. H. Tawney, among others) often contained vivid anecdotes of warlord depredations but—except for one chapter in Ramon Myers' *The Chinese Peasant Economy*—made little effort to assess how important politics was, or was not.[17]

As both the new social history and the new economic history made their way into Chinese studies, new macrolevel economic syntheses emerged, syntheses in which the state was largely absent. Writing from an essentially neoclassical perspective, economists such as Thomas Rawski and Loren Brandt have described a process of economic growth in which ongoing commercialization, the world market, and new technologies powered an early-twentieth-century economic expansion. In this framework, no one actor—not even the state— mattered much.[18] (Indeed, one of Rawski's early contributions was a challenge to the then-accepted wisdom that warlordism had devastated the interwar Chinese economy.[19]) Writing from an eclectic perspective heavily influenced by A. K. Chayanov, Philip Huang has offered a macrolevel picture that includes certain institutional factors—rural class structure and particularly the peasant family—but treats the state, foreigners, and nonfarmers in general as relatively minor factors

16. See, for instance, Albert Feuerwerker, *China's Early Industrialization: Sheng Hsuan-huai (1844–1916) and Mandarin Enterprise* (Cambridge, Mass., 1958); Ellsworth Carlson, *The Kaiping Mines, 1877–1912* (Cambridge, Mass., 1957); and portions of Stanley Spector, *Li Hung-chang and the Huai Army* (Seattle, 1964), and Samuel Chu, *Reformer in Modern China* (New York, 1965).

17. Myers, *Peasant Economy*; Chen Hanseng, *Landlord and Peasant in China* (New York, 1936); Richard Henry Tawney, *Land and Labor in China* (1932; reprinted Armonk, N.Y., 1966).

18. Rawski, *Economic Growth*, esp. 9–32; Brandt, *Commercialization*.

19. This discussion is updated in Rawski, *Economic Growth*, 32–48. For criticisms of an earlier version, see James Sheridan, "Chinese Warlords: Tigers or Pussycats?"; Jerome Ch'en, "Local Government Finance in Republican China"; and Diana Lary, "Violence, Fear, and Insecurity: The Mood of Republican China," all in *Republican China* 10:2 (April 1985), 35–41, 42–54, 55–63.

in a story propelled by the internal dynamics of agriculture and demography.[20]

By contrast, this book is filled with the activities of nonfarmers, particularly officials and local elites. As the above summary suggests, I argue that the state had enormous impact on the rural economy: manipulating currency conditions and affecting local interest rates; aggressively promoting certain new crops; helping some areas, but not others, deal with resource crises; and shifting the massive problems of flood control from some communities to others. Moreover, I argue that these interventions were not primarily determined by the greed, ignorance, or idiosyncrasies of particular officials but were governed by a systematic logic that itself linked economics and politics: its two central tenets were the need for more revenue to fuel the process of state building and the need to reduce foreign debt and the political pressures it created. Although efforts toward these ends sometimes took bizarre and awful forms—particularly since state power was often fragmented and because the unequal treaties ruled out tariffs as an instrument of economic nationalism—the underlying logic seems straightforward enough.

The economic actions of powerful nonofficials, I argue, are also often best understood in terms of political economy. For instance, whether or not local elites cooperated in the spread of new cotton varieties had a great deal to do with how they thought commercialization would affect their political positions vis-à-vis both local government and their poor peasant "clients" and with how exclusively local their interests were. Other analysts have also sometimes noted the potential of local ecology and economics to shape the horizons of local elites; Philip Huang's observation that in North China, land alone could not finance participation in the imperial civil service exams is an important example.[21] However, these insights have not hitherto been followed up with an analysis of how the aims, horizons, resources, and choices of local elites in turn shaped crucial variables: their communities' future importance to the state and their access to state-distributed resources; their willingness to risk weakening their local political power in return for wealth useful in a wider arena; the ability of outsiders sponsoring change to gain a local foothold; and the

20. Huang, *Peasant Economy*; idem, *Peasant Family*, esp. 115–17, 123–43, 152–56.
21. Huang, *Peasant Economy*, 178–79.

capacity of different groups to resist the destruction of private dikes, being forced into providing unpaid labor, and so forth. Here, those connections become vitally important and the relationships between society and economy more truly reciprocal: thus, for instance, ecology and infrastructure are not just an initial "setting" for my story, but a result of the story as well.

Political economy, therefore, not only reintroduces recently neglected variables into our account of Chinese economic development but also opens a search for a whole new class of regularities: the covariance, based on regions' differing social structures and positions in the state's geopolitical calculations, of outcomes in a number of distinct social, economic, and political spheres. In our case, it explains why North and South Huang-Yun produced clusters of opposite outcomes spanning a range of important matters. North Huang-Yun displayed successful agricultural innovation, the spread of new credit and trade arrangements, particular vulnerability to the exactions of warlords and other outsiders, fiscally weak but often surprisingly influential local governments, an almost total loss of state-sponsored infrastructure, and bottom-up insurgencies. South Huang-Yun featured limited agricultural innovation, greater "closure" against predators, local governments that did better at extraction but worse at regulation, slightly greater access to state-financed infrastructure, and strong cross-class, village-based resistance to efforts at coordinated planning.

Thus, the assortment of topics here represents more than just an attempt at broad coverage of social and economic change in Huang-Yun. It is also an attempt to show that even a simple political economy model can uncover unsuspected regularities and relationships among the development paths of seemingly separate markets, institutions, and problems; and it roots those regularities in preexisting social and ecological variation on the one hand and pressures from the international economy and state system on the other.

WATER CONTROL AND STATE MAKING: A THEORETICAL PERSPECTIVE

Our discussion of the failures of early-twentieth-century state making, the ill effects of imperialism, and the destruction of old networks draws heavily on a case study of water control. Insofar as this book is only a study of the area near where the Grand Canal and Yellow River meet, this choice needs no justification. But having made larger claims, I end this Introduction by raising other reasons for this emphasis. In particular, studying water control provides a different perspective on state making from that generated by the favorite topics of most state-making literature: taxation, conscription, standardizing law enforcement, and (especially in the twentieth-century Third World) promoting industrialization.

State making and industrialization are central to the ways in which many retrospective analyses—from "modernization" theory to "dependency" and "world-systems" theories—evaluate states; they were also prized by most of the early-twentieth-century Chinese elite, who saw these efforts as China's only hope for survival. Recent scholarship suggests that the early-twentieth-century Chinese state was doing much better at amassing the modern sinews of power than most historians had previously realized. Government revenues soared at every level, from counties to national governments. At least in some areas, government also increased its penetration of local communities significantly.

Recent research also suggests that the government did far better than we had previously realized at promoting economic growth, and especially industrial growth. For instance, it now appears that banking and transport—two of the crucial sectors in which Dwight Perkins had argued that the Chinese state failed to play a necessary modernizing role—were actually quite dynamic and that the modern sector in general grew very rapidly in early-twentieth-century China.[22] The second chapter of this book even shows the government successfully promoting synergistic changes in agriculture and industry. The new cotton varieties discussed there, which benefited growers and coastal mills alike, required both a major agricultural extension effort and new coercive measures against gleaners, whose exercise of rights rooted in local custom threatened the new crop. The eventual adoption of the new cotton, at least in North Huang-Yun, testifies to a surprising state capacity to influence grass-roots society on behalf of economic development.

The government's major failures appear to have been in its tradi-

22. Dwight Perkins, "Government as an Obstacle to Industrialization: The Case of Nineteenth-Century China," *Journal of Economic History* 27:4 (Dec. 1967), 478–92; on the period's successes, see Rawski, *Economic Growth*; Brandt, *Commercialization*.

tional tasks—maintaining public order and providing water control, famine relief, military defense—and to have been concentrated in specific hinterland regions. Because they hit hardest in areas that were already poor and often at activities (such as fuel gathering) that were largely outside the cash economy and outside those activities included in gross national product (GNP) statistics, these failures may have had limited impact on long-term growth rates. Nonetheless, they had great impact on popular welfare and people's lives. Most likely, they also compromised the government's legitimacy in the eyes of "ordinary" people far more than its limited successes in modern tasks did. Probably few peasants cared much about industrialization; even fewer thought that increasing government revenues and penetration of villages were good things in themselves. When and to what extent peasants became concerned about a strong national defense is controversial,[23] but it is unlikely that this was a high priority for many peasants before 1937; certainly very few wanted more effective conscription.

In contrast, preventing "natural" disaster was probably much closer to most peasants' ideas of what government was supposed to do. And it was in regions that counted for little in China's new statecraft that peasants abandoned the regime in droves, many eventually supporting the Communist revolution. Thus our focus on traditional tasks highlights a subject of particularly great concern to those people and regions who have left the fewest accounts of how they experienced early-twentieth-century state making and helps us balance the emphasis of sources written by core-area elites and foreigners on China's efforts to join the "developed" world; it may even help explain the new direction taken by mid-twentieth-century China.

A focus on water control also allows us to combine new material on the oft-stressed subject of how states extract labor and resources with an analysis of a far less studied issue: how the post-1850 state functioned as a donor of services.[24] Furthermore, stopping floods—unlike building armies or even factories—was something local com-

---

23. Chalmers Johnson, *Peasant Nationalism and Communist Power* (Stanford, 1962), and Donald Gillin, " 'Peasant Nationalism' in the History of Chinese Communism," *Journal of Asian Studies* 23:2 (February 1964), 269–89, represent the original contributions to what has since become a very large literature.

24. The last decade has seen a burgeoning literature on the state as a donor of services in the high Qing, produced by Pierre Etienne Will (*Bureaucracy and Famine in Eighteenth-Century China* [Stanford, 1990]), Peter Perdue (*Exhausting the Earth: State*

munities would and often did attempt on their own. These local efforts give us a baseline for measuring to what extent the state's efforts were more efficient than those that occurred without it: something we might call administrative integration. In some cases, emergency state making led to systems that forfeited the administrative advantages a large-scale state has over isolated communities while retaining all the problems of requisition by command; consequently, such systems used more resources to do less for popular wlefare than had the Qing practices, which partisans of the new statecraft—and historians influenced by them—decried as "wasteful."[25] A prime example is the way the Huang-Yun Yellow River was managed after the state turned its attention elsewhere. Informal, off-budget organizations outside bureaucratic discipline were created; this system kept government costs down but used huge quantities of local, noncash resources to little effect.

Such examples also cast a new light on what Prasenjit Duara has called "state involution":[26] the extraction of more resources and expansion of the government payroll (especially at the local level) without a "breakthrough" to a state that could do more, had more committed personnel, or was more autonomous from civil society. Many of Duara's insights are confirmed by our findings. However, his model requires significant modifications once we look at the state as a donor of services and at the sharp differences between how it handled new and old tasks and core and hinterland regions. While he suggests a pattern all across North China of greater extraction by a new class of low-level, government-employed, "entrepreneurial brokers" and stagnation in government capabilities, my evidence suggests that this

---

and Peasant in Hunan, 1500–1850 [Cambridge, 1987]), R. Bin Wong and Pierre Etienne Will (*Nourish the People: China's State Civilian Granary System, 1650–1850* [Ann Arbor, 1991]), and others. Thus far, however, we have little such material on the nineteenth century and almost none on the twentieth; what accounts of disaster relief, water control, and the like that we have after the mid-1800s focus on private efforts (e.g., Mary Rankin's *Elite Activism and Political Transformation in China: Zhejiang Province, 1865–1911* [Stanford, 1986] and Rowe's *Hankow*), or on foreigners.

25. Hu Ch'ang-t'u, "The Yellow River Administration in the Ch'ing Dynasty," *Journal of Asian Studies* 14:4 (Aug. 1955), relying heavily on the writings of the nineteenth-century "statecraft" thinker Wei Yuan; memorial of 2/21/GX 28 from Xiliang in LFZZ, GX 28, packet 44–45; and documents in Wu Tongju, ed., *Zai xu xing shui jin jian* (Taibei, 1966), 10:4142–46, 4176–78.

26. Prasenjit Duara, "State Involution: A Study of Local Finances in North China, 1911–1935," *Comparative Studies in Society and History* 29:1 (Jan. 1987), 132–61.

picture may be an average of two distinct patterns of development. On one hand, greater extraction may in fact have produced important improvements in public services in core areas. Meanwhile, hinterlands were increasingly ignored by the state and lacked the opportunities for greater administrative integration that existed in areas that were experiencing greater market integration; the hinterlands suffered both greater extraction (mostly by traditional powerholders) and sharply declining services.

Thus, while people as far apart as "modernization" and "dependency" theorists often argue that imperialism's worst political legacy was that it left twentieth-century China (or other Third World countries) with a state incapable of promoting development, it may be more accurate to acknowledge that much was done to develop certain modern sectors and regions and to look instead at how state strategies adopted under foreign pressure shortchanged other policy and geographic areas. Thus, while what follows diverges from "dependency" and "world systems" analyses by placing far more stress on Huang-Yun's preexisting social structure and on the state's failure at old tasks, it also adopts one central insight of both those theories: that instead of saying that some countries (or regions) have "modernized" while others have not, we need to remember that rich and poor areas are both part of the modern world and that rapid development in one area can entail stagnation or degeneration elsewhere.

Thus, a focus on what became of such traditional services as water control during modernization efforts may help us understand the paradox of economic growth with no clear reduction in misery—a paradox with enormous significance for subsequent political events. By placing traditional and modernizing tasks side by side, I hope to provide an account that slights neither such long-term transformations as state and market making nor the welfare and perspective of people living at the time and that avoids unhelpful assertions of global success or failure. Such assessments are common in Western literature on "modernization" and "dependency" and in work that draws on the Chinese idea of a "dynastic cycle"; the latter model often implies that the state's performance changes consistently across all its tasks and territories.[27] More modestly, it is worth noting that

27. Gilbert Rozman, ed., *The Modernization of China* (New York, 1981); Immanuel Wallerstein, *The Modern World-System* (New York, 1976), vol. 1; Frances Moulder,

post-1850 water control remains largely unexplored, despite the millions it affected.[28]

A focus on hydraulics ultimately leads back to the mutual dependence of state making and market making. Water control was central to two more broadly defined government tasks—the prevention of "natural" disaster and ecological decay and the maintenance of infrastructure for transportation—that can rarely be handled by markets alone and that also set limits on economic integration. There is an abundant literature on why infrastructure for transportation is generally best provided by the state and not financed by users' fees;[29] inadequate or expensive transportation clearly limits market integration. Arresting environmental decay also usually requires nonmarket means, such as rules against the thousands of individually convenient acts that create a collective problem.[30] (Tree cutting on public land, for instance, was common in Huang-Yun.) Environmental problems may limit integration across either space or time by increasing "natural" disasters, thus making it harder to move resources and riskier to put them into projects with future rewards.

Finally, in a less rigorous sense of "placing limits on the market," the increased frequency of disasters in Huang-Yun canceled out the welfare gains generated by new opportunities to trade with a wider world and ultimately undermined governments that promoted production for larger markets. In this broadest sense, the services lost by peripheries in the new political economy may have helped set the stage for yet another kind of statecraft.

Japan, China, and the Modern World Economy (Cambridge, Eng., 1977); for a cyclical view, see, for instance, John K. Fairbank, Edwin O. Reischauer, and Albert M. Craig, *East Asia: Tradition and Transformation* (Boston, 1973), 435; Ichiko, "Role of the Gentry," 297–316. Skinner has led the way in suggesting separate cycles for different regions, but these are largely economic rather than political: see "Presidential Address: The Structure of Chinese History," *Journal of Asian Studies* 44:2 (Feb. 1985), 271–92.

28. The surprisingly scant literature on Yellow River control in the Qing and thereafter includes Hu Ch'ang-t'u, "Yellow River Administration," 505–13; Shuilibu Huang He Shuili Weiyuanhui, *Huang He shuili shi shuyao* (Beijing, 1984), a survey covering twenty-five hundred years; and Charles Greer, *Water Management in the Yellow River Basin of China* (Austin, 1979), which emphasizes developments after 1949. Work now in progress by Randall Dodgen should eventually provide a much-needed addition.

29. For a summary of the argument, see Donald N. McCloskey, *The Applied Theory of Price* (New York, 1985), 199–200.

30. For a textbook treatment of this problem by neoclassical economics, see ibid., 331–41.

CHAPTER I

Local Interest Story

*Political Power and Regional Patterns
in the Credit and Currency Markets*

Until recently, historians rarely thought about Chinese credit markets except at two extremes: treaty-port high finance and the village usurer. More recent work makes it clear that we need to look more closely at capital markets at all levels. Interregional capital markets are central to the relationships among richer areas, poorer areas, and economic change. Understanding more local credit markets is an essential part of seeing what options people in different economic positions actually had and thus is crucial for either a quantitative or qualitative assessment of local economies.

This chapter analyzes relationships among capital markets, local interest rates, and regional development, focusing heavily on the Shandong portion of Huang-Yun. And since numerous currencies with varying ranges of acceptance circulated in Shandong, an analysis of supralocal capital markets leads to an analysis of domestic currency markets. Currency and capital markets turn out to be strongly affected by local government finance, raising a third set of questions about relationships between state making and market making in early-twentieth-century China.

None of Shandong's three regional capital markets—the north coast, the heartland (including most of North Huang-Yun), and the southwest (essentially South Huang-Yun)—follows Huang-Yun's borders precisely; this is no surprise, since Huang-Yun was not a functionally integrated region. However, this overlapping regional schema contributes to our understanding of Huang-Yun in at least four ways.

First, it places Huang-Yun in the context of the larger North China economy and of provincial and national administration. Much of this chapter deals with attempts to manipulate interactions between the coastal and the hinterland economy, which met along the Tianjin-Pukou railway—the eastern boundary of Huang-Yun. Second, it outlines limits on the mobility of funds that had enormous influence on all the forms of economic and political integration discussed in this book. Third, it points out the need for a model besides those of physiographic macroregions or a national market to explain the extent of economic networks in early-twentieth-century North China.

Finally, and perhaps most important, it points to a crucial division within Huang-Yun. The northwestern parts of the heartland region comprise most of North Huang-Yun; the southwest region, most of South Huang-Yun.[1] These two parts of Huang-Yun faced essentially the same challenges: the rise of a coastal-centered economy and the state's withdrawal from hydraulic and other key services in inland areas. Their different social structures, however, led to very different responses. North Huang-Yun was easily penetrated by outsiders and became a periphery firmly linked to the new coastal-centered economy. South Huang-Yun, in contrast, became more isolated, in part because local powerholders chose to resist many aspects of incorporation into larger networks. That North Huang-Yun wound up as part of the heartland capital and currency markets while South Huang-Yun wound up in a small zone all its own is a crucial illustration of these different tendencies.

Two groups of issues concerning Chinese capital markets need particular attention. First, if some areas were left out of the growth that occurred in certain regions, we need to explain why funds did not flow from prosperous areas with relatively low interest rates to more "backward" regions, where credit commanded a higher price. It has been a staple of much of the literature on prewar China that large parts of the country gained little from the dynamism of Manchuria,

---

1. The Zhili parts of Huang-Yun clearly divide into those that belong with Shandong's heartland region and those that belong with the southwest. Inadequate data—particularly problems with the grain price reports that are used below to estimate interest rates in Shandong and Zhili—make it impossible to treat the Henan parts of Huang-Yun here.

Shanghai, and other boom areas.[2] Explicitly or implicitly, this literature maintains that very little of the money made in the economy's
most "advanced" regions was invested in the hinterland. Known examples of such investment are indeed rare, but our fragmentary evidence cannot establish a general pattern, much less explain it.

Moreover, some scholars have recently argued that there was a
growing national capital market, in which investment did flow from
coastal cities to the hinterlands.[3] This inference rests on three points:
(1) investors seek the highest return they can find, and changing circumstances (such as the coming of telegraphs) made it easier for people to learn about distant opportunities; (2) there is evidence that interest rate spreads between different parts of China were narrowing;
and (3) without such investment, the imbalances of urban-rural trade
(Shanghai, for instance, sold far more than it bought) would have led
to money shortages and deflation in the countryside, causing a divergence between urban and rural prices that has not been observed.

The second cluster of issues involves local credit markets. Since
North China had far less tenancy than the South, much of the discussion of economic exploitation and coercion in the north has centered
on credit and marketing.[4] Here, too, there are conflicting views of
how capital markets worked.

On the one hand, a wealth of anecdotes show moneylenders abus-
ing local monopolies. Others argue that local credit markets were not
necessarily manipulated by creditors but that they nonetheless provided very expensive credit, in part because they could only draw on a
narrow pool of local savings. Either view assumes a lack of significant

2. Rhoads Murphey, *The Treaty Ports and China's Modernization: What Went
Wrong?* (Ann Arbor, 1970); Fei Xiaotong (Fei Hsiao-t'ung), *China's Gentry: Essays on
Rural-Urban Relations* (Chicago, 1968); and Victor Lippit, "The Development of
Underdevelopment in China," *Modern China* 4:3 (July 1978), for instance, agree on
little besides the claim that the treaty port economy did little to stimulate the Chinese
economy as a whole. Moulder argues that the West drained capital out of China (*Modern World Economy*, 118–19). A rare effort to actually measure market integration
for a single province in the twentieth century is Barbara N. Sands, "An Investigation
of the Nature and Extent of Market Integration in Shanxi Province, China, 1928–1945"
(Ph.D. dissertation, University of Washington, 1985).

3. See, for instance, Rawski, *Economic Growth.*

4. For different views of Northern tenancy rates see Myers, *Peasant Economy*, 217–
27; Joseph Esherick, "Number Games: A Note on Land Distribution in Pre-
Revolutionary China," *Modern China* 7:4 (Oct. 1981), 387–411; and Randall Stross,
"Number Games Rejected: The Misleading Allure of Tenancy Estimates," *Republican
China* 10:3 (June 1985), 1–17. Nobody, however, suggests that a majority of north-
erners were tenants.

credit flows between localities. Two other arguments, however, assume that funds did flow between localities. First, some recent work uses aggregate data and a smaller body of anecdotes to argue that the cheaper credit available in coastal cities (and ultimately, abroad) did "trickle down" to enough rural outlets to give peasants access to a competitive credit market. Another view suggests that before the Opium War, government money deposited with local pawnshops provided outside funds, with the same benefits for rural borrowers that the argument above attributes to twentieth-century treaty-port funds.[5] The account here is based on county and prefectural data, and since credit markets were often segmented at even lower levels, our picture is incomplete.[6] It is, however, a necessary step toward understanding these questions, which are central to the economic dynamics of pre-revolutionary China.

Since the analysis in this chapter is at times technical, it may be useful to list its main conclusions in advance. They are:

1. The province included three distinct regional capital markets. Interest rates in the poorest market (southwestern Shandong) were about 1.5 percent per *month* higher than in the most prosperous region (the area along the north Shandong coast, which faced Manchuria and included two treaty ports) and approximately 0.6 percent higher than in the middle, or heartland, zone. With about one-fifth of Shandong's thirty-four million people, the north coast area was hardly the "fly on an elephant" that some have said the treaty-port economy was.[7] However, the isolated southwest, with about the same population, was hardly a trivial "pocket" of backwardness, and the three-fifths of the province that comprised the heartland was significantly less integrated into "national" money markets than the north coast was.

---

5. For a view of local creditors as exploitative monopolists, see, e.g., Tawney, *Land and Labor*, 58–63, esp. 60–61. On the local loan market as expensive because it was limited to local funds, see Thomas Wiens, *The Micro-Economics of Peasant Economy: China, 1920–1940* (New York, 1982), 123–55. On the growth of a national capital market, see Rawski, *Economic Growth*, 145–55. On subsidization and regulation of pawnshops in the early Qing, see Pan Mingde, "Zhongguo jindai diandangye zhi yanjiu (1644–1937)" (Master's thesis, Guoli Taiwan Shifan Daxue, 1983), esp. 39–65.

6. In Gaomi county for instance, prevailing interest rates were reportedly 2.5 percent in the north district, 3 percent in the east and west, and 5–6 percent per month in the south. See "Shandong Gaomi, Wei xian zhi nongcun jiehuo," *Gong shang banyuekan* 6:4 (Feb. 15, 1934), 49.

7. Murphey, *Treaty Ports*, 31.

2. These interest rate differentials changed little between 1900–11 and the 1930s.

3. These lasting differences cannot be explained by geographic factors. Instead, they resulted primarily from the ability of politically powerful people to restrict the flow of money into and out of their own county. This power over money flows allowed them to manipulate local silver to copper exchange rates while limiting access by others to the cheaper credit and silver available in more prosperous areas.

4. These currency manipulations not only made private profits for the politically connected; they were also a crucial source of public funds for certain county governments.

5. Though county governments gained the most from obstructing currency flows, provincial officials were also caught between the perceived advantages and disadvantages of Shandong's integration into a larger economy.

6. Not only did these artificial barriers keep the return on loans and stored assets in poor areas higher than elsewhere, but the ability of the politically connected to cross these barriers enabled them to make profits trading currency that far exceeded those available in either purely local commerce or in those commodities for which national and international markets existed.

7. Limitations on the capital and currency markets had important, and largely harmful, effects on inland areas, especially southwest Shandong. However, price divergence between the north coast and other regions was not marked because most heartland counties exported enough cash crops to avoid a silver drain, while the southwest, with fewer exports, balanced its books by buying few imports and by exporting laborers, who sent or brought silver home. When Japan seized Manchuria in 1931 and curtailed migratory labor, the southwest experienced a deflation distinct from the more widely felt effects of the world depression.

8. Political and social factors played a central role in shaping local participation in growing supralocal markets. The limits on market integration also handicapped governments trying to move resources between regions. These difficulties strongly affected relations between local and higher-level governments.

SHANDONG'S REGIONAL CREDIT MARKETS

We have numerous interest rates from particular times and places in Shandong. Most cannot be used in systematic comparisons, however, because they omit information about who was charged a particular rate, what security there was, how interest was paid, and so forth. There is, however, a 1933 survey of "average" and "maximum" rates in each county for loans from various kinds of lenders.[8] For 1900–11, we can estimate interest rates using monthly grain prices for each prefecture of Shandong, as McCloskey and Nash did for medieval England.[9] The method assumes that over time, holding grain and selling it a few months later will be no more or less profitable than selling grain immediately and holding money; if a difference emerged, people would turn to the more profitable activity, until it ceased being so.[10] Thus, on average, the appreciation of grain prices after the harvest should represent a good approximation of the interest rate plus other storage costs (for example, losses from rotting, rats, or theft).

This method involves looking at pairs of grain prices a month or a few months apart (table 1). Eliminating pairs that end in or pass through harvest months—when prices represented the influx of new grain rather than the accrued value of whatever little grain remained from the previous year—leaves fifty to sixty pairs for each of six grains in each of the eleven prefectures with reliable data. In ten prefectures the results for the different grains are quite close. The similarity tends to confirm the reliability of the underlying data; special factors explain the odd results in the other.[11] We do not know exactly how much of the price appreciation of stored grains represents interest and how much represents other storage costs, but the other costs were

8. *SSYZ* 5:91–97; for a discussion of this data, see dissertation, appendix B.
9. Donald N. McCloskey and John Nash, "Corn at Interest: The Extent and Cost of Grain Storage in Medieval England," *American Economic Review* 74:1 (March 1984): 174–87, esp. 178–83. The grain prices used here come from monthly reports of the highest and lowest prices during the month of each of six grains collected from each prefecture and now held in the First Historical Archives of China, Beijing. This analysis is based on the high prices only, for technical reasons that are explained further in dissertation, 463. For a further discussion of the data base, see dissertation, 397–98.
10. Even peasants apparently moved their assets back and forth between cash and grain to shield themselves from price fluctuations and seek a better return. See, for instance, memorial from Tang Pin in *Da Qing li chao shilu*, Gaozong (Qianlong) reign, 286:24b–25a (4154–55). I am grateful to Pan Mingde for bringing this example to my attention.
11. See dissertation, chapter 1, n. 10.

TABLE 1   AVERAGE MONTHLY RETURN ON
STORED GRAIN, OCTOBER 1900–DECEMBER 1911

	Wheat	Sorghum	Soybeans (2 kinds)		Millet	Corn	Average of all crops
North coast	.40	.43	.75	.52	.29	.06	.41
Qingzhou	.62	.44	.63	.94	.53	.28	.57
Laizhou	.49	.60	2.25	.89	−.07	−.06	.68
Dengzhou	.16	.43	.13	.03	.48	−.10	.19
Wuding	.32	.25	−.02	.23	.24	.13	.19
Southwest	1.85	1.86	2.30	1.83	2.21	1.86	1.99
Caozhou[a]	1.57	1.73	2.12	1.81	2.39	2.07	1.95
Yanzhou[b]	2.22	1.99	2.47	1.85	2.02	1.65	2.03
Heartland	1.48	1.43	1.43	1.39	1.54	1.32	1.43
Jinan	1.48	1.45	1.56	1.07	1.39	1.19	1.36
Taian[b]	1.49	1.73	1.55	1.36	1.93	1.37	1.57
Linqing[a]	1.53	1.29	1.08	1.35	1.33	1.53	1.35
Dongchang[a]	1.96	1.54	1.67	1.64	1.98	1.62	1.74
Yizhou[b]	.92	1.15	1.31	1.51	1.05	1.05	1.17

NOTE: Jining (southwest) and Jiaozhou (heartland) omitted because of problems with the data. Data on Zhili prefectures (based on five different grains) are discussed in text. For measures of dispersion/central tendency and further information on the data base and methods used, see Kenneth Pomeranz, "The Making of a Hinterland: State, Society, and Economy in Inland North China, 1900–1937" (Ph.D. dissertation, Yale University), appendix A.
[a] Prefectures wholly within Huang-Yun.
[b] Prefectures of which some portion is in Huang-Yun.

similar across prefectures.[12] Thus, regional differences should reflect relative interest rates. We turn now to examine the results.

The results suggest three regional groupings (map 3). The first, the "north coast area," consists of Laizhou, Dengzhou, Qingzhou, and Wuding prefectures, which cover Shandong's northern coast, including the treaty ports of Yantai and Weihaiwei, and had roughly 6,750,000 people. This area also faced Manchuria across the Bohai Gulf and had

12. There were no differences in the kinds of storage facilities available in different parts of the province; thus, if any part of the province had a bigger problem with rotting, it should have been the more humid coastal areas. Banditry was more serious in the southwest than elsewhere, but in the hundreds of crime reports that I have reviewed, stored grain was almost never a target. (Grain on the road to market sometimes was.)

Map 3. Regional capital markets in late Qing and Republican Shandong

SOURCE: Adapted from Koshimura Eiichi, ed., *Chūgoku Tairiku Shōbetsu Chizu* (Provincial atlas of continental China), Tokyo, 1972, p. 19.

unusually good access to that booming region.[13] With strong ties to Manchuria and the coastal economy of China proper, Shandong's north coast region had relatively easy access to hard currency (to be discussed later) and particularly low interest rates. Holding grain there produced an average return of less than 0.5 percent per month. At the other extreme is the second region: the southwestern prefectures of Yanzhou and Caozhou, where the return averaged 2 percent per month. (Data for the third southwestern prefecture, Jining, are defective.[14]) This area had about 6,400,000 people.

13. At certain times, Manchuria's rulers adopted a variety of currency policies that complicated external trade considerably. (These policies resembled the Shandong provincial policies discussed in this chapter; however, the Manchurian regime seems to have been more successful.) See, for instance, Tsao Lien-en, "The Currency System in Manchuria," *Chinese Economic Journal and Bulletin* 6:4 (April 1930), 389–90, and Eduard Kann, "Copper Banknotes in China," *Chinese Economic Journal* 5:1 (July 1929), 551–61. Certain groups of Shandong and Hebei merchants also had special access to Manchuria because of native-place ties to Manchurian merchants.

14. Technically, Jining and Linqing were "independent districts," rather than prefectures. For our purposes, though, such districts functioned like small prefectures, and I use a single term.

The remaining prefectures, ranging from Yizhou (1.2 percent) to Dongchang (1.7 percent, and adjacent to Caozhou, with which its southernmost counties could conceivably be grouped), average 1.4 percent. Its western third is essentially the Shandong part of North Huang-Yun. As the largest region, with perhaps 21,000,000 people, this one presents the least uniform picture, but it still appears to have been a meaningful capital market. Moreover, these prefectures are clearly separate from the other two groups, and they traded with each other much more than with those areas. They were far more involved in outside trade than the southwest was and more closely tied to the North China regional economy (and less to Manchuria) than were the gulf coast prefectures.[15] I call this region the "heartland" both because it made up the bulk of the province and because, except for the port of Qingdao, it was the area most consistently under the political control of the provincial government in Jinan.

A similar pattern emerges from 1903–11 grain prices in neighboring prefectures of Zhili province.[16] In Daming, adjacent to southwest Shandong, the returns on storing five different grains averaged more than 2 percent per month. Yizhou and Guangping, which border the northwest part of the heartland and include parts of Huang-Yun, had average rates of about 1 percent per month. Rates in Tianjin, Zhili's largest port, which also handled much of northwest Shandong's trade, also averaged about 1 percent. Zunhua, a coastal prefecture that was very close to Manchuria (by both land and water), was Zhili's closest analogue to Shandong's north coast; its rates averaged slightly under 0.8 percent.

The measures of dispersion for the Shandong results confirm the regional pattern. All the prefectures except Laizhou show closely bunched results, indicating that within prefectures, markets did keep returns on storing different grains close to each other, and suggesting

---

There are a number of problems with the Jining data. In addition to wildly differing rates of return on different grains, the most striking peculiarity is the absence of any annual harvest cycle. Unlike grain prices in most other places, the Jining prices do not consistently reach their annual high or low at any particular time of the year. Since storage was costly, grain prices that are no lower right after the harvest than at other times of the year make little sense.

15. On trade, see *SSYZ* 2:156–201; on interdependence of North Coast and Manchuria, see, for instance, Gottschaung, "Migration," 78–81. Yizhou was the one heartland prefecture that had extensive ties to a third regional economy: the Lower Yangzi.

16. See dissertation, chapter 1, n. 15.

that entry and exit from local markets in these grains was fairly easy. To the extent that these grains are a random sample of assets one could hoard, the results suggest that for any given prefecture, there is a two-thirds probability that the average return on any particular asset over these years would be within 0.2 percent per month of the mean return for all assets in that prefecture.[17]

In contrast, we cannot predict the returns on storing any particular grain without knowing what prefecture it was stored in. For only one grain can one make a prediction within 0.6 percent (in either direction from the mean) with a two-thirds probability; on average, one can only come within 0.7 percent per month. Defining a range 1.4 percent wide into which returns would probably fall is not much use when returns averaged 1.6 percent per month. In other words, the concept of a functioning market in savings within each prefecture has predictive power, but the idea of a provincewide market in the storage of any particular grain—much less savings in general—does not. Finally, the regional grouping adopted here is the only one that produces results within each region for any given grain that are as closely bunched as those for all grains within a given prefecture.[18] In sum, individual prefectures showed strong market integration although the province as a whole showed none; and although there were differences between prefectures within each region, they were much smaller than those between regions.

THE DURABILITY
OF REGIONAL ECONOMIC DIFFERENCES

This pattern lasted for many years. A 1933 provincial survey presents the "highest" and "ordinary" rates charged by various types of lenders in each county. Of these, the "ordinary" (*putong*) rates quoted for stores (*shangdian*)—many of which also functioned as local banks—seem the most reliable. North coast store rates averaged 1.9 percent; southwestern ones, 3.5 percent; and heartland shops, 2.5 percent. The southwest becomes less distinct from the heartland if we use the figures for loans from individuals; however, it was probably easier to get an accurate picture of rates charged by stores than by scattered in-

---

17. For the data, see dissertation, appendix A; for a discussion of difficulties with this particular data set, see dissertation, 464, n. 16.
18. See dissertation, appendix A.

dividual lenders. Within the heartland, rates were slightly lower near Qingdao than elsewhere; however, the differences among any plausible subregions created out of this region are significantly smaller than those among the three basic regions. The overall geographic pattern is unmistakably like that of 1900–11.[19]

The 1933 rates themselves are higher than those derived for 1900–11. This does not necessarily mean that interest rates rose, however. Expectations of inflation, for instance, may have changed. More important, the 1900–11 figures represent what one earned simply by transferring grain into the future, without its ever leaving one's courtyard. Consequently, the rates inferred for those years should reflect only minimal compensation for risk—that of loss from one's own premises or of market collapse (not likely unless large outside shipments suddenly appeared) but not that of default by a borrower. Nor would they reflect any difference in bargaining power between lenders and possibly desperate borrowers. Thus, they should resemble the returns on the absolutely safest loans. Our limited evidence confirms this. The safest loans in Laizhou (north coast) were at 0.4 percent per month; loans from trade associations to their own member firms cost 0.6 percent in Jinan (heartland), and the lowest rate I have found for a loan in the southwest was 1.5 percent.[20] The 1933 rates, in contrast, must include substantial risk premiums. For current purposes, "safe" loans from 1900–11 can be compared with "ordinary" loans from 1933; what matters is not absolute levels, but the similar geographic pattern of rate differentials. Moreover, other data confirm these divisions and suggest explanations of them.

CREDIT MARKETS
AND OTHER REGIONAL ECONOMIC BOUNDARIES

It is clear that the north coast was economically separate from the rest of Shandong. The northeasternmost part of the province was largely cut off from the rest of Shandong by mountains, making trade in bulky products difficult. However, this area produced barely half the grain it needed; the rest came across the Bohai Gulf from Manchuria. Many people from here went to Manchuria even when such travel was for-

19. For more on this data, and an earlier use of it by Ramon Myers (who reached somewhat different conclusions), see dissertation, appendix B.
20. *SS*, 1156, 1125; *Shandong quan sheng caizheng shuoming shu* (Jinan, 1913), 28.

bidden. After the prohibition was lifted in the nineteenth century, their numbers soared, and this area provided the largest group of migrants to this frontier. Furthermore, large numbers of north coast people either did seasonal work in Manchuria or spent several years there before returning home. In many ways, then, this area was an economic appendage of Manchuria, not of the rest of Shandong.[21] Once Qingdao became a major port on the southern side of the Shandong peninsula, this division became sharper still: Yantai continued to do a bustling trade with Manchuria but ceased handling many goods from any part of Shandong except the north coast.[22]

However, our statistics outline a north coast region larger than this extreme northeastern part of the peninsula. It spreads westward to include all the area along the Bohai Gulf, including areas near the mouth of the Yellow River from which communication with central and western Shandong was extremely easy. Interest rates and trade patterns alike suggest this broader definition: a preliminary analysis of grain price trends from 1900–11 shows strong correlations within this area but absolutely none between these four prefectures and the rest of Shandong.[23] A broader definition of the north coast also seems economically logical: if access to the Bohai Gulf provided superior economic opportunities, people on the western side of the gulf should want to participate, whether or not they could also trade with the heartland. The question instead is why more of the heartland did not become involved; the answers, as we shall see, have more to do with political economy than physiography.

The broader definition of the north coast is also confirmed by 1911 rate schedules for money transfers from Huangxian, an important

---

21. Gottschaung, "Migration," 77–81.

22. On the impact of the opening of Qingdao on Yantai, see Wang Shouzhong, "Qing mo Shandong shouhui lu kuang li quan yundong," in *Zhongguo difang shizhi luncong*, ed. (Beijing, 1984), 259–61; Gottschaung, "Migration," 91–92, 163; *SDZZ*, no. 76 (10/30/XT 2), 18a.

23. These correlations are based on the same set of grain prices used to calculate interest rates in this chapter. There are very sharp differences between the results obtained when trying to correlate the prices between a North Coast prefecture and a prefecture from elsewhere in the province (almost no cases of correlation) and those obtained when correlating price trends of two prefectures that are either both in the North Coast or both outside it (usually some correlation, and often a strong one). However, the small size of the sample and serious autocorrelation problems limit the usefulness of these results.

banking center near the middle of the north coast region.[24] The ten destinations listed span the four prefectures that are part of our expanded definition of the north coast. The furthest, Xincheng, was 153 miles from Huangxian but only ten perfectly flat miles from the important central Shandong trading center of Zhoucun and seventy-five flat miles from Jinan, the provincial capital. Yet foreign-controlled Qingdao is the only destination listed outside our north coast. That a network with such modest costs—less than 0.5 percent of the shipment for the most expensive destination—would suddenly stop short of other important trading centers strongly suggests that the boundaries of this trading area were set by social or political rather than strictly geographic factors; as we shall see later, such was indeed the case.

Various analysts have also outlined a distinct southwestern zone loosely linked to the rest of Shandong. Its boundaries, however, are disputed.[25] Disagreement centers on whether Jining and Yanzhou—which were agriculturally very much like Caozhou but had larger towns, better transport, more commerce, less banditry, and a stronger gentry—constitute a separate zone or should be grouped with Caozhou in the southwest. In our case, the strong similarity between Yanzhou and Caozhou rates supports the broader definition of this region. Moreover, as we shall see later, Jining was unquestionably the economic capital of Caozhou and the rest of southwest Shandong. Caozhou, Yanzhou, and Jining also share a common trade profile in the 1933 statistics: they have the province's smallest consumption of modern-sector goods and its lowest exports, and they rely heavily on remittances from workers in Manchuria, despite being the part of Shandong farthest from Manchuria.[26]

Here, too, it is noteworthy that no insuperable geographic barriers separate this region from the rest of the province. From 1912 on, Jining and Yanzhou were also linked to Jinan by rail. In addition, contemporary accounts often distinguished the southwest in terms of such cultural factors as "roughness"—its high levels of banditry

24. *SS*, 1145–47.
25. Esherick, *Boxer Uprising*, 12–14; Sun Jingzhi, *Huabei de jingji dili* (Beijing, 1958), 132–34.
26. *SSYZ* 2:151–201; Tōa Kenkyūsho, *Santō Koshōgun Chitai no Chiiki Chōsa* (Tokyo, 1940), report no. 14, class C, no. 158-D, 130–31.

and violence—rather than in terms of any physical differences or barriers.[27] Such definitions confirm what both the map and scholars' disagreements suggest: that its boundaries were human, rather than natural, products and had to be enforced to be perpetuated.

REGIONAL CURRENCY MARKETS

The political underpinnings of market boundaries become clearer when we turn to the currency market. Like all of China, Shandong used numerous silver, copper, brass, and paper currencies during this period, with no fixed exchange rates among them.[28] Elsewhere, silver and silver-denominated paper were increasingly dominant,[29] but in Shandong copper remained very important; consequently, so did the copper-silver market.

According to a 1933 study, farmers received copper for the goods they sold in only 20 percent of places in China and made purchases with copper in only 30 percent of places. In Shandong, however, copper was used for agricultural sales in five of twelve places surveyed and was the only currency farmers received in four locations. Farmers made purchases with copper in eight of thirteen locations. In only one of fourteen places, however, could copper be used to settle debts. People often received loans in copper but had to repay in silver. Prices for large items were generally quoted in silver, and taxes were always set in silver.[30]

Consequently, the exchange rate between silver and copper was crucial for both government and private finance. Had there been a unified provincial capital market, the silver/copper exchange rates in different counties should have converged or at least followed parallel paths as people in places with unusually expensive silver borrowed it from elsewhere, changed it, and then took the coppers to a more favorable

27. For a quick survey of Shandong geography in English, see Esherick, *Boxer Uprising*, 11–20; for greater detail see Hou Renzhi, ed., *Xu tianxia qun guo li bing shu, Shandong zhi bu* (Beijing, 1940), 137–216. For the rail link, see Zhongguo jiaotongbu, jiaotong shi weiyuanhui, *Jiaotong shi* (Nanjing, 1937), 3531–35. For the area's "roughness," see, for instance, *Shandong minzhong jiaoyu yuekan* 5:4 (May 1934), 85–88.

28. Li Guijin, "Qing mo bizhi gaige ji qi shibai yuanyin de qiantan," *Jingji shi*, no. 2 (1984), 129–30, has a summary of the situation as of the late Qing; by 1919, the *NCH* (Oct. 18, 1919, p. 172) had counted 115 new kinds of coinage and untold varieties of paper since 1912.

29. Leonard Hsu, *Silver and Prices in China* (Shanghai, 1935), 68, 75.

30. Ibid., 68, 75, SS, 260–61.

place to turn them back to silver. If, conversely, the flow of currency across county lines had been restricted or if exchange rates could be arbitrarily set and enforced, the resulting currency problems would limit capital market integration.

As figure 1 shows, exchange rates varied wildly from county to county, and trends were often far from parallel.[31] The Shanghai rates may be considered "national" prices, although Tianjin and Beijing rates sometimes diverged slightly from Shanghai's.[32] The available quotations for Yantai and other north coast ports closely tracked Shanghai rates,[33] confirming this area's membership in this "national," or more modestly, "littoral," economy. The heartland and southwest, however, show very different trends.

Even within the heartland region there were significant differences between nearby counties, such as Jinan and Taian. Rates in Linqing and Qingping, two adjacent heartland counties (both in northern Huang-Yun) diverged by as much as 33 percent in the early 1920s. However, after 1926 the difference hovers between 0 percent and 7 percent, only slightly above the cost of shipping copper between the two places.[34] Except for Jinan, rates within the heartland region rarely differed by more than 20 percent, and sharply opposed trends do not last long.

Moreover, until 1927, trends in the heartland (again, excepting Jinan) were not very different from those in Yantai and Shanghai. After that, however, littoral rates leveled off, while those in the Shandong heartland kept climbing. By 1933–34, silver exchanged for about 75 percent more copper in Qingping and Linqing (the only heartland counties for which data are available) than in Shanghai. In

31. The exchange rates used in constructing figure 1 are drawn from gazetteers, newspapers (principally *North China Herald*), Tongji yuebao (Statistical monthly), various Chinese and foreign reports, and, in one case, the records of a large commercial enterprise, reprinted in Hai Shan, "Yutang chunqiu—Jining shi Yutang jiangyuan jian shi," *Jining shi shiliao*, no. 1 (1983), 48–78. A complete list of citations and a brief discussion of problems with the data may be found in dissertation, 402–3.

32. See, for instance, *Tongji yuebao*, Dec. 1929, p. 25; Dec. 1930, p. 52.

33. Hsu, *Silver*, 85; THS, 54 (Yangjiagou), 148 (Ye xian), 252 (Longkou), 286 (Huang xian), 317 (Penglai).

34. SS, 234, gives the day rates charged by Dezhou porters for hauling with different sorts of equipment and the weight and distance they could move in a day with each; since porters in this area were well organized, these rates may have been a bit above average. The weight of a string (1,000 *qian*) of copper cash can be deduced from a report on the copper currency trade in Shandong by the U.S. consul in Jinan from 1922 quoted in Frederic Lee, *Currency, Banking, and Finance in China* (Washington, 1926); this figure matches those implicit in *NCH*, Oct. 27, 1917, p. 216.

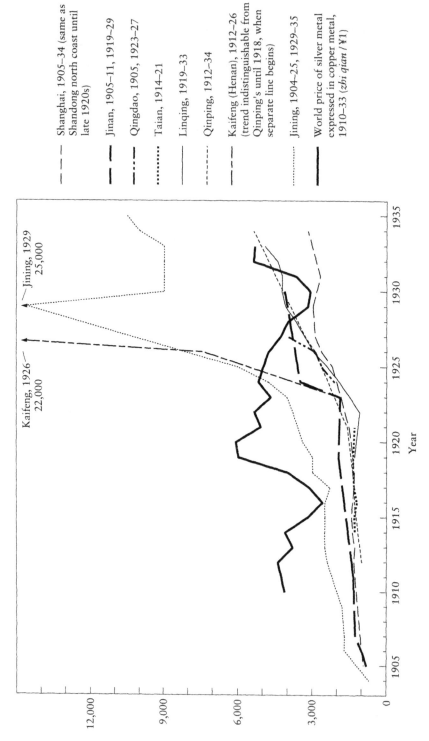

Fig. 1. *Zhi qian* or equivalent in other copper coins per ¥1 of silver in different locations
SOURCES: See dissertation, appendix C.

Shanghai, 1905–34 (same as Shandong north coast until late 1920s)

Jinan, 1905–11, 1919–29

Qingdao, 1905, 1923–27

Taian, 1914–21

Linqing, 1919–33

Qinping, 1912–34

Kaifeng (Henan), 1912–26 (trend indistinguishable from Qinping's until 1918, when separate line begins)

Jining, 1904–25, 1929–35

World price of silver metal expressed in copper metal, 1910–33 (*zhi qian* / ¥1)

most ways, the period after 1928 was more stable than before.[35] However, since, as we shall see, it was governments and their allies that kept the currency market poorly integrated, it is not surprising that with the greater political stability that came after 1928, littoral and heartland rates diverged.

Some evidence suggests that the Shandong government's greater control after 1928 pulled some north coast areas out of the coastal economy and into the heartland zone. A 1928 quotation from Longkou, a small port toward the western part of the north coast region, is very close to those from Jinan and Qingdao and 7–10 percent above those from Linqing and Qingping, but 27 percent above those from Shanghai.[36] Interest rate data also suggest some reabsorption of the western edge of the north coast into the heartland as the Shandong government grew stronger (and less politically connected to Manchuria[37]) after 1928; the five north coast counties with the highest interest rates in 1933 were all from the zone's western end, nearest the heartland.[38]

However, Yantai, the largest north coast port and the one closest to Manchuria, escaped provincial government control and remained part of the littoral economy. Even in 1934, three years after the Japanese seized Manchuria, illegal silver coin shipments from Yantai to Manchuria were large enough to force the government to print more notes; this arbitrage kept Yantai's silver-copper rates within 8 percent of Dalian's,[39] far less than the difference between the coast and the heartland. Thus, while provincial state making expanded the heartland, most of the north coast remained independent.

35. *Qingping xianzhi* (1936), *jingji*, 25a–b; *Linqing xianzhi* (1934), *jingji*, 22b–24a; Shanghai data were created by combining the annual index numbers for trends in copper and silver yuan exchange rates in Shanghai from *Tongji yuebao*, Dec. 1930, p. 51, and combining it with the data on absolute prices for selected dates in Hsu, *Silver*, p. 85. Wherever the two series have data for the same date, they coincide perfectly.

36. Quotation from *Chinese Economic Bulletin* 13:3 (July 21, 1928) (no page number given) in U.S. National Archives, *Records of Former German and Japanese Embassies and Consulates, 1890–1945* (microfilm RG 242 T-179; hereafter *Records*), reel 5, document 4618834.

37. For the reliance of Shandong's early and mid-1920s leadership on Manchurian patronage and on troops recruited among northeast Shandong migrants in Manchuria, see Li Hengzhen, Xu Datong, and Zhang Jinxiu, "Women suo zhidao de Zhang Zongchang," *Wenshi ziliao xuanji*, Jinan edition, no. 13 (1982), 1–2, 12–19, 27, 36–39; Wang Jiaoming, "Zhang Zongchang xing bai jilue," in *Beiyang junfa shiliao xuanji*, ed. Du Chunhe, Li Binsheng, and Qiu Quan (Beijing, 1981), 2:333–37, 346, 348.

38. See dissertation, appendix B.

39. Quotation from *Qingdao Times* of Dec. 7, 1934, in *Records*, reel 5, document 4619093.

The truly astonishing differences, however, are between heartland and southwestern rates. Our most complete set of exchange rate data is for Jining, the commercial center of the southwest,[40] and it resembles nothing else in the province. Jining silver prices were ordinary in 1904, but soared thereafter. By 1909, silver commanded 40 percent more copper there than in Jinan and 60 percent more than in Shanghai; by 1914, Jining rates were roughly double the rate in both Taian (heartland) and Shanghai; by 1921 almost triple; in 1929, nearly six times the Linqing and Qingping rates and about eight times the Shanghai rate; and in 1933, roughly double Qingping and triple Shanghai.

Transport costs cannot explain these differences. Not only was Jining only sixty-five miles by rail from Taian after 1912; even using porters and wheelbarrows to move copper (at roughly 1 percent of the coins' value every eighteen miles) and horses to move silver (at 0.4 percent of the shipment's value for 155 miles),[41] one could clearly make big profits moving coins between various Shandong points. Information problems cannot explain this, either. Late Qing documents reveal active currency exchange markets in Jinan, Weixian, and Yantai that generated publicly available daily price quotations;[42] the same was true in early Republican Jining. By this time, other commercial information was regularly being sent by telegraph even to fairly remote counties.[43]

Warlordism and violence are also inadequate explanations. Provincial governments, as we have seen, were eager to bring more of the province into the heartland currency zone, and for all but a few months of our period, the same government ruled Jinan and Jining.[44]

40. Most of the exchange rate data come from Hai Shan, "Yutang chunqiu," 48–78, which recounts them from the internal records of this factory. For more details, see dissertation, appendix C.

41. *SS*, 234, 1145–47.

42. *Shandong quan sheng caizheng shuomingshu*, 28; *THS*, 462–65; *NCH*, Nov. 22, 1907, p. 455.

43. On Jining, see Chintao Minseibu Tetsudōbu, Chōsa Shiryō, no. 3, p. 88. The first telegraph line was built in Shandong (in Jining) in 1881 (see Zhang Yufa, *Zhongguo xiandaihua de ququ yanjiu: Shandong sheng, 1860–1916* [Taibei, 1982], 490), and by the 1930s there were approximately seventy offices throughout the province (see Zhongguo jiaotongbu youzheng zongju, *Postal Atlas of China* [Nanjing, 1933]). The date of the first telegraph in any given county is usually recorded in its gazetteer.

44. For the 1920s, see Wan Guangwei, "Minguo chunian Shandong zheng dang huodong de neimou yu sheng yihui de chouwen," *Wenshi ziliao xuanji*, Jinan edition, no. 5 (1978), 32–42, and Shao Chuoran, "Tian Zhongyu bachi Shandong sheng yihui xuanju de chouwen," *Wenshi ziliao xuanji*, Jinan edition, no. 5 (1978), 43–50. Lu Weijun, *Han Fuju* (Jinan, 1985) describes provincial-local relations in the 1930s, and pp. 72–73 describe the few months during which different people ruled Jinan and Jining.

Certainly no rival center ever exerted a pull on the southwest comparable to those of Japan and Fengtian on the north coast. And while some parts of the southwest were notoriously unstable and dangerous—perhaps explaining high risk premiums or creating barriers to the movement of money—these conditions did not obtain in Jining and its immediate surroundings,[45] where much of our evidence of aberrant interest and exchange rates comes from. All the conditions were in place for arbitrage to gradually erase these differences; that this did not happen is best explained by the forces of order, not disorder.

THE POLITICS OF ECONOMIC GEOGRAPHY: LOCAL PUBLIC FINANCE

The exchange rate differences could persist because numerous county governments banned the "export" of more than small amounts of certain currencies (usually silver, sometimes copper).[46] This prohibition obstructed both arbitrage and cross-county lending: if it may be difficult to get "hard currency" out of a county, it becomes unattractive to send money in. The barriers that county governments set up protected the profits of certain local money shops and—more important—their own revenues. Although peasants often had only copper on hand, taxes were set in silver.[47] In the 1800s, the exchange rates used for tax payments varied widely; the rate was almost 6,000 copper *jing qian* per silver tael (more than 2,100 *zhi qian* per yuan, in the units used here) in many places.[48] By the 1890s, however, the market rate in coastal cities was less than half that; in 1896, the Shandong governor tried to standardize the tax rate at 4800:1, still roughly double the Tianjin price.[49] If county governments could enforce these high rates on taxes and then dispose of their copper at market rates, they

---

45. Esherick, *Boxer Uprising*, 12–13.

46. See, for instance, *NCH*, Nov. 10, 1905, p. 304, and Nov. 15, 1907, p. 394.

47. An English summary of the Shandong situation is available in John Schrecker, *Imperialism and Chinese Nationalism: Germany in Shantung* (Cambridge, Mass., 1971), 213–16.

48. The late-nineteenth-century situation and some of the fiscal stresses that made the continuation of these techniques important for the Qing court and Shandong governor are summarized by Esherick, *Boxer Uprising*, 170–72; for the early twentieth century, see Governor Sun Baoqi's memorial of 9/25/XT 1, document 4802, file 573, in files of the Huiyi Zhengwuchu, First Historical Archives, Beijing.

49. Esherick, *Boxer Uprising*, 171; see also memorial cited in note 48 above.

would double their real revenue. As silver rose against copper after 1905, the profits that county governments made by preventing free conversion declined, but they remained significant.

Although high exchange rates were imposed on all direct taxes, national and provincial receipts did not increase. Counties collected all taxes and forwarded a fixed amount of silver to the provincial capital.[50] Any profits made by manipulating copper-silver rates went to local government, illegal tax farmers (who undertook responsibility for meeting an area's fixed tax quota, collected as much as they could, and pocketed the difference), and/or local money shops. The Shandong governor even complained in 1903 that since Yellow River control was paid for in copper, the province was suffering from receiving a fixed silver income; he also argued that locally imposed conversion rates led to tax resistance, and so limited the province's ability to collect badly needed new taxes. Although in 1901 the provincial government had decreed that taxes should be computed according to the market exchange rate,[51] counties continued to set their own "market rates" and to enforce them by restricting currency flows.

Because restrictions on currency movement also created periodic currency shortages in inland counties, it was very profitable to issue local coins or paper. While the printing of worthless paper by various provincial and "national" governments during the warlord period (1916–28) is well known,[52] reports from the Shandong Office to Encourage Industry reveal a constant struggle against the proliferation of local government and merchant notes, often copper-denominated and backed by nothing.[53] (Though some warlords passed their notes at gunpoint, local merchants needed a demand for additional currency to give their notes initial acceptability, which they could later exploit by overprinting.) This problem was especially acute in western Shandong,

50. See, for instance, *NCH*, Nov. 15, 1907, p. 394; Schrecker, *Imperialism*, 213–14, notes this same phenomenon in the area near Qingdao.

51. See Wu Tongju, ed., *Zai xu xing shui jin jian* (Taibei, 1966), 10:3748; *Jining zhili zhou xu zhi* (1927), 4:14a–b; *NCH*, March 18, 1904, p. 575; *En xianzhi* (1909) 4:4a; memorial of 9/25/XT 1, document 4802, file 573, files of the Huiyi Zhengwuchu, First Historical Archives, Beijing; *SDZZ*, 62 (6/10/XT 2), 11a–b.

52. For Shandong examples, see *NCH*, May 29, 1926, p. 390; July 2, 1927, pp. 1, 4; Oct. 8, 1927, p. 50.

53. See, for instance, *QYHK*, no. 4 (Jan. 1921), *ge xian shiye zhuangkuang*, 17 (on Shan county); no. 7 (May 1922), *ge xian quanye baogao*, 32–33 (Heze); no. 11 (Feb. 1923), *ge xian chengji baogao*, 20 (Heze again); no. 13 (April 1923), *gongdu*, 41 (Tang Yi), 45 (Linqing). On southwestern Hebei see, for instance, Xu Puqi and Zhang Shouqian, "Daming Xingtai liang xian shicha gaiyao," *Hebei yuekan* 1:3 (March 1933), 4.

and most of all in the southwest and the adjacent parts of Zhili/Hebei and Henan. Closer to the coast, a variety of German, Japanese, English, and (before 1917) Russian silver and paper rushed in to fill any vacuum, leaving little room for local currency.[54]

Jining, the southwestern trading center with the sky-high silver/copper exchange rate, had one of the worst "local currency" problems. The radicals who briefly took over the county in 1928 apparently did not prosecute landlords or employers, but several leaders of the city's Chamber of Commerce and one prominent rural merchant were arrested for their role in issuing—with government approval—nearly worthless "Benefit Jining Copper Notes."[55] This local scam had begun in 1924, before the influx of worthless provincial notes. The payment of workers in local, copper-denominated notes was an issue in two of the city's few major strikes.[56]

THE POLITICS OF ECONOMIC GEOGRAPHY: SUPRALOCAL AUTHORITIES AND POLITICAL SELF-PROTECTION

The potential profit from excess minting or note printing or from artificial exchange rates gave county—and sometimes provincial—governments strong incentives to restrict currency movements across their boundaries. However, local and provincial efforts to quarantine their domains from market forces were not always cynical. Indeed, writings on economic development from early-twentieth-century Shandong have an almost mercantilist tone. Growth is desired because it will help preserve China's independence, not because it will promote individual welfare.[57] Though many of the government's import-substitution and export-promotion projects made sense in terms of comparative advantage, they were generally conceived as ways of

54. See, for instance, *SDZZ*, no. 78 (11/20/XT 2), 14b–15a; *NCH*, Jan. 30, 1909, p. 250.

55. See Tang Chengtao, "Huo guo yang min de 'Li Ji qianpiao,' " *Jining shi shiliao*, no. 1 (1983), 89–91.

56. Wu Guogui, "Yutang xinghuo—Jining Shi Yutang jiangyuan gongyun gai," *Shandong gongyun shi ziliao*, no. 16 (Feb. 10, 1985), 13. The workers won their demand for payment in conventional silver yuan rather than copper notes.

57. See, for instance, the untitled article by Yi Rong in *SDZZ*, no. 88 (4/30/XT 3), 7b–8a; Jing Sheng, "Shandong renmin zhi fudan," in no. 89 (5/15/XT 3), 8a–9b, and no. 90 (5/30/XT 3), 7a–8b; *Nong shang gongbao* 1:5 (Dec. 1914), *zhengshi*, 14; Lin Maoquan (head of the Shandong Office to Encourage Industry in the 1920s), *Wenji* N.p., 1926[?], 2a–b, 71a.

escaping indebtedness, reclaiming concessions from foreigners, or achieving other "self-strengthening" goals that would not necessarily be served by full-fledged integration into the coastal economy.[58]

This emphasis on nationalist political goals made perfect sense in the intellectual climate of early-twentieth-century China. Even liberals in early-twentieth-century China generally saw the liberation of individual energies as a method of strengthening China in its struggle for autonomy more than as an end in itself.[59] The mixture of self-serving and sincere motives for interference with currency flows is exemplified in the provincial government's attempt to block copper coin exports from Shandong.

Even in the late Qing, copper coins had sometimes been worth more as metal than as coins, leading both Chinese and foreigners to buy coins and melt them down. Beginning in 1904, the national government tried to deal with this by slightly debasing its copper currency; when provincial and local mints followed suit, the situation quickly got out of control.[60] German silver coins soon became the standard currency along the Qingdao-Jinan railway in east Shandong, and Russian silver a common currency on Shandong's north coast; the government feared foreign control of its money supply.[61] During World War I, the world price of copper (as metal) climbed rapidly.[62] Japanese merchants, now the dominant foreign group in Shandong, became much more aggressive about buying up copper coins to export and melt down. Since the Japanese now controlled Qingdao, they found it much easier than before to evade provincial restrictions, and this trade quickly spread along the route of the Qingdao-Jinan railway. Between 1915 and 1919, according to the U.S. consul in Jinan, Shandong "was almost denuded of copper currency," with more than ¥22,000,000 worth exported.[63] These coin exports from Shandong

58. See, for instance, Lin Maoquan, *Wenji*, 1a–7b. *NCH*, March 4, 1922, pp. 576, 585, provides an example of actual investment decision making governed by the same logic.

59. See, for instance, Benjamin Schwartz, *In Search of Wealth and Power: Yen Fu and the West* (Cambridge, Mass., 1964), and Joseph Levenson, *Liang Ch'i-ch'ao and the Mind of Modern China* (Cambridge, Mass., 1953).

60. Li Guijin, "Qing mo bizhi," 129–37; see also Zhongguo jindai huobi shi weiyuanhui, eds., *Zhongguo jindai huobi shi ziliao* (Shanghai, 1965), 2:958–61, 970–75, 984–85.

61. *NCH*, Jan. 30, 1909, p. 250; *SDZZ*, no. 78 (11/20/XT 2), 14b–15a.

62. Eduard Kann, *The Currencies of China* (Shanghai, 1926), 408.

63. Lee, *Currency*, 32–33; Kann, *Currencies*, 525.

equaled about 12 percent of the annual capacity of all of China's copper mints or the leakage from the entire country during the currency panic of 1899.[64] The foreign demand for copper coins raised their value further above the levels set by many local authorities, making restrictions all the more important to county finance.

Provincial and national authorities became increasingly worried both about the symbolism of this trade—some of this copper was used for Japanese bullet casings—and about the control it gave Japan over the money supply along the railway.[65] (Losing control over the money supply hurt not only the provincial government's influence, but its purse—minting coins was quite profitable, and printing paper currency even more so.[66]) Complaints about this arbitrage disappeared in the mid-1920s but became common again from 1928 on, with Japanese buyers regularly appearing as far inland as Taian.[67]

Although provincial projects often suffered from restrictions on currency movement between counties, provincial authorities enacted many restrictions on coins leaving the province, including a system of currency "passports"; most exports of copper coins were banned in 1930.[68] In the late 1920s and 1930s provincial-level state makers were caught between the desire for a unified provincial currency and unwillingness to let unification happen through integration into larger, international, markets; at the same time that they redoubled their efforts to limit currency exports, they were (unsuccessfully) ordering all counties to abide by exchange rates for notes that would be set in Jinan.[69]

We know little about how currency restrictions were enforced, but persistent exchange rate differences suggest significant successes. Even in 1933, some counties very close to each other still quoted very different rates.[70] Silver-copper exchange was a major problem for American

64. Li Guijin, "Qing mo bizhi," 134, 131.
65. See p. 19 of the June 1929 report in JD2:AH110.
66. Kann, *Currencies*, 526; *NCH*, Nov. 10, 1905, p. 304.
67. *Records*, reel 5, documents 4619097–134; see esp. 4619130 (quotation from the *China Sphere*, Aug. 15, 1928) on the spread of the trade to inland areas; see also p. 19 of the June 1929 report in JD2:AH110.
68. Lee, *Currency*, 52; for a later repetition of the same phenomenon, see *CZGB* 6:4 (Jan. 1935), *mingling*, 10–12; Lu Weijun, "Han Fuju tongzhi xia de Shandong jinrong," *Shandong shi zhi ziliao*, no. 8 (1985), 58.
69. See *Records*, reel 5, document 4168841, copy of Chefoo *Daily News*, Dec. 1, 1927.
70. *Shouguang xianzhi* (1934), 11:12a–b; *Shandong zheng su shicha ji*, 362, 371, 832.

firms in Shandong, which advanced goods and silver to retailers throughout the province, who were then paid in copper; these retailers often claimed they couldn't get silver to repay in and frequently deducted currency losses from their repayments.[71] While county governments could not fully police their borders, people were searched for currency at train stations and other checkpoints;[72] policing rail and water routes could restrain the largest and most profitable means of arbitrage. (Postal remittances were irregular, and since they used government offices, were easy to monitor.[73]) Rate differentials between Jining and nearby heartland points far exceeded even the costs of moving copper by wheelbarrow, not to mention rail freight.

THE POLITICS OF ECONOMIC GEOGRAPHY: PRIVATE GAIN

Soldiers, however, were often exempt from inspection,[74] and at a higher level, those with political connections could profit handsomely by evading these restrictions. A hint of how currency moved across counties may be gathered from the other service offered by the Huangxian currency-moving company mentioned previously: convoying opium, which required extensive official contacts, bribes, or enough armed force to ignore the state.[75] In Kaifeng, Henan, near southwest Shandong, it was reportedly officials, including the provincial treasurer, who evaded the currency export restrictions; one sent an entire railroad car of copper coins to Hankou for exchange.[76]

One of the most revealing stories of currency arbitrage involves less privileged participants, from Fan county in southwest Shandong. In 1917, huge floods left millions of people in North China destitute. The *North China Herald* sent a correspondent to the southwest Shandong-Henan-Zhili border area, near the original dike break. Here he found

---

71. Quoted in Lee, *Currency*, 56.
72. *NCH*, Nov. 10, 1905, p. 304; Nov. 15, 1907, p. 394.
73. Clifton O'Neal Carey, "Narrative Account of Experiences in China," p. 8, in packet labeled "Letters, Sept.–Dec., 1919," Clifton O'Neil Carey Papers, Bentley Historical Library, University of Michigan; *NCH*, Sept. 27, 1907, p. 720.
74. *NCH*, July 29, 1916, p. 189, describes such a situation in Kaifeng, near southwest Shandong.
75. *SS*, 1145.
76. *NCH*, Dec. 22, 1917, p. 719; March 30, 1918, p. 752.

Japanese merchants who were paying ¥0.155 per *jin* (1 *jin* = 1.3 pounds) for copper coins worth about ¥0.167 back on the coast.[77] This trade had previously been carried on elsewhere, but high water had now allowed it to move further upstream, where silver fetched a higher price. The Japanese were making their fourth trip to the area,

> allowing just enough interval for the natives to take their [silver] dollars upstream or inland and bring all the available [copper] cash to this shipping point. . . . Last year, said the loquacious [village] headman [who was supervising the exchange], this trade did not come so far up stream *and the officials prevented the shipment of cash down to the buyers, but this year the buyers had come themselves and "bought an open road"* [bribed the officials] *so that all was easy*, and the impoverished countryside, under water for three months, was recovering, thanks to the cash trade. (emphasis added)[78]

Several points emerge from this story. First, the people in this village knew about this opportunity, but were normally excluded. Second, official prohibitions and, conversely, bribes, determined who could participate. Third, even after getting by the formal government, the merchants did not deal with individual peasants, but with a village head who had organized "his" people into work teams. Fourth, the biggest profits were made on the inland side of the transaction. If the copper the Japanese bought for ¥0.155 was indeed worth ¥0.167 on the coast, the merchants cleared less than 8 percent between Fanxian and the coast, minus their costs. The peasants who took the coins further inland (on foot), however, received 1,400 cash for a piece of silver that cost them roughly 1,000,[79] a 40 percent profit before accounting for their costs (largely a matter of their time). Moreover, their 40 percent markup was probably less than what officials and their cronies got in "normal" years, when participation was more restricted. Local officials who restricted currency flows preserved hefty profits for a favored minority of local traders, not for the outside merchants who brought in their silver.

77. *NCH*, Oct. 27, 1917, p. 216; the weight-to-value conversion ratio derived from the figures here is confirmed by figures from the American consul in Jinan quoted in Lee, *Currency*, p. 32.
78. *NCH*, Oct. 27, 1917, p. 216.
79. Ibid.

FRAGMENTED MARKETS AND DISTRIBUTION:
THE POWERFUL

Weakly integrated currency and capital markets had various effects on
the distribution of wealth. High interest rates hurt hinterland debtors.
Artificially high silver and copper rates in the hinterland counties redistributed wealth from private citizens to local government. High exchange rates hurt those who were paid in copper but bought at least
some things in silver (or at silver-denominated prices) and benefited
people paid in silver. Finally, restrictions on currency movement benefited those who had the connections to circumvent those restrictions
or to pass local currency, at the expense of everyone else. Determining
who was in each of these groups, however, is difficult, and quantifying
their profits and losses is harder still.

High interest rates clearly favored hinterland creditors over debtors.
Besides banks and pawnshops, certain stores were also significant
lenders. In the heartland and north coast zones, buyers of cash crops,
particularly cotton and peanuts, were also important sources of
credit,[80] but this situation seems to have been rare in the southwest. In
Jining, the shops that doubled as credit institutions were those that
sold modern goods: factory-made thread and yarn, cloth, kerosene,
matches, and cigarettes.[81] Since they often got credit from their suppliers, who were located where money was cheaper, they were probably among the major beneficiaries of the high price of local credit.[82]
Interestingly, a 1942 survey argued that sellers of yarn and other
"foreign" goods had become Jining's mercantile elite and noted a
sharp conflict between them and the grain, leather, and wool merchants[83]—exporters of local products, who lacked access to the importers' relatively cheap credit, were, in turn, surprisingly unimportant as lenders to local farmers.

80. See, for instance, *QYHK*, no. 12 (March 1923), *gongdu*, 30 (on northwest
Shandong in general).
    81. Kokuritsu Pekin Daigaku Fusetsu Nōson Keizaisho, *Santō Sainei Kenjō
o Chushin Toseru Nosam Ryūtsū ni Kanchiru Ichi Kōsatsu* (hereafter, *Santō Sainei*)
(Beijing, 1942), 94–100.
    82. On credit (in both money and goods) from the suppliers of various modern
goods to their agents in the Jining area, see the remarks of British-American tobacco
agent Frank H. Canaday in his letter from Jinan to A. Bassett of May 20, 1925, in the
F. H. Canaday papers, Harvard-Yenching Library, 17:92, 96; such credit was provided
even though their agent in Jining was "the richest man in the city" (vol. 15, letters of
Aug. 20 and 26, 1923).
    83. *Santō Sainei*, 12–13, 10, 31.

While the survey unfortunately does not describe this conflict, it does note that many importers were also local officials, while grain traders were not, and that importers, unlike exporters, did a great deal of business with Jining's two modern bank branches. It also notes that all of Jining's export firms were quite small and most quite new.[84] In the days before modern goods imports, many of Jining's leading families had been involved in the export trades, and these families did not disappear in the twentieth century. Rather, they seem to have moved out of their old businesses and into more lucrative ones or shifted such traditional operations and assets to larger urban centers such as Jinan or even Shanghai.[85] Thus, though some nationally known figures from Jining were still involved in exports from the region, importers held the upper hand in local politics.

These Jining importers, then, appear to exemplify the politically connected oligopolists with access to cheap credit that we are looking for. Moreover, earlier historical material also suggests Jining as a likely center for such collusion. We will return repeatedly to the collaborative relationships among Jining's top merchants and officials, but an introduction is in order here.

There were unusually strong ties between big merchants and officials in Jining as far back as the late Ming, based in part on their cooperation in the farming of transport taxes and proscription of "smuggling" (evading these taxes).[86] At the peak of the Grand Canal trade, Jining and Linqing (the principal port of northwestern Shandong/North Huang-Yun) were roughly equal in importance; yet government complaints about evasions of customs duty, in both the 1700s and 1900s, describe merchants using land transport and back roads to circumvent Linqing, but not Jining.[87] In part this was due to geography,[88] but it was also self-perpetuating: close cooperation be-

---

84. Ibid., 26–27, 68–70.
85. See, for instance, David Buck, *Urban Change*, 28–29, 105, 139. See also Hai Shan, "Yutang chunqiu," pt. 1, pp. 64–65.
86. See Jing Su and Luo Lun, *Qing dai Shandong jingying dizhu jingji yanjiu* (proofs for revised edition; original version translated and abridged by Endymion Wilkinson as *Landlord and Labor in Late Imperial China*, which will be the citation used hereafter, though page numbers will refer to the revised text), 27.
87. Memorial from Tian Wenjing, 10/27/Yongzheng 6, reprinted in Guoli Gu Gong Bowuyuan wenxian bianji weiyuanhui, *Gongzhong dang Yongzheng Chao zouzhe* (hereafter, *Yongzheng Gongzhong dang*) (Taibei, 1978), 11:649–51; see also Madeline Zelin, *The Magistrate's Tael* (Berkeley, 1984), 209, for a different complaint of this sort.
88. Seasonal problems (e.g., low water, ice) at the confluence of the Wei River and

tween merchants and government became the norm in Jining, rather than Linqing's game of hide and seek. Moreover, Jining's collaborating merchants and officials administered a near monopoly over commerce originating in or passing through the city's hinterland. The kind of manipulation described in this chapter depended on having most of the southwest's trade with the outside world pass through Jining, as indeed it did.[89] Linqing exercised no such monopoly, both because of its geography and because of the lack of very close merchant-official cooperation. While much of Jining's hinterland could reach no other port, much of Linqing's hinterland could also reach the Grand Canal at Dezhou or before 1902 at Liaocheng. And while twentieth-century Jining became the closest railroad stop for most of southwest Shandong (it was the end of the branch line going west from Jinan), Linqing never did get a railroad station.

It is also suggestive that Jining's oldest and largest firm—the Yutang food-processing enterprises—was owned by a lineage that had been producing officials since the eighteenth century and had a member on the Qing Grand Council in the late nineteenth century.[90] Though founded in 1776, the company first became heavily involved in financial activities after 1875, when the development of the treaty ports had begun to create the possibilities for arbitrage discussed here. In this period, the company borrowed from foreigners, bought several pawnshops, and developed relationships with local money shops that allowed them to begin issuing their own notes; these new businesses grew much faster than their original food-processing trade.[91] In addition to the official family that owned most of Yutang, many other Jining officials had their families' educational trust funds invested in this company.[92] Moreover, Jining's largest charity, whose directors included the city's leading merchant and gentry families, deposited more than 80 percent of its endowment with the city's major pawnshops and commercial firms and invested less than 20 percent in land.

Grand Canal at Linqing encouraged the growth of land porterage—which could easily be adapted to customs evasion. See, for instance, *NCH*, Nov. 2, 1906, p. 252, and *Linqing xianzhi* (1934) 7:21b–22a.

89. On the dominance of southwest Shandong's trade by Jining, see, for instance, *SSYZ* 2:124, 151–202.

90. Hai Shan, "Yutang chunqiu," 55–56.

91. Ibid., pp. 48, 56, 58; pt 2 in *Jining shi shiliao*, no. 2 (1984), 99.

92. Ibid., p. 56.

Nor was this merely a matter of familiarity and convenience: since the firms with which these funds were deposited paid between 8 percent and 12 percent per year (0.67 percent to 1 percent per month) for these deposits at a time when consumer rates were well over 2 percent per month, this was a very profitable form of self-dealing for the city's elite.[93] Dominating access to cheap funds from the littoral, or even the heartland, provided similarly lucrative spreads.

Though many of these officially connected merchants were importers, this picture of their behavior should be distinguished from the Leninist critique of Chinese "compradors."[94] The goods they sold were often "foreign" only in the senses of being factory products and being imports to the area; many were made in Qingdao, Tianjin, or Jinan. Some firms, such as Yutang, both imported and exported goods, with the net balance unclear.[95] Probably the most genuinely foreign item all these firms offered was credit, which came to them (sometimes directly, more often with intervening steps) from modern banks or suppliers in the treaty ports. However, the problem was not that they conveyed this useful product to the interior, but that they acted as a cartel, offering less credit at a higher price than would have been available were cross-county credit transactions unrestrained. And, as with the currency arbitrage described above, local conduits for outside credit, not would-be or actual outside lenders, profited from there being few such conduits. Certainly treaty-port firms that dealt with them did not find these people to be subservient.[96]

Other people, of course, were also affected by the interest rate. One very strategic group—rural tax collectors, who in southwest Shandong were largely clerks and village heads—also benefited from the restricted flow of credit from outside; they often lent money to taxpayers for their payments and were often the ones who actually collected copper coins.[97] It is not clear from whom, if anyone, these tax collectors

---

93. *Jining zhilizhou xu zhi* 5:10b–11a, 13b, 21b.

94. The general source for this view is Mao Zedong, in writings such as "Analysis of the Classes in Chinese Society" (1926) in *Selected Readings from the Work of Mao Tsetung* (Beijing, 1971), p. 11; for examples from well-known historical works see Harold Isaacs, *The Tragedy of the Chinese Revolution* (Stanford, 1951), 6–7, 10; Marie-Claire Bergère, "The Role of the Bourgeoisie," in *China in Revolution: The First Phase, 1900–1913*, ed. Mary C. Wright (New Haven, 1968), 236–37.

95. Hai Shan, "Yutang chunqiu," pt. 2, 91–92.

96. Lee, *Currency*, 56.

97. See memorial of the censor Gao Xixi on 1/30/GX 28 in LFZZ, GX 28, packet 28–29.

themselves borrowed. However, if they were colluding with politically connected merchants and officials to enforce artificial currency rates, it would be logical for them to borrow from these people, probably at rates that gave them a share of the arbitrage profits.

FRAGMENTED MARKETS AND DISTRIBUTION: THE GENERAL POPULATION

Moving to larger groups, most farmers, laborers, and merchants outside the privileged circle were net borrowers—and therefore losers from restrictions on capital mobility. However, some better-off farmers and merchants were net creditors. While they would not have benefited from high local interest rates nearly as much as those who could borrow elsewhere and realize large spreads, any net creditor gained something from high rates. This applies to more than just cash lending: farmers who did not have to sell their crops immediately at harvest time could hoard instead and earn the area's high interest rate. The only study I know of a southwest Shandong village (one near Jining) indicates that the village's eight wealthiest households (of fifty-one) made more of their sales several months after the harvest than other farmers and received slightly higher average prices, but the evidence is scant.[98]

For government overcharges, the losers are easily identifiable: taxpayers. The winners were local government, tax collectors, and moneychangers, not higher levels of government. The mechanics and extent of their gains, however, are unclear. Most local government expenses were local, and those who collected extra copper by rigging exchange rates had to dispose of it at more realistic rates to realize their profit. At least some southwest Shandong counties appear to have had trouble obtaining silver locally.[99] Thus local governments either had to ship their copper elsewhere to exchange it or force those from whom they made local purchases to value copper more highly than the government did when it computed taxes; they probably used a mixture of both strategies.

In some cases, favored money shops or stores made the profits from

---

98. *Santō Sainei*, 86, 92.
99. *NCH*, Nov. 15, 1907, p. 394.

manipulating the exchange rate, although they probably paid local officials for this franchise. In others, the government tried to force local money shops to convert its money at a rate that gave the government all the profit.[100] Since some of the latter cases led to successful money shop strikes,[101] it appears that merchants had significant bargaining power, but this area remains murky. The sharing of gains between local governments and tax collectors is even murkier, since tax farming, though common, was illegal.

The importance of these profits to local government is clear, even if their exact size is not. One measure of this importance is the tenacity with which local governments clung to the opportunity for currency conversion even when cash crop farmers could have paid their taxes in silver. Several southwest Shandong counties made sure that their citizens did not escape these exactions by requiring that taxes be computed in silver but paid in copper.[102]

Thus, what currency people earned made no difference to them as taxpayers. It did, however, determine whether they gained or lost from the overvaluation of silver in private transactions. An apparently unfinished survey by John L. Buck reported that farmers were paid for their goods with copper in five of twelve Shandong locations and received only copper in four of them, but we do not know which locations these were. Most likely those who grew sorghum, millet, and other crops with purely local markets received copper. Crops destined for urban or coastal markets, such as peanuts, cotton, and wheat, appear to have usually been paid for in silver.[103] Sometimes what currency would be used was a matter of contention. While various docu-

---

100. This would appear to be the case in the situation described in ibid., 393–94, where the government itself had trouble obtaining silver. German observations of this system as it operated near Qingdao also suggested that the locally collected copper never got near Jinan. See, for instance, Schrecker, *Imperialism*, 213, quoting claims that the tax collectors and their cronies profited, but the county magistrate simply received the set amount of silver. In general, see the Shandong provincial assembly's resolution on money shops in *SDZZ*, no. 62 (6/10/XT 2), 11a–11b.

101. See, for instance, *SDZZ*, no. 77 (10/1/XT 1), 14b.

102. *NCH*, Nov. 15, 1907, pp. 393–94.

103. The prices for "export" crops are almost always quoted in silver, but payments were not always made in the quoted currency. For instance, *NCH*, Nov, 11, 1916, p. 307, quotes Taian peanut prices in copper, but just a month later (Dec. 23, 1916, p. 635) explains the relatively cheap silver prices there by referring to the unusually large peanut crop just sold. Given exchange rate differentials, coastal buyers probably paid hinterland producers in silver.

ments allude to urban merchants passing off worthless currency to
rural people in western Shandong, especially during the 1904 and
1935 currency reforms, farmers did not always lack information and
bargaining power.[104] When copper currency hit a new low in Kaifeng
(Henan, beyond Huang-Yun, but still near southwest Shandong),
many peasants refused to sell their grain except for silver, putting
heavy pressure on an already hungry city.[105]

Small retailers and especially laborers depended on earnings in
copper. Porters and day laborers, both urban and rural, were almost
always paid in copper.[106] Southwest Shandong's few factory workers
were paid in copper or, worse yet, in copper-denominated notes that
were heavily discounted by stores.[107] However, such people paid very
few direct taxes and so were probably hurt less than those farmers
who were paid in copper.

Overvalued silver probably had the greatest impact on people con-
templating purchases of capital goods rather than items of daily consumption. Items sold in small, inexpensive units, such as cigarettes or
flour, were usually sold for copper; large purchases, like land or livestock, were priced in silver (a notable exception—a source giving Jining
land prices in copper—highlights again the peculiarities of southwest
Shandong).[108] There were some exceptions even to this generalization,
however. For instance, the government salt monopoly demanded silver. A Jining folk song from the 1930s makes fun of a fool who didn't
realize that *tong yuan*—one type of copper currency—would not be
accepted for either salt or grain and may as well be spent at the local
theatricals (that is, wasted).[109] And all these effects were strongest
where exchange rates were the most unrealistic: primarily in the
southwest.

104. *NCH*, Dec. 28, 1929, p. 507; memorial from Shandong governor Yang Shixiang of 2/16/GX 33 (1907) in *LFZZ*, GX 33, packet 49–50.
    105. *NCH*, Sept. 9, 1916, p. 512.
    106. On porters' rates, see *SS*, pp. 234, 250, 260; on factory workers and day
laborers in construction, see *Records*, reel 37, pp. 4660213–219, 4660230.
    107. Wu Guogui, "Yutang xinghuo," 13.
    108. For examples of flour prices quoted in copper, see *NCH*, May 20, 1911,
p. 484; Jan. 2, 1915, p. 56; July 13, 1918, p. 82; July 14, 1923, p. 93; *SS* 260–61,
315–16; on cigarettes, see F. H. Canaday Papers, vols. 12, 15, 17 passim. (Canaday
recorded copper fluctuations in every town he visited.) On livestock, see *NCH*, July
18, 1914, p. 235. The one example of a land price in copper is in *SS*, 315.
    109. Dong Taisheng, ed., *Shandong ge yao ji* (Jinan, 1933), 35.

FRAGMENTED MARKETS
AND REGIONAL ECONOMIC PERFORMANCE

These highly imperfect markets kept capital scarcer and more expensive in the heartland, and especially the southwest, than it would have been had money been easier to move. Thus, certain projects in those regions were never carried out, even though they would have paid as well as projects that were carried out in the north coast zone. In all likelihood, heartland projects that would have generated exports were not affected much, while projects that would have earned money locally were hard hit; in the southwest, all kinds of projects were seriously affected.

Unlike the southwest, the heartland had its own access to the international economy through Qingdao. That port, however, was always dominated by one power (first Germany, then Japan) that tried to monopolize its foreign trade, and credit and silver were never quite as cheap there as in Yantai, Weihaiwei, or Shanghai.[110] The northwestern parts of this region also had connections to Tianjin.[111] The heartland sent some goods and people to Manchuria but received fewer remittances than the north coast; those remittances seem to have pushed interest rates to particularly low levels in the north coast and similar parts of Zhili.

Some significant infusions of outside capital did reach the heartland and helped its economy. We will look at one of these in the next chapter: improved cotton varieties, the introduction of which was financed by Qingdao and Tianjin mills and which then became a crop against which their agents regularly advanced working capital.[112] There is little information about rates on these loans; at times these buyer/suppliers established local monopolies that probably let them overcharge for advances against the crop. At one point, well-entrenched Japanese buyers who had given a partial advance on a local cotton

110. On Qingdao rates, see *SSYZ* 5:90; *Jiao-Ao xianzhi* (1928), *shihuo*, 85–88.
111. On, for instance, Tianjin's pivotal role in northwest Shandong's cotton (the area's largest crop) trade and peanut trade, see Cheng Shouzhong, ed. *Shandong kaocha baogaoshu* (Jinan, probably 1934), 6–18.
112. *Gong shang banyuekan* 6:3 (Feb. 1, 1934), 108; *Nongye zhoubao* 2:48 (Nov. 27, 1933), 766–67, 5:27 (July 16, 1926), 581; *QYHK*, no. 4 (Jan. 1921), *gongdu*, 1–5; Matsuzaki Yujiro, *Santō Shō no Sai Nishiki* (Qingdao, 1941), 478–79; Mantetsu, *Santō no Mensaku* (Tianjin, 1942), 47–54; Kambe Masao, ed., *Dō A Keizai Kenkyū* (Tokyo, 1942), 1:118–20.

crop even tried to pay for the balance in opium rather than money.[113] Some well-entrenched tobacco buyers were also abusive creditors.[114] In general, however, the influx of outside funds meant that such farmers got cheaper credit and generally did better than farmers growing for more local markets.

Cash crop farming enabled the heartland to avoid the southwest's frequent silver shortages. As of 1933, most heartland counties sold more goods beyond their boundaries than they bought from beyond them; thus they should have had enough silver left for taxes and for repaying whatever cross-county loans did exist. There is no reason to expect deflation or marked price divergence from the north coast in the heartland, in contrast to what we will see in the southwest.

Still, the persistent interest rate differences between the heartland and the north coast are strong indicators of this area's limited gains from development on the coast and in Manchuria. The heartland's semi-integration with the coast might be compared to contemporary China's relation to the world economy. Numerous projects in the People's Republic of China would offer returns high enough for would-be foreign investors to find attractive, but because profits in local currency cannot be converted or removed, investors are primarily interested in projects that will produce exports. Similarly, the early-twentieth-century heartland received outside loans for export-oriented projects like cotton improvement but not for projects that might have earned even more, but only locally.

Shandong provincial and local authorities often sounded like mercantilists, emphasizing the balance of payments and "independence" as economic goals. Since these goals seem to have mattered more to them than did increasing local consumption levels, they may have been content to have no outside loans to the heartland except for those that financed exports, thus decreasing rather than increasing the area's debt. However, this situation did not maximize the region's growth or welfare. The infusion of new capital was limited by the extent to which the heartland specialized in exports—a specialization that depended on a limited and vulnerable transport network.[115] The move-

113. *Shandong shiye gongbao*, no. 3 (Sept. 1931), *xunling*, 27.

114. See, for instance, the case of Tian Qunquan described in Sherman Cochran, *Big Business in China: Sino-Foreign Rivalry in the Cigarette Industry, 1890–1930* (Cambridge, Mass., 1980), 144.

115. See, e.g., *NCH*, June 10, 1916, p. 571; "Shantung Groundnut Trade," *Chinese Economic Bulletin* 9:29 (Sept. 11, 1926), 157.

ment of money in and out of this area remained more dependent than it had to be on the movement of commodities that were harder to store and move than money itself.[116]

The southwest was hurt much more. Even here, some outside capital flowed in. Two of Jining's factories were partially financed by outsiders, though these were special cases that resulted from unusual political conditions.[117] And we would not expect investors from other areas to have made many retail loans to individual southwest Shandong peasants for weddings, funerals, and the like.[118] Even without currency restrictions, difficulties in getting information about borrowers and in enforcing payments would have discouraged remote lenders. This reluctance would be especially true in disorderly places such as Heze or Shanxian. Jining and its immediate surroundings were not particularly unstable or bandit ridden, however;[119] their credit and currency problems were the same as those in the rest of the southwest because they had the same government policies.

What is most striking in the southwest—aside from interest and exchange-rate differentials themselves—is the absence of outside credit for production and marketing, even of crops purchased by firms from areas with lower interest rates. In heartland Shandong, as noted above, those who grew cotton, peanuts, and tobacco often got loans from those who bought their crops. These buyers, in turn, were often financed by the larger merchants they sold to, and so on in a chain stretching back to the treaty ports and beyond.[120] In northern Jiangsu, just south of southwest Shandong, wheat growers were financed by merchants who depended on bank loans, with the funds originating in Shanghai.[121] Although southwest Shandong exported less than the rest of the province did, large quantities of wheat, soybeans, and

---

116. Market price-to-weight ratios for Shanxi province, 1929–36, which should not be too different from contemporaneous ones for Shandong, are calculated in Sands, "Investigation," 64. Some goods (cotton, kerosene, and cooking oil) were actually worth more per unit weight than copper cash would have been, but most agricultural goods were worth less, and all goods were worth far less than silver.

117. These circumstances are discussed at length in dissertation, chapter 1, n. 129.

118. These were among the most common reasons for peasant borrowing throughout North China and are cited as among the major reasons that peasants wanted cash at all in the only village study from southwest Shandong that I am aware of; see *Santō Sainei*, 93.

119. See, for instance, Rolf Tiedemann, "The Persistence of Banditry: Incidents in Border Districts of the North China Plain," *Modern China* 8:4 (Oct. 1982), 397.

120. See, for instance, "The Peanut Trade of Tsingtao," *Chinese Economic Bulletin* 11:348 (Oct. 22, 1927), 213–14.

121. See, for instance, Chen Bozhuang, *Xiaomai ji mianfen* (Shanghai, 1936), 52.

other products were collected from the rest of the region in Jining and shipped to Jinan and to coastal ports.[122] This traffic seems not to have been disrupted even in the worst years of warlordism and banditry; thus, even if risk factors affected retail lending in the more remote parts of the southwest, they should not have mattered here.

However, a 1921 report by the Ministry of Agriculture, Industry, and Commerce noted that finance was a particularly serious problem in Jining, a problem that was preventing the area from increasing its agricultural exports.[123] A survey of Jining and nearby villages twenty years later makes it clear that at each level of trade, credit for production and marketing came from "below" rather than "above." Farmers in the village surveyed generally borrowed from fellow villagers.[124] Poor peasants brought the village's wheat and beans to the nearest market town or, occasionally, directly to Jining. Other villagers provided barebones financing for the trip; the producers were paid after the seller returned. The description of the market in Jining emphasizes how eager these *xiao banzi* were to get back to their villages; this eagerness presumably weakened their bargaining power and was probably due in part to pressures from producers who needed cash quickly for debts and taxes. These *xiao banzi* rarely borrowed from Jining grain shops and did not give advances against crops.[125]

Other potential sources also failed to relieve southwestern farmers' dependence on local (primarily village) credit. Jining's grain and bean/nut oil firms were very small; only three of the thirty-two wholesale oil buyers, and one of thirty-seven grain buyers, had ¥1,000 in capital.[126] They were poor candidates to receive or dispense large amounts of credit, and they got no loans from Jining's two modern banks.[127] The Taian, Jinan, and other merchants who bought southwestern crops did not arrive in Jining until after the harvest; at that point, they did borrow from modern bank branches, but this was too late for them to pass these funds on as credit for producers.[128] Southwestern peasants and local traders lacked the option of financing im-

122. *Santō Sainei*, 4–8, 47.
123. *NSGB*, no. 85 (Aug. 1921), *zhengshi*, 57.
124. *Santō Sainei*, 13, 106; this pattern is confirmed by the figures in John L. Buck, *Land Use in China: Statistical Volumes* (New York, 1982), 404.
125. *Santō Sainei*, 33–40.
126. Ibid., 26–27, 68–69.
127. Ibid., 13.
128. Ibid., 68.

provements with credit cheaper than that generated locally, even when their crops were processed by firms that could have borrowed more cheaply.[129]

With even producers of cash crops unable to attract cheap credit, southwest Shandong suffered frequent, serious silver shortages. This area responded in part by making do with fewer modern-sector goods than the rest of the province. According to the 1933 provincial survey, the southwestern counties "imported" far fewer outside goods than any other part of the province:[130] ¥2 per person for seventeen southwestern counties (¥10,673,020 for 5,338,260 people) versus ¥5.75 per head (¥19,498,900 for 3,388,396 people) in eighteen equally remote counties in the northwestern heartland (northern Huang-Yun). Most southwestern counties, in fact, imported so little that they had modest trade surpluses. The key to most of those surpluses, however, was running large surpluses with Jining; and Jining, despite reexporting much of what it imported from the rest of the southwest, ran by far the largest deficit of any Shandong county. Thus, the southwest as a whole ran a substantial trade deficit.[131]

With a trade deficit, taxes to pay, and little credit from outside, the southwest was heavily dependent on a different export—labor, particularly labor in Manchuria. Although no part of Shandong or Hebei (the two provinces that accounted for 95 percent of migration to Manchuria) was farther from Manchuria, southwest Shandong sent tens of thousands of people per year there.[132] In 1934, after migration was disrupted by Japan's seizure of Manchuria, a study of 16 southwestern counties estimated their lost remittances at ¥4,000,000 per year;[133] at about the same time, remittances from Manchuria to all 215 Shandong and Hebei counties were estimated at ¥30,000,000.[134] According to one source, Jining alone lost ¥3,000,000 per year from the closing of Manchuria.[135]

Before 1931, these Manchurian remittances masked the expected

129. Ibid., 47–48, 65–72.
130. *SSYZ* 2:151–201.
131. *SSYZ* 2:165–189, gives the county-by-county figures; the figures for Jining are on p. 167.
132. For estimates, see Tōa Kenkyūsho, *Santō Koshōgun Chitai no Chiiki Chōsa,* report no. 14, class C, no. 158-D, pp. 127–29, based on figures for 1933.
133. "Luxi ge xian nongcun jingji xianzhuang," *Nongcun jingji* 1:11 (Sept. 1, 1934), 75.
134. Gottschaung, "Migration," 137–38.
135. "Luxi jingji xianzhuang," 76.

effects of poorly integrated currency and credit markets. Normally, there would be price divergence between areas with trade deficits and those with surpluses, unless money was recycled through net flows of investment to poor regions. Thus the absence of such divergence would imply integrated capital and currency markets, contrary to the argument here. In this case, however, price divergence is absent for a different reason: before 1931, remittances from workers in Manchuria made up for the trade deficits of most Shandong counties that ran them, at least before we factor in taxes.[136] Thus, instead of deflation or price divergence the southwest's currency problems before 1931 are reflected in high interest rates, relative austerity, and massive temporary and permanent emigration.

Political and fiscal strategy may have forced many southwesterners to do without kerosene lamps and machine-made cloth and made some of them work in Manchuria rather than near home. And—as we shall see in the next chapter—the politically motivated actions of southwestern rural elites also sometimes prevented export growth.[137] Nonetheless, the quasi-mercantilist goals often enunciated by local and provincial government officials were met as long as Manchuria stayed open. Local government and its allies generally found enough silver to meet obligations to higher authorities while keeping enough control over the money supply to manipulate exchange and interest rates.

This delicate balance collapsed after 1931. Between 1930 and 1934, the Shanghai price of wheat—southwest Shandong's biggest crop and main export—declined 40 percent.[138] In southwest Shandong, however, things were much worse. Of thirteen southwestern counties that reported price trends in 1934, one reported a 50 percent decline in wheat and land prices; four reported 60 percent declines; one a 75

---

136. *SSYZ* 2:156–201 has the trade figures; see also "Luxi jingji xianzhuang," 75–77.

137. One such example—the unwillingness of village leaders in the southwest to cooperate with the dissemination of new cotton varieties that were very successful elsewhere in the province—is discussed in chapter 2.

138. Wu Chengming, "Wo Guo ban zhimindi ban fengjian guonei shichang," *Lishi yanjiu*, no. 168 (April 1984), 115. Opium might have been close to wheat as a southwestern export in the late Qing, but by the 1920s most of this market had been lost to morphine and heroin imported under Japanese protection. Lu Weijun, *Han Fuju*, 211. See letters of Jan. 24, 1919, and April 29, 1919, from U.S. legation in Beijing to Secretary of State, plus copies of articles from *Peking Leader* (Dec. 21, 1918), *North China Daily News* (Dec. 17, 1918), and *Chinese Literary Digest* (April 12, 1919), all in U.S. Department of State, *Records Relating to the Internal Affairs of China, 1910–1929*, reel 114; interview notes, Liaocheng, Dezhou, and Linqing, November 1985.

percent drop; and seven reported 80 percent declines.[139] The Jining price of silver money (in copper, which might serve as a proxy for all goods sold for copper) also suggests price divergence between the southwest and other areas. After retreating from the dizzying heights of the late 1920s, that price stabilized in 1930–33, but then took off again, rising faster in Jining over the next two years than in any other place for which we have data. Moreover, this price divergence was occurring at a time when the provincial government's presence in the southwest was the strongest it had been in years.[140]

At the very least, it is clear that three years after Manchurian remittances dried up and a silver drain began, the high rates being offered for credit and hard currency in the southwest were not drawing in outside funds. Thus, the area's relative "independence" became debilitating economic isolation. By contrast, the north coast counties—which also had merchandise trade deficits in 1933 and traditionally received even larger remittances from Manchuria—do not seem to have experienced a shortage of hard currency after Manchuria was closed;[141] even in a worldwide depression, this region's continued participation in larger markets appears to have brought in enough funds to fill the gap.

CODA:
FRAGMENTED MARKETS AND STATE MAKING

These economic effects of government activities in turn affected the state itself. Local and provincial officials alike in Shandong usually emphasized decreasing imports and increasing exports as economic goals. Far less attention was paid to commodities that circulated only locally. This emphasis on trade balances will figure prominently throughout this book, affecting policies toward agriculture, forestry, transportation, water control, and other services. But in another sense officials' economic orientation was profoundly localistic: both the provincial government and many county governments tried to make their jurisdictions economically meaningful units in which they could

---

139. "Luxi jingji xianzhuang," 75–77.
140. Government initiatives in southwest Shandong at this time included a massive river control project on the Wanfu He, a large-scale experiment in local government reform (which had its own journal, *SDXZJSSYQGB*), and Liang Shuming's Heze project (discussed briefly in chapter 2). See, for instance, Lu Weijun, *Han Fuju*, 222–37.
141. *SSYZ* 10:189–201.

control matters such as currency without interference from broader markets.

Many government policies aimed at greater economic integration. In some matters, such as road building, important advances were made.[142] County Offices to Encourage Industry in the 1920s gave up on retiring all the local notes issued by merchants, but they did try to centralize issuing authority, usually in the county Chamber of Commerce.[143] In the 1930s, the provincial government did seriously try to eliminate local paper money, although with limited success, at least in western Shandong.[144] However, these efforts generally aimed at concentrating control at that particular level of government; control was not supposed to pass to a larger political unit or broader market. The simultaneous efforts of the Shandong government to standardize currency rates within Shandong and to restrict currency exports from the province are a good example.

As we have seen, these activities did not produce the best results for economic growth in Shandong, particularly in its poorest regions. But how did the government affect itself?

This question will recur in different guises throughout this book. Some general outlines, however, are worth noting here. The provincial government had some success in protecting its prerogatives in currency matters against broader markets. While it could not control currency transactions with the outside world at Yantai or along the Jinan to Qingdao railway (two of the wealthiest areas of the province), it was fairly successful in the rest of the province, thus protecting its own autonomy and revenue. However, the appearance of Japanese copper buyers in Taian, along Shandong's other rail line, and increased government warnings about these activities after 1928 indicate that provincial control of money markets was always contested, even in the heartland.[145]

142. County-by-county road-building reports are available in *Shandong zheng su shicha ji*.

143. See, for instance, *QYHK*, no. 4 (Jan. 1921), *ge xian shiye zhuangkuang*, 17 (on Shan county); no. 7 (May 1922), *ge xian quanye baogao*, 32–33 (Heze); no. 11 (Feb. 1923), *ge xian chengji baogao*, 20 (Heze again); no. 13 (April 1923) *gongdu*, 41 (Tang Yi), 45 (Linqing).

144. Luo Ziwei, "Zouping si chao mian guan," *XCJSXK* 4:29 (July 1935), 26–31; *CZGB* 6:3 (Dec. 1934), *mingling*, 41; *SDXZJSSYQGB*, no. 14 (Nov. 27, 1935), 6–7; no. 23 (Dec. 15, 1935), 3 (page numbers supplied; original is unpaginated).

145. *Records*, reel 5, documents 4619097–134, esp. 4619130 (quotation from the *China Sphere*, Aug. 15, 1928), on the spread of the trade to inland areas; also see p. 19 of the June 1929 report in JD2:AH110.

Meanwhile, many county governments were able to maintain independent monetary policies even into the 1930s; they used this to increase local, not provincial or national, revenues. Even heartland Zouping county ignored numerous provincial orders to suppress local paper currency and adopt standard exchange rates until it became a showcase county run by outsiders.[146] The national currency reform of 1935 came too shortly before the outbreak of war for us to judge its success in Shandong, but in 1937 the province's heartland still had only limited access to littoral currency and capital markets, and the southwest was still only loosely tied to either the littoral or heartland economic systems. Unwilling to accept integration into larger markets, the province was also unable to impose full integration on its own system.

This failure does not seem to have seriously lowered provincial government revenue. Returns to the government from greater growth would have come slowly. The southwest was an unlikely area in which to raise more revenue: it was poor, local taxes were high, and provincial control was incomplete.[147] However, the provincial government could not simply ignore Huang-Yun, or even south Huang-Yun. Two of the area's biggest problems—the Yellow River (the first 80 of whose 250 miles in Shandong went through the southwest) and unusually serious banditry—were quickly felt in the rest of the province if not checked locally. In dealing with these problems, the southwest's economic isolation came back to haunt provincial officials. Water control will be discussed in detail in chapters 4 and 5. Problems of public order run throughout all the chapters. Throughout this book, we will see effects of the concentration of fiscal—and to some extent monetary—power at lower levels of government.

In sum, one critical part of state making in early-twentieth-century Shandong—the search for greater revenue—interfered with market integration. This is a marked contrast to early modern Europe, where state and market making usually reinforced each other and market in-

146. Luo Ziwei, "Zouping si chao mian guan," *XCJSXK* 4:29 (July 1935), 26–31.
147. Southwest Shandong remains the poorest part of the province; see, for instance, the figures in Shandong sheng nongye qu hua weiyuanhui, *Shandong sheng zonghe nongye qu hua* (Jinan, 1982), 215–16. The provincial government's weakness in the southwest did lead to a massive administrative reform there in the 1930s, but there was not enough time for this to take root before the Japanese invasion; see, for instance, Xu Shuren, "Wo zai xiang jianshe pai de huodong yu jian wen," *Wenshi ziliao xuanji*, Jinan edition, no. 2 (1982), 50–68, for an account of these reforms that emphasize their connection to a provincial grab for control over the southwest.

tegration made state extraction and movement of revenue easier.[148] One crucial difference was that in Europe, both the amount of government revenue and the central government's control of that revenue increased; in Huang-Yun, exactions increased, but it was primarily local governments that benefited. Thus the political limitations placed on credit market integration in Shandong not only limited the area's economic development; they also forced local governments in the southwest to rely heavily on nonmonetary exactions such as corvée labor and in-kind contributions of construction materials. Thus limits on the movement of money hindered the development of an administrative system that could move and exchange resources easily, thereby accomplishing things that isolated localities could not.

Yet it would be too simplistic to blame these problems entirely on the governments involved. Government in early-twentieth-century China did not consume a particularly large part of the country's income,[149] and further market integration and economic growth surely required that some government provide more of various public goods (social stability, flood control, and the like) than could have been provided without all levels of government finding additional revenue somewhere. Some local officials may have favored the methods discussed here because they were profitable for themselves and their allies, but they probably also felt these methods were less disruptive than many alternatives and may have considered them important to defending Chinese authority against foreign economic power. Finally, the foreign political threat that helped provoke these measures (and that, in taking Manchuria, also disrupted currency flows) was inseparable from the stimulus that made economic links to the coast so useful.

148. See, for instance, the discussion in Charles Tilly, "Reflections on the History of European State-Making," in *The Formation of National States in Western Europe*, ed. Charles Tilly (Princeton, 1975), 17, 30–31, 52–57.

149. Estimates of the government's share of GNP in this period vary, but most are in the area of 3–5 percent. See, for instance, Huang, *Peasant Economy*, 280–84.

CHAPTER II

Community, Coercion, and Cotton

Agricultural Innovation and Social Stratification

Agricultural specialization in Huang-Yun increased considerably but unevenly after 1890. These changes were part of a miniature "green revolution" that swept much of North China from 1890 to 1937. Like the larger and later Green Revolution, this transformation increased agricultural output significantly, but had ambiguous, sometimes divisive, social consequences.[1] Thus, at least in Huang-Yun, its implementation required increased coercion. Organizing coercion, disseminating new knowledge, providing a secure supply of hybrid seeds, and other such tasks posed major challenges for the state and for local elites. Eventually, however, organizations emerged in much of Huang-Yun—especially its northern half—that handled all these matters successfully. In view of the state's outright hindrance of capital market integration, described in chapter 1, and its ineffective management of ecological problems, discussed in the next three chapters, it is striking that the state found new and effective ways to promote agricultural change.

The results of state and private efforts to link Huang-Yun agriculture with world markets depended much more on rural social structure than on such narrowly economic factors as soil quality or trans-

1. For material on the social aspects of the Green Revolution see, for instance, James C. Scott, *Weapons of the Weak* (New Haven, 1985); Francine Frankel, *India's Green Revolution: Economic Gains and Political Costs* (Princeton, 1971), esp. 8–10, 191–95.

port costs. The relevant social differences parallel differences in the organization of trade discussed in chapter 1, but at the village rather than the county level. Like its cities, North Huang-Yun's villages were far less tightly controlled and more "permeable" to outsiders than those of South Huang-Yun. Consequently, the story of these agricultural innovations introduces a recurring theme of the rest of this book: though the urban elites of South Huang-Yun were stronger and more tightly knit than those of the North, they could not force unwanted changes on South Huang-Yun village elites, who were also stronger than their northern counterparts.

This story also highlights the influence of social and political factors on economic choices in a way that most other work on China has not done. Discussion of peasant cropping and labor allocation in China can be divided into what one might call "single-logic" and "multiple-logic" approaches. Single-logic proponents (Ramon Myers, Thomas Rawski, Loren Brandt) argue that although different farmers had different resources, they all decided how to employ those resources in the same way: as the constrained profit maximizers of classical economics.[2] Multiple-logic proponents (Jing Su and Luo Lun, Chen Hanseng, Philip Huang) disagree on many other points but agree that different classes behaved according to fundamentally different logics. Huang, for instance, argues that those who ran large "managerial farms" were profit maximizers, but peasants who were closer to subsistence were not. Some were so desperate to gain security from their own small farms that they engaged in "self-exploitation," putting in additional hours long after the marginal returns on such labor had gone below the prevailing wage. Others sought to eke out subsistence from too small a plot of land by gambling very heavily on high-risk, high-return crops.[3] Other multiple-logic scenarios abound; what unites them is the idea that a household's economic reasoning varies with its position in a given socioeconomic structure.

The material discussed in this chapter does not include nearly enough microlevel data to confirm or dispute Huang's assertion that many poor peasants farmed according to a rationality different from

2. For examples of the "single logic school," see Myers, *Peasant Economy*; Wiens, *Micro-Economics*; Rawski, *Economic Growth*; and Brandt, *Commercialization*. For examples of "multiple logic" approaches, see Jing Su and Luo Lun, *Landlord and Labor*; Huang, *Peasant Economy*; and Chen Hanseng, *Landlord and Peasant*.

3. Huang, *Peasant Economy*, 162.

that of the neoclassical firm. It does, however, make claims that both bear on this debate and add another dimension to it. First, we will see that poor people took collective action to enforce norms that restricted the maximizing efforts of other farmers. In South Huang-Yun, they succeeded; in North Huang-Yun they were defeated, but only through a highly coercive campaign encouraged by the state. Second, once this campaign had succeeded, the contested new cotton varieties began to be grown on all sizes of North Huang-Yun farms; while poorer peasants may have had different risk tolerances, there are no signs that they were averse to market involvement per se. Third, and perhaps most important, our story shows that it was not only the poor who may have farmed with goals besides profit maximization in mind.[4] The rural elites of South Huang-Yun, concerned about various ways in which the new cotton varieties might undermine their social and political position, did not cooperate with those who promoted the new varieties, even though such cooperation would have increased their farm profits. And by taking this course, South Huang-Yun's rural elites powerfully shaped the environment in which their neighbors acted.

Thus, this chapter goes beyond the existing debate on "single" versus "multiple" logics by insisting on points that have often been made in the literatures on economic development elsewhere. In general it reminds us that whether the economic logic of particular groups or families varies with their social positions may depend on the type of community they live in; thus this question requires context-specific answers, based on an analysis that treats social structure itself as a variable.[5] South Huang-Yun villages had strong elites who were determined to retain their political dominance; North Huang-Yun villages did not. Consequently, poor or even middle peasants in North and

4. This point has methodological as well as substantive implications. Among other things, it suggests that Brandt's failure to find a strong inverse correlation between farm size and labor intensity does not necessarily refute Huang's "multiple logic" scenario. See Brandt, *Commercialization*, 144–55.

5. Examples of arguments that elite actions and social structures influence the extent to which other members of the community follow market "rationality" may be found across the globe and across the political spectrum. For two radically different historical accounts, see Clifford Geertz, *Agricultural Involution* (Berkeley, 1963) and the essays in T. H. Aston and C. H. E. Philpin, *The Brenner Debate: Agrarian Class Structure and Economic Development in Pre-industrial Europe* (Cambridge, Eng., 1985). Several examples from the contemporary development literature are briefly surveyed in Milton Esman and Norman Uphoff, *Local Organizations: Intermediaries in Rural Development* (Ithaca, 1984), 116–17.

South Huang-Yun faced different opportunities and threats. And because the varying strength and goals of local elites affected peasants'
"economic" strategies, we can expect certain outcomes to occur
together. It is no accident, we will see, that new cotton varieties took
hold where the old village elite fled office in the 1920s, 1930s, and
1940s and not where established rural bosses survived the strains
created by warlord and Japanese extraction.

This chapter begins by describing the opportunity represented by
new cotton varieties. Next it looks at how these new plants interfered
with gleaning patterns and with the subsistence strategies of the very
poor more generally. Third, it examines the "cotton societies" that
formed to promote these new crops and protect them against gleaners
and contrasts these organizations with older crop-watching methods.
Next, it analyzes the social reasons why the new cotton varieties took
hold in North Huang-Yun but not in South Huang-Yun. Finally, it examines the broader implications of this case for social change in rural
North China.

NEW CROP VARIETIES

Individual Chinese officials had long promoted crops that they thought
would benefit their jurisdictions; around 1900, the new Ministry of
Agriculture, Industry, and Commerce began more systematic efforts.[6]
Private parties were also active. Missionaries had begun promoting
new crop varieties in the 1870s, partly to provide alternatives to
opium growing on certain soils.[7] New industries that processed agricultural goods, particularly cotton and cigarette mills, often went to
the countryside to try to expand the supply of the crops they used.[8] In
the case that most affected Huang-Yun—cotton—state efforts were

6. On traditional efforts to introduce new crop varieties, see, for instance, Francesca
Bray, ed., *Agriculture*, vol. 6, pt. 2 of *Science and Civilization in China*, ed. Joseph
Needham (Cambridge, Eng., 1984), 598–600; and Ho Ping-ti, *Studies on the Popula-
tion of China* (Cambridge, Mass., 1959), 178–83; for material on the new efforts, see *ci*
from Shandong governor, sent 1/29/XT 2, file 110, Nong gong shang bu, nong wu si,
Huiyi Zhengwuchu, First Historical Archives, Beijing; Kambe Masao, *Dō A Keizai
Kenkyū*, 1:77–78; Cheng Shouzhong, ed., *Shandong kaocha baogaoshu*, 13–18.

7. Lin Maoquan, *Wenji*, 6a, 80a. Helen S. Coan Nevius, *The Life of John Livingston Nevius* (New York, 1895), 421–31.

8. Matsuzaki Yujiro, *Santō Shō no Sai Nishiki*, 478–79 on cotton; for tobacco, see
Cochran, *Big Business*, 22–27, 141–45, 160, and 281 n. 119.

closely linked to those of Chinese and British mill owners after 1918 and competed with parallel efforts by Japanese-owned mills.[9]

The government generally promoted industrial rather than food crops.[10] There were many reasons for this. In a competitive market, consumers capture most of the benefit of increased agricultural productivity,[11] and the buyers of industrial crops were far better organized to encourage increased cash crop production (and capture its benefits) than were the millions of dispersed food consumers. Moreover, there was little progress in wheat production between the 1890s and the 1930s, even in countries where intensive efforts were made.[12] North China wheat varieties do not seem to have been markedly inferior to those available elsewhere at this time. Even in the 1930s, when far more research was done, experiments with foreign wheat and sorghum varieties in China produced much more modest gains than did research with other crops.[13]

Perhaps most important, government officials were less interested in raising rural income for its own sake than in "national strengthening." That meant, above all, promoting crops that could be used in either import-substituting or export-promoting industries.[14] New cotton varieties fit both these categories: they were introduced as an import-substitution measure, but since growing them in China cost 20 percent

9. The Chinese efforts will be the subject of most of this chapter. For brief accounts of Japanese efforts, see Mantetsu, *Santō no Mensaku*, 4, 6, 28, 106; also Matsuzaki Yujiro, *Santō Shō no Sai Nishiki*, 478–79.

10. See the records of the Huiyi Zhengwuchu for the late Qing; *Nong shang gongbao* for the national government, 1914–26; *Shandong quanye huikan* for the Shandong provincial government, 1921–25; H. H. Love papers, Olin Library, Cornell University, for the 1920s and early 1930s.

11. See, for instance, the discussion of the effect of this distribution of gains from changes in agricultural technology on investment in agricultural research in Japan during the early twentieth century in Hayami Yujiro, *A Century of Agricultural Growth in Japan* (Minneapolis, 1975), esp. 139–40.

12. Theodore Schultz, *Transforming Traditional Agriculture* (New Haven, 1964), 22. U.S. agricultural productivity increased only 6 percent between 1910–12 and 1917–19, despite massive investment; significant gains did not come until the 1930s.

13. Letter of Jan. 15, 1930, from T. H. Shen to Charles A. Stanley in box no. 1, folder no. 16, and report from Shen and R. G. Wiggins of trip through North China, July 26–Aug. 19, 1930, in box no. 13, folder no. 40, H. H. Love papers; Nanjing University, College of Agriculture and Forestry, *Bulletin*, no. 27 (June 1932), 4, and no. 30 (March 1933), 4. These studies report that after years of work and numerous failures, experimental varieties of wheat and sorghum were now yielding 10–15 percent more per acre than varieties already in use by farmers under controlled conditions; this is a much smaller gain than was achieved earlier with cotton.

14. *NSGB* 1:5 (Dec. 1914) *zhengshi*, 14; Lin Maoquan, *Wenji*, 71a; *SDZZ*, no. 90 (5/30/XT 3), 7a–b.

less than in the United States, they had export potential, too.[15] While various other crops were promoted briefly in response to special situations,[16] the two lasting favorites of Qing and Republican officials were cotton and mulberries (for silk production).[17] Their efforts to promote another primary product—timber—also stressed import substitution and national strengthening rather than general improvement of the standard of living, as we shall see in the next chapter. The main Chinese agricultural extension effort in Nanjing, provincial efforts in North China, and later efforts in Shaanxi all emphasized crops that could improve China's balance of trade and thus, it was hoped, help protect its autonomy;[18] rural living standards per se got far less attention.

In Huang-Yun, by far the most important new crops were versions of North American cotton varieties. These strains had several advantages. Their longer fibers were more suitable for mechanized spinning than indigenous Chinese cotton. As China's modern cotton industry boomed during and after World War I, the new cotton came to sell for about 20 percent more per pound than native varieties.[19] The new plants could also grow on the sandy soil that was so common in the lower Yellow River Valley.[20] In most cases, these varieties also produced more cotton per acre than Chinese varieties.[21] The gain in yields

15. Kambe Masao, *Dō A Keizai Kenkyū* 1:142.

16. *NSGB* 3:2 (Sept. 1916), *zhengshi*, 15–23; *jinwen*, 1.

17. *Ci* of 2/29/XT 1, file 110, and *ci* of 9/13/GX 30, file 120, Nong gong shang bu nong wu si, Huiyi Zhengwuchu; *NSGB* 2:2 (Sept. 1915), *xuanzai*, 31; *QYHK*, no. 10 (Jan. 1923), *lunshuo*, 1; for similar views expressed by intellectuals not necessarily in government, *SDZZ*, no. 90 (5/30/XT 3), 7a–7b; Yan Guangyao, Sun Bocai, and Zhou Chengpeng, "Diaocha Shandong zhi nongye zhuangkuang," *Kexue* 4:5 (Jan. 1919), 465, 471; *QYHK* repeats these three priorities for almost every county—see, for instance, no. 5 (July 1921), *ge xian shiye zhuangkuang*, 8–12, 19–21.

18. On agricultural extension work done at Nanjing's Jinling University, see esp. Randall Stross, *The Stubborn Earth: American Agriculturalists on Chinese Soil, 1898–1937* (Berkeley, 1986), 92–160; on Shaanxi, see E. B. Vermeer, *Economic Development in Provincial China: The Central Shaanxi since 1930* (Cambridge. Eng., 1988), 250–52, 290–96, 325–35.

19. Lin Maoquan, *Wenji*, 65b; *QYHK*, no. 10 (Jan. 1923), *zhuanjian*, 1.

20. Lin Maoquan, *Wenji*, 5a, 28b, 64a, 65b; Matsuzaki Yujiro, *Santō Shō no Sai Nishiki*, 478–79; Imai Shuin, "Kōnichi Konkyochi no Keisei Katei ni tsuite no Ichi Kōsatsu," *Shichō*, no. 108 (June 1971), 25; "Zhenxing Shandong Shiye," in *SDZZ*, no. 92 (6/30/XT 3), 6b.

21. Lin Maoquan, *Wenji*, 64b–65a, has a detailed chart of yield differences in different Shandong counties; Hu Zhangzhun, "Shandong zhi mianye," *Shandong wenxian* 1:3 (Dec. 1975), 22, says the varieties finally settled on for most of Shandong yielded about 30 percent more than domestic varieties. More information is available in Ren Jimin, "Heze xian tuikuang Mei mian yi yu minsheng yi," *XCJSXK* 3:18–19 (Feb. 1934), 14–15, and in Mantetsu, *Santō no Mensaku*, 2 (also reporting a 33 percent increase).

was even greater when the new varieties were compared, not to pure Chinese strains grown experimentally, but to the mix of different seeds that most farmers used; many agronomists felt that their most important task was to get farmers used to planting a whole field with a single variety—any variety—of cotton from a seed farm instead of using whatever seed they had available.[22]

Together, these advantages were such that even in 1934—a bad year for cotton prices—rural reconstruction workers in Heze(S) estimated that this crop would produce four times the profit per acre of the next best option.[23] Other estimates varied, but all of them agreed that where it could be grown, U.S. cotton was the most profitable crop.[24] The new cotton was aggressively promoted by missionaries in the 1890s; from 1905 on, it was promoted and subsidized by the national, provincial, and county governments and by Tianjin and Qingdao cotton mills. Meanwhile, cotton mills stopped sending buyers to counties that produced only native cotton; as with tobacco, seed distribution and crop purchasing became closely linked.[25]

Yet the new cotton varieties were accepted only fitfully. In northwest Shandong and southwest Zhili they made little progress until the 1920s, when county governments became more actively involved; but then they became dominant by the early 1930s.[26] In southwest Shandong, the new varieties never caught on; and as buyers from urban mills disappeared from that area, growers were left to either sell to a shrinking local market or to turn to less lucrative crops, usually

22. Stross, *Stubborn Earth*, 124–27; M. L. Darling, *The Punjab Peasant in Prosperity and Debt* (Oxford, 1947), 151.

23. *XCJSXK* 3:18–19 (Feb. 1934), 14–15. Because this chapter emphasizes differences between northwestern and southwestern Shandong, county names will be followed by either (N) or (S). Northwest Shandong composes the bulk of North Huang-Yun and corresponds to the westernmost part of the "heartland" capital market described in chapter 1; southwestern Shandong takes in most of South Huang-Yun and corresponds to the "southwest" capital market. A list of counties in the northwest and southwest appears in appendix A.

24. Mantetsu, *Santō no Mensaku*, 47–54; Lin Maoquan, *Wenji*, 71a; Leonard G. Ting, *Recent Developments in China's Cotton Industry* (Shanghai, 1936), 14; Kambe Masao, *Dō A Keizai Kenkyū*, 1:118–20. On trends of cotton prices versus grain prices (the main alternative), see Wu Chengming, "Wo Guo guonei shichang," 115, 121.

25. See, for instance, Cheng Shouzhong, *Shandong kaocha baogaoshu*, 13–18. On tobacco seed distribution, see Hsu Ying-sui, "Tobacco Marketing in Eastern Shandong," reprinted in *Agrarian China: Source Materials From Chinese Authors* (London, 1939), 172.

26. See figures in dissertation, appendix D; Imai Shuin, "Kōnichi Konkyochi no Keisei Katei ni tsuite no ichi Kōsatsu," 25–27, describes a similar phenomenon in southwest Hebei.

gaoliang or wheat. Overall, despite aggressive promotion, no more than 40 percent of the cotton land in prewar Shandong and 70 percent in Zhili/Hebei was planted with the new varieties.[27]

The switch to U.S. cotton in northwest Shandong and southwest Hebei after 1920 proceeded at about the same pace as a contemporaneous switch to similar varieties in the Punjab. Punjabi farmers, in turn, responded to new information about the yields and prices of various cotton varieties at approximately the same rate as farmers in the American South.[28] Thus, despite all the obstacles posed by warlordism and other disruptions, North Huang-Yun cotton farmers seem to have been as responsive to new options as any others in the world. (One might have expected North Huang-Yun's adoption of new cotton to outpace the Punjab's, however, since the difference in net profitability between foreign and domestic cotton was probably larger in North Huang-Yun.[29]) Thus it is all the more striking that promotional efforts that succeeded so well in northwest Shandong failed utterly in the southwest. This divergence was already evident in the mid-1920s, but it became much more marked after the Northern Expedition and collapse of warlordism in 1928; the establishment thereafter of relative stability in Shandong created an opportunity for innovation that was seized in the northwest, but not the southwest.

Native cotton production appears to have shrunk all over Shandong

27. Doi Akira and Tonō Fumino, *Hokushi Jijō Soran* (Dalian, 1936), 262; Mantetsu, *Santō no Mensaku*, 17–18, gives figures for ten northwestern counties that work out to 81 percent; the figures are said to come from the Linqing Chamber of Commerce. Figures for 1930–32, quoted on pp. 14–15 from *Mianye tekan* for the same counties, work out to only 56 percent. See also *HBMCLB*, no. 7 (Aug. 1, 1936), 6.

28. Raj Krishna, "Farm Supply Response in the Punjab (India-Pakistan): A Case Study of Cotton" (Ph.D. dissertation, University of Chicago, 1961), 1, 9, has the figures needed for this comparison; for the American South, see p. 24.

29. While U.S. cotton in Shandong sold for at least 20 percent more per unit than Chinese cotton (Lin Maoquan, *Wenii*, 65b), the difference in the Punjab was 14 percent or less in eighteen of the twenty years from 1922 to 1941, and usually about 5 percent (Krishna, "Farm Supply," 95). Differences in net profitability are harder to fix, since cost accounting methods vary, but for the two districts of the Punjab for which Krishna supplies figures, the average differences in net profitability over these years are roughly 16 percent and 25 percent, well below the compound effects of price and yield differentials in North China even after allowing for any plausible cost differential. The highest net profit difference for a year in Krishna's thirty-eight observations is slightly under 100 percent (in one year in one district) (104). Shandong figures for various counties in 1922 and for Heze in 1934 show much larger differences. See Lin Maoquan, *Wenji*, 88b–100a, and *XCJSXK* 3:18–19 (Feb. 1934), 14–15.

in the middle and late 1920s, probably because of warlordism; south-western production appears to have fallen more than northwestern.[30] After 1928, cotton acreage rebounded throughout Shandong; by 1932, the southwest was again producing about 45 percent as much cotton as the northwest in disaster-free years, as it probably had in 1911.[31] However, total cotton output now included two very different products, and the southwest lagged far behind in the new, more profitable one. In 1932, the southwest's cotton farms had fully recovered from the problems of the 1920s, and total output had reached previous levels. Less than 20 percent, however, was the U.S. variety; in the flood year of 1933, this fell to 3 percent. By comparison, 55 percent of northwestern production and 30 percent of other North Shandong production in these same two years was the more lucrative, hard-currency-earning U.S. variety.[32]

Southwest Shandong's failure to participate in the most profitable and growing part of the cotton market eventually affected its total out-put, too. Once peace had enabled it to recover from the 1920s, south-western output leveled off (except for a slight statistical effect caused by having fewer disasters than in the mid–1920s), and northwest Shandong increased its lead again. Two different data sets put the southwest's 1932 production at almost one half (47.2 percent and 44.2 percent) the northwest's, but the two data sets available for 1934–37 put southwestern production at barely one third (33.5 per-cent or 34.7 percent) of northwestern output.[33] Moreover, the north-west's lead was still growing at the onset of World War II; if we consider 1936–37 alone, southwestern production had slipped to

---

30. See the 1922 and 1926–29 figures in dissertation, appendix D and the note on 1930 figures; see also Cheng Shouzhong, ed., *Shandong kaocha baogaoshu*, 19–20.

31. See dissertation, appendix D.

32. *HBMCLB*, no. 7 (Aug. 1, 1936), 6; the 1932 data in appendix D for our sample counties yields figures of 17.2 percent for the southwest and 57 percent for the north-west, confirming this. On the question of American cotton but not Chinese cotton hav-ing a market outside the area and earning hard currency, see *XCJSXK* 3:18–19 (Feb. 1934), 15.

33. Photocopied data from the Second Historical Archives, Nanjing, analyzed in dis-sertation, appendix D, give total southwestern production for 1934–37 as 33.5 percent of northwestern production and 34.7 percent for the sample counties in those years. *HBMCLB*, no. 7 (Aug. 1, 1936), 6, using very slightly different samples (including all the significant producer counties), gives southwestern production in 1932 as 44.2 per-cent of northwestern production, while the original sample counties for that year pro-duced 47.2 percent of the original northwestern sample counties.

29 percent of northwestern levels.[34] By the end of the decade, a
Japanese study of machine-spinnable cotton referred to the existence
of only two principal Shandong zones—north and northwest—rather
than the traditional three cotton zones.[35] Indeed, the spread of U.S.
cotton in northwest Shandong is an important reason why that
area, long considered poorer than southwest Shandong, had a much
higher per capita income by the late 1930s.[36]

What accounts for this peculiar pattern? Southwest Shandong had
long been a major cotton producer.[37] It included huge areas suitable
for the new varieties, and these were targeted by the Shandong Office
to Encourage Industry (Quanyesuo; hereafter, OEI) and by foreign
and domestic cotton mills.[38] OEI workers and Tianjin and Qingdao
mill agents reached even the most remote southwestern counties, distributing free seed and promoting this crop; in the 1930s Shanghai
mills (which had rail and canal links to southwest, but not northwest,
Shandong) had a shortage of the new cotton and complained that
Shandong did not grow enough of it.[39] True, the new cotton bloomed
later than the old and thus was harder to fit into a two-crops-a-year
system. However, the southwest had only slightly more double cropping than the northwest; the predominant regime in both areas was
three crops in two years.[40] Moreover Jiangsu, which had far more
double cropping than any part of Shandong, did adopt new cotton
varieties.[41] Transport costs to major mills were about equal for north-

---

34. See dissertation, appendix D, figures for sample counties in 1934–37: the ratio
is 392,950 to 898,200, or 44 percent, for 1934–35 and 474,960 to 1,621,970, or 29
percent, for 1936–37.

35. Mantetsu, *Santō no Mensaku*, refers to the southwest once (p. 2) as the third
cotton area in the province but describes no efforts or procurement of U.S. cotton there,
while going on at great length about efforts in the north and northwest; the other general surveys of cotton in Shandong, such as *Shandong kaocha baogaoshu*, also pass
over the southwest as a source of cotton for mills.

36. See dissertation, appendix E.

37. On southwest Shandong as a traditional cotton area, see Yan Zhongping,
Zhongguo mian fangzhi shi gao 1289–1937 (Beijing, 1963), 75 (Dingtao, for instance,
had been a major cotton producer as early as the middle Ming; see also Huang,
Peasant Economy, 118); see also *XCJSXK* 3:18–19 (Feb. 1934), 13, and QZ1038:
AH2034, p. 10 (early 1920s).

38. See, e.g., *QYHK*, no. 12, *gongdu*, 36, on Tianjin cotton mills distributing seed
in remote southwestern *xian*; every issue of *QYHK* contains some discussion of OEI
efforts in the southwest.

39. *Shandong shiye gongbao*, no. 4 (Oct. 1931), 37; *Nongye zhoubao* 3:7 (Feb. 23,
1934), 158.

40. Comparative cropping indices from *Santō Sainei*, 18.

41. Ting, *Recent Developments*, 13–18.

west and southwest Shandong, and even the most remote and bandit-ridden southwestern counties sold wheat to urban flour mills.

Most important, numerical comparisons from various years and sources all show that U.S. cotton would have been more profitable for southwestern farmers than what they were growing.[42] Even before the new varieties were perfected, their per *mu* cash value exceeded that of domestic cotton in eighteen of the twenty-two southwestern counties for which we have figures (in two they were equal). In thirteen of these counties, the per *mu* premium was 50 percent or more. The additional income averaged 33 percent, almost the same as for eleven north-western counties in the same source (36 percent).[43] The only additional input that OEI agents recommended was one extra layer of rotten grass, surely not enough to negate these gains.[44] Moreover, the new cotton could also grow on land currently planted with crops that were still less profitable than domestic cotton, and even on some waste land. Reformers and mill agents worked hard to spread this information, in both the northwest and the southwest.

The failure of the new cotton varieties in the southwest stemmed from two features that loomed large in that area's particular social context. First, these hybrids degenerated rapidly: thus successive good crops required frequent inputs of new seeds from overseas to mill agents and provincial experiment stations; from those stations to the county storehouses, experiment stations, and seed farms; and from the county OEI to farmers. Farmers had to trust that the new seeds would be on time and affordable the next year; if they saved seed from one year's crop, they would be sorely tempted to use it the next.[45] The use of impure seeds could set back the new cotton varieties for several years in a given locality: farmers who wound up with stunted plants were not eager to keep experimenting. However, this problem had been conquered by the mid-1930s, at least in North Huang-Yun; similar and perhaps even more severe problems that dogged early Punjabi

42. *XCJSXK* 3:18–19 (Feb. 1934), 14–15; Doi Akira and Tonō Fumino, *Hokushi Jijō Soran*, 261; *QYHK*, no. 28 (Aug. 1924) *shiye gongdu*, 26; Lin Maoquan, *Wenji*, 65a–b.

43. Lin Maoquan, *Wenji*, 88b–100a.

44. *QYHK*, no. 7 (May 1922), *gongdu*, 18.

45. Matsuzaki Yujiro, *Santō Shō no Sai Nishiki*, 478–79; Mantetsu, *Santō no Mensaku*, 35; *Gong shang banyuekan* 6:7 (April 1, 1934), 47. Also see *Gong shang banyuekan* 6:23 (Dec. 1, 1934), 154–56; *HBMCLB*, no. 41 (Aug. 1, 1938), 29; no. 16 (Dec. 16, 1936), 18; no. 12 (Oct. 16, 1936), 13.

efforts were under control by the late 1930s.[46] These organizational and logistic challenges may have been particularly hard to handle in some of the more insular and disorderly parts of South Huang-Yun, where endemic banditry often made travel and transport dangerous; however, we lack evidence on this point.

Some people were more threatened by the possibility that these new networks would *not* fail. If the cotton did take hold, the seed suppliers—whether mills or extension agents—would become very important to the peasants. Few people seemed to worry about this in North Huang-Yun, unless the mills were Japanese owned. But in South Huang-Yun the prospect of switching to U.S. cotton meant that the area's entrenched rural bosses—who had no real counterparts in the North—might soon have bothersome new rivals.

The coolness of southwestern rural bosses was a particularly serious impediment in the social setting of that region. Only they could guarantee the safety of—or an audience for—those who came from the county capital or beyond bearing seeds, pamphlets, and exhibits. Moreover, the southwest's reputation for disorder probably meant that the new cotton needed particularly vigorous promotion there. Though available crime reports suggest that bandits rarely seized bulky agricultural goods on their way to market, this restraint may have been predicated on unreported protection payments. If this was the case, the willingness of powerful patrons to arrange such protection would have been crucial to any peasants considering a new cash-cropping venture.

Moreover, the possibility of transport interruptions must have increased the desire of all classes to grow crops that could be eaten if necessary. Certainly an emphasis on food production suited the political goals of southwestern rural elites, whose local power was partly based on their ability to protect people and stockpiled grain during violent periods[47] as well as to offer preharvest food loans to hard-pressed individuals. The advantages of having food on hand for maintaining local political dominance have sometimes made local elites

46. *Gong shang banyuekan* 6:7, p. 47; for the Punjabi situation, where the seed problems were sufficiently serious that yields per irrigated area were higher for domestic than U.S. cotton in seven of twenty-three years (and twelve of twenty-three in one district), see Krishna, "Farm Supply," 70–73.

47. See, e.g., Elizabeth J. Perry, *Rebels and Revolutionaries in North China* (Stanford, 1980), 89–93.

elsewhere unresponsive to lucrative cash-cropping opportunities;[48] such a preference for food over money as a medium for patronage would have made perfect sense in a bandit-ridden region like south-west Shandong.

Reports from officials promoting cotton, however, focused on the need for elites to help them overcome a different type of "disorder": opposition from the unarmed poor. As we shall see shortly, the new cotton varieties provoked considerable opposition from the very poor. In northwest Shandong, these protests were suppressed by newly formed "cotton societies." In the southwest, where the very poor were especially numerous and solid middle peasants especially few, cotton societies had little chance of succeeding without the wholehearted support of the rural elite. We will look first at this problem of class conflict and then return to other ways in which southwestern social structure posed special obstacles to the introduction of new cotton varieties and other innovations that were brought to its villages by outsiders.

The objections of the poor to U.S. cotton stemmed from a seemingly innocuous feature of the new plants: they took two to four weeks longer to ripen than native cotton.[49] Thus the new varieties were not yet ripe on the traditional day for completing the harvest in western Shandong and ran afoul of the local practice of allowing gleaners to enter the fields after that day and take whatever remained.[50] This problem delayed the spread of the new varieties in northwest Shandong in the 1920s and continued to frustrate promoters of the new varieties in southwest Shandong at least as late as 1934.[51] (It appears to have been less a problem in Henan and Hebei,

---

48. See, for instance, Norman Owen, "Abaca in Kabikolan: Prosperity without Progress," in *Philippine Social History: Global Trade and Local Transformations*, ed. Alfred McCoy and Eduard de Jesus (Honolulu, 1982), 191–216, esp. 207–8.

49. *QYHK*, no. 7 (May 1922), *ge xian quanye baogao*, 22; no. 11 (Feb. 1923), *ge xian chengji baogao*, 18; Mantetsu, *Santō no Mensaku*, 28.

50. *QYHK*, no. 7 (May 1922), *ge xian quanye baogao*, 22–23, 30; no. 9 (Dec. 1922), *ge xian chengji baogao*, 25; no. 10 (Jan. 1923), *ge xian shiye zhuangkuang*, 1–2; no. 11 (Feb. 1923), *ge xian chengji baogao*, 18–19; no. 12 (March 1923), *gongdu*, 38, 40; *ge xian chengji baogao*, 27; no. 16 (July 1923), *gongdu*, 41; no. 22 (March, 1924), *gongdu*, 1, 16; no. 28 (Aug. 1924), *shiye gongdu*, 26; also Yang Junan, ed., *Nong yan he nong ge* (Beijing, 1932), 38, which lists from the "lower Yellow River" area both a proverb saying that "after the traditional gleaning date (*shuang jiang*) you should leave nothing in the ground but peanuts" and another saying that "*li dong* (fourteen days later) is the time to collect your foreign cotton to take it to market." In Jihe, slightly east of Huang-Yun, the opening of the cotton fields to gleaners on this date was still marked by a public festival in 1933: *Jihe xianzhi* (1933), 12:5a.

51. *XCJSXK* 3:18 (Feb. 1934), 13–19.

but the evidence is too scant to be sure.[52]) Analyzing how this situation arose illuminates the mutual dependence of political and economic integration and the social structure of rural Huang-Yun.

GLEANING AND SUBSISTENCE

Gleaning was extremely important to the poor of western Shandong. The area had an acute fuel shortage, which we shall discuss in detail in chapter 3. Thus, once the fall harvest was in (late October or early November), people had only a short time in which to gather enough fuel for the winter.[53] Even an efficient gleaner who found adequate supplies available would need sixteen to twenty-five days in the fields to gather enough leavings to meet the annual fuel supply needs of a family of five (depending on whose estimate of "minimum needs" we use).[54] Indeed, fuel was so scarce and expensive that a woman who actually managed to gather as much straw as she physically could in a day would earn the in-kind equivalent of a male coal miner's day wage, and much more than she could earn as an agricultural worker.[55]

However, people who started their gleaning late (or were denied access to prime fields) might take much longer to find adequate supplies. Worse yet, they might simply not find them, since, as we shall see, Huang-Yun as a whole did not have nearly enough burnable material to meet everyone's needs. Further, fuel gathering that continued into

52. I have not found nearly as much material on the introduction of U.S. cotton in the Hebei and Henan parts of Huang-Yun, so this conclusion must be tentative; however, the material from these provinces makes almost no mention of this problem. For a rare instance of a Henan report describing this as a major challenge, see Quan guo jingji weiyuanhui, mianye tong zhi weiyuanhui, *Henan sheng mianchan gaijinsuo gongzuo zong baogao* (1936), 145. Security was also a problem when these varieties were introduced to Shaanxi in the 1930s: see Vermeer, *Economic Development*, 200.

53. Mantetsu, *Hokushi Nōson Gaikyō Chōsa Hōkoku* (Tokyo, 1940), 200; Arthur Smith, *Chinese Characteristics* (London, 1900), 22.

54. On mimimum fuel needs, see Asian Development Bank, *Asian Energy Problems* (New York, 1982), 114, 360; and Vaclav Smil, *The Bad Earth: Environmental Degradation in China* (Armonk, N.Y., 1983), 150. For the daily capacity of an energetic fuel gatherer in North Huang-Yun, see Kita Shina Hattatsu Kabushiki Kaisha Chōsaka, *Rosai Mensaku Chitai no Ichi Nōson ni Okeru Rōdoryoku Chōsa Hōkoku* (1943), 92. Fuel gathering and requirements are discussed at much greater length in chapter 3 and in dissertation, appendix F.

55. At anywhere from ¥1 to ¥1.66 for 100 *jin* of straw (see chapter 3 for more details), the 30 *jin* that could be gathered in a day (Kita Shina, *Rosai Mensaku*, 92) was worth ¥.3–.5. Coal miners in North China earned anywhere from ¥.22 to ¥.55 per day (Rawski, *Economic Growth*, 319) and female farm workers about ¥0.3 or ¥0.4, even in peak season.

the winter meant additional exposure to the cold, and such exposure made the project largely self-defeating even if supplies could still be found; numerous proverbs and folk songs from Huang-Yun advise against going out at all during winter if at all possible.[56] Finally, fuel was hard to buy; markets were poorly developed, and elsewhere in North China supplied less than 20 percent of total fuel needs.[57] In short, a successful gleaning season was vital to poor families' welfare, and success depended on being allowed into the right fields early enough.

While cotton residues were mostly used as fuel, other gleanings were also used to feed animals or, in particularly hard times, humans.[58] Gleaners could also take whatever usable produce had been missed or dropped by the harvesters; bits of cotton too small to spin were still useful as padding. Where the hired harvesters included the gleaners-to-be or their spouses, there were many ways to take a little extra at the expense of the landowner.[59]

Huang-Yun's poverty, fuel shortages, and weak law enforcement meant that gleaning had long been practiced on an unusual scale. In the 1600s some peasants from the Dezhou(N) area went as far as Jining(S)—125 miles—to glean.[60] The missionary Arthur Smith reported in 1896 that some women went from village to village for more than ten days just gleaning cotton.[61]

Most gleaning, though, took place close to home. As a postharvest activity in which poor people, often working in groups, claimed part of others' crops, it bears some resemblance to other "predatory survival strategies" described by Elizabeth Perry;[62] and as with banditry, particularly poor people often found it worthwhile to go a long way in search of more, or more inviting, targets. But unlike bandits, gleaners faced no moral pressure from their neighbors to do their work elsewhere. It was widely recognized that the poor had a right to some sort of gleaning and that this right began in their home village. Indeed, when the promoters of U.S. cotton wanted to suppress

---

56. See, for instance, Dong Taisheng, ed., *Shandong ge yao ji*, 27.
57. John L. Buck, *Chinese Farm Economy: A Study of 2866 Farms in Seventeen Localities and Seven Provinces in China* (Chicago, 1930), 399.
58. Mantetsu, *Santō no Mensaku*, 39.
59. See, for instance, Gamble, *North China Villages*, 235–36; Perry, *Rebels and Revolutionaries*, 82.
60. Esherick, *Boxer Uprising*, 27.
61. Arthur Smith, *Village Life in China* (New York, 1899), 167.
62. See Perry, *Rebels and Revolutionaries*, passim.

"cotton rushing" in the 1920s, they had to ask county magistrates to declare it illegal.[63]

This should not conjure up an image of a pre-twentieth-century "moral economy" with uncontested subsistence rights for all. Conflicts over gleaning were legion, and the elaborate rules that many villages had—specifying who could glean, when and for how long, and even the length of the stubble the harvesters were obliged to leave in the field—demonstrate the absence of any easy consensus about the limits of gleaning.[64] As we shall see, many villages placed new restrictions on gleaning near the end of the Qing, and the state encouraged the formation of crop-watching societies that enforced these limits (and guarded against outright theft). Far from being matters of timeless "custom," gleaning rules were frequently revised and continually tested by gleaners and property owners.

Even before the new varieties, cotton scraps and leavings were intensely contested. Smith noted in the 1890s that cotton was the crop gleaners coveted most and thus was the hardest to protect; nonetheless, his only example of a family trying to completely exclude gleaners from their fields involved cotton.[65] Routine cotton stealing kept some peasants from even trying the new varieties:

> Although the farmers in the province of Anhui were amazed at the size of the American boll, and were fully convinced of its greater yield and value, they were reluctant to raise it for fear that it would be stolen by their less fortunate neighbors. A quiet investigation revealed the facts that petty banditry and thieving were so prevalent in parts of the area that the cotton was picked from the field at night, unless gathered by the farmer himself.[66]

Thus even old cotton was especially attractive to gleaners and petty thieves who got to it early enough; new cotton was even more so. But the new cotton offered slim pickings to anyone forced to wait until after its late harvest date. The 1934 Heze(S) report extolling U.S. cotton's superior profitability gives the value (in yuan) of both the "main product"—the harvest—and the "secondary products" of various crops that would be available to postharvest gleaners. The comparison is

63. QYHK, no. 22 (March 1924), gongdu, 16; QYHK, no. 10 (Jan. 1923), ge xian shiye zhuangkuang, 1.

64. See Smith, Village Life, 166–67; Gamble, North China Villages, 71, 236.

65. Smith, Village Life, 163, 166–68.

66. George Smith, "Improving China's Cotton," China Weekly Recorder, Dec. 12, 1923, p. 128.

instructive:[67]

	main crop	leavings
U.S. cotton	15.60	1.00
wheat	5.39	1.38
soybeans	3.84	1.00
millet	3.60	2.40
sorghum	3.00	3.00

Furthermore, although the new cotton varieties needed more labor than most other crops, these needs were more evenly spread through the season, so farmers could use less hired labor; in particular, harvest labor needs were anywhere from 28 percent to 44 percent per *mu* lower than for the other crops listed above.[68] One survey also found that fear of theft led households growing U.S. cotton to use more of their own female and child labor for this particular crop, rather than hiring others.[69] (These concerns apparently overcame moral strictures against "respectable" women being in the fields, at least when accompanied by family members rather than hired hands.) Since those who depended most on gleaning were often also those who most needed to work for wages—and since harvesting was often a chance to start gleaning early—the new cotton varieties represented a serious threat to their livelihood.

To the dismay of OEI officials, gleaners all over western Shandong refused to abandon their traditional gleaning date. In the mid-1920s, Qingping(N), Puzhou(S), Heze(S), Qiu(N), Linqing(N), Guancheng (N), Wucheng(N), Xiajin(N), Tang Yi(N), and Juye(S) all reported U.S. cotton being ruined by people who rushed the fields before the crop was fully ripened; another report said that typically only 60 percent to 70 percent of the bolls had opened when people

67. *XCJSXK* 3:18–19 (Feb. 1934), 14–15. Figures in Mantetsu, *Santō no Mensaku*, 47–54, are generally similar for costs and harvests, but lack information on residues. Unfortunately, precisely comparable figures for Chinese cotton are not available, but other sources suggest that the main product of U.S. cotton was usually worth 50 percent more than that of native cotton. Comparable figures on residues are unavailable, but since U.S. cotton had to be planted slightly farther apart than Chinese cotton (in compensation, it had more and larger bolls on each plant), it seems likely that it produced fewer, or at least no more, cotton stalks per *mu*; these stalks, which were the principal residue, were burned for fuel.

68. *XCJSXK* 3:18–19 (Feb. 1934), 14–15. For a similar phenomenon in Weixian, Shandong, see *Chinese Economic Journal* 3:2, p. 660.

69. Kita Shina, *Rosai Mensaku*, 51.

rushed the fields and that the practice threatened the new crop's prospects in much of western Shandong.[70] Farmers victimized by cotton rushing not only lost one crop, but were reluctant to plant American cotton the next year. Others might reasonably conclude that an organization that could not even guarantee their crop against the limited forces of gleaners could hardly be counted on to ensure that either seeds or the crop itself arrived safely and on time. Many county OEI reports listed improved security against cotton rushing as the first prerequisite for making the new crop succeed.[71]

At first glance, the larger number of northwestern counties reporting cotton rushing might seem to suggest that the problem was more severe there than in the southwest. However, these reports come from 1922 to 1925; and as of 1922, Heze and Juye, two of the three southwestern counties reporting cotton rushing, had 88 percent of all southwestern acreage sown to U.S. cotton. No figures are available for Puzhou, the third southwestern county making such reports, during this period; and no other overall figures on southwestern plantings of U.S. cotton are available until 1930, by which time U.S. cotton had roughly the same small share of the total crop throughout the southwest.[72] It appears, then, that cotton rushing appeared wherever U.S. cotton did in western Shandong; it is the coverage of our records that is incomplete.

While the northwest and southwest began with comparable cotton-rushing problems, they did not make comparable progress against them. By 1930, cotton rushing was under control in northwest Shandong[73] and was no longer a serious obstacle to U.S. cotton in that region. But there is not a single report claiming any progress against this custom in the southwest. In 1934, the rural reconstruction group in Heze(S) was still trying to promote American cotton and reported that

---

70. *QYHK*, no. 7 (May 1922), *ge xian quanye baogao*, 22–23, 30; no. 9 (Dec. 1922), *ge xian chengji baogao*, 25; no. 10 (Jan. 1923), *ge xian shiye zhuangkuang*, 1–2; no. 11 (Feb. 1923), *ge xian chengji baogao*, 18–19; no. 12 (March 1923), *gongdu*, 36, 38, 40; *ge xian chengji baogao*, 27; no. 16 (July 1923), *gongdu*, 41; no. 22 (March 1924), *gongdu*, 1, 16; no. 28 (Sept. 1924), *shiye gongdu*, 26; the second to last of these references, p. 1, also gives the 60–70 percent figure.
71. *QYHK*, no. 7, *ge xian quanye baogao*, 22; no. 10, *ge xian shiye zhuangkuang*, 2; no. 11, *ge xian chengji baogao*, 18; no. 12, *gongdu*, 36, 38, 41; no. 22, *gongdu*, 15–16; no. 28, *shiye gongdu*, 26.
72. See dissertation, appendix D, 406–19.
73. "Lubei shi xian nongye diaocha baogao," *Shandong nongkuang gongbao*, no. 13 (Jan. 1930), 34.

cotton rushing was still a major obstacle; the farmers, they said, "did not dare resist" this practice, and special organizations would have to be created to combat it.[74]

Cotton rushing—and the conflicts it spawned—went far beyond ordinary cases of poor peasants exceeding what property owners considered to be acceptable gleaning. Most earlier cases in which gleaning was held to have crossed over into theft involved individuals acting surreptitiously. Smith reported that in Shandong in the 1890s a farmer could usually make somebody picking at the edge of a cotton field move on just by yelling "Who are you?"[75] Sidney Gamble's survey of twenty-four North China villages in the 1930s deals at length with conflicts over crop watching, gleaning, and theft, but very few of the cases recorded involve open defiance of the gleaning rules, much less open defiance by groups.[76] A gazetteer from Luyi county, Henan, a bit south of Huang-Yun, reports that in the late nineteenth century, so many people exceeded what cultivators considered tolerable gleaning that family crop watching was replaced by villagewide patrols. Even here, though, the gazetteer attributes the provocation to the actions of "cunning" women; this seems a far cry from open, mass defiance.[77]

By contrast, accounts from the 1920s and 1930s note that cotton rushers approached in groups including both men and women[78] and that tens or even hundreds of people sometimes entered the fields together.[79] Using extensive organized force against cotton rushers therefore would often have been morally awkward; resisting them without such force, however, was impossible.

If cotton rushing in the 1920s went beyond "normal" attempts to expand gleaning, it still resembled old practices enough to be referred to as a "custom" and was usually distinguished from "banditry." The gleaning date itself derived much of its power from tradition. However, the high stakes that the new cotton varieties represented and the

74. *XCJSXK* 3:18–19 (Feb. 1934), 13; *QYHK*, no. 9 (Dec. 1922), *ge xian shiye zhuangkuang*, 25.

75. Smith, *Village Life*, 163.

76. Gamble, *North China Villages*, esp. 87–96, 301.

77. Quoted in Hsiao Kung-ch'uan, *Rural China: Imperial Control in the Nineteenth Century* (Seattle, 1960), 288.

78. *QYHK*, no. 22 (March 1924), 15; *HBMCLB*, no. 12 (Oct. 16, 1936), 13; see also Smith, *Village Life*, 167, 276 on the importance of women in cotton picking and gleaning generally.

79. *QYHK*, no. 10 (Jan. 1923), *ge xian shiye zhuangkuang*, 2.

open challenge of cotton rushing produced very new kinds of security efforts. To these we now turn.

CROP WATCHING AND "COTTON SOCIETIES"

Crop-watching organizations sprang up in many North China villages near the turn of the century, replacing family-based crop watching. The late Qing government encouraged this development, hoping that curbing theft would allow property owners to pay higher taxes.[80] Many of these crop-watching organizations also moved to restrict gleaning; for instance, after 1900, when more tax and administrative burdens were assigned based on the village unit, some Zhili villages began excluding outsiders from gleaning.[81] Organized village crop watching appears to have increased gradually throughout the disorderly years of the early twentieth century.[82] However, we should not overestimate its strength, particularly in Huang-Yun.

In the first place, village crop watching was far from universal. In some counties the practice was well established by the 1890s, but in others it was still unheard of.[83] Of fifty-three available reports of Huang-Yun murders arising from land or money disputes between 1900 and 1908, nine involved crop watching. In seven of the nine, the crop watching was still done by families; in the eighth, a village crop watcher tried to evade an assignment away from his own home.[84] A spotty pattern of family and community crop watching persisted through the 1930s.[85]

Moreover, organized crop watching was usually limited to grain. As we shall see, people had good reasons to keep their crop-watching

---

80. Myers, *Peasant Economy*, 261.
81. Prasenjit Duara, "Power in Rural Society: North China Villages, 1900–1945," (Ph.D. dissertation, Harvard University, 1983), 254–56; Duara, "The Political Structure of a North China Village in Late Imperial and Republican Times," *Stone Lion Review*, no. 5 (Spring 1980), 50; Myers, *Peasant Economy*, 260–61.
82. Gamble, *North China Villages*, p. 77; Duara, "Power in Rural Society," 162.
83. Smith, *Village Life*, 163.
84. The relevant cases can be found in the Xing Bu files, Shandong Si and Henan Si, listed under the category "tu di fangwu, qian cai zhaiwu anjian," in record books 475 16–19 and 475 16–21 of the First Historical Archives, Beijing, China. The nine cases involving crop watching are 15603, 15672, 15652, 15657, 15666, 15714 (Shandong cases); 13795, 13800, 14379 (Henan cases). Case 15603 is the account of the villager who did not want to leave home.
85. Gamble, *North China Villages*, 69–70.

duties brief, which often meant protecting only one harvest.[86] In Shulu, a Huang-Yun county in southwest Hebei, none of the 1930s village crop-watching groups covered cotton, which was considered the most difficult crop to protect.[87] (Orchards, melons, and peanuts were also omitted.[88])

"Ordinary" village crop watching also often mixed enforcement with concessions to gleaners and the village poor. By banning gleaning by outsiders, a village protected and placated its own poor. At least one northwest Shandong crop-watching society went a step further, preventing outsiders from coming in to work in the village's harvest;[89] no reason is recorded, but the ban had the effect of reserving jobs as well as chaff for poor villagers.

Crop watching itself provided jobs, which were limited to the village's own members. Even in villages with crop watching, it was rare for all the villagers to stand guard in the fields. Instead, they often pooled their money and hired poorer villagers.[90] Thus, some of those hurt by tightened restrictions on gleaning and theft received added wage income; in fact, many observers said that precisely those men who had been involved in stealing were most likely to be hired.[91] The crop-watching societies may have also contributed to village solidarity by hiring youths with an interest in martial arts; Joseph Esherick argues that such employment gave young men who had earlier been inclined to pursue this interest in towns or on the open road a chance to aspire to "local heroism" instead of "knight-errantry."[92]

Crop-watching societies had reasons besides a taste for community to make these concessions to the poor and restless. Crop watching was difficult and unpleasant, and it strained individuals and the community. People often became sick from sleeping night after night in the fields.[93] In one southwest Zhili village, opium addiction spread to the peasantry in 1920, when farmers of this village, forced by crop failures

86. Ibid., 74, 78.
87. Ibid., 279.
88. Smith, *Village Life*, 162, 276.
89. Chūgoku Nōson Kanko Chōsa Kai, *Chūgoku Nōson Kanko Chōsa*, 4:14.
90. See, e.g., Gamble, *North China Villages*, 69; Perry, *Rebels and Revolutionaries*, 82; for an earlier scheme explicitly linking crop watching to relief for the poor, see Philip Kuhn, *Rebellion and Its Enemies in Late Imperial China* (Cambridge, Mass., 1970), 33.
91. See, for instance, Perry, *Rebels and Revolutionaries*, 82.
92. Esherick, *Boxer Uprising*, 65.
93. Smith, *Village Life*, 168.

in nearby areas to put in especially long hours guarding their successful crops, used the drug to stay awake.[94] An OEI official in Linqing(N)
in 1924 feared that the cotton rushers would prevail because the strain
of prolonged crop watching was simply too great.[95] The same late
Qing murder records that show five cases in which crop watchers
killed intruders show six in which crop watchers died. Two were
killed by thieves; two died in disputes over who should watch; one
well-off man (whose home, in this area, would have been in a walled
compound) was kidnaped from the thatch hut he used for crop watching; and in one case a killer with an unrelated grudge sought out a
crop watcher he knew would be alone and vulnerable.[96]

Three more murders arose from events that began when men left
their wives or daughters alone to go watch crops. Only long-term
labor—with five cases—was a more common reason for men to have
been away when "family problems" leading to murder began.[97] Such
samples are obviously too small to rely on. However, various writers
have argued that long-term labor by poor peasant males made them
less able to control access to their wives and so contributed to a
stereotype of poor peasants as "loose" that further marginalized
them.[98] If sexual relations leading to murder often began when men
were crop watching, then it, too, presumably strained families and
contributed to the desire of "respectable" men to avoid this duty.

In sum, even peasants concerned about crop theft knew that discre-
tion was often the better part of valor. If relatively light levies could
turn potential thieves into paid crop watchers and decrease the number of nights one spent in the fields, such payments made good sense.
Moreover, since people often needed a respected "guarantor" to be
hired as crop watchers,[99] such jobs could serve as an inducement to
better behavior (especially by the young and poor) all year round.
Finally, farmers had to continue to live with not only the potential

94. Guo Yizhi, "Pochan shengzhong de yige Jinan nongcun," in *Zhongguo nongcun
jingji lunwen ji*, ed. Qian Jiaju (Shanghai, 1935), 514.
95. *QYHK*, no. 22 (March 1924), *gongdu*, 16.
96. Cases 14379, 15672, 15652, 15657, 15666; 13795, 13800; 15603, 15714;
16683; and 15638, respectively.
97. Cases 16902, 16907, 16911; 16913, 16917, 16945, 16951, and 14845.
98. Victor Nee, "Toward a Social Anthropology of the Chinese Revolution," *Bulletin of Concerned Asian Scholars* 11:3 (July–Sept. 1979), 42–43; Huang, *Peasant
Economy*, 256, quoting among others Mao Zedong, "Report on an Investigation of the
Hunan Peasant Movement."
99. Gamble, *North China Villages*, 82.

thieves "paid off" with crop watching jobs, but even the people actually caught stealing.[100] Under the circumstances, punishments for
those caught tended to be light: usually small fines, an occasional beat-
ing (usually reserved for outsiders), or even just a lecture.[101]

In the 1930s, children in Yanggu(S) and Ciyang(S) counties played
a version of tag called "taking the sorghum stalks" that reflected the
kind of ordinary gleaning conflicts suggested by Smith forty years
earlier. In this game, there were several "crop watchers" at a time, but
only one "gleaner." (The games in which several people were chased at
a time cast them as fleeing or deserting soldiers.) Before beginning the
chase, the crop watchers ask "What are you doing?" and the gleaner,
who stands behind them, replies truthfully, using a word (*chu*) that refers specifically to postharvest residues. The crop watchers then ask
"Why are you still here?" to which the gleaner replies, "I'm afraid."
The crop watchers then sarcastically reply, "We'll get a lamp and
accompany (*song*) you," making clear that the imaginary event takes
place at night. Of course, children's games need not reflect the adult
world precisely. Still, the mock courteous conversation and the references to a single stealthy perpetrator and to crop residues in particular
suggest that this game mimicked a world of limited conflict. Moreover, this game had no "punishment" for those who were caught; in
the other chase games, they were forced to spend a turn in "jail," were
insulted, or were beaten.[102]

Thus, while organized village crop watching represented an escalation of already serious conflicts,[103] this escalation happened in only
some villages and still stopped far short of outright class war. It is also
significant that the fines assessed against violators were often spent on
incense burning or theatricals for the whole village:[104] here, too, crop-
watching societies mixed coercion, concessions, and gestures toward
"village unity."

The more confrontational tactics of 1920s cotton rushers brought a
qualitatively different response. The provincial OEI ordered each

100. Perry, *Rebels and Revolutionaries*, 83; Smith, *Village Life*, 163.
101. Gamble, *North China Villages*, 87–96, 296, 301; Smith, *Village Life*, 163,
168; *Chūgoku Nōson*, 4:430.
102. Shandong shengli minzhong jiaoyuguan, *Shandong minjian yule* (Jinan, 1933),
1:17, 20–21, 23, 64, 77, 80–81, 84–87.
103. Smith, *Village Life*, 164, 168; Gamble, *North China Villages*, 77, 85; see
generally Hatada Takashi, *Chūgoku Sonraku to Kyōdotai Riron* (Tokyo, 1973).
104. Gamble, *North China Villages*, 85; Smith, *Village Life*, 168.

county to establish a "cotton society" (*mianye gonghui*) with as many branches as possible. These organizations were supposed to distribute U.S. cotton seeds and promotional literature, conduct lectures, inspect crops, collect harvested seeds (to keep them from being re-planted), and award prizes; however, their principal task was to pro-tect cotton against rushing. All the recorded branch societies were multivillage, even though one had only eighteen members. The num-bers of villages included in each branch strongly suggest that they were based on subcounty administrative units, which were much larger than such "natural" units as standard marketing areas. In theory, they could all be summoned by the county magistrate or the county OEI head, though this was probably rare. One report, however, distin-guished the cotton societies from nearby Red Spears by noting that they were far better organized[105]—and the Red Spears were by far the most impressive federation of village-based defense groups.

Cotton societies also differed in other ways from all other village-based security arrangements. The county OEI heads and their assis-tants were all fairly young (usually under thirty) sons of members of the county elite; they had all been educated in modern technical schools elsewhere in Shandong, but served in their home counties.[106] Their leadership of cotton, forest, and mulberry societies that had budgets—albeit modest ones[107]—technical and organizational re-sources, arms, and legal authority represented an extension of their power down toward the villages, not an initiative by the villages. In this sense, such societies were completely unlike older crop-watching groups. In fact, they were more like the reformist schools and "peasant organizations" being organized at the same time by radicalized young

105. *QYHK*, no. 4 (Jan. 1921), *gongdu*, 1–6; no. 7 (May 1922), *ge xian quanye baogao*, 23–24, 33; no. 13 (April 1923), *ge xian chengji baogao*, 1–8; no. 16 (July 1923), *gongdu*, 44; for the power vested in the county magistrate, see, for instance, *QYHK*, no. 9 (Oct. 1922), *gongdu*, 22; no. 15 (June 1923), *ge xian chengji baogao*, 42; for comparsion with the Red Spears, see "Lubei shi xian nongye diaocha baogao," 22.

106. *QYHK*, no. 6 (Jan. 1922), appendix.

107. On the budgets of county *quanyesuo* for cotton promotion, see Lin Maoquan, *Wenji*, 77b–78a. Few of these counties spent more than ¥300 of public funds; two of the three largest expenditures came in the southern counties of Dingtao and Dengxian, where U.S. cotton nonetheless made little progress. The budgets of the cotton societies themselves are harder to fix, but until they succeeded enough to begin farming the rev-enues from the cotton-brokerage tax, they were dependent on dues that were usually only ¥1 or ¥2 per member and on an occasional merchant contribution. Puxian, a bor-derline county with an unusually vigorous Quanyesuo, did its early 1920s cotton work through an "agricultural society" that spent ¥340 in 1922 (*QYHK*, no. 12 ([March 1923], *gongdu*, 37).

members of the county elite in Jiangxi as they returned home from schooling and sought to build themselves political bases.[108]

In some Shandong counties, these reformist political entrepreneurs joined forces with missionaries: old antagonists of South Huang-Yun rural elites and the quintessential outsiders with big plans. Indeed, China's first agricultural education fair—held in Linyi, east of Huang-Yun, in 1922—featured a staged drama that symbolized this alliance and how different its values could be from those upheld by most village leaders. In the play, peasants, upset by the low price their native cotton fetches, resort to "idolatrous worship." They are rescued from this blind alley by an American missionary (playing himself); he directs them to the county agricultural official (playing himself), who solves their problems by giving them U.S. cotton seeds.[109] Most county OEI heads probably did without such allies; no missionaries are mentioned in the extant OEI reports from Huang-Yun. Still, the willingness of an OEI head to frontally attack popular religion reminds us how much these associations, based in the county capital and guided by young men with "modern" educations, were part of a reformist thrust that came from outside the village and could not easily base itself on village traditions, institutions, or leaders.

As we shall see, the cotton societies did not rely on village solidarity and did not take the steps that village crop watchers took to shore up community solidarity. Cotton societies were also far more likely to be organizations of the relatively prosperous. In Xiajin(N), for instance, members had to have more than ten *mu* of U.S. cotton.[110] In a county with less than eighteen *mu* for an average-sized family,[111] such a requirement excluded the poor, unless they gambled on putting well over half of their land in U.S. cotton at a time when only 13 percent of the county's farmland was in this high-risk, high-return crop.[112]

Had Xiajin's 1922 acreage of U.S. cotton been divided up into even ten-*mu* plots, about 5,000 families would have been eligible to join;

108. See Stephen Averill, "Party, Society, and Local Elite in the Jiangxi Communist Movement," *Journal of Asian Studies* 46:2 (May 1987), 279–303, esp. 282–85, 299.

109. "China's First Agricultural Institute," *China Weekly Recorder*, May 12, 1923, p. 382.

110. *QYHK*, no. 16 (July 1923), *gongdu*, 42.

111. Based on figures from John L. Buck, "A Statistical View of Shantung," *Chinese Economic Journal* 1:1 (Jan. 1927), 41.

112. See dissertation, appendix D, for cotton figures, and Buck, "Statistical View," 41, for total acreage.

since any late-ripening cotton raised by nonmembers would have been easy prey for cotton rushers, there were strong incentives for all eligible families to join. But in 1923 the twelve oldest branch societies in Xiajin had 850 members; this number suggests that the "twenty-plus" branch societies in the county had fewer than 2,000 members.[113] Thus either the cotton societies excluded large numbers of peasants who had small plots of U.S. cotton—an exclusion that would have made it very risky indeed for them to stick with this crop—or those farmers who were members had an average of more than twenty-five *mu* each in just this one crop. Such holdings hardly make the cotton society members magnates, but they probably were among the wealthier farmers in Xiajin, which, like the rest of northwest Shandong, had very few large landholders.[114] A 1929 provincial report said that more than half the cotton society members in Linqing(N) had magazine rifles,[115] an item few peasants could afford. Heze(S) required only five *mu* of land in U.S. cotton to join a branch of the cotton society, but since most Heze peasants had less land than those farther north, this lesser requirement may have excluded just as many people.[116] There are also some hints that many county societies expected their members to be literate.[117] The Shandong provincial government eventually reversed the course charted by these exclusionary requirements, trying to bring all cotton growers into new cotton cooperatives, but not until shortly before World War II.[118]

Cotton societies also dropped the village crop-watching societies' practice of co-opting some of the poor by hiring them. While members did pay dues, there is no mention of wage payments being made. The

113. *QYHK*, no. 16 (July 1923), *gongdu*, 44–46.
114. For general surveys of land distribution in this area see Esherick, *Boxer Uprising* (esp. 24, 206); Huang, *Peasant Economy*; and Myers, *Peasant Economy*, 49, 71, 106, 154, 201.
115. "Lubei shi xian nongye diaocha baogao," 21.
116. *QYHK*, no. 7 (May 1922), *ge xian quanye baogao*, 35.
117. Many cotton societies' rules say that all members must "have knowledge" (e.g., *QYHK*, no. 16 [July 1923], *gongdu*, 41), but it is unclear whether this refers only to a knowledge of how to plant U.S. cotton or refers to more general matters as well. According to the provincial guidelines for these organizations (*QYHK*, no. 4 [Jan. 1921], *gongdu*, 4), members were obligated to submit "detailed reports" on their cultivation methods and results, and could be fined and denied future seed supplies if they failed to fill out the appropriate forms. Of course an illiterate member might receive help. The heavy reliance on pamphlets—several organizations report printing pamphlets as their principal promotional effort, though many also arranged lectures and demonstrations—is also interesting.
118. *HBMCLB*, no. 12 (Oct. 16, 1936), 13–14.

TABLE 2 DISTRIBUTION OF COTTON
WATCHING IN QIZHAI, GAOTANG

Landholding category (no. of *mu* in cotton)	% of families in village	% of cotton security work done	Cumulative totals	
			Population	Work
0–4	17.7	0.0	17.7	0.0
5–14	28.8	15.3	46.5	15.3
15–24	33.1	35.1	79.6	50.4
25–34	9.3	14.9	88.9	65.3
more than 34	11.0	34.7	99.9	100.0

only positions these organizations had, aside from head and two deputy heads, were "inspectors." Along with their security responsibilities, inspectors had record-keeping and quality-control tasks that required literacy; they were to be selected from among the "gentry and people" (*shen min*) and confirmed by the county magistrate.[119] Consequently, inspectors must have been of much higher status than the guards hired by village crop-watching groups. Even if a few were not, these positions could not be used by village leaders to placate their own poor; whatever patronage was involved was controlled at a higher level.

A 1943 survey of one Gaotang(N) village (the home of the head of the county Cotton Improvement Society, presumably a successor to its cotton society) with 66 percent of its land in cotton shows that cotton security still bore the marks of the 1920s cotton societies. While the village collected money and paid people to fulfill its corvée and militia obligations, it handled cotton security quite differently. Families with fewer than five *mu* of cotton were not involved at all; the others were assessed a number of nights on duty according to their holdings; paid substitutes were almost never used. Applying the rules on cotton security obligations to village land-holding figures shows just how much of this one type of work was done by solid middle peasants and those above them (table 2).[120]

Some of the heavy burden falling on the richest families may have been done by their long-term laborers; these people may even have

119. *QYHK*, no. 7 (May 1922), *ge xian quanye baogao*, 33, 35.
120. Kita Shina, *Rosai Mensaku*, 47, 51, 52, 104–7, 117.

been listed as part of the family, and so not considered "paid substitutes." Nonetheless, including such work in the duties of a privately
hired worker on long-term contract is a far cry from the village as a
whole hiring its poor to do this specific task, and it does not have
the same effect of "buying off" those being excluded from gleaning.
The contrast to "ordinary" village crop-watching arrangements could
hardly be sharper.

Cotton society members could earn money watching cotton. Chi-
ping(N), for instance, paid the person who caught an illicit gleaner 30
percent of the gleaner's fine. The other rewards this group dispensed
were for people who planted twenty, forty, or a hundred *mu* of U.S.
cotton, which would exclude even most middle peasants; the group's
outlays as a whole were clearly not a way to buy social peace or
strengthen community.[121] The cotton societies' shares of the "heavy
fines" mandated for early gleaning went for general expenses (leaflets,
seeds, and so forth);[122] by contrast, village crop-watching groups
spent the fines they collected for theatricals, incense burning, or other
events that brought the entire village together, at least superficially.

The cotton societies confronted gleaners with far more coercion
than village crop-watching groups ever had. Some became huge fed-
erations: in 1929, the cotton society in Linqing(N) claimed more than
twenty thousand members and more than ten thousand modern rifles
just in the eastern part of the county. (Significantly, cotton societies
were weak in the western part of the county, where the Red Spears
dominated security affairs.)[123] Even individual branches often had formidable forces.[124] The charters of most county-level societies also
specified that the county police and militia would work with them at

121. *QYHK*, no. 9 (Oct. 1922), *gongdu*, 22.
122. This is nowhere explictly stated, but many of the organizations have no other
apparent source of funds, or only one obviously inadequate for their expenditures.
There is also no mention in any of the cotton society reports of a villagewide feast to
mark the end of the crop-watching season such as was common with "regular," village-
based crop-watching groups (see, for instance, Gamble, *North China Villages*, 74).
123. "Lubei shi xian nongye diaocha baogao," 21–22; however, Meng Da, "Zhang
gu shang jiang Zichong jia shi ji Linqing fengguang," *Shandong wenxian* 1:1 (June
1975), 75–76, gives the total number of metal rifles available to Linqing protective
organizations as eight thousand.
124. See, for instance, the membership figures for some of the larger branches in
QYHK, no. 16 (July 1923), *gongdu*, 44; Imai Shuin, "Kōnichi Konkyochi no Keisei
Katei ni tsuite no Ichi Kōsatsu," 38–39, outlines a sharp increase in both militia and
police expenditures and armaments connected with the rise of cotton and peanut planting in southwestern Hebei, where conditions were broadly similar, though he does not
say anything about the practice of cotton rushing in particular.

harvest time; some were also joined by the county's forest patrol, a paid, armed force also created in the early 1920s at the behest of the provincial OEI. County forestry societies (discussed in chapter 3) also helped out; these were organized along similar lines to the cotton societies but were generally even less egalitarian, more at odds with customary ideas, and more dependent on force. This unusual level of force in the hands of the relatively prosperous made it possible for county OEI reports to speak of "abolishing" cotton rushing, not just controlling it.[125]

The cotton societies also possessed one nonviolent, unpredictable, and utterly revolutionary weapon: the experiment and extension stations. These county-level stations collected seeds from U.S. cotton grown locally, received seeds bought abroad by the province or developed at regional stations, and served as demonstration and seed farms. They also tried to breed better locally adapted strains; many laid particular stress on creating strains that would mature a little earlier.[126] (Local experimentation was required both to cope with soil peculiarities and to reduce reliance on the underfunded provincial OEI network.)[127] Where varieties that matured before the traditional rushing date were developed, the issue was settled: gleaners did not push beyond the calendar-based definition of their rights.[128] In the environment created by the cotton societies, only one side dared to make unprecedented claims. Moreover, it appears that none of these stations was ever attacked, despite their centrality to cotton promotion—or perhaps because of it. Such a raid might have slowed down the new plant varieties, but it would have escalated a conflict in which gleaners did not want the state to get any more involved.

125. See, for instance, *QYHK*, no. 9 (Dec. 1922), *gongdu*, 22; no. 16 (July 1923), *gongdu*, 41; no. 12 (March 1923), *gongdu*, 38; no. 22 (March 1924), *gongdu*, 16; *HBMCLB*, no. 12 (Oct. 16, 1936), 13.

126. See, for instance, Hu Zhangzhun, "Shandong zhi mianye," 22; report of Shandong governor of 2/29/XT1 (1909) in file 110 Nong gong shang bu, Huiyi Zhengwuchu; *Nongshang gongbao* 2:3 (Oct. 1915), *baogao*, 47; *NSGB* 2:6 (Jan. 1919), *diaocha*, p. 2; *Gong shang banyuekan*, 6:23 (Dec. 1, 1934), 154–56; *HBMCLB*, no. 12 (Oct. 16, 1936), 13; no. 16 (Dec. 16, 1936), 18; no. 41 (Aug. 1, 1938), 29.

127. Most counties carried on some research of their own, even though the province funded larger scale research centers in Linqing, Jinan, Jidong, and Yi xian (slightly east of our "southwest" region). On the size of the provincial network's seed distribution (which was not intended to be sufficient by itself) see, for instance, Mantetsu, *Santō no Mensaku*, 6; on problems of one county's seeds not working in others, see QZ1038: AH2034, 11a–b; and see *QYHK*, passim, on the province's insistence that each county do some cotton experimentation of its own.

128. *XCJSXK* 3:18–19 (Feb. 1934), 13.

Unfortunately, we have only fragmentary descriptions of this conflict. It is clear, however, that the cotton society patrols were effective in many northwestern counties and that some counties also eventually obtained cotton that ripened slightly earlier.[129] The latest source I know of that treats cotton rushing as a serious problem in northwest Shandong is from 1930, and it says that protection was getting increasingly effective.[130] Cotton rushing is mentioned only once in the surviving late 1930s reports from the cotton stations in Linqing, Jinan, and Jidong, which served north and northwest Shandong,[131] and not at all in the many other reports from this area after 1930. Instead we are told that once the cotton-rushing problem was solved, peasants in north Shandong "fought with each other to get their cotton seeds first"; by the 1930s, all strata of peasants in north Shandong had some land under the new cotton varieties, and total cotton output reached record levels.[132] This is not surprising. Cotton prices rose 40 percent more than wheat prices during the expansionary years from 1913 to 1920 and fell 13 percent less between 1929 and 1933, as the Great Depression made itself felt.[133] Furthermore, since cotton marketing was more efficient than grain marketing, peasants received a higher percentage of cotton's final selling price.[134] U.S. cotton was still riskier than other crops: it required more fertilizer and thus more credit, and it left people dependent on other people for seed and on the market for food.[135] However, there were ample rewards to com-

129. *QYHK*, no. 9 (Dec. 1922), *ge xian chengji baogao*, 25; no. 10 (Jan. 1923), *zhuanjian*, 1; no. 12 (March 1923), *ge xian chengji baogao*, 27; Ting, *Recent Developments*, 13–14, 17–18.

130. "Lubei shi xian nongye diaocha baogao," 34.

131. *HBMCLB*, no. 12 (Oct. 16, 1936), 13, is a rare example. Moreover, petty thievery by individuals continued to be a problem; in Qizhai, Gaotang, peasants would not plant their furthest outlying fields in cotton because they could not protect them. Kita Shina, *Rosai Mensaku*, 73.

132. *XCJSXK* 3:18–19 (Feb. 1934), 13–14; for output figures, see dissertation, appendix D.

133. Figures derived from data on price changes for different crops given in Wu Chengming, "Wo Guo guonei shichang," 115, 121; see also *SSYZ*, 5:180–82.

134. Wu Chengming, "Wo Guo guonei shichang," 114. More efficient networks mean lower costs, which, if there is competition among merchants, should benefit the farmers. While having many different organizations involved at different stages of a process does not necessarily make it inefficient, it is worth contrasting the relatively direct path of cotton from field to mill with the far more circuitous path of wheat, as described, for instance, in Mai Shudu, "Hebei sheng xiaomai zhi banyun," *Shehui kexue zazhi* 1:1 (March 1930), 73–107, and in a subsequent Japanese study of marketing in the Jining area in *Santō Sainei*.

135. For a general summary of these problems, based on southwest Hebei's experi-

pensate for such risks, especially if a peasant also kept some land in safer crops. Because it was so labor intensive, this new commercial crop may even have benefited families with small farms (though not, as we have seen, the landless) more than it benefited the more prosperous farmers who adopted it first.

By contrast, the only account we have from people still promoting U.S. cotton in southwest Shandong in the mid-1930s still describes cotton rushing as their key problem.[136] Significantly, the report comes from the Heze rural reconstruction team, a nongovernmental group of determined outsiders focused on one county, who often complained that they got little cooperation from local elites. In general, the return of relative stability in the 1930s allowed the OEI's official successor—the Shandong Reconstruction Office—to undertake infrastructural projects spanning several counties; consequently, they left most of the promotion of agricultural change to local organizations. In the northwest, many such local organizations were by then well established: Gaotang's Cotton Improvement Society, as we saw, was still organizing village-level projects during the Japanese occupation. In the southwest, however, the equivalent organizations had never taken firm root; most had disappeared soon after their formation. The Heze report said that organizations would have to be created to deal with cotton rushing, not even mentioning the cotton societies created there in the 1920s. Without determined and powerful local sponsors, new cotton varieties did not spread in the southwest, and the area lost access to the cotton market.

In the early phase of the cotton boom, between 1914 and 1922, southwestern cotton acreage actually increased more than northwestern acreage—11.7 percent versus 5.6 percent. However, the area's acreage of U.S. cotton reached only 352 *qing* (less than 5 percent of the area's cotton land) versus 3,970 *qing* (about 15 percent) in the northwest. (U.S. varieties had been trivial in both areas in 1914.) The switch to U.S. varieties helped the northwest increase its yield 23.1 percent per acre versus 4.7 percent in the less innovative southwest; total output rose 30 percent in the northwest versus 17 percent in the southwest.[137] As the discrepancy between the acreage devoted to

---

ence, see Imai Shuin, "Kōnichi Konkyochi no Keisei Katei ni tsuite no Ichi Kosatsu," 22–40.

136. *XCJSXK* 3:18–19 (Feb. 1934), 13.

137. See dissertation, appendix D, for raw figures.

U.S. cotton in these regions increased in the 1920s and 1930s, cotton
buyers concentrated on the northwest and some areas east of Huang-
Yun. In 1921 Japanese mill owners had been so interested in buying
cotton from the southwest that they asked a Japanese bank that
planned to finance a major land reclamation project there (see chapter
5) to make sure the new land would be used for cotton; but by World
War II, the Japanese had given up on southwest Shandong as a cotton
source.[138] In the 1930s, northwest Shandong and southwest Hebei recovered from warlord depredations to reach record output levels, with
U.S. varieties making up ever higher percentages of the crop. But since
southwest Shandong's output remained native cotton, it had no external market and consequently never grew much further once it regained
its pre–civil war (1922) level.[139] In the People's Republic, with security much less a problem, the percentage of land under cotton in southwest Shandong has moved much closer to northwestern levels than
ever before in this century; only high-yield, machine-spinnable
varieties are grown.[140] Since many noneconomic factors have affected
post-1949 cropping patterns, this change alone does not demonstrate
that the southwest would have joined in the cotton boom had security
problems been solved; moreover, this evidence does not help us dis-
tinguish cotton rushing from other security problems that may have

138. On the enthusiasm of Japanese mills in the early 1920s, see the letter of
Vice-President Ono of the Industrial Bank of Japan to Charles Stone of American
International Corporation, June 1, 1921, in U.S. Department of State, *Records of the
Department of State Relating to the Internal Affairs of China, 1910–1929* (hereafter,
Department of State), reel 216, document 3424, p. 199. By contrast, the southwest is
mentioned only once, briefly, in the extensive accounts of efforts to obtain and promote
machine-spinnable cotton in Shandong in Mantetsu, *Santō no Mensaku*, and is treated
as a minor crop in *Santō Kōshogun Chitai no Chūki Chōsa*, the Japanese army's 1940
study of southwestern Shandong.

139. See dissertation, appendix D, on the general rising trend of Shandong cotton
production; on the attainment of new output highs, see, for instance, Ting, *Recent Developments*, 13–14.

140. The percentages were roughly 18.5 percent of all cultivated land in cotton in
southwest Shandong and 25 percent in northwest Shandong, according to Shandong
sheng nongye qu hua weiyuanhui, *Shandong sheng zonghe nongye qu hua*, 215. This
ratio of 1.35:1 compares with a ratio of close to 2 to 1 in the 1930s. (See dissertation,
appendix D, giving an output ratio [acreage figures unavailable] of 2.56:1 while the
northwest had 1.27 times as much land; total cultivated land figures are from John L.
Buck, "Statistical View," 1:1 [1927], 33–47.) In 1932, a particularly good year for
southwestern production, the sample counties of the northwest, with almost precisely
the same area as the sample counties of the southwest (11,555,818 *mu* versus
11,038,082), had 1.72 times as much land under cotton (see dissertation, appendixes D
and E). However, the boundaries of the two regions as described in the 1982 study are
not the same as the ones used here.

had an influence, such as highwaymen. However, the post-1949 trend is one more piece of evidence supporting those contemporaries who saw the struggle between gleaners and cotton societies as a crucial factor.

REGIONAL VARIATION
AND LOCAL LEADERSHIP

At first glance, the failure of South Huang-Yun cotton societies seems unsurprising. After all, southwest Shandong had always had the most banditry, salt smuggling, and opium growing in Shandong (though the northwest had pockets that were comparable where the new cotton was nonetheless adopted).[141] The OEI's failure in the southwest might seem to be just another instance of that area's famed disorder.

A second look, however, uncovers many reasons to expect the opposite outcome. Peasants in the more densely populated southwest, who had traditionally had higher yields, might have felt more pressure to maximize per *mu* returns.[142] They also had far more irrigation, a major advantage for growing the new cotton varieties. Even though the new varieties were somewhat more drought resistant than native cotton,[143] northwestern farmers had to switch to other crops if the spring rains were inadequate, but southwesterners would not be as seriously affected.[144] (When the same cotton varieties were introduced in Shaanxi in the 1930s, they took hold where there was irrigation, but not elsewhere.)[145] The southwest had more floods than the northwest,[146] but this flooding could have actually aided the OEI. Few things favored outsiders bringing in new seeds so much as people having no seed of their own because the previous year's crop had failed;[147] such a situation also minimized the mixing of old and new

---

141. See the area around Linqing on the map in Tiedemann, "Banditry," 397.

142. Esherick, *Boxer Uprising*, 12–14; Huang, *Peasant Economy*, 63.

143. Lin Maoquan, *Wenji*, 66a.

144. The relationship between irrigation and adoption of the new cotton varieties (which need water at the time of the first fertilizer application) is explained in the Indian context by Krishna, "Farm Supply," 1, 10; for the same phenomenon in Huang-Yun, see QH1038: AH2034, 27b, which describes peasants in Ningjin county, Hebei, abandoning cotton production because of inadequate irrigation.

145. See Vermeer, *Economic Development*, 332.

146. See chapter 4.

147. *HBMCLB*, no. 4 (June 16, 1936), 8.

varieties. Credit, as we have seen, was more expensive in the southwest, but cotton mills would have been quite willing to advance money against a crop of U.S. cotton.

Southwest Shandong's social structure might also seem more conducive to cotton promotion than northwestern society. Jining dominated the southwest's trade and commerce far more than Linqing or Liaocheng did the northwest's, and its powerful elite strongly supported the new cotton. Several of them, including sometime prime ministers Pan Fu (of whom more in chapters 3 and 5) and Jin Yunpeng, owned shares in a Jinan cotton-spinning mill, for which Pan had "solicited everyone in political and military circles"; the mill was founded in 1915 with the express purpose of gaining a foothold in this industry while foreigners were occupied elsewhere.[148] Pan Fu had headed the provincial OEI's late Qing predecessor, which had itself tried, though more feebly, to promote U.S. cotton. He was also heavily involved in making Jining an open city for foreign trade, bringing the railroad to Jining, and promoting regional exports, even organizing an exhibit for the 1914 Panama world trade show.[149]

Thus the cream of the southwest's elite had much to gain from the expansion of U.S. cotton in their home area. Some members of county elites who lacked the broad connections of Jining's top leaders might have feared that increased lending by mills would undermine the currency manipulation rackets described in chapter 1; however, there is no evidence that such fear affected county-level cotton promotion efforts. County OEI offices in the southwest appear to have been just as vigorous as their northwestern counterparts, and they were supported by a regional urban elite far more powerful than any urban elites in the northwest.

Moreover, southwestern rural society was much more stratified than northwestern,[150] and one might have expected that whatever fac-

148. On the cotton mill organized by Pan Fu, see *NSGB* 2:2 (Sept. 1915), *xuanzai*, 31. On another of his efforts to make Jining a significant exporter, see *NSGB* 8:1 (Aug. 1921), *zhengshi*, 56–58. His involvement in efforts to promote rail and water transport in the area are discussed in chapters 3 and 5, respectively.

149. *NSGB* 2:2 (Sept. 1915), *xuanzai*, 31, and subsequent discussion here.

150. For a general survey contrasting conditions in these two areas, see Esherick, *Boxer Uprising*, 12–14, 17–19. However, it is important to note two critical differences between his definition of these regions and mine. First, Esherick separates the Jining area from his "southwest" region. Following Sun Jingzhi's *Huabei de jingji dili* and what seems to me to be the pattern of economic and political activity in southern Shandong, I have treated them as one region. Second, Esherick's "northwest" region

tors sustained this greater inequality would have made it easier to introduce a new crop with inegalitarian consequences. More specifically, as Joseph Esherick demonstrates in his study of the Boxer movement, village leaders in the southwest controlled their villages much more thoroughly than did leaders in the northwest, despite the southwest's rampant intervillage violence. Some have described the area as particularly "feudal"; many southwestern villages were dominated by a family or families who controlled forts, granaries, and other protective structures.[151]

Southwest Shandong's tenancy rates were high for North China (though not for the country as a whole); the landlords were local residents, and the tenants had nonfarming obligations. By contrast, northwest Shandong had the lowest tenancy rates in the province; where northwestern villages did have high tenancy rates, the landlords were usually nonresident moneylenders, and there were no noneconomic obligations on either side. Southwestern villages were more likely to be single-surname units and to have few "outsiders" in them.[152] In sum, while most Huang-Yun villages were relatively "closed" compared to the more market town–oriented villages common in East and South China,[153] differences within Huang-Yun were still very significant: southwestern villages were generally more militarized, more "closed," and more tightly controlled than northwestern ones.

These patterns initially seem to suggest a promising base for sup-

---

continues east of the railroad line (not built until after the Boxers) to where the Yellow River meets the sea. (It remains "western" in contrast to the Shandong peninsula.) Because of my interest in areas once closely linked to the Grand Canal and the influence of railroad development on some of these counties, I have not extended my area that far to the east. Differences in regional boundaries and time period studied (rather than interpretive disagreement) also explain the one seeming difference between Esherick's north-south contrast and my own. Since between 1855 and the early 1890s the part of the Yellow River most likely to flood was its last hundred miles, Esherick's definition of the northwest leads him to conclude that the northwest was more prone to disaster than the southwest. In the twentieth century, as chapter 4 will show, most flooding occurred in the upriver sections of Shandong; thus, even had I extended my "northwest" or "North Huang-Yun" to match Esherick's, the characterization of the southwest as more disaster-prone than the northwest after 1900 would not have changed. See also dissertation, appendix E.

151. Esherick, *Boxer Uprising*, 23, 162; Amano Motonosuke, *Santō Nōgyo Keizairon* (Dalian, 1936).

152. Esherick, *Boxer Uprising*, 12–13, 19, 23, 24, 27; Myers, *Peasant Economy*, 90–93, 107–11.

153. See, for instance, the figures on average number of days per year spent on marketing in John L. Buck, *Land Use*, 343.

pressing gleaning in the southwest, with powerful village elites using their control to make their land more profitable. The contrast Esherick draws between southwestern Big Swords and northwestern Boxers in the 1890s—the Boxers having numerous lower-class leaders and eluding the control of both village elites and the government, the Big Swords being led by local elites and collapsing when the state pressured those elites into withdrawing—might seem a useful parallel.[154] As for the opium growing and salt smuggling of the southwest, these kinds of illegality hurt neither ordinary villagers nor the village elite; thus, their continued vitality tells us little about the ability or desire of local leaders to suppress cotton rushing.

But as we have seen, southwest Shandong never brought cotton rushing under control, while northwestern cotton societies did. This contrast serves to reinforce the point made earlier: unlike earlier crop-watching societies, cotton societies worked against, not with, village solidarity. The southwestern microgeography Esherick describes—walled villages situated so they straddle jurisdictional boundaries[155]—symbolizes beautifully how a strong village elite might prefer to frustrate control by county government, even in a climate of banditry and disorder. And cotton societies, sponsored by elites based at the county capital, represented an extension of county-level power into the countryside.[156]

But—as their very successful collaboration with the government in suppressing the Big Sword Society also shows—southwestern village elites could follow the lead of officialdom if they wanted to; when this happened the combined county and village forces were able to establish stronger control than existed in the northwest.[157] The Heze(S) regulations—with lower property qualifications than in Xiajin(N) and the provision of a "supervising" role for village heads—suggest some attempt by the county to adjust to and make use of the strong villages of this area.[158] So do the provincial guidelines for new cooperatives promoting U.S. cotton in the late 1930s, when this task was largely finished in the northwest but still faltering in the southwest.[159]

154. Esherick, *Boxer Uprising*, 319.
155. Ibid., pp. 20, 27, 99.
156. *QYHK*, no. 6 (Jan. 1922), appendix; Lin Maoquan, *Wenji*, 40b–42a.
157. Esherick, *Boxer Uprising*, 107, 146–48, 161, 224, 234, 319.
158. *QYHK*, no. 7 (May 1922), *ge xian quanye baogao*, 33–35.
159. *HBMCLB*, no. 7 (Aug. 1, 1936), 9–10; no. 12 (Oct. 16, 1936), 13–14. On the

However, village leaders simply did not have the same reasons to promote new cotton varieties as they had had to help end the Big Sword uprising. As tax farmers who often advanced money for peasants' payments (see chapter 1), they had an incentive to keep new lenders, such as mill agents, out. However, social and political motivations were probably the crucial ones.

Southwestern village leaders had reluctantly joined the government's suppression of the Big Swords because they were convinced that otherwise further anti-Christian incidents would lead to more forceful intervention (either Qing or, more likely, foreign) and a further loss of their control over local society; it had been the erosion of that control by missionaries that had led village elites to back the Big Swords in the first place.[160] In contrast, allowing the new cotton varieties to fail might cost rural bosses some potential earnings, but it did not threaten their grip on local society. Joining with the government in this case, however, did pose such a threat and might have led to further erosion of the local elites' hegemony. In many twentieth-century North China villages, crop-watching societies became the most important political institution in the village, often replacing weakening temple organizations.[161] Thus, even if cotton societies had simply been a new security system based outside the village, they would have given many village leaders cause for concern.

The societies, however, also raised other threatening possibilities. Where U.S. cotton did become widespread, it changed local society considerably. Peasants became dependent on people outside the village for seed. Some needed more credit, which often came from mill agents. They needed safe passage on the roads for their crop, and such passage—unlike safe storage for their grain in a local fort—had to be organized at the ward or county level.[162] A growing cotton trade also meant new commercial taxes to be farmed, strengthening the hands of those with ties to the mills, those with ties to the county governments

---

enormous difference in percentages of U.S. cotton in the northwestern and southwestern cotton crops in the 1930s, see dissertation, appendix D, and *HBMCLB*, no. 7 (Aug. 1, 1936), 6.

160. Esherick, *Boxer Uprising*, 87–89, 121.

161. Duara, "Power in Rural Society," 159, 162; Gamble, *North China Villages*, 2–4.

162. On the importance of local forts, see Perry, *Rebels and Revolutionaries*, 89–93.

that licensed commercial tax collection, and the county government itself.[163] Often the same organization supplied the seeds, supplied credit, organized crop protection, purchased the crop (the loans having been secured against it), ginned the crop (giving it control of the seed supply), made sure the crop met the mills' quality standards, and took charge of forwarding the sales taxes to the county government.[164] The cotton cooperatives that the Shandong provincial government was promoting on the eve of the Japanese invasion were explicitly granted control over all these matters.[165] Even where the same organization did not do all these tasks, they were closely connected: indeed, one reason why Shandong officials viewed the direct distribution of seeds and purchase of crops by Japanese-owned mills with such alarm is that they feared Japanese control of the taxes on cotton transactions.[166] Hebei provincial officials in the late 1930s complained that village elites opposed their cotton improvement efforts because they feared that new credit and marketing arrangements (and presumably taxing arrangements, since sales taxes on cotton were particularly important in Hebei) threatened their local position.[167] Southwest Shandong village elites in the 1920s and 1930s apparently saw the same threats and reacted the same way.

Moreover, county governments that obtained extra revenues from the growth of cotton and other trades expanded their operations. The most common addition when county governments got more money was more police. County police were a mixed blessing for village elites like those in the southwest, whose power often derived from their con-

---

163. See, for instance, Imai Shuin, "Kōnichi Konkyochi no Keisei Katei ni tsuite no Ichi Kōsatsu," 36; there is a lengthy discussion of the sociology of the cotton trade and cotton tax farming in northeastern Henan and southwestern Hebei in JD2:AH124, 3082, 3083, and 3084 of the Second Historical Archives, Nanjing, pursuant to accusations of corruption lodged between 1931 and 1935.

164. See, for instance, Guy Alitto, *The Last Confucian* (Berkeley, 1979), 256–57, for an account of how this worked in Zouping; *Gong shang banyuekan* 6:3 (Feb. 1, 1934), 108; *Nongye zhoubao* 2:48 (Nov. 27, 1933), 766–67; *NYZB* 5:27 (July 16, 1926), 581; *QYHK*, no. 4 (Jan. 1921), gongdu, 1–5, Matsuzaki Yujiro, *Santō Shō no Sai Nishiki*, 478–79.

165. *HBMCLB*, no. 12 (Oct. 16, 1936), 13.

166. For one example, see *Shandong shiye gongbao*, no. 3 (August 1931), 27–28.

167. *HBMCLB*, no. 15 (Dec. 1, 1936), 8; on the especially large role of commercial taxes in Hebei, see, for instance, Zhu Bingnan, "Zhongguo zhi yingye shui," *Shehuixue zazhi* 6:3 (Sept. 1935), 343–463, esp. 367–70, 373–76, 400–2, 405–7, 413; Feng Huade, "Hebei sheng xian caizheng zhi chu fenxi," in *Zhongguo jingji yanjiu*, ed. Fang Xianting (H. D. Fong) (Changsha, 1938), 2:1039–55; idem, "Hebei sheng yashui xingzhi zhi yanbian," in ibid., 1067–79.

trol of brick protective structures and who also often had relations—not always voluntary—with illegal land reclaimers, opium growers and smugglers, and bandits. At the same time, any southwestern village leader whose village switched some land from food crops to the new cotton would have found that his local fort was much less useful—against either bandits or the state—when it could not be filled with locally grown grain. In sum, the county OEI represented the cutting edge of both state making and market making in rural Huang-Yun, a position that promised unwelcome changes for South Huang-Yun rural elites.

Thus, village leaders had only money to gain but perhaps both money and power to lose by helping to promote U.S. cotton; when they had helped to suppress the Big Swords, they had been preempting a crackdown that might have eliminated the political space they worked in. In North Huang-Yun there had been no strong rural elite to either vie with the missionaries or suppress the Boxers; now there was no such elite to worry about the growth of county and merchant power or about the loss of village control over crop watching.

Moreover, in the 1920s, when the cotton societies' big effort began, village elites had other problems. Since it is impossible to get precise figures on the warlord depredations, irregular surtaxes, and other exactions of this period, it is no wonder that opinions about their macroeconomic significance vary.[168] What is clear is that these exactions caused enough strain to alter at least the official political leadership of many villages. As early as 1922, the provincial OEI explained its reluctance to rely on village heads to organize tree planting by arguing that since village heads more often apportioned surtaxes than represented their fellow villagers, they were widely resented.[169] The heads of many North China villages fled their responsibilities; in some villages only local toughs (or their hired tools) were willing to serve as heads.[170] While the severity of this problem and the time it emerged

---

168. For a debate on the importance of warlord disruptions of the Chinese economy in particular and the significance of warlordism generally, see the articles by Jerome Chen, Diana Lary, and James Sheridan in *Republican China* 10:2 (April 1985), and Thomas Rawski, *China's Republican Economy: An Introduction* (Toronto, 1978).

169. *QYHK*, no. 7 (May 1922), *lunshuo*, 4; the same point is made with regard to security tasks as well as tree planting in Lin Maoquan, *Wenji*, 42b.

170. See, e.g., Gamble, *North China Villages*, 294–95, and Duara, *Culture, Power, and the State*, 192–93, 218–30. Huang, *Peasant Economy*, 228–29, sees this trend beginning earlier.

differed from place to place, the phenomenon of higher requisitions making the village headship more difficult was widespread.

In North Huang-Yun, the old village elite—never nearly as strong as in South Huang-Yun anyway—almost all fled office in the 1920s or thereafter, as demands from above got out of hand.[171] This flight clearly marked an end to any obstacle they might hypothetically have presented to penetration by the OEI and cotton societies, who in this sense may have even benefited from the chaos of the warlord years.

In the southwest, requisitions were even higher. Eleven southwestern counties had local land surtaxes that exceeded the basic land tax in 1935, while only two counties in the northwest—both along its southern fringe—did.[172] However, many southwestern village elites seem to have stayed around, apparently arranging for these greater exactions to be met in an orderly fashion. I have found no evidence of southwestern villages being "shell-shocked"[173]—that is, having their entire social structure destroyed by military exactions—the way some northwestern villages were. During the Japanese occupation, the Jining area was one of the very few to exceed Japanese grain procurement quotas, and it suffered far less terror than the northwest did.[174] One survey even found that the livestock population of villages near Jining increased under Japanese rule, while the animal populations of accessible villages in the northwest were devastated.[175] Although few details are available, this pattern would seem to suggest that southwestern rural elites reached an accommodation with the occupiers and were then able to implement the enormous exactions from the peasantry that this required without arousing enough effective opposition to require retaliatory raids by Japanese troops. In sum, southwestern village elites not only had greater staying power than their north-western counterparts; they apparently wanted to stay.

One reason for this desire to stay—in addition to the "feudal" aspects of southwest Shandong society already noted—was the role that southwestern village leaders played as farmers of the land tax.

171. Duara, *Culture, Power, and the State*, 219–23; Gamble, *North China Villages*, 294–95.
172. *CZGB* 6:7 (April 1935), *zhuanzai*, 11.
173. For this term, see Huang, *Peasant Economy*, 46, 313, 320.
174. Myers, *Peasant Economy*, 283; *Santō Sainei*, 104–12.
175. On the increases near Jining, see *Santō Sainei*, p. 110; on the loss of animals in the northwest during warlord fighting, *NCH* Dec. 28, 1929, p. 507; on improvements in the southwest after 1937, *Santō Sainei*, 104, 109–10.

The 1859 gazetteer for Jining district (which included Yutai, Jiaxiang, Jinxiang, and Jining counties) notes that the old Ming *li zhang* (tax headman of roughly a hundred families, part of a system that was defunct in most of the country after 1712), allied with yamen runners, remained in control of tax collection in this area long after they had nominally been replaced; and while the gazetteer claimed that there had eventually been reforms, people with the same title still handled the land tax in the 1930s.[176] When the eighteenth-century tax reformer Tian Wenjing complained that Shandong had done little to break the power that rural strongmen had gained over tax collection during the Ming, he cited some counties in east Shandong and some in the southwest as examples, but none in the northwest.[177] In 1902 a censor complained that collusion between "rural bosses" and yamen runners in farming land taxes was especially serious in Shandong; he named no specific counties, but another memorial he sent at about the same time places him slightly southeast of Jining.[178] The late Qing and Republican archives I saw had very little material on the land tax, but the three specific reports of abuses by land tax farmers are from Heze and Fanxian, both in the southwest; one of the Fanxian documents states that the land tax farmer was a village head.[179] As late as the 1930s the term *li zhang* was still used for village heads in southwest Shandong, though not for those in northwest Shandong.[180]

Even the salt tax, a quintessential commercial levy, reached many southwestern peasants through their village heads. In late Qing Heze(S) and Shouzhang(S) people had to buy a quantity of official salt based on the number of *mu* they owned.[181] Since village leaders played a critical role in determining what land was registered, and in whose name, they probably controlled the incidence of this tax as well.[182] In

176. *Jining zhilizhou zhi* (1859), 3:19a–b, 20b–22a.

177. Memorial of 10/27/Yongzheng6 in *Yongzheng zhupi zouzhe bulu* (Taibei, 1965), 3311–33; generally, see Zelin, *Magistrate's Tael*, 149–52, and "Huo-hao Kuei-kung" (Ph.D. dissertation, University of California, Berkeley, 1979), 189–97.

178. Memorials of 1/30/GX 28 in LFZZ, GX 28, packet 51–55 and 32–35; also undated *pian* from summer of GX 28 (1902) in packet 64–68.

179. Xingbu, Shandong Si, case 15604; *CZGB* 5:3 (Dec. 1933), *gongdu*, 3, 10–12.

180. *HWTK*, no. 2 (Jan. 1930), *gongdu*, 15; no. 6 (Jan. 1934), *gongdu*, 2; no. 8 (Jan. 1936), *gongdu*, 2; *Jining zhilizhou xuzhi* 4:1a; *QYHK*, no. 7, *ge xian quanye baogao*, 33.

181. *SDZZ*, no. 79 (11/30/XT 2 [1910]), 14b, on Heze; no. 62 (6/10/XT 2), 16a, on Shouzhang.

182. For a brief discussion of the role of village heads in registering land and farming land taxes, see chapter 5. At least in the case of Shouzhang, assigning the salt tax

North Huang-Yun, by contrast, the government used mobile salt intendants based in administrative centers to harass the salt smugglers, apparently assuming that this practice would assure purchase of the official product. These widely hated salt patrols are described in reminiscences and literature as "toughs," "vagabonds," or "bare sticks" and as creatures of administrative or market towns; there are no references to village elite involvement in salt enforcement in northwest Shandong, northeast Henan, or southwest Hebei.[183] The southwest used very few roving intendants until the mid-1930s.[184]

The crucial role that southwestern village elites played in various sorts of tax collection was likely a major source of their staying power; the opportunities for profit help explain why many of them wished to stay in office (or at least choose the nominal village head) through the hard years of the 1920s, 1930s, and 1940s. In North Huang-Yun, in contrast, even groups who did have a strong base in the villages did not base their revenue gathering on that unit. Even the Red Spears, a confederation of independent village self-defense units that elsewhere (including South Huang-Yun) relied on contributions assessed by each village branch on the basis of land ownership, turned to commercial taxes in the Henan and Hebei parts of North Huang-Yun: they created a levy on the wholesale cotton trade, a

---

according to land quotas apparently did involve setting quotas that added up to more than the county's total quota, with the difference retained by tax farmers along the way, including the magistrate.

183. On northwest Shandong salt intendants and opposition to them, see, for instance, Li Shizhao, "Ji Gaotang Guguantun baodong de lingdao ren," *Wenshi ziliao xuanji*, Jinan edition, no. 10 (1981), 47–49. A fictional version of these conflicts, which describes the intendants in similar terms, is "Sha yanxun," which claims to describe an actual murder of an abusive salt patrolman near Xiajin in the late Guangxu period; it is collected in *Shandong minjian xiaoshuo* (Jinan, 1984), 258–68. Since the records of the Changlu salt monopoly, unlike those of the Shandong monopoly, are available at the First Historical Archives, Beijing, we have a much more detailed picture of events just across the border in southwestern Zhili. These documents make clear that the focus here was on interception of illegal salt by patrols (see, for instance, *bing* from merchant Zhong Jusheng of 10/6/GX 30, in file 231 for a particularly detailed account, and *bing* from merchant Yu Changmao of 6/11/GX 29, which deals specifically with the Shandong-Hebei border trade); there were raids into villages to try to destroy illicit salt wells, but there is no mention on smuggling in southwestern Zhili of any attempt to assign quotas through village heads or to establish any sort of permanent presence in the village, except through the attempts to improve alkaline soil and get people to grow crops on it.

184. *SDZZ*, no. 79 (11/30/XT 2 [1910]), p. 15a; Alexander Armstrong, *Shantung* (Shanghai, 1891), 126. On roving intendants being introduced to South Huang-Yun see *SDXZJSSYQGB*, no. 28 (Dec. 25, 1935), 16.

levy that county governments took over after the Red Spears were suppressed.[185]

When we look at water control in chapters 4 and 5, we will see further evidence that village heads remained unusually powerful in South Huang-Yun at least until the anti-Japanese War. Village leaders (either individually or collectively) in southwest Shandong retained substantial control of land reclamation, dike building (both the informal but legal and the illegal varieties), and the incidence of corvée and surtaxes for flood control. For instance, after the rural reconstruction group in Heze(S) had mobilized fewer than two hundred people on its own for emergency dike work in one district in 1933, it announced a quota system of one laborer per fifty *mu* of land, with fines for village heads who did not meet their quota. Within days this produced 1,300 workers. If these 1,300 workers represent an addition to those already mobilized—the text is unclear about this—the district's quota of 1,493 was perfectly filled. If not, it was 87 percent filled.[186]

The village elite's continued successes in water control activities, however, were chiefly in matters that required either inaction (for example, ignoring orders to destroy illegal dikes) or sporadic mobilizations of labor in the face of evident threats. Had they taken on cotton rushing, southwestern village leaders would have had to organize more lengthy, strenuous, and divisive mobilizations. Indeed, given the polarized class structure of the southwest, suppressing cotton rushing would have required great efforts by the elite, who lacked the broad base of solid middle peasants and rich peasants who joined northwestern cotton societies. And despite the economic benefits of the new cotton, southwestern rural elites had little incentive to make special efforts on its behalf. The political results of success would have favored urban mills and county-level statemakers at their expense, while angering many of their peasant clients. And had elites tried to profit from the new cotton, they too would have become dependent on outsiders. On the contrary, if southwestern rural elites annoyed mill agents, returned agricultural school graduates, and an occasional missionary by failing to suppress cotton rushing or to otherwise promote

185. On the Red Spears generally, see Perry, *Rebels and Revolutionaries*, 198–203; on the Red Spear origins of the cotton-trading tax of southwestern Hebei (which apparently also affected much of northeast Henan's cotton trade), see the petition to the Caizhengbu of Dec. 12, 1934, in Xingzhengyuan mishuchu gao xuan, file 22121, in JD2:AH3084.
186. *XCJSXK* 4:14 (Jan. 1935), 10, 19.

the new crop, such (in)action might lead to increased tensions, but it would hardly threaten their positions; failing at other suddenly more difficult tasks—such as meeting tax quotas—might. Thus, at least noncooperation with the OEI was called for. Given the social structure of South Huang-Yun, noncooperation was more than enough to ensure that the new cotton would fail; even in the more equal northwest, better-off farmers had had to take the early lead in both innovation and the organization of repression.

Rural elites in the southwest remained strong enough to keep the state at arm's length throughout our period; the riverworks chapters will provide many more examples. And as long as revenue was not withheld, the state was rarely inclined to press the point. Even during the 1905–13 campaign against opium—which many southwestern village heads were known to tolerate or protect—the state trod very lightly in this region. The opium suppression effort in southwest Shandong relied heavily on *li zhang* to assess the fines, strictly limiting the number and authority of inspectors from the county capital who went into the countryside, lest they "incite violence."[187] Accounts of anti-opium efforts in En(N) county mention no such provisions, and accounts of enforcement problems in Gaotang(N) focused on the relations between influential opium traders (not growers) and county-level officials.[188]

The various waves of privately organized urban-educated reformers that twentieth-century China generated also found rural South Huang-Yun particularly inhospitable. New schoolteachers with "modern" ideas and manners were physically chased out of Cao(S) and Heze(S) counties in the last years of the Qing.[189] Later groups did little better. Liang Shuming's rural reconstruction group in Heze(S), for instance, never established village-level "school centers," which were the core of its program in Zouping (slightly east of North Huang-Yun). This failure is partially attributable to a difference in outlook between those who ran Zouping and those who ran Heze; nonetheless, these reformers clearly found southwestern villages much harder to penetrate.[190] The Heze cadres complained that the village leaders and

187. *SDZZ*, no. 26 (1/30/XT 2), 19a–b.
188. *SDZZ*, no. 92 (6/30/XT 3), 31a–b; no. 93 (7/15/XT 3), 32b; *Shuntian shibao*, 6/27/XT 3 (unpaginated).
189. *SDZZ*, no. 91 (6/15/XT 3), 31a–32b; no. 92 (6/30/XT 3), 30b.
190. Alitto, *Last Confucian*, 265–66.

landlords there were impossible to work with and that new village heads would have to be selected before progress could be made; to find people willing to "cooperate," they said, it was necessary to go below the villages' normal leadership class. In Zouping, it had been much easier for outsiders to gain a foothold in the villages. The Heze group also noted that there was unusually little unmediated contact between Heze villagers and local market towns, and much cultural contrast: mutual hostility was strong, and villagers rarely participated in even those town activities (such as gambling) that they enjoyed within their own villages.[191]

Early Chinese Communist Party (CCP) organizers also found southwest Shandong villages particularly impenetrable. During the Party's urban phase, they appear to have been stronger in Jining(S) than in Liaocheng, their largest northwestern base. Many of the early Party recruits in both cities were normal-school students. Recruits such as these who returned home as teachers were central to the CCP's later rural activity in western Shandong,[192] just as they were in its more successful efforts in Jiangxi; and although these students were generally of lower status than the returned provincial graduates who became county OEI officials, there is an interesting parallel between these cases. Though probably more teachers-to-be were radicalized in Jining than in Liaocheng, all the stories of rural CCP activity in western Shandong before 1937 take place in the northwest, except for one at the very northern edge of a borderline county.[193]

191. *XCJSXK* 5:3 (Sept. 1935), 3–4; 4:28 (May 1935), 18–20; 6:2 (Sept. 1936), 1–5; 4:14 (Jan. 1935), 15–16, 18.

192. See, for instance, Wu Guogui, "Yutang xinghuo—Jining shi Yutang jiangyuan gongyun gai," *Shandong gong yun shi ziliao*, no. 16 (Feb. 10, 1985), 12–17, esp. 13; "Jining xing huo," *Jining shi shiliao*, no. 1 (1983), 40–51; *Shandong gongyun shi ziliao*, no. 6 (Dec. 10, 1982), 33, 37, 39–40; and Liu Nanyun, "Yi Dang zai Jining shi de zaoqi huodong," in *Jining shi shiliao*, no. 1 (1983), 5–17, indicating that in Jining, the CCP played a significant role both in strikes and in students' protests and study groups. By contrast, the northern groups during the urban phase seem to have had a more limited following and smaller projects: Wang Ruizheng and Zhi Bi, "Wei Chi, Xiu Zhi, tongzhi zai Linqing de geming huodong huiyi," *Liaocheng diqu dangshi ziliao*, no. 10 (1984), 3–10; Li Shizhao, "Jie Zhanbo tongzhi shilue," in ibid., 61–65; "Dang zai Dezhou diqu zaoqi huodong de jijian da shi," *Dezhou shi zhi tongxun*, no. 2 (1986), 24–26; and Xie Xinhou, "Liaocheng Shifan xuesheng de geming fengchao," and Xu Yunbei, "Lu Xibei dang de jianshe pian duan huiyi," both in *Guang you Chunqiu: Shandong geming douzheng huiyi congkan*, ed. Liaocheng diqu xingzheng gongzhe chuban bangongshi (Jinan, 1981), 1–3, describe much more limited and abortive urban operations in Liaocheng and Linqing.

193. Zhong Zhongming, "Yanggu Poli baodong huiyi," in *Guang you Chunqiu*, ed. Liaocheng diqu xingzheng gongzhe chuban bangongshe, 27–35; Li Shizhao, "Zhao

PERMEABILITY, OPENNESS,
AND SOCIOECONOMIC CHANGE

The "permeability" of a village—that is, the relative ease with which agents of outside organizations can penetrate it—should not be confused with the village's "openness," a term usually used for villages whose members leave relatively often and build up contacts with the wider world. G. William Skinner's classic statement of the openness of Chinese villages during periods of stability emphasizes that while most possibilities for upward mobility required leaving the village—at least briefly to do some marketing and often at length to take an urban job, official exams, or the like—those pursuing these paths were still considered village residents. Moreover, somebody who successfully climbed the social ladder would eventually bring wealth and goods back to his home area, where he and his kin would enjoy the fruits of success. When a dynasty was in decline, however, external opportunities would shrink, the state and/or those it could not control would become more predatory, and villages would tend to "close."[194]

However, there is no necessary relationship between a particular community's sending people out to seek advancement—and perhaps help shape the changes initiated in centers of power—and its receiving and being changed by outsiders itself. Moreover, only a small minority of people entering a community to promote their own fortunes were doing anything with much potential to disturb the power of local elites or significantly change life in the host community. Thus, the ease with which people who did have disruptive transformative aims could func-

---

Yizheng lieshi zhuanlue," *Shandong dangshi ziliao*, no. 2 (1981), 167–77; "Jindai Lu Xibei diqu nongmin douzheng shilue," *Liaocheng difang shizhi*, no. 2 (July 1983), 11–15; Li Shizhao, "Ji Gaotang Guguantun baodong de lingdao ren," 43–60; "Du Buzhou tongzhi yi zhong gong Jin Nan tewei de jijian da shi" *Dezhou shi zhi tongxun*, no. 1 (1984), 17–19. Xu Yunbei, "Xuzhuang dang zhibu de zaoqi huodong," *Guang you Chunqiu*, 54–64, esp. 55, notes some rural organizing as far south as Fan and Pu counties; interestingly, however, this organizing was done by a Party member whose brother was the local *xiang zhang* and in a village that bore their surname. Thus, this was probably more a struggle among rural bosses (even if one of them had radical plans) than a challenge to them by an outsider. See also David Paulson, "War and Revolution in North China: The Shandong Base Area" (Ph.D. dissertation, Stanford University, 1982), 26–36.

   194. G. William Skinner, "Chinese Peasants and the Closed Community: An Open and Shut Case," *Comparative Studies in Society and History* 13:3 (1971), 270–81; see esp. 273–75.

tion in a particular place—showing its "permeability"—should be separable from that place's "openness."

This distinction seems borne out by the case of Huang-Yun. North Huang-Yun villages may have been no more open than those in South Huang-Yun, but they were certainly more permeable. Philip Huang has argued convincingly that middle peasants in North China spent the least time away from their villages, since they were not rich enough to participate much in the business or entertainments of the market towns and not so poor that they needed to hire themselves out away from home.[195] Since northwest Shandong villages were less stratified than southwestern ones,[196] it is at least plausible that northerners, on average, left their villages less. Many of the rural counties near the canal, however, in both North and South Huang-Yun, had long-standing traditions of occasional migrant labor connected to the waterway;[197] we do not have enough evidence to be sure whether people were more geographically mobile in North or in South Huang-Yun.

More importantly, as Huang also notes, we cannot equate trips to the market town (or elsewhere) with receiving outside influences—people often went there without talking to anyone but their fellow villagers.[198] Late Qing Caozhou(S) provides an example of how travel could actually reinforce village closure: a 1907 report claims that people there who were traveling any substantial distance would gather a group of knife-carrying neighbors and go together.[199] Conversely, Houxiazhai village in En county, in the heart of northwest Shandong cotton country, shows that a predisposition to stay at home need not entail creating barriers to outsiders. This village's overwhelmingly middle-peasant population considered themselves "above" long-term wage labor and so brought in people from Taian, more than eighty miles away.[200] Finally, the Chinese in the countryside of the 1950s through 1970s, who may well have left their home villages and social-

195. Huang, *Peasant Economy*, 222–23, 308–10.

196. Esherick, *Boxer Uprising*, 17, 25, 103, 206.

197. See, e.g., Susan Naquin, *Shantung Rebellion* (New Haven, 1981), 11, 18, 21–22.

198. Huang, *Peasant Economy*, 221.

199. *SDZZ*, no. 2 (1/15/GX 34), *min feng*, 1. A somewhat similar argument has been advanced about certain groups of rural migrants in nineteenth-century France. See, for instance, Martin Nadaud, *Mémoires de Leonard, Ancien Garçon Maçon* (Paris, 1948), 13–14, 69–78 (esp. 74), 81–82, 101.

200. *Chūgoku Nōson* 4:178.

ized with people from other villages less than ever[201] but were
nonetheless influenced by outside agents far more than any of their
ancestors, also remind us that a village's permeability to outside organizers (be they agents of the state, of firms, of a religion, or something
else) is distinct from its residents' geographic mobility.

Many Huang-Yun peasants were receptive to agricultural innovations that were brought to their door, but it would have been very difficult and expensive for them to go out looking for suitable innovations (even if a whole village paid for such a venture cooperatively).
Thus, permeability probably would have been more important for
agricultural change than openness even where changes did not require
new, county-initiated coercion and seed distribution.[202] This fact may
help explain why new varieties of peanuts, promoted by missionaries
but not the state, also spread faster in the northwest than the southwest.[203] One could even argue that the greater tendency of southwestern than northwestern peasants to seek work in Manchuria—despite probably higher travel costs—was partly a result of
southwestern villages' "impermeability,"[204] which hindered local economic development and so made it harder for the poor to find new
opportunities close to home.

Tightly knit South Huang-Yun villages might be better situated to
take advantage of certain opportunities that came to them. One
thinks, for instance, of the Fanxian village head described in chapter 1,
organizing "his" villagers in teams to plug into the cash trade temporarily; such teams may have maintained the common price necessary to
keep profits up better than separate profit seekers from a more loosely
knit community would have. However, most of the more promising
new opportunities were more compatible with a more permeable social structure. Thus the desire and power of village leaders to preserve
their positions as nearly exclusive "brokers" between their villages and

201. Huang, *Peasant Economy*, 308.
202. The argument that it makes little sense for even the most receptive peasants to
go out looking for such innovations is drawn from Schultz, *Traditional Agriculture*,
169.
203. See dissertation, appendix E.
204. Figures are hard to come by, but all accounts of rural distress in the southwest
in the 1930s stress the closing of Manchuria as an important factor, while accounts of
problems in the northwest mention it briefly or not at all. For more details, see chapter
1. Twenty years earlier, on the contrary, one finds more references to northwesterners
going elsewhere for work; see, for instance, *NCH*, Nov. 16, 1912, p. 433. The peculiar
reliance of southwest Shandong on hard currency remitted by migrants to Manchuria
because of its limited exports is discussed in chapter 1.

the outside world was a crucial variable determining the extent to which different types of Huang-Yun villages were brought into new networks. In these terms, missionaries, Boxers, mill agents, rural reformers, and early Communist activists all found northwest Shandong more permeable than the southwest.

The particular importance of permeability rather than openness in facilitating change is in part a function of the period we are dealing with. Since 1949, for instance, the state has been able to exert considerable influence on even the most impermeable villages, while outside organizers not backed by the state have been few and extremely weak; thus openness may be the only local factor that introduces much variability into a village's relations with the outside world. The high Qing state never penetrated villages as much as the CCP has, and the variety of nonstate organizers (sectarians, merchants, and so forth) was greater than it has been for most of the post-1949 period; still, an argument could be made that varying degrees of circulation by locals (that is, of openness), especially through the civil service, mattered more in the high Qing than in our period, and differences in permeability less.

The very late Qing and Republican periods, however, combined the economic opportunities usually associated with dynastic peaks and the exceptionally predatory environment associated with dynastic collapse. During these years, a remarkable variety of organizers sought to incorporate villages into various new networks. At the same time, almost no outside agents, even of the state, were so strong that they could make themselves a consistent presence in any village they chose. Finally, the severe dislocation of the period gave many villages an incentive to try to keep outsiders away, just as Skinner's cyclical model of open and closed stances suggests. Consequently, for this period it seems reasonable to place the greatest stress on permeability rather than openness in explaining variations among different types of villages' relations with the wider world.

In the end, then, social and political factors largely explain why agricultural innovations caught on in northwest but not southwest Shandong. At the turn of the twentieth century, the northwest was in most ways more "backward" than the southwest: more of its population worked in agriculture, it had lower yields per acre, its cities were smaller and (as we shall see in chapter 5) declining rather than holding their own. Its access to transport was no better than the southwest's.[205] And while the southwest was more notorious for banditry than the northwest, some officials thought the two areas were close on this score during the crucial 1920s.[206] Moreover, it was the northwest that had recently given birth to uncontrollable disorder during the Boxer rising. However, this uncontrollability held the key to the northwest's success with the new cotton varieties: its lack of dominant village elites and consequent greater permeability to outside organizers—in this case, both those who brought new seeds and those who helped found cotton societies. These organizers constituted the visible, sometimes brutal hand knitting Huang-Yun and the coast into a more integrated agricultural market.

Economic and political integration were never completely separate, voluntary, or costless. Nor were their costs necessarily limited to a "transitional" period such as the one in which cotton rushing was suppressed. Northwest Shandong would again suffer greatly from its permeability, as it had in the Christian-Boxer clashes. Many North Huang-Yun villages repeatedly suffered horrible violence when they failed to meet invaders' demands in the 1920s, 1930s, and 1940s; the more tightly organized villages of the southwest appear to have done better, though they paid heavily for relative peace.[207] Permeability had its perils even in stable times, since those who moved in were often as bent on domination as the elites of impermeable villages were. In the late 1920s, for instance, Japanese cotton buyers who had established themselves as vital sources of credit and seeds began making part of their postharvest payments to peasants in opium.[208] And although other factors were far more important, North Huang-Yun's heavy concentration in cotton can hardly have helped in the famines of 1920

205. The trip from Linqing to Tianjin was cheaper than the southwest's canal access to Shanghai, but the southwest generally had easier access to Jinan and Qingdao than the northwest did. While a few counties in the southwest were farther from Jining than any place in the northwest was from transport, they did manage to export products such as wheat via Jining, though wheat was far less valuable per pound than cotton. For price-to-weight ratios for many standard commodities in early-twentieth-century China, see Sands, "Investigation," 64; for lists of what various counties did export in the 1930s, see *SSYZ*, pt. 2, passim.

206. *SDXZJSSYQGB*, no. 12 (Nov. 23, 1935), 11; telegram from Shandong governor Han Fuju, received by Xingzhengyuan on Nov. 29, 1930, in JD2:AH1832. Zhongguo dier lishi danganguan, eds., *Zhi An zhanzheng* (Nanjing, 1980), 275.

207. See *Santō Sainei*, 104–12; Myers, *Peasant Economy*, 283, on the relative stability of southwestern Shandong under Japanese occupation; on the northwest, see Duara, *Culture, Power, and the State*, 219–23.

208. *Shandong shiye gongbao*, no. 3 (Sept. 1931), *xunling*, 27.

and 1928, in which it suffered more than South Huang-Yun.[209] In general, however, northwestern villages gained far more from their penetrability than southwestern villages did from their impenetrability. In later chapters, we will see that weak integration into administrative networks had even greater costs for Huang-Yun villages—especially those in South Huang-Yun—than did failures to be more fully linked to larger commercial networks. However, firm incorporation into those administrative networks would also have threatened traditional arrangements even more than the new cotton varieties did.

209. See, e.g., *NCH*, Oct. 2, 1920, p. 24; Nov. 24, 1928, p. 301.

CHAPTER III

Ecological Crisis and the Logic of "Self-strengthening"

The government's promotion of new cotton varieties, discussed in chapter 2, was its most successful effort to develop the economy of Huang-Yun—or at least of North Huang-Yun. Even that success, as we have seen, led to unanticipated problems. Most of the government's other rural development efforts involved managing North China's ecological problems. These efforts were far less successful.

MARKET, STATE, AND ECOLOGY

Huang-Yun's deepening ecological crisis was partly a result of specific shocks it suffered, such as the shift of the Yellow River, the decay of the Grand Canal, and the loss of access to timber and stone that this region had once received in long-distance trade. However, these difficulties also had more systemic roots. At the same time that mounting transport problems dimmed Huang-Yun's prospects for market solutions to problems such as obtaining an adequate wood supply, new ideas about economic development were becoming popular among officials; these ideas led them to slight or even sacrifice areas such as Huang-Yun. Until the nineteenth century, Ming-Qing statecraft had subsidized ecological stabilization in this area and had used state resources extensively to guarantee reproduction in areas in which the private economy failed to do so; the new statecraft, however, exacerbated regional differences. This chapter analyzes how the essentially mercantilist priorities of the Chinese state in the late Qing and Republic added to Huang-Yun's ecological problems, focusing on deforestation. Chapters 4 and 5 will focus on water control.

Much of China suffered severe environmental degradation in the late nineteenth and early twentieth centuries, but Huang-Yun's problems were especially serious. Most of China's most densely populated areas are also its most prosperous regions; poverty-stricken Huang-Yun was an exception. It included the most densely populated part of Shandong, one of China's most densely populated provinces; the Henan and Hebei parts of the area were comparably dense.[1] Populations throughout China had soared in the high Qing, setting the stage for the ecological problems of our period.[2] Malthusian pressures alone, however, do not explain why ecological problems greatly worsened after the mid-nineteenth century: after the wars, floods, and droughts of the 1850–80 period, Huang-Yun did not significantly exceed its 1840s population until after 1949.[3]

Aside from population pressures, Huang-Yun had three serious ecological problems. First, it lost contact with old sources of key raw materials and failed to find new ones. Second, the same isolation that made market solutions difficult also caused Huang-Yun to be given a low priority by governments, which were most concerned with problems that threatened their ability to compete against other governments. Thus priority was given to conservation efforts that could act as a form of import substitution, such as reforestation in areas that would otherwise import wood. Moreover, the imports that the state hoped to make unnecessary by increasing local supplies were not limited to U.S., Canadian, or Russian timber. As we saw in chapter 1, provincial governments also worried about their own balance of payments, currency flows, and independence; consequently, provincial governments also viewed coastal North China's heavy purchases of

---

1. Zhongguo haiguan zong shuiwusi, *Decennial Report, 1912–1921*, 189; Tōa Kenkyūsho, *Santō Kōshogun Chitai no Chiiki Chōsa*, 127–30; *SSYZ*, 5:35–60.

2. Research into when, if ever, Chinese population has bumped up against "Malthusian" restraints has, reasonably enough, concentrated on the issue of food supply. Generally speaking, people have concluded that food production kept pace with population growth, but there are some indications that population density may have been reaching "natural" limits in the early nineteenth century. See Ho Ping-ti, *Studies on the Population of China, 1368–1953* (Cambridge, Mass., 1959), esp. 183–95, 229; and Dwight Perkins, *Agricultural Development in China, 1368–1968* (Chicago, 1969), esp. 25, 27, 29.

3. See, e.g., Zhang Yufa, *Zhongguo xiandaihua*, 11; *SSYZ*, pt. 1, p. 35.

Manchurian timber as "imports" to be replaced with local production. (After Japan seized Manchuria in 1931, it became "foreign" to the national government as well.) On the other hand, areas such as Huang-Yun, which did not have transport adequate to import a bulky item like wood, had no imports to replace, and the state paid little attention to their problems. Third, Huang-Yun itself had no organizations that could limit what people took from ecologically crucial areas outside the villages—riverbanks, hillsides, wastelands, and former forest lands.

The first two of these problems were peculiar to areas that lacked both modern transportation and navigable rivers. The third was more widespread, but it was particularly severe in Huang-Yun, parts of which were especially disorderly. Naturally, raids on growing trees were an especially serious problem in an area where locally grown fuel supplies were the only ones available.

Poor transportation, unclear property rights, and general instability intensified Huang-Yun's ecological crisis and ruled out market solutions. We will begin by looking at why this was the case and at the extent of deforestation, a particularly severe environmental problem created by market failure.

The second and third parts of this chapter will examine why the government's remedial efforts did not help Huang-Yun: the reasons are a combination of objective difficulties, the limited abilities of local government, and the mercantilist priorities of higher levels of government. Local governments, acting at the behest of the province, created "forestry societies" much like the cotton societies discussed in the previous chapter; the forestry societies carried out large though sporadic planting campaigns and, occasionally, severely punished "tree bandits." However, they were not able to apply more modest amounts of resources consistently to give saplings steady care and protection. Since trees are more dispersed and take far longer to mature than cotton plants, the use of unpaid patrols staffed by those with property rights in the growing plants—an approach that was stretched to its limits in protecting the new cotton varieties—was wholly inadequate for protecting trees.

Meanwhile, higher levels of government paid little attention to deforestation in Huang-Yun. This area's particularly acute fuel shortage—evident in fuel prices far higher than those in more accessible areas—meant that successful reforestation in this region would have considerably improved the general welfare. In terms of the principal economic goals of provincial and national governments, however—improving their balance of payments by reducing imports or stimulating exports—it did not matter what happened in a region whose weak transport links to the coast already ruled out importing bulky goods such as fuel. State efforts wound up being concentrated in precisely those areas that could spend hard currency to address their ecological crises through the market.

In fact, the quickest and probably best way of alleviating Huang-Yun's fuel crisis—improved transportation—might have actually interfered with some government aims, since it probably would have increased imports more than exports. The last part of this chapter will look at government priorities and the politics of transportation, explaining why Huang-Yun did not get the infrastructure it needed.

The patterns emphasized here—local governments' inability to move resources across time and space, the low priority that mercantilist officials above the county level gave to Huang-Yun even when resources used there would have done more for popular welfare than in coastal areas, and the state's failure to penetrate South Huang-Yun villages—will reappear on a larger scale in the last two chapters. Those chapters expand the story of ecological decay to the area of water control, particularly Yellow River control. The three chapters together describe a shift from a state that had helped reproduce the ecological basis of Huang-Yun's economy—albeit inefficiently and at great expense to the South China tax and tribute payers—to a state that, under foreign pressure, wrote off Huang-Yun to concentrate on more accessible and generally wealthier regions.

ISOLATION, FUEL SHORTAGES, AND DEFORESTATION

When the hydraulic system was at its peak, Huang-Yun received a number of useful raw materials from elsewhere—materials it was too densely populated to supply for itself. The decline of both Grand Canal and Yellow River shipping in the mid-1800s meant that Huang-Yun lost access to this trade, with devastating ecological consequences.

One such material was stone, which was desperately needed for dike construction. Chapter 4 will look at this problem in more detail. Here, two points are worth noting. First, financial problems in the

1830s and 1840s—before the Yellow River shift—led the Qing to try to economize on shipping expenses for riverworks projects; this policy would eventually have disastrous effects on the stone-short parts of Huang-Yun near the Yellow River.[4] Second, stone is a single, though particularly important, case of a more general attempt to cut shipping expenses on government projects—including that of feeding Beijing.[5]

The government's retreat from regional division of labor by command was not a problem in coastal areas or along easily navigated rivers. There, water routes required little maintenance and would soon be invigorated by the arrival of steamships, enabling private trade to maintain or expand the benefits of integration. Elsewhere, however, private parties did not take up the slack. Where—as in Huang-Yun—dense populations were forced to do without materials they had once obtained by trade, the use of such inferior substitutes as Yellow River dikes built with stalks could lead to disaster.

Even greater problems ensued when the commodity involved had more varied uses than stone. One crucial instance of Huang-Yun's limited economic integration with the wider world was the timber trade, or lack thereof. While much of China tapped ever more distant timber sources beginning in the mid-nineteenth century, Huang-Yun had less and less access to outside wood and saw its own supplies dwindle rapidly.

This decline had varied repercussions, including an acute fuel shortage. Even the most generous estimates of all questionable data still give southwest Shandong in the 1930s a total per capita fuel supply (including straw, grass, and so forth) that was only 27 percent of what present-day researchers consider the bare minimum for "subsistence," which as defined here includes fuel for cooking, boiling water,

---

4. The most important examples of this economizing were proposals to commute grain tribute to cash, which became more frequent and insistent beginning in the 1820s. Proposals to save on the shipping of dike-building supplies were a constant theme of reform proposals in the Daoguang (1821–50) period. The effects of one such change—the substitution of local materials for stone on the dikes of the Huang-Yun Yellow River—is discussed in detail in chapter 4. However, these concerns were not limited to times of fiscal crisis; Shandong reduced its use of willow branches in dike making as early as the 1720s to save on transport. A summary of where different river control supplies were obtained may be found in *Shandong tongzhi* (1915), *juan* 124, pp. 3442–44. See also Jane Kate Leonard, "Grand Canal Grain Transport Management," *Modern Asian Studies* 22:4 (1988): 665–99.

5. See chapter 4; James Polachek, "Gentry Hegemony in Soochow," in *Conflict and Control in Late Imperial China*, ed. Frederic Wakeman and Carolyn Grant (Berkeley, 1975), esp. 223–24, 226–27, 252–53.

and preparing animal feed, but not for heating (except as a byproduct of cooking) or lighting.[6] A supply of 27 percent of that minimum is slightly smaller than that available in particularly poor areas of contemporary Bangladesh (36 percent), which has a population density about triple that of 1930s Shandong and a fuel shortage rivaled only by parts of Sahelian Africa and a few other such regions.[7] Northwest Shandong was only slightly better off than the southwest, at 31 percent of the minimum.[8]

The fuel shortage led to enormous suffering, to countless hours of extra work for the women and children responsible for gleaning and cooking, and to social conflicts as well.[9] It is unclear which personal conservation measures were most common, but all of the likely options—doing without fires on some cold days, trying not to leave the *kang* (a combination bed/stove/sitting platform) during winter,[10] eating fewer cooked meals—involved serious discomfort and health risks.

It is even harder to measure the fuel crisis in economic terms. For one thing, relatively little fuel was bought and sold (19 percent in North China as a whole, according to J. L. Buck[11]); consequently, the volatile prices of the small proportion that was marketed are poor measures of the value people placed on the fuel they gathered themselves. But if we accept the market price of stalks—an inferior fuel and construction material—as a rough measure of the value of fuel, we can generate some guesses.[12] Making the admittedly dubious

6. See dissertation, appendix F, for calculations. The estimates of minimum fuel supply come from Smil, *The Bad Earth*, 150, and Asian Development Bank, *Asian Energy Problems*, 114. See also Smil, *Energy in China's Modernization* (Armonk, N.Y., 1988), 47–48. Obviously, many people continue to live below "subsistence"; inadequate fuel does not have the same immediate and inevitable impact that inadequate food does. However, the things that people living below these levels have to give up— cooked food, boiled water, and the like—do have obvious health effects and would certainly be considered "necessities" almost anywhere.

7. See Asian Development Bank, *Asian Energy Problems*, 116; Smil, *Energy*, 52–53. Bangladesh, with an area of 55,126 square miles (versus slightly under 60,000 for Shandong—see Shandong sheng nongye qu hua, *Shandong sheng zonghe nongye qu hua*, 1) had a population of 110,000,000 in 1991.

8. See calculations in dissertation, appendix F, esp. 433.

9. On fuel gathering, see, for instance, Arthur Smith, *Chinese Characteristics*, p. 22; Clifton O'Neal Carey, letters of Dec. 16, 1918 (from near Dong'a) and May 18, 1919 (from near Dezhou) in papers of Clifton O'Neal Carey.

10. See, e.g., Dong Taisheng, ed., *Shandong ge yao ji*, 27.

11. John L. Buck, *Chinese Farm Economy*, 392.

12. The estimates of fuel supplies and needs on which these calculations are based may be found in dissertation, appendix F, 431–32; the agricultural output estimates are

inference that since Huang-Yun still had significant forests in the
1840s, most peasants were probably obtaining enough fuel to meet
subsistence needs, the drop to less than one-third that level by the
1930s represented a loss of in-kind income equivalent to anywhere
from ¥3.4 to ¥8.8 for a family of five; where in this range the result
falls depends on what price we use for stalks and whose estimate of
subsistence fuel needs we adopt. In other terms, this lost noncash income amounted to a fall of between 1.8 percent and 4.7 percent of our
somewhat high estimates of gross farm output for an average North
Huang-Yun family of five and 2.9 percent to 7.5 percent for their
South Huang-Yun counterparts.

It becomes clear that these estimates are extremely conservative
when we compare them to actual consumption figures from areas not
far from Huang-Yun, which include at least some fuel use for lighting and winter heating. Fairly detailed data are available from Dingxian, an experimental model community roughly 120 miles north of
Huang-Yun. Household budgets for Dingxian—which include in-kind
income—virtually eliminate the low end of our Huang-Yun loss estimates. In that more accessible and somewhat more prosperous community, the average cost of self-gathered and purchased fuel together
ranged from ¥13.8 for the poorest group of families to ¥24.0 for the
richest group; this represented 8.3 percent and 5.3 percent of total income for these groups.[13] Buck's average figure for North China is ¥21
worth of fuel or 11 percent of all consumption.[14]

Our Huang-Yun calculations, by contrast, price the subsistence fuel
needs of a Huang-Yun family at an extraordinarily frugal ¥5.9 to
¥15.0. Dingxian was no colder than most of Huang-Yun, fuel was
more plentiful and thus cheaper there, and people kept heating and
lighting to a minimum;[15] thus it seems unlikely that an adequate
Huang-Yun fuel supply would really have cost less than the ¥19.6 that
the average Dingxian family spent. Were we to assume that when
Huang-Yun still had forests, its residents consumed as much fuel as

---

from dissertation, appendix E. Prices are a questionable measurement of value here in
part because where auto-consumption is high and probably fairly inflexible, small
changes in total supply or demand will create greatly exaggerated fluctuations in the
prices of the small part of the crop that is marketed.

13. Sidney Gamble, *Ting Hsien: A North China Rural Community* (Palo Alto,
1954), 108, 118.

14. John L. Buck, *Chinese Farm Economy*, 399.

15. Gamble, *Ting Hsien*, 109.

Dingxian families did in the 1930s, then the in-kind income lost as their fuel supply disappeared would be much larger: 7.3 percent of total income for the average North Huang-Yun family of 5 and a whopping 11.3 percent for their South Huang-Yun counterparts. By comparison, even the high end of the lost-income estimates we derived from "cooking only" energy budgets—4.7 percent of gross output for North Huang-Yun and 7.5 percent for South—seem quite cautious.

The lost-income figure for North Huang-Yun is less than what such an "average" family gained by adopting U.S. cotton; thus, if such a family was able to find fuel to purchase, its members could avoid suffering from the area's fuel crisis.[16] Some such families, like better-off families in Dingxian, even began to buy some kerosene, a preferable fuel for many purposes. Still, the money spent to compensate for lost gleaning income would have been close to the annual clothing budget of an average Dingxian family.[17] And given the overall fuel shortage, many families, especially in North Huang-Yun's least accessible areas, were obviously unable to either gather or buy enough fuel.

The southern figure of 7.5 percent, meanwhile, represents a large loss not offset by any gains from the new political economy. Much of this lost income had previously been earned by women and children, who were particularly unlikely to find equivalent new opportunities.[18] Smaller families could not cut back proportionately on fuel costs and thus were likely to be even harder hit.[19] And, as we shall see later, the fuel crisis was just the tip of the iceberg; the decay of Huang-Yun water control in the new political economy caused far greater losses.

Naturally, damage from the fuel crisis went beyond immediate suffering; people's desperate responses exacerbated long-term environmental problems. As peasants ran through not only wood, but chaff from their crops, and twigs, roots, and grass from the surrounding land, they were forced to burn dung—an inefficient fuel and a desperately needed fertilizer. Digging up peat, which was just below the surface in many areas, was another popular way of supplementing the

16. Kita Shina, *Rosai Mensaku*, 91, notes that in the North Huang-Yun county of Gaotang some cotton farmers purchased fuel to make up for their inability to gather enough; there was not, however, enough for all.

17. Gamble, *Ting Hsien*, p. 118.

18. On women's wages in the area, see *SSYZ* 1:62–69.

19. A fire meant to keep three people warm or cook food for three cannot be made with only three-fifths the fuel of a fire for five. Thus, if a small family had the same per capita income as a larger one, fuel would be a larger part of their budget.

fuel supply. Despite rigorous security measures, reforestation was wrecked by peasants cutting down very young trees for fuel. Wood shortages made pit props hard to come by in Shandong, thus handicapping the development of coal mining, which could have eased the fuel problem a bit.[20] Treelessness and the gleaning of grass and other plants increased erosion and flooding, decreasing future crops and crop residues. Increased flooding also increased soil salinity, causing lasting damage to agriculture.

Like many intensely farmed regions, Huang-Yun's ecological problems had been growing for a long time. Thus, it may seem pointless to try to specify when these problems reached a "critical" point. However, identifying such a point is useful for weighing the causes of these problems and understanding the more general relationships between "natural" and "social" factors in Huang-Yun. Despite some evidence for earlier dates, I believe the mid-nineteenth century was the most critical period.

The Grand Canal caused ecological problems in southwest Shandong that affected the local economy as early as the 1600s; one scholar has suggested that such problems explain the steady decline in western Shandong's share of Shandong *juren* degree winners.[21] The seventeenth-century historian and geographer Gu Yanwu observed that "the Ming [through their canal work] blocked the rivers to bring rice to the capital"; in other words, the canal slowed the drainage of the area's rivers, causing increased sedimentation.[22] This not only increased waterlogging and flood dangers, but added additional salt to the area's soil. Huang-Yun still suffers today from poor drainage, waterlogging, and saline soil.[23]

However, the problems the canal caused before 1853 were not even remotely comparable to what happened after the Yellow River shift. And before the 1850s, any problems the Grand Canal caused were more than compensated for, even in ecological terms, by the useful inputs and government attention the canal brought to Huang-Yun.

Twentieth-century Huang-Yun's lowest yields and biggest salinity

20. Generally, see Smil, *The Bad Earth*, 149–53; Smil, *Biomass Energies* (New York, 1983), 340, 343; Yan Guangyao, Sun Bocai, and Zhou Chengpeng, "Diaocha Shandong zhi nongye zhuangkuang," *Kexue* 4:5 (Jan. 1919), 471–72; *NSGB* 8:3 (Oct. 1921), *xuanzai*, 17.
21. Esherick, *Boxer Uprising*, 31–34.
22. Ibid., 32–33.
23. See, for instance, *Shandong sheng zonghe nongye qu hua*, pp. 45, 154, 157.

problems are in northwest Shandong and adjacent parts of Hebei; until 1853, the Yellow River had not touched this area for centuries, and canal-related floods, though frequent, were fairly small.[24] It was after 1855 and especially 1890 that North Huang-Yun experienced heavy flooding. Drainage problems also worsened dramatically at that time. The Grand Canal had slowed the meeting of local rivers with the sea even before 1853. However, drainage became a much greater problem after the Yellow River arrived and, with its much stronger current and higher bed, blocked the flow of various small rivers and of the Grand Canal itself. Developments in the far northwest also changed the nature of Yellow River sediment in the nineteenth century, so that floods deposited far less soil-enriching silt than before and far more useless sand.[25]

The drainage of numerous little streams was also slowed by people encroaching on riverbanks and cutting down trees. This problem was at least partially a product of declining political control. The "under-rule" of Huang-Yun became much more serious in the mid-1800s, both because the Qing were weakening and because they began to give less attention to the Yellow River, the Grand Canal, and the areas near them. Though Shandong's far southwest had a centuries-old reputation for "roughness," it is only after 1884 that the number of military incidents recorded there greatly exceeds that in the rest of the province (even as the number of incidents throughout the province rose).[26] The concentration of Shandong's flood problem within Huang-Yun, as chapter 4 will show, actually began a little later yet, in the 1890s.

Furthermore, the number of *juren* degrees that an area's residents won is not a sufficiently sensitive index of when its wealth—and, by inference, its ecological base—began to decline. Such statistics represent some combination of total wealth, concentration of wealth, and control of that wealth by local residents—as opposed to, say, Linqing and Liaocheng "guest merchants," whose children would have taken the exams elsewhere. Linqing, for instance, produced few higher degree winners even during the years when it was indisputably one of

24. On low yields and salinity, see ibid., 45–46; Esherick, *Boxer Uprising*, 11–14, 31–34. On Shouzhang see, for instance, Naquin, *Shantung Rebellion*, 12–14; north and east of Shouzhang, problems were probably less frequent, and no bigger when they did strike.

25. See Perry, *Rebels and Revolutionaries*, 19.

26. These statistics are tabulated in Zhang Yufa, *Zhongguo xiandaihua*, 102–12.

North China's richest cities. A combination of these factors would also explain the southwest's continuing lead over the northwest in *juren* and in producing far more important Republican leaders, even though the northwest led in per capita income.[27] Moreover, most accounts suggest that Linqing and Dongchang peaked economically in the middle or late eighteenth century, but their production of *juren* began to fall much earlier.[28] It is not clear why western and especially northwestern Shandong produced ever fewer members of the national elite, but it seems not to have been a simple result of ecological/ agricultural decline. It seems at least equally true that political and social problems triggered the area's particularly severe ecological problems: increasingly, local elites neither organized successful protection and maintenance for vulnerable resources nor fared well in the scramble for government aid. Even the Yellow River shift, as we shall see, was heavily influenced by politics: the Qing did not try to put the river back in its old bed in part because Jiangsu interests were more powerful than Shandong interests.[29]

Thus, there are strong reasons to doubt that the economic and political decline of Huang-Yun stemmed from ecological change caused by the Grand Canal during the period when the canal functioned well. Recent research suggests that such damage was relatively slight until the late eighteenth century; even the great Yellow River shift was preceded not by recurrent disasters, but by a quarter century with relatively few floods.[30] The "disasters" that were worsening before 1850 were primarily fiscal: Yellow River control was becoming extremely expensive, and it was the Grand Canal and the grain tribute, rather than local welfare, that justified those expenditures.[31] Thus, the Grand

27. On per capita income, see dissertation, appendix E; on production of degree holders, see Esherick, *Boxer Uprising*, 11–12, 31; on the prominence of southwest Shandong leaders in the Republic, see Xia Lianju, "Shandong duli qianhou," *Wenshi ziliao xuanji*, Jinan edition, no. 12 (1981), 22, 29, 40; Shao Chuoran, "Tian Zhongyu," 43–44; and especially Wan Guangwei, "Minguo chunian Shandong zheng Dang huodong de neimou yu Sheng yihui de chouwen," 33–40.

28. Yang Zhengtai, "Ming Qing Linqing de sheng shuai yu dili tiaojian de bianhua," *Lishi Dili*, no. 3 (1983), 117, on the peak of Linqing's commerce; for *juren* numbers, see Esherick, *Boxer Uprising*, 11–12, 31.

29. Esherick, *Boxer Uprising*, 14; Polachek, "Gentry Hegemony," passim; see also 175, 179–81.

30. See Randall Dodgen, "Hydraulic Evolution and Dynastic Decline: The Yellow River Conservancy 1796–1855," *Late Imperial China* 12:2 (Dec. 1991), 36, 43–46, 53–54, 57.

31. See Dodgen, "Hydraulic Evolution," 36–37, 53–54, 58; also Hu Ch'ang-t'u,

Canal not only brought needed wood and stone to Huang-Yun, as we shall see below, but attracted huge state water control efforts, staving off massive ecological damage. Contrary to the picture of the Grand Canal as an ecological liability that sacrificed northern Jiangsu and Shandong to the feeding of Beijing (much as huge areas were despoiled to provision Madrid, Berlin, and other capitals whose immediate surroundings could not do so), it seems more likely that Ming-Qing statecraft lightened the ecological burdens of the areas crossed by the Yellow and Huai rivers. If any areas were sacrificed they were Jiangnan and other rich Southern regions, which paid for this system through the canal-borne grain tribute.

This notion that the Grand Canal was largely beneficial is in some ways a return to an older view of it. However, it also fits well with recent scholarship emphasizing that the Ming-Qing state targeted its interventions in the economy at vital functions that the market failed to perform on its own and thus wound up concentrating much of its efforts in "backward" regions—for example, helping to develop the northwestern grain trade and to extend water control on the southwestern frontier while leaving Yangzi River control and the Yangzi Valley grain trade in largely private hands.[32]

One could doubt that the state had any beneficent motives and argue that its only interest in the Grand Canal and Yellow River was one analogous to those of its European contemporaries: provisioning the capital at all costs. Indeed, the fact that the government made little effort to prevent frequent small floods near the canal should caution us against too rosy a picture of its intentions. Nonetheless, the effect of the Ming-Qing tribute system was that for four hundred years rich southern regions paid to maintain an overall ecological balance in poorer areas such as Huang-Yun, a sharp contrast to the usual results of European provisioning strategies.

A somewhat closer analogue—though still very imprecise—might be Mughal India; the limits of the analogy suggest the roles of geopoli-

"The Yellow River Administration in the Ch'ing Dynasty," *Far Eastern Quarterly* 14:4 (August 1955), 505–13.

32. On the northwestern grain trade see Terada Takanobu, *Sansei Shōnin no Kenkyū: Mindai ni okeru Shōnin oyobi Shōgyo shihon* (Kyoto, 1972), esp. 5–6, 101–6, 120–57. On various aspects of frontier water control and irrigation see, e.g., Susan Naquin and Evelyn Rawski, *Chinese Society in the Eighteenth Century* (New Haven, 1987), 24; James Lee, *State and Society in Southwest China, 1250–1850* (Cambridge, Eng., forthcoming).

tics and Confucian ideas in the Chinese case. There, too, the tribute a conquest dynasty extracted forced accessible, well-watered, and commercialized southern regions to subsidize the ecologically more fragile northern plain, which otherwise could not have supported the empire's capital; and since much investment from the cities that this tribute made viable went into irrigating nearby lands, the tribute indirectly made intensive farming of certain northern areas sustainable. But while the Mughals shared the Ming-Qing problem of a huge capital and army placed far from the regions that could best support them, they seem to have had no comparable ideology of imperial benevolence or support for subsistence farming—and they made no comparable state effort to stabilize more remote and truly fragile areas, where market stimuli would not prompt investment in wells.[33]

Regardless of the exact mix of motives that had driven high Qing statecraft, its benefits for needier regions were thrown into sharp relief by the contrasting logic that came to dominate policy making from the late nineteenth through the twentieth century. As fiscal strains mounted and China faced a world of competing nation-states, its statecraft began to emphasize such goals as efficiency and national strength above stability and the reproduction of a Confucian society; and it was at this point that state policy began to exacerbate regional inequalities rather than work against them. (To cite another case, most of the state's interest in underwriting settlement and secure subsistence in the far northwest and southwest undoubtedly stemmed from military priorities rather than a concern for these backward regions per se. Nonetheless, as long as China worried about military threats from Central Asia or its own unassimilated minorities, funds flowed to poor areas; once the principal threat was Westerners along the coast and in other commercially attractive areas, the government focused its attention on such relatively well-off areas as Fengtian, Tianjin, the Yangzi delta, and the southeastern coast.) The general reorientation toward rich and newly contested parts of China marked something much more basic than the triumph of any particular regional "lobby": the acceptance of a new logic that would govern statecraft for years to come.

Transportation and trade were essential to Huang-Yun's ecology: it

33. See, for instance, C. A. Bayly, *Rulers, Townsmen, and Bazaars: North India in the Age of British Expansion, 1770–1870* (Cambridge, Eng., 1983), 63–64, 83–84.

was simply impossible for such a densely populated area to supply itself with such quintessential "hinterland" inputs as stone and wood. With much of China suffering from increased pressure on resources in the mid-nineteenth century, coastal North China got a reprieve through the opening of Manchuria, which beginning in the 1840s became a major supplier of lumber to eastern Shandong, Zhili, and elsewhere.[34] (Jiangnan's overworked soil had begun to get relief from Manchurian beancake a century earlier.[35]) By the early twentieth century, Manchurian timber was not only the mainstay of coastal North China, but was transported inland as far as Jinan. By 1920, more than twenty locations in eastern and central Shandong imported more than ¥1 million each of Manchurian logs per year, enough to meet the fuel needs of a minimum of thirty thousand families of five in each of these locations. Numerous places along the Hebei coast depended on lumber from North America. If the wood imported at Qingdao alone in 1935 had all been used for fuel, it would have met the needs of almost one-third of Shandong's population.[36]

When shipping goods up the Yellow River from the coast became too unreliable in the 1890s, Shandong salt merchants diverted some of their usual donations for Yellow River work to making the Xiaoqing He navigable from the coast to Jinan. Naturally, this eased the shipping of items besides salt, too, although not as much as had been hoped.[37] At any rate, rafts could not go beyond Jinan on either waterway, and no other transportation linked most of Huang-Yun to Manchurian timber supplies. Merchant groups formed in 1911 and 1919 both tried developing motorboat navigation all the way to Puzhou (where the Yellow River enters Shandong); both quickly obtained government permits, but not support, and neither became important.[38]

Meanwhile, the decline of the Grand Canal cut this area off from its traditional southern timber sources.[39] A missionary in Xuzhou, north-

34. Norman Shaw, *Chinese Forest Trees and Timber Supply* (London, 1914), 114.
35. Adachi Keiji, "Daizuhaku Ryūtsū to Shindai no Shōgyo Teki Nōgyo," *Tōyōshi Kenkyū* 33:3 (1974), 360–89, esp. 365–71.
36. For import figures, see *NSGB* 8:2 (Sept. 1921), *xuanzai*, 17. For more import figures and discussion of forest resources, see Kōain Kijitsubu, *Hokushi ni okeru Rinsan Shigen Chōsa* (Tokyo, 1940), 11, 39.
37. David Buck, *Urban Change*, 32.
38. Zhongguo jiaotongbu, jiaotong shi weiyuanhui, *Jiaotong shi* (Nanjing, 1937), 877–81; *SDZZ*, no. 90 (5/30/XT 3), 25b.
39. Hoshi Ayao, *Dai Unga* (Tokyo, 1971), 203; interview notes from Linqing and Liaocheng, November 1985.

ern Jiangsu, described in 1908 a situation similar to the one across the border in Shandong:

> Lumber, both native and foreign, has become almost impossible to get. This district has always depended on Southern pine poles for house roof beams, which now can be brought up only with the greatest difficulty and expense (owing to the silting up of the Grand Canal and *likin* exactions). This also compels the use for building purposes of what is ordinarily sold for stove-wood, thus demoralizing the fuel market and causing great distress among the poor. It also affects the price and supply of fuel for burning bricks, which are therefore very high.[40]

This was not the first contraction of timber shipments to Xuzhou. In the eighteenth and early nineteenth centuries large amounts of timber had entered the Xuzhou market (and thus at least indirectly affected Shandong supplies) by being floated down the Yellow River from Shaanxi. However, overcutting in Shaanxi forests and the Yellow River shift ended this trade after the mid-nineteenth century.[41]

In the eighteenth century, Yanzhou (slightly east of Jining) still sent large amounts of wood up the Grand Canal to brick kilns in Linqing. This area still had significant forests in the mid-nineteenth century, when supplies in east Shandong were becoming strained. But in the late 1800s the patterns of trade and shortage shifted: Manchurian and later foreign lumber provided new alternatives for eastern Shandong, while the decline of the Grand Canal and Yellow River timber trade from their early-nineteenth-century peaks destabilized Huang-Yun's timber market.[42]

We do not know how big the lost canal-borne lumber trade had been. The few available figures seem far too small to account for Huang-Yun's fuel crisis.[43] However, we need to consider not only

---

40. Quoted in Shaw, *Chinese Forest Trees*, 80.

41. Wu Chengming, *Zhongguo zibenzhuyi de mengya* (Beijing: Renmin chubanshe, 1985), 435–36.

42. Xu Tan, "Ming Qing shiqi de Linqing shangye," *Zhongguo jingji shi yanjiu*, no. 2 (1986), 138; A. A. Fauvel, *La Province Chinoise du Chan-toung: Géographie et Histoire Naturelle* (Brussels, 1892), 270; Shaw, *Chinese Forest Trees*, 131; Hoshi Ayao, *Dai Unga*, 202–3.

43. Hoshi Ayao, *Dai Unga*, 203, gives the number of logs, but not their size. If these logs were of the size described as typical for transportation from Jiangxi (the ultimate source of some, though not all, of them) in Shaw, *Chinese Forest Trees* (318), they would total approximately 70,000 cubic meters of timber per year, equivalent to about 84,000,000 *jin* of crop residues, or perhaps 10 percent of the residues available in southwestern Shandong after feeding farm animals but before doing any construction, dike repair, or cooking. The figures used to convert cubic meters of timber to tons (and

the lumber trade that ceased to exist but the increased imports that this area needed—and that, unlike coastal areas, it never got. Indeed, Huang-Yun became so isolated from larger markets for these resources—and its fuel supply, therefore, so inelastic—that during twentieth-century crop failures, the price of fuel often rose faster than that of food.[44]

The coming of the Yellow River and the decline of stone and wood shipping also placed a new burden on Huang-Yun's supply of millet and sorghum stalks—crucial parts of the rural fuel supply that were now increasingly used for dike repair and for civilian construction as well.[45] The number of pounds of stalks thus removed from the fuel supply in the Shandong part of Huang-Yun is impossible to calculate precisely, but the amount used for dikes alone was almost certainly more than 100,000,000 *jin* (one *jin* equals about 1.33 pounds) per year, and possibly more than 400,000,000 *jin*.[46] This constitutes only a small percentage of all the biomass (trees, crop residues, and human and animal wastes) that was close enough to the western Shandong Yellow River dikes to be used by a very vigorous bureaucracy. In fact, however, this burden—like that of most flood control requisitions—fell on a much narrower area very close to the river.[47]

More importantly, stalk exactions—even if they had been widely shared—were a larger percentage of what we might call the discretionary biomass supply: the amount left for use as fuel, fertilizer, or construction material after keeping essential farm animals alive.[48] Even a generous estimate of this figure would give residents of southwest Shandong in the 1930s less than one-third the average fuel supply of rural Chinese today, which is still unanimously considered

---

thence to *jin*) of crop residues are derived from Smil, *Bad Earth*, 149–50. See also Vaclav Smil and William Knowland, *Energy in the Developing World: The Real Energy Crisis* (Oxford, 1980), 363.

44. See, for instance, *NCH*, Oct. 23, 1920, p. 230, reporting chaff selling at a staggering 50 cash per *jin* and people eating uncooked food, drinking unboiled water, and tearing down homes for firewood. These chaff prices represent an increase of at least 150 percent, while food prices had risen roughly 40 percent. For more on prices of auto-consumed products, see n. 12.

45. On stone as a substitute for other construction materials in civilian use, see Jing Qi, "Dong'a xian luxing jian wen ji," *Shandong wenxian* 2:3 (Dec. 1976), 153; on its crucial role in dike construction, see chapter 4, "Stalks and Stones," and dissertation, appendix G.

46. See dissertation, appendix G.

47. This problem will be discussed in detail below.

48. See dissertation, appendixes F and G.

inadequate.[49] Thus, people probably replaced at least some of the stalks delivered for Yellow River dike repair by using more of the only fuels remaining—peat and dung.[50] Had residents replaced all the stalks needed for repair (according to a "middle range estimate") by burning dung, they would have consumed about 11 percent of southwest Shandong's solid wastes—an astonishing 38 percent of the solid wastes of the ten counties in which these dikes were located, fertilizer the area could ill afford to lose.[51]

Moreover, even peasants who did not burn dung wound up losing some of its benefits if they were very short of stalks. A 1936 soil survey found that the biggest problem with fertilizing and composting in North China "is to find sufficient organic material to properly absorb the nitrogen liberated in the composting of manures. Wheat and rice straw are too valuable as roofing material, for the making of ropes, and for use as fuel, to be used in compost." An American agronomist in Jinan imported a composting method from India that addressed this problem, but it required wood ash; thus, it was probably of little use in Huang-Yun.[52] In fertilizer, as with lumber, Huang-Yun suffered from not being well tied to coastal cities. Night soil from Tianjin was shipped down the Grand Canal as far as Dezhou (about a hundred miles), but, like wood, this cheap fertilizer quickly became uneconomical if carried overland.[53] Without imported materials, Huang-Yun's already depleted soil worsened steadily throughout the early twentieth century.[54]

49. For the estimate, see dissertation, appendix F; for comments on the contemporary fuel supply in rural China see Smil, *The Bad Earth*, 149–53; Wang Mengshang, "Zhuyi jiejue nongcun nengyuan wenti," *Guangming ribao*, July 19, 1980, p. 4.

50. See dissertation, appendix G; on contemporary burning of dung in China, see Smil, *Biomass Energies*, 343.

51. See dissertation, appendix G.

52. James Thorp, *Geography of the Soils of China* (Nanjing, 1936), 424–25 (for quote, 424). On the geographic pattern of wood availability in Shandong, see section "Isolation, Fuel Shortages, and Deforestation" in this chapter; on the availability of some wood on the hills outside Jinan, see Harry A. Franck, *Wandering in Northern China* (New York and London, 1923), 269.

53. On the shipping of night soil from Tianjin to Dezhou (on the Grand Canal) see "Lubei shi xian nongye diaocha baogao," 9. At the porterage rates prevalent in the area fifteen years earlier (see *SS*, 234) shipping this fertilizer twenty miles from the pier by land would have added two-thirds to the price of the low-grade night soil, one-third to the price of the higher grade. Since going much further than that would have added the expense of overnight accommodations, such shipments would have rapidly become uneconomical without motorized transport.

54. *XCJSXK* 3:18–19 (Feb. 1934), 15; John Earl Baker, *Explaining China* (London, 1927), 246.

By this time both foreign and Chinese observers were noting that Shandong had no forests left, even on hillsides.[55] There were some trees along riverbanks and along the railroad lines; most families had one or two in their own courtyard.[56] However, travelers in western Shandong repeatedly noted the total absence of trees outside walled villages in the southwest and outside family courtyards in the north-west (where villages were rarely walled).[57] The rest of Huang-Yun was no better off. One survey called Henan the least forested province in China.[58] The Maritime Customs reported in 1931 that only 1/38,000 of Hebei province was still forested.[59] That such an implausible num-ber could be printed at all gives an idea of how desperate the situation was.

Most trees were behind walls because trees out in the open were extremely hard to protect and getting more so as fuel became more scarce. Meanwhile, other changes further decreased the number of places where trees could endure. Monasteries and temples had pre-viously protected some trees: these institutions lost much of their land to the new "local self-government" organizations created after 1901, which often sold the trees.[60] Abandoned river beds—of which Huang-Yun had many—or the banks of existing rivers, which were often good for nothing else, had long been another important area for trees. The early-twentieth-century peanut boom, however, suddenly created a very profitable use for this land, touching off numerous battles be-tween foresters backed by the county and peanut-growing squatters who often had the support of their village.[61] The reform atmosphere and foreign contacts that produced these added strains, however, also sparked official interest in augmenting timber resources nationwide.

55. Shaw, *Chinese Forest Trees*, 130; Franck, *Wandering*, 269; Fauvel, *Chan-toung*, 270; *NSGB* 1:3 (Oct. 1914), *baogao*, 2.

56. Nanjing University, College of Agriculture and Forestry, *Bulletin* 1:3 (Jan. 1924), 3; Esherick, *Boxer Uprising*, 1; Carey, letter of May 18, 1919.

57. See, for instance, Fauvel, *Chan-toung*, 270; Esherick, *Boxer Uprising*, 1; Franck, *Wandering*, 269; Shaw, *Chinese Forest Trees*, 21, 130.

58. Shaw, *Chinese Forest Trees*, 54.

59. Imperial Maritime Customs, *Decennial Report, 1922–1931*, 356.

60. See, for instance, Shaw, *Chinese Forest Trees*, 16; *NSGB* 1:3 (Oct. 1914), *baogao*, 1; Zhang Yufa, *Zhongguo xiandaihua*, 15–16.

61. John L. Buck, "Cost of Growing and Marketing Peanuts in China," *Chinese Economic Journal* 5:3 (Sept. 1929), 768; Ji Bin, "Nongcun pochan sheng zhong Jinan yige fanrong de cunzhuang" in *Zhongguo nongcun jingji lunwen ji*, ed. Qian Jiaju (Shanghai, 1935), 502–3; *QYHK*, no. 13 (April 1923), *gongdu*, 23. For an actual in-stance of trees being cut down by squatters to plant peanuts (in Enxian), see "Lubei shi xian nongye diaocha baogao," 13–14.

THE FUEL SHORTAGE
AND THE LOGIC OF "SELF-STRENGTHENING"

The national officials who began promoting reforestation were not particularly interested in the rural fuel crisis. They sometimes acknowledged it, but they emphasized other points: erosion, the cost of wood imports, or the ways in which a lack of wood hampered such "modernizing" activities as railroad, telegraph, and mine construction.[62] These priorities (which have persisted down to the present time[63]) derived from a larger program that we have already noted: the government's emphasis on projects that officials believed would do the most to help China maintain its political autonomy (and often, help their unit of government maintain its own power), rather than those that would do the most for popular welfare in economic terms. In what follows, I refer to this program as "self-strengthening": although this label is usually applied to late-nineteenth-century policies, I believe there is enough continuity in the logic of government-supported development measures to justify extending this term to cover the otherwise nameless outlook of early-twentieth-century reformist bureaucrats. This outlook might also be labeled "mercantilist," since aside from favoring modernization, one of its chief features was a preoccupation with improving the country's (or sometimes the province's) balance of trade and currency reserves; this goal was clearly more important to officials than increasing the quantity of goods available to the population. Given how much of China's huge debt was imposed at gunpoint and how often it was used to infringe further on Chinese sovereignty, it is not surprising that economic self-strengthening was defined in terms of improving the balance of trade.

Of course, governments in other times and places have also had these concerns. However, early-twentieth-century China's political fragmentation and its lack of tariff autonomy ruled out many of the protectionist measures that are usually part of import substitution strategies. Instead, import substitution could only be achieved by improving Chinese production of the commodity in question or by using nontariff barriers against imports. For areas that already bought

---

62. See, for instance, Lin Maoquan, *Wenji*, 5b; Yan Guangyao, Sun Bocai, and Zhou Chengpeng, "Diaocha Shandong zhi nongye zhuangkuang," 471–72; *NSGB* 8:3 (Oct. 1921), *xuanzai*, 17–22.

63. On the priority of industrial uses over rural needs in recent forestry policy, see Lester Ross, *Environmental Policy in China* (Bloomington, 1988), 82–83.

foreign wood, government efforts to increase the available supply of home-grown wood were the obvious answer; for areas that had no means of importing such a bulky product, no such efforts were necessary.

Thus, this self-strengthening orientation gave government forestry officials strong reasons to think that some areas were much more important than others. In 1914, the Ministry of Agriculture and Commerce gave three reasons for making Taian a focus of its Shandong forestry work: (1) the need to reverse the intensifying erosion caused in recent years by farmers who had cleared and terraced hillsides, (2) the closeness of these hills to the railroads, and (3) the possibilities this situation created for involving merchants in reforestation.[64]

Reforesting where the hillsides were most eroded had the advantage of not decreasing any other sort of production. Since areas with many bare hillsides were often near current or potential mining sites, which in turn tended to be near foreign-built railroads, these priorities were mutually reinforcing. These areas also often overlapped with those in which foreigners had undertaken pioneer reforestation efforts: hillsides near their concessions (principally Qingdao and Weihaiwei) and areas along the railroads, where they needed wood for ties and had the police power to protect saplings.[65] Finally, areas that were accessible and had at least an infant modern sector usually received some supplies from Manchuria or abroad. (Most Shandong railroad ties were made with Japanese lumber; American and Russian timber were also imported.[66]) Thus, government-sponsored reforestation was, among other things, an import-substitution measure designed to preserve precious hard currency.[67]

Foreign advisers to the Chinese forestry service shared this orientation. A 1923 bulletin from the new College of Agriculture and Forestry, for instance, did not even mention the fuel crisis in areas cut off from the coast. Moreover, its calculation of the benefits of refores-

64. *NSGB* 1:10 (May 1915), *zhengshi*, 9.

65. *NSGB* 1:3 (Oct. 1914), *baogao*, 2; Deutschland Reichsmarineamt, *Denkschrift Betreffend die Entwicklung des Kiautschou-Gebiets*, 1902:12, 46, 47, 52; 1903:38; 1904:47; 1905:49; 1906:70; 1907:58; 1908:56; R. Rosenblith, "Forests and Timber Trade of the Chinese Empire," *Forestry Quarterly* 10:4 (Dec. 1912), 655; Shaw, *Chinese Forest Trees*, 132.

66. On the importance of Japanese imports in Shandong, see, for instance, Shaw, *Chinese Forest Trees*, 121; on other foreign timber sources in coastal North China (before 1937) see Kōain Kijitsubu, *Hokushi ni okeru Rinsan Shigen Chōsa*, 11, 13.

67. See, for instance, *NSGB* 8:3 (Oct. 1921), *xuanzai*, 17–22.

tation did not include any increase in consumption: it estimated the amount of lumber imports China could replace through reforestation and how much of its railroad system China could either buy back from foreigners or duplicate with these savings.[68]

Sun Yat-sen voiced similar views, though in more emotional, less economic terms. Sun did not mention the widespread rural fuel crisis and the severe problems of inland areas like Huang-Yun (or northwest China, where the situation was even worse). Instead, he made two points about the importance of forestry to "people's livelihood." First, deforestation contributed to flooding. Second, China's coastal cities had become dependent on foreign lumber for construction. This dependency wasted foreign exchange and—seemingly more important to Sun—made the people of these cities dependent on foreigners even in death (for coffin wood). Although Sun never had much power in the north, his ideas suggest that many people framed the deforestation problem more in terms of national strength than popular welfare. Sun's ideas also seem to have influenced later Guomindang reforestation efforts.[69]

The emphasis on self-strengthening concerns led the national government to emphasize forestry work in areas that already had the most options for alleviating fuel shortages: in Shandong, they set up forestry centers in Jinan, Qingzhou, and Taian.[70] Except for places along its edges like Taian and Dong'a—relatively accessible areas with many bare hillsides—the Shandong part of Huang-Yun was in the "western plains" section of the province, which was considered particularly difficult to plan for and given last priority.[71]

While such an emphasis fit in well with the mercantilist priorities discussed in chapter 1, popular welfare would have been better served by a focus on less accessible areas like Huang-Yun. In 1920, the Shandong Yellow River Office was paying almost twice as much for stalks in western Shandong as it paid on the section of the river nearest the coast.[72] In 1934, *gaoliang* (sorghum) stalks sold for ¥1.66 per 100 *jin*

---

68. University of Nanjing, College of Agriculture and Forestry, *Bulletin*, no. 2 (Dec. 1923), 4. See also Rosenblith, "Timber Trade," 656–57.

69. See Wu Jinzan, "Zhonghua Minguo linye fazhi zhi yanjiu—Minguo yuan nian zhi Minguo sanshiwu nian" (Ph.D. dissertation, Zhongguo Wenhua Daxue, Taibei, 1982). Sun's views are summarized on 71–73.

70. Imperial Maritime Customs, *Decennial Report, 1922–1931*, 444.

71. *NSGB* 8:3 (Oct. 1921), *xuanzai*, 19.

72. *Hewu jibao*, no. 3 (Oct. 1919), 134.

in Heze; since wood was better for both burning and building, it presumably cost at least as much.[73] These figures are particularly striking since Heze's fuel supply was probably above average for southwest Shandong; in the late Qing the Shandong Yellow River Office used Puzhou and Heze as its principal wood sources for the Huang-Yun section of the river.[74] By contrast, in Dezhou, at the northeastern edge of Huang-Yun and near rail and canal links to Tianjin, wood cost only ¥1 per 100 *jin*.[75] The price of locally decocted black market salt also suggests that fuel cost 60 percent more in southwest Shandong than near Dezhou.[76]

In the eighteenth century, northwest Shandong had imported wood from the southwest, and northwesterners had gone to the southwest to glean.[77] A 1930s biomass/energy budget for northwest Shandong (which omits imports, for which we have no figures) suggests that its fuel shortage was by then less severe than the southwest's, but only slightly.[78] Thus, fuel prices near Dezhou that were five-eighths of those in the southwest most likely reflect Dezhou's links to the coast. In general, because relief from the fuel shortage arrived through ports, fuel prices in North China resembled those of a manufactured good: cheaper in more developed areas (which were linked to these ports) than in less developed ones. (In a self-sufficient macroregion, by contrast, fuel would be less expensive in the periphery, where it is extracted, than in core cities, to which it has to be shipped.) Fuel, however, was far less valuable per pound than manufactured goods, so the price differences between areas were still too small to bring imported lumber to all the remote places that manufactured goods reached.[79]

Thus, reforestation would have gone furthest toward meeting

73. *XCJSXK* 3:18–19 (Feb. 1934), 14–15, gives a value of ¥3 for the crop residue of one *mu* of *gaoliang*; since the residue from one *mu* would be about 180 *jin*, the price per 100 *jin* would be ¥1.66.

74. *Shandong tongzhi* (1915), *juan* 124, p. 3442. See also dissertation, appendixes F and G.

75. "Lubei shi xian nongye diaocha baogao," 9.

76. On southwestern prices of illegal salt, see *SDXZJSSYQGB*, no. 28 (Dec. 25, 1935), 5; on Yucheng prices and the amounts of materials needed for illicit production, see Sun Zhuomin, "Yucheng xian shehui diaocha," *Nongye zhoubao* 4:19 (May 17, 1935), 668–69. The only other supplies needed were alkaline soil and reeds (usually from riverbank land that was unsuitable for crops and often unclaimed) and water.

77. Xu Tan, "Ming Qing shiqi de Linqing shangye," 138; Esherick, *Boxer Uprising*, 27.

78. See dissertation, appendix F, esp. 433.

79. For the weight-to-value ratios of various widely traded products in early-twentieth-century China, see Sands, "Investigation," 64.

human needs—and performing the old state function of making up
for market failures—if it had emphasized more isolated areas. The
national government, however, emphasized areas where the payoff
would be largest in mercantilist terms. More wood in Huang-Yun
would have improved life there but would have done little to decrease
the area's imports (cotton goods, kerosene, cigarettes) or increase its
exports (peanuts, beans, cotton, cattle, laborers).[80] Only in the long
term (through decreasing ecological damage, saving on flood relief,
and improving the soil) could it turn into the hard currency or taxes
the government wanted; and the government was not much interested
in such a remote payoff in such uncertain times.

LOCAL EFFORTS:
REFORESTATION AND ITS DISCONTENTS

Provincial governments also encouraged local reforestation efforts. Beginning in 1922, the provincial OEI not only made seedlings available
but ordered each county to set up a nursery, sell subsidized saplings
and seedlings to people who wanted to plant them, organize mass
plantings on public land at Qing-Ming Festival, and create a county
forestry society with subcounty branches.[81]

The forestry societies were primarily designed to protect trees: each
and every report emphasized that this task was much more difficult
than planting or caring for trees.[82] Between 1918 and 1920, most
Shandong counties planted more than fifty thousand trees per year;
some planted more than five hundred thousand each year.[83] However,
in a 1933 survey only two counties in the Shandong part of Huang-
Yun reported having more trees than they had reported planting in
1918–20.[84] The Heze rural reconstruction group estimated in 1934
that at most 2 percent of the trees planted reached maturity.[85] This
figure is particularly striking since Heze had not only twenty-seven

80. For lists of the products imported and exported by various Shandong counties,
with approximate values, see *SSYZ* 2:151–201.

81. *QYHK*, no. 11 (Feb. 1923), *lunshuo*, 1–7.

82. See, for instance, *QYHK*, no. 4 (Jan. 1921), *ge xian shiye zhuangkuang*, 2; no.
5 (July 1921), *ge xian shiye zhuangkuang*, 19–20; no. 6 (Jan. 1922), *gongdu*, 27;
XCJSXK 4:18 (Feb. 1935), 12.

83. *QYHK*, no. 11 (Feb. 1923), *gongdu*, 3–9.

84. For planting figures, see note 63 above; for 1933 numbers, see *SSYZ* 5:384–
402.

85. *XCJSXK* 4:18 (Feb. 1935), 10.

forestry society branches and the local militia protecting trees, but a larger-than-average squad of twenty-four full-time mounted "tree police."[86] Many counties set up paid forest patrols of twenty to thirty members (most Huang-Yun counties had fifty to a hundred paid police in the 1930s), but the forestry societies had the main responsibility for tree security.[87]

If cotton societies were more coercive, less village-based, and less egalitarian than crop-watching societies, tree protection went still further in these directions. In Xiajin, for instance, forest society membership required owning two *mu* of trees, far more than most people had. Counties without property requirements charged membership dues.[88]

Forestry societies also took a much harder line toward fuel gatherers than crop-watching or even cotton societies. County reports to the provincial OEI routinely referred to tree cutters as "bandits" (*fei*) or at least "thieves" (*zei*); by contrast, cotton rushing was merely termed a "bad custom," and participants were distinguished from "bandits."[89] Regular crop-watching societies generally assessed light penalties for stealing grain, as we saw in the last chapter, while cotton societies aimed at slightly higher penalties (about ¥1) for cotton rushing.[90] By contrast, the fine for harming a tree less than three years old began at ¥1 per tree and escalated rapidly if the tree was older or if it was actually cut down. Penalties for not cooperating in planting began at ¥100, payable in money or labor, and went up to ¥1,000. (These penalties were presumably intended for whole villages, although the text refers to "people," probably meaning village leaders.)[91] According to the province's model rules for forestry societies, those who had "harmed" more than ten trees were to be sentenced by the county magistrate to hard labor; anyone who set fire to more than ten trees (as one might to clear a piece of land) would theoretically be sentenced to life at hard labor.[92]

86. *QYHK*, no. 7 (May 1922), *ge xian quanye baogao*, 29.

87. For the approximate size of the Gonganju in each Shandong county in 1933 see *Shandong zheng su shicha ji*.

88. *QYHK*, no. 16 (July 1923), *gongdu*, 42; 15 (June 1923), *gongdu*, 13.

89. *QYHK*, no. 16 (July 1923), *quanye baogao*, 10.

90. *QYHK*, no. 22 (March 1924), *gongdu*, 16. During the Japanese occupation, penalties in Houxiazhai, En xian, got as high as ¥3–¥5 (see *Chūgoku Nōson* 4:431), but this appears to have represented a recent increase.

91. *QYHK* no. 29 (Sept. 1924), *shiye gongdu*, 2, 4.

92. *QYHK*, no. 29 (Sept. 1924), *shiye gongdu*, 4.

There is no reason to think that these harsher penalties were a result of violence by fuel gatherers (who were often children). Rather,
they appear to reflect frustration at the high cost and near universality
of "illegal" fuel gathering. Of course, by labeling such widespread behavior "banditry" and setting very harsh penalties, the forest patrols
cut themselves off further from any possibility of popular cooperation.
This spiral is a familiar pattern in the enforcement of forest regulations
in numerous "early modern" societies.[93] That the problem was common, however, did not make it any easier to solve.

Little is known about how closely these rules were followed; in
many places, the chaos of the years after their promulgation (1923)
must have made them a dead letter. Still, in some places, the patrols
may have been fairly effective; several counties claimed survival rates
of more than 60 percent, compared with less than 10 percent in the
counties with the worst security problems.[94] Many tree societies stipu-
lated that 50 percent or more of a mature tree's value belonged to
them, rather than to the owner of the land it was planted on. Thus
societies that planted trees and thereafter provided nothing except
security for this "crop" received 50 percent of it, while tenants who
farmed annual crops in this area generally received 40 percent or
less.[95] Even at this rate, though, the societies could claim they were
offering a bargain. In Deng county a three-year-old sapling was worth
three times as much as a two-year-old one; if it lasted longer, it would
appreciate even faster.[96]

It is also important to note how far these organizations were from
the late-nineteenth-century model of village crop watching discussed
in chapter 2. Although crop-watching organizations were often pro-

93. For a general discussion, see dissertation, 168–79. On New England, see William Cronon, *Changes in the Land: Indians, Colonists, and the Ecology of New England* (New York, 1983), 110–11; see 196, n. 4, for various references to the same phenomenon in early modern Europe, particularly England. Even Europe's relatively strong
states had problems of this kind as late as the nineteenth century; see, for instance, John
M. Merriman, "The Demoiselles of the Ariège, 1829–1831," in *1830 in France*, ed.
John M. Merriman (New York, 1975), 87–118.

94. *QYHK*, no. 12 (March 1923), *ge xian chengji baogao*, 32; no. 13 (April 1923),
gongdu, 14, 54, *ge xian chengji baogao*, 8; no. 14 (May 1923), *quanye xiaoxi*, 8.

95. See, for instance, He Yunlong, "Heze nongcun de shishi," *Nongye zhoubao* 4:14
(April 12, 1935), 489, and "Lubei shi xian nongye diaocha baogao," 13; more generally, see Huang, *Peasant Economy*, 205, 209–12. Fifty percent was probably the
single most common rate, but higher rates were not uncommon and lower ones were.
See also Mantetsu, *Santō no Mensaku*, 55.

96. *QYHK*, no. 25 (June 1924), *gongdu*, 8.

moted by higher officials, they remained firmly village-based, village-led, and village-controlled: they protected the crops they chose, to the extent they chose, through a mixture of threats, concessions, and (usually small) penalties they chose. Forestry societies, in contrast, were formal organizations that were not based on the village, often restricted membership, and claimed the lion's share of the value they protected. Essentially, the provincial government, recognizing that counties could not provide security for trees, instructed local governments to charter profit-seeking organizations to do this work. The governments then granted such organizations the power to give orders both to village heads and to the new, salaried, forest patrols—that is, to both the formal and informal subcounty government.[97] The Heze tree societies created by Liang Shuming's rural reconstruction group in the 1930s, all of which were based in market towns rather than villages, went still further in relying on the profit motive for their members and coercion for others.[98]

Evidence of comparative efficacy is spottier for tree protection than for protection of U.S. cotton varieties, but here, too, northwest Shandong organizations appear to have been more successful than their southwestern counterparts.[99] The only other successes were those of private companies guarding consolidated plots of trees. In Dong'a, a forestry company created by Jining investors was very successful for several years, but it frequently clashed with nearby communities; when local government was weakened by nearby military clashes during the 1928 Northern Expedition, there were riots and arson on the company's property.[100] The new county government then dissolved the company for being "unvirtuous" (*bu shan*). Although the provincial government gave permission in 1929 for the company to be reconstituted "under party [Guomindang] supervision," it was less effective

97. *QYHK*, no. 11 (Feb. 1923), *ge xian chengji baogao*, 1; no. 12 (March 1923), *ge xian chengji baogao*, 23; no. 13 (April 1923), *gongdu*, 63; no. 15 (June 1923), *gongdu*, 14.

98. See dissertation, 176–77, and accompanying notes for an extended discussion of this case; the original source is *XCJSXK* 4:18 (Feb. 1935), 10–11.

99. On northwestern counties, see *QYHK*, no. 7 (May 1922), *ge xian shiye zhuangkuang*, 13; no. 10 (Jan. 1923), *ge xian shiye zhuangkuang*, 4; no. 12 (March 1923), *gongdu*, 23, 32, 44; no. 13 (April 1923), *gongdu*, 14, 44, 54, *ge xian chengji baogao*, 8; no. 14 (May 1923), *quanye xiaoxi*, 8; on southwestern counties, no. 5 (July 1921), *ge xian shiye zhuangkuang*, 20; no. 22 (March 1924), *quanye xiaoxi*, 3–7, 13.

100. Ibid., no. 22 (March 1924), *gongdu*, 22; also *NSGB* 2:2 (Sept. 1915), *zhengshi*, 13; *Dong'a xianzhi* 7:2a–2b.

thereafter, and Dong'a reported less forest in 1933 than in 1918.[101] The close organization of the tightly knit villages of southwest Shandong, so useful for traditional crop watching and defense, was of no help with these new security problems.

The different degrees of failure in different parts of Huang-Yun, however, are much less significant than the failure of reforestation in Huang-Yun as a whole. People's desperate needs for fuel created extreme, often unmanageable security problems in most areas. And science could not provide a technical fix for trees as it had for cotton, making plants mature before some culturally significant day arrived. Ultimately, any hope for reversing Huang-Yun's environmental decay lay outside the region.

ECOLOGY, TRANSPORTATION, AND MARGINALITY

Failures like these led a 1936 Japanese study to conclude that improved flood control throughout inland North China required railroad building: railroads, it said, were the only way to give people in these areas an alternative to burning everything that could slow erosion.[102] Certainly the fuel price difference between, say, Heze and Dezhou would have made it attractive to ship between them were a means better than the ox-cart available. Moreover, if more of Huang-Yun had been able to spend hard currency on fuel from elsewhere, the provincial and national governments might well have been more interested in providing alternatives.

Huang-Yun's waterways will be discussed in the next two chapters. Before that it is worth looking at why most of the area was left outside the rail network. The story helps explain how the region wound up being isolated and thus marginal to the logic of self-strengthening; it also illustrates that logic at work.

Along with the lines actually built in Shandong before 1949—the Tianjin-Pukou railway along the eastern edge of Huang-Yun and the Qingdao-Jinan railway—the Germans, who had the railway concession for the province until 1914, originally planned four other lines; two would have gone through the middle of Huang-Yun.[103] The only

101. See p. 13a of October 1932 report in JD2:AH119.
102. Mantetsu, *Santō Chihō no Kōka Suisai Jōkyō* (Tianjin, 1936), 59.
103. Vera Schmidt, *Die Deutsche Eisenbahnpolitik in Shantung* (Wiesbaden, 1976),

line that eventually did touch Huang-Yun was not originally included. In all these cases, local interests wanted the railroad, but higher authorities were more concerned that the wrong party not build the railroad than that the railroad be built. The one success for local interests—the creation of a spur line to Jining—came about precisely because this line was an alternative to a route that many powerful people saw as a threat to China's sovereignty. Where this political element was absent, provincial and national figures were generally indifferent to linking Huang-Yun to the coast and hostile to having foreigners do it.

The Sino-German agreements on railroad concessions were re-negotiated several times in the last decade of the Qing. Aside from finances, the principal issues were mining rights along the railroads, management of completed railroads, plans for routes announced by Germany in 1898 but not begun during the next decade, and the precise route of the Tianjin-Pukou railroad.[104] The first two issues did not affect Huang-Yun since its railroads were never built. Two planned railroads concern us: a southern one from Yanzhou to Kaifeng via Jining and Caozhou and a northern one from Jinan to Xundefu (Zhili) via Changqing, Chiping, Zhangdefu, Nanle, Wei-xian, and Pingxian, with a spur line to Linqing and Xiajin.[105] These lines would have brought most of Huang-Yun firmly into the rail network.

After much dispute, Germany agreed in 1913 to allow these lines to be Chinese-built with German financing and with mining rights reserved for Germany.[106] During World War I, Japan claimed Germany's rights in Shandong. Eventually, the Chinese government decided that it preferred not building these lines to building them with the Japanese. Over the next twenty-five years, there were periodic flurries of interest in the Jinan to Xundefu line as an all-Chinese project, and the Japanese listed it as a planned construction project during

---

136–40; see also Li Yushu, ed., *Zhong Ri guanxi shiliao* (Taibei, 1976), 6:14–15, 43–44, 134–37.

104. Zhongguo jiaotongbu, *Jiaotong shi*, 3531–38; Schmidt, *Deutsche Eisenbahn-politik*, 138–40.

105. Zhongguo jiaotongbu, *Jiaotong shi*, 3533. On an early plan to build part of the southern line as a Chinese project, see *Dongfang zazhi* 1:8 (8/25/GX 30), jiaotong, 85.

106. Li Yushu, *Zhong Ri guanxi shiliao*, 6:135–36; see also Lee En-han, *China's Quest for Railroad Autonomy, 1904–1911* (Singapore, 1977), 171–72.

World War II; but no work was ever done.[107] Moreover, there was not much pressure from North Huang-Yun communities to have the line built; during the only such campaign, Linqing and Liaocheng petitioners could not agree on a route to suggest.[108] As we shall soon see, this is quite different from what happened in South Huang-Yun.

Plans for the southern line quickly became entangled in disputes over the route of the Tianjin-Pukou (Shanghai) line. Germany wanted this line to veer to the east in southern Shandong and wanted to build a spur line to Qufu, so that their mining rights would be in the most promising areas.[109] A group of Jining degree-holders, some of whom held public office and some of whom were also involved in commerce, wanted the trunk line to go through Jining; they feared for the city's future if it did not at least get a spur line. The omnipresent Pan Fu—of whom more in chapter 5—led the charge.[110]

The group took the routing issue to the gentry of all four provinces the Tianjin-Pukou line would go through and connected it to the burgeoning "rights recovery movement."[111] In doing so, they placed more emphasis on denying mining rights to Germany than on the commercial advantages of bringing the railroad to Jining, the hub of southwest Shandong and a place where railroad and canal shipping could meet.[112] The one Jining petition to higher authorities that made a positive case for Jining did so in terms of another self-strengthening idea: it argued that concentration of commerce in Jining rather than

107. Matsuzaki Yujiro, *Santō Shō no Sai Nishiki*, 12–13, 33–36; Wu Xiangxiang, ed., *Lu an shan hou yuebao tekan—tielu* (Taibei, 1971 [1923]), 94–95.

108. Interview notes, Linqing and Liaocheng, November 1985.

109. Yuan Jingbo, "'Yan Ji zhixian' yu 'Jining huochezhan' xiujian xiao shi kaolue," draft dated Sept. 25, 1982, for inclusion in *Jining wenshi ziliao*, no. 1 (March 1986?); see esp. 5, and *Shandong zazhi*, no. 79 (11/30/XT 2), *lunshuo*, 2a.

110. Yuan Jingbo, "Jining huochezhan," is the most complete account of this affair (the author's grandfather, Yuan Jingxi, played a major role in these events). A more readily accessible account is included in *Jining xianzhi* (1929), 3:56a–68a. On Pan Fu's participation, see *SDZZ*, no. 4 (2/29/GX 34), *shiye*, 15; no. 5 (3/15/GX 34), *zhuanjian*, 1–5; no. 11 (6/15/GX 34), *zalu*, 1–2; no. 44 (10/30/XT 1), 26b; no. 45 (11/15/XT 1), 11a; lists of other prominent participants may be found in no. 41 (9/15/XT 1), 24b–25a, and no. 45 (11/15/XT 1), 11a.

111. Yuan Jingbo, "Jining huochezhan," 5–6; Wang Shouzhong, "Qing mo Shandong shouhui lu kuang li quan yundong," 258–59. See also *SDZZ*, no. 5 (3/15/GX 34), *zhuanjian*, esp. 1, 3, 5.

112. *SDZZ*, no. 4 (2/29/GX 34), *shiye*, 15; no. 5 (3/15/GX 34), *zhuanjian*, 1–5; no. 11 (6/15/GX 34), *zalu*, 1–2; no. 44 (10/30/XT 1), 26b. *SDZZ*, no. 41 (9/15/XT 1), 24b–25a; no. 45 (11/15/XT 1), 11a; no. 79 (11/30/XT 2), 2b, all include public statements with this emphasis. For a similar argument about the northern line, made in 1913 by Shandong governor Zhou Ziji, see Zhongguo jiaotongbu, *Jiaotong shi*, 3535.

Yanzhou or Qufu was desirable because a further accumulation of commercial profits there might spur industrialization.[113] Above all, however, the petitioners emphasized that the original route threatened China's sovereignty and its control of resources (especially coal) necessary for modernization. This argument, and numerous elite connections, rallied the gentry and governors of Jiangsu, Anhui, Shandong, and Zhili behind the Jining proposal.[114]

These pressures eventually forced a compromise in which the main route was somewhere between the two original positions, and a spur line to Jining was built.[115] This line was to be the first stage of the Yanzhou to Kaifeng line—which, at last report, has still not been completed.[116]

The Jining organizers of this battle were eager to tie their home area into the coastal economy and were adept at reaching elites elsewhere with nationalist appeals. Well-attended meetings were held in Tianjin, Beijing, Kaifeng, and Yantai, and signatures for the petition were gathered all along the planned Tianjin-Pukou route.[117] The strength of this group contrasts not only with the weakness of Linqing and Liaocheng's lobbying for a railway, but with the absence of any public campaign in favor of Yanzhou. This unusual unity and effectiveness doubtless owed much to energetic, skillful organizing. However, it was also rooted in the unusually close ties between merchant and official circles in Jining, which we saw in our discussion of credit markets and will see again when we look at the politics of water control.

Neither the nationalist nor the mercenary arguments of the Jining elite seem to have mobilized rural people or Jining city's less elite citizens, however: the campaign never developed nearly as broad a base as did comparable movements in Zhejiang, Jiangsu, Sichuan, and other provinces.[118] The local weakness of Jining's nationally well connected elites will remain an important theme through the rest of this book. Some of the conflicts between more locally oriented and more outwardly oriented elites were touched upon in our discussion of

113. *SDZZ*, no. 45 (11/15/XT 1), 11a.
114. Yuan Jingbo, "Jining huochezhan," 6–8.
115. Ibid., pp. 7–8.
116. See "Foreign Funds for Railways," *Beijing Review* 29:21 (May 26, 1986), 28.
117. *SDZZ*, no. 4 (2/29/GX 34), *shiye*, 15; no. 8 (4/30/GX 34), *zalu*, 1; no. 11 (6/15/GX 34), *zalu*, 1–2; no. 41 (9/15/XT 1), 25a.
118. See, e.g., Wang Shouzhong, "Qing mo Shandong shouhui lu kuang li quan yundong," 262.

credit, and especially in the discussion of why crop improvement schemes failed in southwest Shandong. As we shall see at length in the case of water control, these divisions made figures like Pan Fu much less effective when the projects they promoted required more rural cooperation than the railroad campaign did.

It is also noteworthy that the effective appeals these gentry and merchants made to the national elite were based almost entirely on China's political needs rather than their region's economic predicament. Huang-Yun needed to be incorporated into the "coastal" political economy to get help for its environmental and economic problems, whether from the government or the market. To get the infrastructure that would bring more of Huang-Yun into that world, its leaders had to argue in terms of "self-strengthening" concerns— that is, sovereignty or hard currency—rather than local welfare.

Thus, these appeals had to stress what Huang-Yun could export rather than what it needed to import. None of the many Chinese pleas I have seen for improving transport in Huang-Yun mentions access to badly needed imports as an expected benefit, though foreigners sometimes mentioned this. And, as we have seen, specialization in cotton could proceed without modern transportation. As long as the area's exports—which, contrary to the usual pattern for a hinterland, were less bulky than certain imports it desperately needed—did not need new infrastructure to get to market, economic arguments would not help Huang-Yun.[119]

Huang-Yun's banditry did attract the attention of higher levels of government, in part because it was "exportable" to areas in which the government had a greater stake.[120] Surviving Republican-period

119. For a summary of the argument that areas far from major population centers ("peripheries" in our terms) will normally specialize in products that are bulkier per unit of value and produce less income per unit of area, see Donald McCloskey, *The Applied Theory of Price* (New York, 1985), 416–17; conversely, "core" areas are likely to produce items worth more per bulk and to sell at least some of them to places that do not produce such things—probably peripheries.

120. See, for instance, Xia Lianju, "Shandong duli qianhou," 49, who claims that in the early post-1911 period, the control of banditry in Shandong (and thus control of the garrison there) was considered the key to control of Shandong as a whole. Esherick (*Boxer Uprising*, 20) also notes that western and especially southwestern Shandong "exported" bandits. The southwest produced the antimissionary incident that led to German intervention in 1897 (see, e.g., Esherick, *Boxer Uprising*, 110–30), the Lincheng bandit incident that ousted Tian Zhongyu as governor (*NCH*, April 5, 1924, p. 8), and the only important internally generated challenge to a Republican regime in Shandong (Lu Suwen's rebellion; see *NCH*, Dec. 20, 1924, p. 487, and follow-up in succeeding issues).

appeals from western Shandong for provincial or national help in suppressing banditry say less about the region's own plight than about the threat that spreading banditry might pose to the Tianjin-Pukou railway.[121] Higher authorities took the petitioners at their word and prepared plans for defending the railroad.[122]

In fact, suppression of banditry in general provides an excellent example of how sovereignty-preserving logic could affect the distribution of public services. Bandits who kidnaped foreigners during the Republic could be reasonably sure that they would be paid off quickly by Chinese governments, which feared foreign reprisals; for the same reason, bandits who actually killed foreigners met with unusually swift and determined suppression. The suppression of "ordinary" banditry and kidnaping, however, was left to local authorities.[123] Regions such as Huang-Yun, which were just barely touched by China's rail network, were only slightly better served by the sovereignty-preserving logic of self-strengthening than they were by its economic logic.

In sum, Huang-Yun's ecological decline was far from just a Malthusian process. Nor was it a result of problems created by the Grand Canal. On the contrary, it was the abandonment of the old hydraulic system that hurt Huang-Yun. More broadly, Ming-Qing statecraft before the mid-nineteenth century helped maintain Huang-Yun's precarious ecological stability in the face of intense demographic pressure. In part, this assistance was simply a byproduct of the state's execution of a self-interested task—feeding its capital and army—according to a logic no different from that of state makers elsewhere. In part, though, it may also be seen as an intentional result of a "benevolent" statecraft, which consciously concentrated its efforts in places where market forces were inadequate to assure subsistence: aiding the development of the northwest grain trade, maintaining the "ever-normal" granaries, subsidizing well digging in Shaanxi, or promoting the creation of infrastructure in the southwest. Whichever motives

121. See, for instance, the lengthy undated petition (probably April 29, 1918) from Pan Fu, Zhou Ziji, and twenty-eight others and the follow-up petition of May 1, 1918, in JD00:AH1164.

122. See Neiwubu jingzheng si 3 hao ke, "Pi Shandong tongxianghui Ma Long biao deng," May 18, 1918, in JD00:AH1164; for a later, more detailed instance, see the lengthy plans for defending the railroad (and nothing else in western Shandong) in JD00:AH1166 (Sept.–Oct. 1923). See also Franck, *Wandering*, 303.

123. For a general discussion, see Philip Billingsley, *Banditry in Republican China* (Stanford, 1988).

one stresses, the result was that Huang-Yun got wood through long-distance trade, stone shipped on government-maintained waterways, and funds for flood control from southern taxpayers.

In the mid-nineteenth century, however, all of this changed. The Chinese state, faced with foreign enemies and insurrection in its richest regions, turned toward a self-strengthening logic. In that scheme, what mattered was whether a project contributed to maintaining control of contested areas of China, building China's modern sector, or reducing the debt that threatened the state's sovereignty over China as a whole. As both fragmentation and indebtedness worsened in the twentieth century, these priorities became still more insistent. The state shifted its attention to key regions rather than laggard regions; and with the rise of ocean shipping, Huang-Yun ceased to be a key region of any sort. This shift meant the end of the Grand Canal subsidy of Huang-Yun, with devastating ecological consequences.

Moreover, the mercantilist logic by which the balance of trade came before welfare meant that coastal areas would get help in replacing imports, while such areas as Huang-Yun would receive little help in obtaining needed imports from Manchuria or elsewhere. Since no strong argument could be made within this logic of self-strengthening for tying Huang-Yun more firmly into the new coastal-centered networks, the new transport grid bypassed it; thus it became increasingly isolated and marginal. And given that marginality, there was less reason than ever for the state to worry about providing other services—water control, suppression of banditry, and the like—to Huang-Yun, unless its problems threatened to touch more strategic areas.

Relative isolation also meant greater autonomy, however, from which some local power holders benefited. Examples of this were evident in the cases of credit and cotton. Such groups largely stood aside as more outward-oriented groups tried to secure rail links between Huang-Yun and the larger political economy. But when the issue was what to do about the area's hydraulic system—which the state was abandoning for the same self-strengthening reasons—everyone from big traders to peasants to clerks who were paid to ignore reclaimed land had a stake, and all of them influenced what happened. This larger case of state abandonment and varied local responses concludes our study of Huang-Yun's transformation into a periphery.

Sowing cotton near Linqing, 1919. The whole family participates, with the daughter-in-law and children doing the pulling. Photo by Clifton O'Neal Carey; Clifton O'Neal Carey papers, Michigan Historical Collections, Bentley Historical Library, University of Michigan.

Member of a local forest patrol with sign forbidding entry to a grove of saplings, Shandong, 1924. The caption that accompanied this photo in *China Weekly Recorder* (February 16, 1924, p. 431) says that these signs and patrols were "more feared than the mandates" and regular troops of the government.

Woman and children resting while gathering stalks for fuel. Everyone has a rake and a basket; the ground itself is nearly bare. Photo by Clifton O'Neal Carey, 1919; Clifton O'Neal Carey papers, Michigan Historical Collections, Bentley Historical Library, University of Michigan.

Crowd gathered on the lower lock of the Grand Canal at Jining to watch the arrival of American engineers drawing plans for the ill-fated Grand Canal restoration project, 1919. Though slow and plagued by high fees, the canal remained a significant commercial waterway from Jining as far south as Jiangnan—and a major flood hazard for surrounding farms. Photo by Clifton O'Neal Carey; Clifton O'Neal Carey papers, Michigan Historical Collections, Bentley Historical Library, University of Michigan.

Boats carrying roots on Grand Canal, 1919. After 1901 large boats could not use the canal between Jining and Linqing, but it was still used by smaller vessels for local transport of bulky commodities such as these roots, destined to become fuel or animal feed. Photo by Clifton O'Neal Carey; Clifton O'Neal Carey papers, Michigan Historical Collections, Bentley Historical Library, University of Michigan.

Stalks and wood used to protect an earthen dike on Grand Canal, 1919. When properly built and maintained, such works could be fairly effective; but even then they were no match for stone and brick, and they were not suitable for the most dangerous places on the canal or Yellow River. Photo by Clifton O'Neal Carey; Clifton O'Neal Carey papers, Michigan Historical Collections, Bentley Historical Library, University of Michigan.

Work party repairing earthen dike near Grand Canal, 1918. Note the large party, simple tools, and the near absence of trees, which were supposed to be planted all along the canal to strengthen the banks. Photo by Clifton O'Neal Carey; Clifton O'Neal Carey papers, Michigan Historical Collections, Bentley Historical Library, University of Michigan.

CHAPTER IV

Sold Down the River?

The decay of North China's hydraulic system will take up the next two chapters and conclude our discussion of the marginalization of Huang-Yun. This chapter focuses on the political, social, and physical sources of decay; chapter 5 looks at the impact of this decay on Huang-Yun and on attempts to reverse it. Thus this chapter continues a central theme of chapter 3: how changes in Chinese state-making strategy led to the "sacrifice" of Huang-Yun as the state concentrated on more strategic regions. It then discusses how this change in high-level policy altered the configuration of local interests that affected Huang-Yun water control. This analysis of the state's differential impact on different regions and of the state's role as a provider of services will also be used to refine current approaches to modern Chinese state making, which tend to focus more narrowly on the state's extractive capacities.

This chapter first looks at the political realities that caused the national government to single out inland hydraulics for massive budget cuts. It then describes the extent of these cuts and explores their significance by estimating what could have been done with old levels of funding and newly available techniques. The following section shows how the central government's withdrawal also weakened precisely those local interests that the state had hoped would take up the slack. This was particularly true in North Huang-Yun, where elites concerned with water transport were particularly weak, and the central government's withdrawal from water control was almost total. Next the chapter examines the technical problems of Huang-Yun water control and explains how declining interest in inland water transport led to disastrous corner cutting in inland flood control, in particular the adoption in the Huang-Yun part of Shandong of techniques known to be inferior to those used nearer the coast and in most of Henan and Zhili. It also shows that while these techniques involved lower state spending, they were actually more expensive for peasants, whose "informal" deliveries of local goods and labor soared under the new system. The next section connects this choice of techniques to administrative problems and corruption inherent in the ad hoc river control system that replaced central government efforts in much of twentieth-century Huang-Yun and to general patterns of state making.

The final section brings us full circle, merging the discussion of government priorities in water control with our earlier discussions of self-strengthening and regional priorities. It shows that the funding cuts and institutional changes imposed on the hydraulic system at the end of the nineteenth century not only shifted the burden of water control (especially Yellow River control) but redistributed the flood problem itself from areas near the coast (and, later, areas near the railways) to inland areas that had become less important to both Jinan and Beijing. This shift and its results, in turn, link inland hydraulic problems to China's changing place in the international state system and to the different degrees to which different regions had become part of larger marketing networks. Chapter 5 will finish the story, looking at the consequences of hydraulic decay and at local responses to this prolonged crisis.

THE CENTRAL GOVERNMENT'S WITHDRAWAL

Huang-Yun's hydraulic problems long predate 1890. Although the entire region was touched by the Grand Canal, the Yellow River, and the canal's tributaries, it never knew the full-fledged system of large-scale public works described by Qing statutes and theorists of the "hydraulic society."[1] But after 1890, a combination of new challenges and decreased attention from the central government created a new crisis in the region.

---

1. See, for instance, Karl Wittfogel, *Oriental Despotism* (New Haven, 1957).

The central government's withdrawal had two components. First, the government's priorities and the pressures it faced changed, and riverworks funds were diverted to other things: in the 1860s to tax reduction in the Lower Yangzi Valley and the defeat of rebels, and in the 1890s to the New Army, foreign indemnities, and modernization projects in Beijing and Tianjin. Second, "reforms" in the 1890s reshuffled the remaining riverworks funds and personnel in ways that did not reduce flooding but did change where floods occurred: to a great extent the flood problem was redistributed from higher-priority areas to Huang-Yun.

In 1852–55, the Yellow River shifted its bed to Shandong; for centuries before, it had gone through Jiangsu to the sea. The Yellow River posed enormous flood control problems in its own right. Moreover, its new course turned the previously reliable Shandong section of the Grand Canal into the most technically difficult one and complicated the control of the area's smaller rivers.[2] Huang-Yun had no institutions capable of handling these massive new problems, and the Qing government, preoccupied with the Taiping and Nian rebellions, was not about to create one. Instead, grain tribute was shifted from canal to sea transport. Areas along the Yellow River's new course—many of them occupied by the Nian, anyway—were left to fend for themselves. Fortunately, the river caused very little trouble during the first decade in its new bed.[3]

Many important figures favored institutionalizing this interim solution. Ending canal-borne grain tribute was a boon to the Lower Yangzi provinces and was crucial to the tax cuts that were supposed to help restore stability there.[4] Yangzi Valley elites had long wanted to abolish canal-borne tribute, which had been growing steadily more expensive. (The cost of a "sample" trip from Hubei, for instance, had risen from 130 ounces of silver [*liang*] in 1732 to 700–800 *liang* in 1821.) Now they had their chance.[5]

Others also found the old tribute system hard to deal with. The hereditary soldiers who staffed the tribute boats found it harder and

---

2. *NYHH*, pt. 1, pp. 2–3; Hou Renzhi, ed., *Xu tianxia qun guo li bing shu, Shandong zhi bu* (Beijing, 1940), 24.

3. *HH*, 358–59; Wu Tongju, ed., *Zai xu xing shui jin jian* (Taibei, 1966), 10:4129, 4143. These two basic sources agree on listing three "major" floods between 1855 and 1879.

4. Polachek, "Gentry Hegemony," 211–56, esp. 226–27, 253–54.

5. Hoshi Ayao, *Dai Unga*, 223–27.

harder to survive on their rations; and despite increases in the amount of private goods they could legally carry and trade, they turned increasingly to smuggling, raiding nearby villages, or fleeing. When canal personnel fled, canalside counties had to provide substitutes, at a cost that could run into thousands of *liang*. These problems seem to have grown especially rapidly during the Daoguang reign (1821–50).[6] However, post-1855 discussions of tribute and canal policy do not explicitly mention them.

The long wars of the 1850s and 1860s put inertia on the side of those urging an end to canal-borne tribute. So did nineteenth-century progress in ocean shipping. The growth of Tianjin and Shanghai created powerful commercial and political interests favoring ocean transport; Li Hongzhang, among others, depended on commercial taxes from these ports.[7]

Finally, the court's mid-nineteenth-century shift to promoting Manchurian development gradually created an alternative source of grain for the capital and the northern troops. Even in the early Qing, growing private shipments of Manchurian grain had made Beijing less dependent on grain tribute than it had been in the Ming.[8] These shipments might eventually have surpassed southern grain in the capital's food supply even without the mid-nineteenth-century shocks, but this displacement would not have occurred soon. As it was, those shocks greatly accelerated this switch, as the interruption of tribute in the 1850s and the threat of foreign encroachment in the northeast helped convince the Qing that they should settle more Han farmers in the Manchus' ancestral home.[9]

The centuries-old system did not disappear without an argument, however. As rebellions subsided in the mid-1860s, discussion of what to do about the Grand Canal and the Yellow River resumed at full volume.

One side advocated forcing the Yellow River back into its old course. This strategy would have three advantages. First, the old offi-

6. Ibid., 196–206, 210–13; David Kelley, "Temples and Tribute Fleets," *Modern China* 8:3 (July 1982), 361–91.

7. Polachek, "Gentry Hegemony," 242–43; Spector, *Li Hung-chang*, 213–16.

8. Wu Jianyong, "Qingdai Beijing de liangshi gongying," in *Beijing lishi yu xianshi yanjiu* (Beijing, 1989), 167–86, esp. 172–73.

9. Robert Lee, *The Manchurian Frontier in Ch'ing History* (Cambridge, Mass., 1970), 76, 116–19, 185. Lee emphasizes that although the Taiping Rebellion began the "period of transition" in Manchuria, settlement accelerated much more rapidly after foreign encroachment intensified in 1895.

cial dikes (*guan di*; hereafter, "official embankments") on that route could be used, with only minor extensions and reinforcement. By contrast, accepting the river's new route would eventually entail building a comparable set of dikes all along both sides of the river's new three hundred plus–mile "tail."[10] For the time being, that section was lined with dikes built by "the people" under official "supervision" (*min nian*). These were much smaller bulwarks, and they cost the central government nothing; local communities built and maintained them.[11] Since the river had not yet seriously silted up its new bed, these barriers were still adequate, but eventually, accepting the new course would require large-scale, centrally financed and organized construction. Second, this group argued that the river's old course was more natural and stable; they feared that no matter what sorts of works were built, there would be endless flooding along the new course, until the river forced its way back to its old bed.[12]

Finally, this group argued that returning the Yellow River to its old course would vastly simplify Grand Canal management and would allow the grain tribute to function as of old. While the old intersection of these waterways near Huaian had often flooded, the canal had rarely been dry—a more serious obstacle to transportation. The shifting of the Yellow River had cut off the smaller rivers that used to provide water for the roughly seventy miles of canal between the new Yellow River crossing at Dong'a and Linqing, leaving China's only north-south inland waterway with a dry patch in the middle. The easiest temporary expedient—flooding this part of the canal with Yellow River water as the tribute fleet approached—deposited huge amounts of silt in the canal bed and so made things worse in the long run. It would be better, these officials argued, to face the costs of restoring the only truly workable system before they became still higher.[13]

The opposing position—accepting the Yellow River's new course and its consequences for the canal—was most consistently and effectively represented by Li Hongzhang. It was supported by a de facto coalition of "restorationists" interested in reducing taxes in the Yangzi Valley heartland and those with interests in the development of the

10. Wu Tongju, *Zai xu*, 4133–34; see also Polachek, "Gentry Hegemony," 252.
11. See the explanation in Wu Tongju, *Zai xu*, 3939.
12. Ibid., 4134.
13. *HH*, 351–52; see also Arthur Hummel, *Eminent Chinese of the Ch'ing Period* (Washington, D.C., 1943–44), 1:464–71, 554–56, 2:642–44, 723–25, 751–56, on specific participants in the debate and the positions they took.

treaty ports and coastal shipping. Li argued that dredging the nearly filled in old bed and doing dike repairs would be at least as expensive as diking the new route; more important, such a project might well fail, inviting a repeat of the 1852 disaster.[14] As early as 1857, Li said that the government should get on with the work of building official embankments along the new course.[15]

The new set of official embankments was not begun until 1872, after the last serious campaign to return to the old river bed had been defeated. Even then, the work went slowly. Delay had been costly; the new course already had large sediment deposits. The first half of the Guangxu reign (1875–91) saw several very bad Yellow River floods, particularly along the river's last 150 miles, from Jinan to the sea (that is, east of Huang-Yun). By 1884, *guan di* had been completed along the new course. Even then, interest in returning the river to its "natural" course did not disappear—Shandong governor Zhang Yao raised the idea again in 1886, and one last time after a huge Henan dike break in 1887 provided an opportunity to reroute the river out of Shandong. Once again, Li Hongzhang condemned this idea, and this time it died for good.[16]

But where did this leave the Grand Canal? During these years, the canal had been kept open; some tribute was shipped on it, but the vast majority now went by sea. While many argued that ocean freight was a cheaper and more reliable means of supplying the capital, they did not advocate abandoning the canal;[17] such a position would have been unacceptably radical. This left them in a peculiar position, at least implicitly. Canal upkeep was largely paid for by charges levied against the grain tribute shipped on the canal.[18] Thus, shipping tribute by sea would save little money as long as the canal was to be kept open anyway. At any rate, those who preferred the new course of the Yellow River generally passed over the Grand Canal issue quickly,

14. *HH*, 353; also Harold C. Hinton, *Grain Transport via the Grand Canal, 1845–1901*, Harvard Papers on China, no. 4 (Cambridge, Mass., 1950), 40.

15. *HH*, 357.

16. Ibid., 352–53, 356, 357.

17. Hoshi Ayao, *Dai Unga*, 219, 248, 250; Hinton, *Grain Transport*, 4:33; *qing dan* accompanying memorial of 8/2/GX 29 submitted by Zhou Fu, in LFZZ, GX 29, packet 26; *qing dan* dated 12/10/GX 31, no longer connected to its memorial, in LFZZ, GX 31, packet 39C.

18. Hoshi Ayao, *Dai Unga*, 248; *Shandong tongzhi*, 1915 edition, 1934 reprint (Governor Han Fuju listed as "editor"), 3463.

either keeping to the narrower issue of sea freight (or silver payments) versus canal-borne tribute or discussing only the Yellow River.

The canal was also a tricky subject for supporters of the old course. While they often argued that national security required an inland route for provisioning the capital and noted the economic benefits of a north-south canal, they could not deny that the Canal, Yellow River, and grain tribute administrations were cumbersome, expensive, and often corrupt.[19] Even the canal's principal beneficiaries were often dissatisfied. Jining merchants, for instance, were eager to see nearby locks maintained, but complained that the officials and troops in charge of them did poor work and demanded high "customary fees."[20] As noted above, the boatmen were often a problem for counties along the canal. Sharp cuts in Yellow River spending (1891) and Grand Canal spending (1901) were part of reforms aimed at reducing the number of troops and lower officials involved by substituting local, often semiprivate efforts. Publicly, many people argued that these cuts would therefore not hurt hydraulic maintenance. Some did worry that the cuts would cause problems, but nobody seems to have defended the old system.[21]

By 1890, then, the issue of where the Yellow River would flow—or at least where humans would try to make it flow—had been settled and dikes built. The Grand Canal issue was in limbo: the canal stayed open, and a small part of the tribute fleet continued to use it, but no major repairs were done.[22] However, continuing Yellow River floods and mounting fiscal problems soon forced further decisions.

In the late Guangxu period (1891–1908) water control budgets were cut sharply to free money for debt and indemnity payments, railroads, the New Army, and other "modern" projects.[23] Yellow River spending had been extremely loosely controlled until 1891; essentially,

19. For the national security argument, see note 75 below; for a later example, see the memorial of Gao Xixi, 1/30/GX 28 in LFZZ, GX 28, packet 51–55. For the economic benefits of a north-south canal, see memorials from censor Gao Xixi, 1/30/GX 28 (GX 28, packet 51–55); from Zhou Fu, 11/7/GX 29 (GX 29, packet 40); from Wu Tingyi, 10/21/GX 33 (GX 33, packet 56), all in LFZZ.

20. Chen Yunlong, ed., *Qiu pu Zhou shang shu (yu shan) quanji, Zhou Fu* (Taibei, 1966), 151–52, 165–66.

21. Wu Tongju, *Zai xu*, 3712, 4142, 4177; memorial from Zhou Fu, 11/7/GX 29 (GX 29, packet 40), in LFZZ.

22. Hinton, *Grain Transport*, 33, 37–38, 40.

23. Wu Tongju, *Zai xu*, 3860; memorial from Chen Kuilong of 7/4/GX 31, in LFZZ, GX 31, packet 62–66; more generally, see the following section of this chapter.

the relevant provincial governors spent whatever they thought necessary.[24] In 1891, however, the Shandong and Henan Yellow River budgets were set at 600,000 *liang* apiece, and Shandong changed its river control system (particularly for the westernmost part of the province) to concentrate diminished resources where it thought they were most needed.[25] Governors, particularly of Shandong, kept exceeding these budgets, requesting authority to spend more, and trying to reallocate other revenues.[26] However, no reliable sources were found, and expenditures declined steadily; *Shandong gongbao* estimated Yellow River expenditures at 992,000 *liang* per year for 1894–1900 and 670,000 per year for 1900–6.[27] Henan expenditures, more than 1,500,000 per year in the Daoguang period, declined to 423,000 by the end of the Qing.[28] Changing exchange rates also worked against Yellow River control, at least during the first part of the austerity period. The copper value of one (silver) tael fell 31 percent between 1891 and 1903; since most river supplies and wages were paid in copper, this was equivalent to cutting the Shandong budget further, from 600,000 to 412,500 *liang*.[29]

Further reforms and budget cuts came in 1901–2. The Boxer uprising had disrupted the remaining grain tribute and prevented even routine repairs on the increasingly dilapidated canal. During the disorder, people occupied the driest parts of the canal as farmland. The Boxer Indemnity greatly increased the financial strain on the Qing: in 1903, for instance, China had to make indemnity payments of more than 50,000,000 *liang*.[30] Grain tribute was abolished; the Shandong Grand Canal budget was cut from more than 160,000 to 75,000 *liang*.[31]

Once again, the announcements of these decisions ignored the ways in which the tribute system subsidized canal maintenance. The memorials made it clear that the canal should stay open but said nothing about how.[32] As we would expect, the results were quite different in North and South Huang-Yun. The North Shandong Grand Canal,

24. Chen Yunlong, *Zhou Fu*, 179; Wu Tongju, *Zai xu*, 3945.
25. *HWJB*, no. 1 (Fall 1919), 104–5.
26. Chen Yunlong, *Zhou Fu*, 205; Wu Tongju, *Zai xu*, 3729, 3734, 3748, 3806.
27. *Shandong gongbao*, no. 106 (Sept. 17, 1912), *wendu*, 2.
28. Wu Tongju, *Zai xu*, 3846, 3851–53, 4178.
29. Chen Yunlong, *Zhou Fu*, 204.
30. Immanuel Hsu, *The Rise of Modern China*, 2d ed. (New York, 1975), 496.
31. Chen Yunlong, *Zhou Fu*, 237–38.
32. Undated *qing dan*, probably originally accompanying Xiliang memorial of 2/21/GX 28; memorial from 22 Board of War and other capital officials of 1/17/GX 28, both

whose engineering needs were too complex for local solutions, was abandoned by the central government. In South Shandong, the problems were easier, local interests had more clout, and the central government continued to help manage the situation.

Funds and personnel for the South Shandong Grand Canal (from the Yellow River to the Jiangsu border) were cut but not eliminated, and the remaining river troops (*ying*) and the Jining canal office were made responsible for this section.[33] Thus, South Huang-Yun still received some state help in maintaining its infrastructure. As was the case with railroad building, Jining's place in the new order was less central than it had once been; it became the last stop on both the northbound canal and the westbound railroad, rather than a station between Beijing and the south. Still, South Huang-Yun remained linked to some of China's most economically dynamic areas through physical networks subsidized by others.

No authority comparable to the Jining canal office was ever created for the North Shandong Grand Canal. The subject was not discussed in any now extant memorial. Shandong governor (1901–4) Zhou Fu rarely mentioned this section either, despite his tremendous interest in waterways. A few allusions to Jining's commercial importance and its interregional trade[34] are as close as the memorials ever get to explaining why the reforms made provision for the southern but not the northern section (*beiyunhe*). As in the case of railroads—and the cases of wall building and other local infrastructure alluded to in chapter 1—North Huang-Yun elites lacked the strength and connections that would obtain significant state help in building infrastructure. And though, as we saw with credit and cotton, North Huang-Yun would be more successful than South Huang-Yun in profiting from new economic networks centered on the coast, these gains were widely dis-

---

in LFZZ, GX 28, packet 44–45; from Zhou Fu, 11/7/GX 29 (GX 29, packet 40), and from Wu Tingyi, 10/21/GX 33 (GX 33, packet 56), in LFZZ; Wu Tongju, *Zai xu*, 3713, 3717.

33. Chen Yunlong, *Zhou Fu*, 237–41; undated *qing dan*, probably accompanying Xiliang memorial of 2/21/GX 28, and memorial from 22 Board of War and other capital officials of 1/17/GX 28, in LFZZ, GX 28, packet 44–45; and from censor Gao Xixi, 1/30/GX 28, in LFZZ GX 28, packet 51–55.

34. Memorial from 22 Board of War and other capital officials of 1/17/GX 28, in LFZZ, GX 28, packet 44–45; memorial from censor Gao Xixi, 1/30/GX 28, in LFZZ, GX 28, packet 51–55. Memorial from Zhou Fu, 11/7/GX 29 (GX 29, packet 40), and from Wu Tingyi, 10/21/GX 33 (GX 33, packet 56), in LFZZ.

persed and did not lead to either large concentrations of wealth or political influence at higher levels.

Meanwhile Beijing continued to press for more cuts. Henan's Yellow River expenditures were cut particularly sharply, mostly to free money for the Boxer Indemnity, but also to help fund modernizing projects, mostly in the Beijing-Tianjin area.[35] Shandong's governors resisted cuts more vigorously than Henan's, pointing out that their hydraulic tasks were particularly difficult.[36] However, they never regained their early Guangxu funding levels; they merely staved off further cuts while spending more than their official budget. They had to plead every year for extra funds; and although they sometimes got them, they could never count on them.[37]

Henan governor Chen Kuilong complained in 1905 that these funding shifts were bleeding inland areas to finance coastal development. Nothing came of this complaint, but there is much truth to it.[38] In the long run, some inland areas also benefited from the development of facilities in Tianjin and Manchuria and could have benefited along with everyone else from an army capable of resisting foreign aggression. However, there is no question that there was a massive transfer of government funds away from hydraulics, centered in inland areas, to other projects, centered on the coast.[39] Moreover, as shown in the final section of this chapter, the funds still allocated for hydraulics were increasingly spent on projects near the coast.

Riverworks budgets shrank further after 1911. In the 1920s Shan-

35. Wu Tongju, *Zai xu*, 3845–51.

36. Memorial from Zhou Fu of 9/27/GX 29 (GX 29, packet 40); from Yang Shixiang, 9/15/GX 32, and attachment (*pian*) to Yang Shixiang memorial of 6/11/GX 32 (both in GX 32, packet 37–38), and Yang Shixiang memorial of 8/6/GX 33 (GX 33, packet 56), all in LFZZ; Wu Tongju, *Zai xu*, 3729, 3733–34, 3748, 3809–10, 3826, 3835.

37. Wu Tongju, *Zai xu*, 3729, 3733–34, 3748, 3756, 3806, 3809, 3813, 3822, 3835–36; Yang Shixiang, *pian* of 6/11/GX 32 in LFZZ, GX 32, packet 37–38.

38. For Chen's complaint, see memorials of 7/4/GX 31 from Chen Kuilong, GX 31, packet 62–66, and from Chen, date of issue illegible, received 5/8/GX 31 (GX 31, packet 40), both in LFZZ. As far as I was able to discover from searching in the First Historical Archives in Beijing, any reply that may have been made to Chen's memorial is no longer extant.

39. See the memorials from Chen Kuilong, above, and the undated *qing dan* summarizing contributions from other provinces (chiefly Shandong) to Manchurian troops 1874–1905 in LFZZ, GX 31, packet 45B. Esherick, *Boxer Uprising*, 170, notes the importance of Shandong as a "surplus" province for the Qing and (131) quotes Beijing praising one Shandong governor for saving money from the Yellow River budget, but assumes that those particular savings came from limiting corruption, not undermining river control.

dong spent ¥520,000 (or 371,429 *liang*) of provincial funds per year on the Yellow River; ¥380,000 of that came from surtaxes levied in eighteen riverside counties.[40] Funds were requested from the other ninety counties but were not forthcoming,[41] except for relief and stop-gap repairs after huge floods. Henan (¥400,000), Hebei/Zhili (¥250,000), and Shandong together spent less than Henan alone had in the 1840s.[42]

The intricate fiscal system complicated money shortages: conservancy funds came from specific, earmarked sources.[43] Thus, if one county failed to send its contribution, work might not get done, even if there was no shortfall in general revenue. Such problems were particularly serious for hydraulic work, where all the requirements—available materials, peasants who had free time, and proper conditions on the river itself—might coincide only briefly. Timing was especially tricky for stone, which could be brought in only after the river thawed, leaving little time before farm work picked up.[44]

In the Qing, these problems were dealt with by borrowing from other local funds—usually salt funds—and from other provinces. Late Qing Yellow River reports refer to borrowing not only from nearby provinces with a stake in this work, but from faraway Zhejiang, Jiangxi, and Guangdong.[45] In fact, though the documents refer to this money as "borrowed" from other provinces,[46] much of it probably represented transfer payments, with the "lending" provinces remitting that much less to Beijing instead of being repaid out of funds from Shandong, Henan, or Zhili.

40. *HWTK*, no. 1 (Oct. 1928), *ji shi*, 3, *gongdu*, 21. The *liang*, equal to approximately ¥1.4, was an accounting unit used widely during the Qing but much less so during the Republic.

41. See, for instance, *HWTK*, no. 2 (Jan. 1930), *mingling*, 18, *gongdu*, 14, 31–32; *HWTK*, no. 7 (Jan. 1935), *mingling*, 62.

42. *HH*, 367.

43. *HWTK*, no. 1 (Oct. 1928), *gongdu*, 21, *jishi*, p. 3.

44. Memorial of Zhang Renjun, 2/8/GX 28 (GX 28, packet 44–45); memorial from Zhou Fu, 11/28/GX 29 (GX 29, packet 40); from Zhang Renjun, 6/22/GX 29 (GX 29, packet 40), and *pian* from Yang Shixiang, 7/9/GX 32 (GX 32, packet 37–38), all in LFZZ; *HWTK*, no. 2 (Jan. 1930), *gongdu*, 16, 44–45; no. 6 (Jan. 1934), *bu gao*, 1–2.

45. Memorial from Hu Tinggan, 6/3/GX 27, and memorial from Yuan Shikai, 4/26/GX 27 (both in GX 27, packet 42–43); memorial from Zhou Fu, 7/2/GX 29 (GX 29, packet 40), all in LFZZ; Guoli Gu Gong Bowuyuan wenxian bianji weiyuanhui, eds., *Gongzhong dang Guangxu chao zouzhe*, 14:161, 15:204.

46. See, for instance, memorial from Zhou Fu of 7/2/GX 29, in LFZZ, GX 29, packet 40; memorial from Yuan Shikai of 4/28/GX 27 in *Guangxu gong zhong dang*, 14:161–62.

Republican records are too spotty to prove that such borrowing ceased, but I have found no cases of it, and it is easy to see why. Until 1890, the provinces could count on all Yellow River spending being refunded by Beijing; and even after that date, the Qing would probably not have let one province leave another with a large unpaid loan of public funds, which in principle all belonged to Beijing.[47] After 1916, when provinces were often ruled by mutually hostile cliques, it is small wonder that only neighboring provinces, which would be hurt by major floods, would make interprovincial riverworks loans.

THE CENTRAL GOVERNMENT'S WITHDRAWAL: NEW PRIORITIES, NEW AUSTERITY, AND MISSED OPPORTUNITIES

Ironically, the hydraulic system became impoverished just as China was gaining access to new techniques that might have dramatically improved conservancy at no more cost than the old system. After the 1887–88 Yellow River floods, the Qing consulted foreign engineers for the first time. The foreigners endorsed the minority position among Chinese experts: that the Yellow River should be forced to narrow its channel so the channel would deepen and so the river could not shift back and forth, striking dikes at odd angles. Keeping the river within such bounds required stone dikes.[48] In places such as Lekou (east of Jinan, near the Shandong Yellow River quarry), where the river was naturally contained between two limestone walls only one-third mile apart, it had deepened its channel considerably, and flooding was minimal.[49] Later engineers also endorsed this basic approach, although details were continually modified; "river training" was quite new in the West as well, and the Yellow River became an early test case for laboratory simulations of this new technique.[50]

We have no direct calculations of what river training would have

47. On the intricacies of what funds officially belonged to the provinces (relatively few) in the high Qing and which ones, even if they never left the province, belonged to Beijing and had to be spent according to its instructions, see Zelin, *Magistrate's Tael*, passim. For a concise account of interprovincial transfers in the late Qing, see Mann, *Local Merchants*, 109–10.
48. Freeman, "Flood Problems," 1141, 1154; Walter Mallory, *China: Land of Famine* (New York, 1926), 52; Shen Yi, ed., *Huang He taolun ji* (Taibei, 1971), 1–17.
49. Freeman, "Flood Problems," 1141.
50. Shen Yi, *Huang He taolun ji*, passim.

cost in the 1890s, but a rough estimate is possible. In 1898, Li Hong-zhang, after consulting foreign surveyors, estimated that repairing the entire Yellow River would cost 30,000,000 *liang*; 9,300,000 of this would be needed rapidly, the rest gradually over many years.[51] (These sums equal ¥42,000,000 and ¥13,020,000 respectively. Henceforth, all sums will be converted to yuan, the twentieth-century unit of account.) This plan did not include all the narrowing involved in river training, but it did include using stone dikes wherever transportation allowed and building kilns and brick dikes elsewhere. Zhou Fu cut the estimate for the Shandong section to ¥7,840,000 over three years, though this involved reducing plans for narrower, stone-faced banks on the upper section of the river.[52]

In 1932, Shandong, Hebei, and Henan agreed to cooperate on a massive Yellow River overhaul. In addition to thorough dredging with new equipment, the plan included all the stonework needed to train the river; where necessary, it called for buying motor launches and building narrow-gauge railways to bring in stone. The stonework required was calculated at 1,788,000 *fang*; the entire project would cost ¥76,620,400 over twenty years.[53]

Based on information in this plan and elsewhere, it appears that the stonework envisioned in the comprehensive 1932 plan could have been done in the late 1890s for between ¥17,500,000 and ¥20,300,000.[54] This does not include dredging costs, but such costs would exist anyway and would have declined as the channel became narrower and deeper.

Moreover, these figures do not include the enormous savings that would result from reduced annual dike work. All the river control plans from the 1890s to the 1930s calculated that reduced annual expenditures for river control would more than pay for the initial outlay, even before counting the benefits of flood prevention.[55] (Exactly how much could have been saved on future construction is unknowable, however.[56]) And under any assumptions, preventing even a fraction

51. Chen Yunlong, *Zhou Fu*, 210.

52. Wu Tongju, *Zai xu*, 3822, 3836, 3756–57.

53. *HWTK*, no. 4 (Jan. 1932), *jihua*, 2–3.

54. For calculations, see dissertation, 203–4, and accompanying notes.

55. Wu Tongju, *Zai xu*, 3835–36; Freeman, "Flood Problems," 1113–14; *HWTK*, no. 4 (Jan. 1932), *jihua*, 3–4; William Tyler, "Notes on the Hoang Ho or Yellow River" (Shanghai, 1906), 10–12.

56. Even if we accept the government's estimates of future expenditure reductions as precisely accurate, the actual amount of savings would depend on how much was spent

of the losses from Yellow River floods would have made large-scale repairs worthwhile, as numerous observers pointed out at the time.

The problem was financing this work. After all, other massive construction projects that were probably worthwhile (such as further railroad building) were also left undone. Neither the government nor its lenders could have undertaken all worthwhile projects at once. Unlike the case of the railroads, however, in this case money was not lacking because the government had never funded riverworks on this scale or because there were disagreements about the merits of the project. Major repairs went undone because a new austerity was imposed on official water control. Moreover, as chapter 5 will show, river control would have yielded a much higher rate of return than railroads and other modernizing projects.

While the costs described above are substantial, they are far from extravagant compared to water control spending before 1891. Routine expenditures were ¥2,100,000 per year for Henan alone in the 1830s and 1840s and averaged about the same amount for Shandong in the 1880s.[57] Compared to this, planning to spend less than ¥21,000,000 (or even Li Hongzhang's ¥42,000,000 for the whole river) over twenty years for stonework that would gradually obviate the largest routine expense (repairing stalk dikes) was quite reasonable. Moreover, as late as 1930, the Shandong Yellow River Office (Hewuju) estimated that the worst trouble spots on the Yellow River dikes could be converted to stone at just ¥200,000 per year over fifteen years, offering almost equal benefits at a much lower price.[58] If the people's dikes used after 1891 consumed anywhere near the amounts of stalks I have estimated,[59] they alone were costing much more than the most ambitious stonework plan, and many times the smaller one; spending on official embankments was extra. During the Republic, Zhili treated all its Yellow River dikes as official responsibilities and controlled the river very effectively. Treating all the upper section of the Shandong Yellow River, by far the most neglected and flood-prone section, the

---

at precisely what dates and on the real or implicit cost of borrowing. However, the project would have been worthwhile at any rate the national government could conceivably have been charged.

57. Wu Tongju, *Zai xu*, 4178; *Shandong gongbao*, no. 106 (Sept. 17, 1912), *wen du*, 2.

58. *HWTK*, no. 2 (Jan. 1930), *zhuan jian*, 4.

59. See dissertation, appendix G.

same way and at the same cost per *li* as in Zhili would have cost about ¥750,000 per year; such a sum was not trivial, but it still would have been much less than the cost of stalk dikes, and a small burden for the province as a whole; moreover, it would have left Shandong's total river spending still far below that of Henan a hundred years earlier.[60] In other words, provincial or national government funds could have done more than a much larger amount of local, informal spending achieved in Huang-Yun.

Before 1890, major Yellow River repairs were done roughly every twenty years, often at enormous expense. As early as 1815, almost ¥5,600,000 was spent for work in the Sui district of Henan alone, though that district had had a "big job" (*da gong*) done sixteen years before. In 1820, more than ¥14,000,000 was spent on a Henan *da gong*. In 1888, after the Yellow River break at Kaifeng, ¥15,444,000 had been spent on Henan repairs alone—repairs done almost exclusively with stalks and dirt.[61] However, only one such major repair was undertaken after 1890: a ¥4,200,000 overhaul of the main Zhili dikes in 1914, after which this area avoided major flooding until the 1940s.[62]

The new austerity imposed on the hydraulic system after 1891 is also visible in the percentage of spending going to water control. Qing budget figures are hard to find and hard to interpret, but it is clear that the percentage of spending going to water conservancy shrank drastically. One study, which unfortunately cites no sources, says that the central government's water conservancy outlays declined from 12 percent of total spending before 1850 to 3 percent between 1850 and 1900 and to 1.38 percent in 1905.[63]

This shift in priorities is apparent even in the Yellow River provinces themselves. In 1855, the Grand Council rejected Shandong's request for additional funds to cope with effects of the Yellow River shift, saying that Grand Canal and Yellow River expenses in the province were "only" 10–20 percent of Shandong's revenue.[64] By 1911 the

60. See dissertation, chapter 4, nn. 48 and 290, for the sources and numbers used in this calculation.

61. Wu Tongju, *Zai xu*, 4178.

62. Xu Shiguang, *Puyang heshang ji* (N.p., 1915), *hou xu*, 1b.: Hou Renzhi, *Xu tianxia*, 151.

63. Kōain Kijutsubu, *Hokushi Rinsan*, 100.

64. Quoted in petition from southern Shandong Grand Canal Intendant (name illegible), 4/12/Xianfeng 5, in archives of the Shandong governor (no packets or files yet), First Historical Archives, Beijing.

budget for riverworks in Shandong had shrunk to ¥938,000—less than 7 percent of the province's tax receipts and less than half the province's annual contribution to the Boxer Indemnity.[65] Had half of Shandong's indemnity payments been available to supplement riverworks spending, major repairs could have been done,[66] and the percentage of Shandong's budget going to riverworks would still have been toward the low end of the range that the Grand Council considered reasonable in 1855.

Hydraulic problems had increased since 1855 but had not become unmanageable. What changed most were the state's interest in managing these problems and the degree to which its revenues were available for water control. "National development," military strength, resisting foreign control, and escaping indebtedness replaced the older priorities of subsistence and reproduction, and Huang-Yun was left behind. Moreover, the lack of national funds was only part of the problem. The state's withdrawal also weakened local interest in maintaining the hydraulic system; this and other factors made it impossible for Huang-Yun even to muddle through.

ACCELERATED DEPRECIATION:
SOCIAL AND POLITICAL BASES OF LOCAL PARALYSIS

HYDRAULICS AFTER 1902:
INSTITUTIONAL ORPHANHOOD AND FINANCIAL CRISIS

Not surprisingly, waterways decayed rapidly once the Qing became less involved. Numerous sources emphasize that although the Shandong Grand Canal was in poor condition in 1902, it was still usable; the section from the Yellow River to Linqing became impassable, thus ending long-distance transport, after grain tribute stopped and the central government pulled out.[67] Many officials thought it had been understood that the hydraulic system was to be maintained even after

65. *SDZZ*, no. 88 (4/30/XT 3), 7a, 8a; no. 89 (5/15/XT 3), 23b.

66. Wu Tongju, *Zai xu*, 3756. Zhou Fu's somewhat scaled-down version of Li Hongzhang's plan called for spending 800,000 *liang* per year, but for only three years.

67. *SDZZ*, no. 3 (2/15/GX 34), 9–11; no. 66 (6/15/XT 1), 22a–b; *JSYK* 1:3 (March 1931), *gongdu*, 33; *HWJB*, no. 5 (Fall 1921), 15; *Jiaotong shi*, 1787; *Linqing xianzhi*, 2:20b; memorial from Zhou Fu, 11/7/GX 29 (GX 29, packet 40), and from Yang Shixiang, 2/23/GX 32 (GX 32, packet 37–38), in LFZZ.

tribute shipments ended.[68] The rescript on the memorial suggesting the 1901–2 cuts specified that the canal should be maintained, though not by whom.[69] Foreigners in the affected area, while applauding the end of inland tribute, generally assumed that the canal would be maintained, or even improved.[70] Instead, it decayed rapidly.

The partial successes and larger failures of post-1901 hydraulic repairs followed patterns that persisted into the 1930s. The efforts made in the Republican era were more extensive, however, and more records of them exist. I will review the Qing efforts quickly here, returning to some of them when I discuss the Republican hydraulic system in chapter 5.

Shandong governor Zhou Fu submitted several plans for improved riverworks. However, only one request was ever granted: a three-year diversion of a small part of Shandong's payments for troop rations in Beijing and Manchuria to urgent Yellow River repairs.[71] When the authorization to withhold these surtaxes ran out, Beijing firmly rejected pleas for extensions.[72] Zhou's larger plans closely followed Li Hongzhang's 1898 plan, which the court had requested; they were praised, but not funded.[73]

In 1906, Zhou's successor, Yang Shixiang, pleaded for funds to save the north Shandong Grand Canal while it was still possible; this plan also depended on withholding a small amount of money from surtaxes earmarked for extraprovincial soldiers.[74] Among other things, Yang argued that China needed an inland shipping route for security. One might have expected this rather common argument to be well received: after the Western invasion of 1900, the Qing had moved the Tianjin arsenal to Dezhou, on the north Shandong canal, for

68. Memorial from censor Gao Xixi, 1/30/GX 28 (GX 28, packet 51–55); from Zhou Fu, 11/7/GX 29 (GX 29, packet 40); from Yang Shixiang, 2/23/32 (GX 32, packet 37–38); from Yang Shixiang, 7/27/GX 33 (GX 33, packet 56); and from Wu Tingyi, 10/21/GX 33 (GX 33, packet 56), all in LFZZ.

69. Memorial from 22 Board of War and other capital officials, 1/17/GX 28, in LFZZ, GX 28, packet 44–45.

70. *NCH*, April 2, 1903, p. 634; April 16, 1903, 729; May 21, 1903, 984.

71. Memorial from Yang Shixiang, 12/11/GX 32, in LFZZ, GX 32, packet 37–38; Chen Yunlong, *Zhou Fu*, 179–80, 203, 209–11.

72. Memorial from Yang Shixiang, 9/15/GX 32, in LFZZ, GX 32, packet 37–38; Wu Tongju, *Zai xu*, 3806, 3809, 3811.

73. Wu Tongju, *Zai xu*, 3756–57; memorial from Zhou Fu, 11/8/GX 29 (GX 29, packet 40); memorial from Yang Shixiang, 12/11/GX 32, both in LFZZ, GX 32, packet 37–38; *Shandong tongzhi* (1915), 3442; Chen Yunlong, *Zhou Fu*, 683–91.

74. Memorial from Yang Shixiang, 2/23/GX 32, in LFZZ, GX 32, packet 37–38.

security reasons.[75] Instead, however, Yang Shixiang was sharply rebuked for even suggesting that Beijing forgo revenue so he could save this section of the canal.[76] Since Beijing's reaction to Yang could hardly have encouraged future governors to worry about the canal, and since nobody else had any responsibility for the section from Dong'a to Linqing, official statements that the whole canal should be kept open were meaningless.

Even without significant funding, putting somebody in charge might have helped a great deal. While fully refurbishing the Grand Canal would have been very costly, maintaining the level of the previous fifty years would not have been. In the last years of tribute, the Dongchang prefect had made sure that enough was done to allow "clear sailing" (*chang xun*) for the fleet through northern Shandong; the annual cost was a mere 50,000 *liang*.[77]

In southern Shandong, where an office—headed by a resident salt official[78]—and a small river battalion remained, much was accomplished. In 1903, the south Shandong Grand Canal (Nanyunhe) Office received prefectural funds to keep it going.[79] At the same time, the merchants who used the Shandong Nanyunhe were consulted on how to reorganize the lock personnel and security forces and how to decrease corruption; the merchants, in turn, agreed to contribute 13,000 *liang* per year.[80] In 1908, the office financed major repairs by borrowing 215,000 *liang* (interest free) from their appropriations for the next ten years of annual canal work (75,000 *liang* per year). Two years later, the Shandong governor reported that routine maintenance was being done with only 54,000 per year of central funds, allowing this loan to be repaid on schedule.[81] Thus, though maintaining this office was a minimal gesture by the central government, it created a vital focal point for the efforts of local government and private interests,

75. Memorial from Yang Shixiang, 7/27/33, in LFZZ, GX 33, packet 56.

76. Memorial from Yang Shixiang, 2/23/32, in LFZZ, GX 32, packet 37–38, with rescript; for a fuller discussion, see dissertation, 209–10, 213, and nn. 97, 98.

77. *Guangxu gong zhong dang*, 14:167; Dominique Gandar, *Le Canal Impériale: Étude Historique et Descriptive* (Shanghai, 1903), 56.

78. Shandong tongzhi (1915), 3464.

79. Memorial from Zhou Fu, 11/7/GX 29, in LFZZ, GX 29, packet 40.

80. Chen Yunlong, *Zhou Fu*, 239–40.

81. Report of Nong gong shang bu of 4/19/XT 2, enclosed with memorial of 4/22/XT 2, document 6560 in files of the Huiyi Zhengwuchu, First Historical Archives, Beijing.

allowing for a relatively successful delegation of central government responsibilities.

The north Shandong Grand Canal lacked both institutional sponsorship—it became the responsibility of the distant Shandong governor—and local funding sources. Here again, this area's lack of a group of powerful merchants closely tied to officialdom meant that, despite being richer per capita than South Huang-Yun, the area lacked both patrons for its infrastructure and the means to get help from the state. The Linqing customs were more often evaded than those at Jining, and their use was decided by the state, without any local input; they were earmarked for remote recipients, mostly garrisons in Beijing and Manchuria.[82] Salt merchants in northwest Shandong—called the "salt drain" because of its rampant smuggling[83]—were neither as wealthy nor as influential as those who used the south Shandong canal. Both northwest and southwest Shandong merchants had trouble filling their sales quotas, but the southwestern quotas were much larger to begin with and thus more lucrative for both the state and the merchants.[84] In general, the merchants of north Shandong's more open society did less to lobby for or support infrastructure than Jining's bigger, more organized, better connected, and more monopolistic ones.

Yellow River control in Huang-Yun also moved toward a more informal, semiprivate system. The 1891 reforms abolished many of the battalions of troops (*ying*) who specialized in river control. Many official embankments were transformed into people's dikes; these were to be maintained by local effort, supervised by commissioners (*weiyuan*) sent by the governor.[85] These changes proved disastrous, as we will see subsequently. The switch to people's dikes affected only certain areas, but these areas included almost all of the upper portion of the Shandong Yellow River, which was the part in Huang-Yun. Once made, this change proved lasting—in the 1930s this area still

82. On the Linqing customs funds and their diversion to the northeast, see, e.g., undated *qing dan* covering GX 23–26 in LFZZ, GX 29, packet 27A; *qing dan* of 12/14/GX 29 in GX 29, packet 27A; and accompanying memorial from Zhou Fu.
83. *NYHH*, Appendix, p. 11.
84. See the two memorials of 3/17/GX 33 from Yang Shixiang in LFZZ, GX 33, packet 42B. It should be remembered that the northern circuit included far more than northern Huang-Yun, while the southern circuit included only a part of southern Huang-Yun.
85. *HWJB*, no. 4 (Spring 1921), 75; no. 1 (Fall 1919), 107–9.

had most of Shandong's people's dikes and very few official embankments.[86] The centralized Yellow River Administration was
abolished.[87]

Thus, the institutional bases for cooperation between provinces,
between counties in the same province, and between subcounty powerholders were all weakened; the more local problems proved to be the
most important. We will look at this situation in more detail in chapter 5; for now, two brief stories suggest how hard it was to produce
coordinated action under the new system, even across a small area.

One example comes from the north Shandong Grand Canal. After
major floods on a 130-*li* section of the canal in Xiajin, Qinghe, and
Wucheng in 1891, the relatively prosperous people on the west bank
of the canal quickly organized themselves, rebuilt the dikes, and did
not have another flood for more than forty years. The east bank was
poorer and more sparsely populated, in part because the land's east-
ward slope made it more prone to flooding in the first place. The
people there could not maintain adequate dikes, and they suffered
almost annual flooding thereafter. These floods, in turn, affected other
streams, until approximately 400,000 *mu* of farmland was lost. The
east bank got no aid from the more lightly burdened people on the
west bank—who benefited from the outlet that a weak east bank created for high waters—or from the relevant county governments,[88]
though even a very light tax on the reclaimed land would have easily
paid for flood control. Elsewhere, too—for instance, along the north
and south banks of the Yellow River in Shouzhang—local governments allowed a very uneven allocation of burdens to persist, even
though it resulted in frequent floods and lost revenue.[89]

At times, the lack of coordination even turned to sabotage. The
people in charge of dikes were always in charge of only one side of the

86. See, for instance, the Hewuju's memo to Governor Han Fuju of December 5,
1933, in *HWTK*, no. 6 (Jan. 1934), *gongdu*, 25–26.

87. The Yellow River Administration continued to exist formally long after it had
ceased to function. The 1891 reorganization of the Shandong Yellow River meant that
the administration was no longer responsible for the whole river in even a purely formal
way; in 1898 it was briefly abolished during the Hundred Days reforms; and in 1913 it
was finally abolished for good. See Immanuel Hsu, *Modern China*, 456, on 1898; and
Jiaotong shi, 1746, on 1913.

88. *JSYK* 3:5 (May 1933), *lunzhe*, 1–3.

89. See Shandong sheng gongzhe jiaoyuke, *Shandong sheng ge xian xiangtu diaocha*
(Jinan, 1920), 138.

river; the *North China Herald* said that diverting the river toward the opposite bank (by building concave dikes, for instance) was "an old Chinese practice." Moreover, once high water arrived, flooding another area was often the easiest form of self-protection. In the huge 1917 floods, some villagers from the west bank of the Grand Canal near the Dezhou-Enxian border deliberately broke the dikes on the east bank, flooding 500 square miles (almost 2,000,000 *mu*) to a depth of up to five feet. Four of them were caught and lynched, but they were hardly the only people trying to divert floods from their own area. During the same flood, observers noted that for Puzhou and Fanxian people who had depended on people's dikes near the Yellow River, it was no consolation that the official embankments a few miles back were holding nicely; on the contrary, this made their own land slower to drain. Officials also deliberately broke several dikes during the 1925 Yellow River floods; while such flooding was not always a bad tactic, it could be disastrous if not coordinated.[90]

THE CANAL AND LOCAL POLITICS

The devolution of hydraulic responsibilities to more local, informal bodies not only made water control efforts harder to organize; it also changed their goals. Increasingly, land reclamation and local flood control were emphasized over transport. In Jining (1902), Dong'a (1904), and Liaocheng (1910) the end of grain tribute was quickly followed by reclamation and irrigation projects that would have been forbidden before, since they interfered with transport on the canal; in Liaocheng and Linqing, local officials sold the canal bed itself as farm land. In the Jining area, urbanites wanted the canal full of water, while rural dwellers preferred a useless, but nonthreatening, dry canal.[91] As long as the canal had carried grain tribute, the great fear of those responsible for it had been obstacles to transport; therefore, water was channeled into it and merchants benefited, while farmers suffered from

90. *NCH*, Oct. 27, 1917, pp. 217–19; Oct. 6, 1917, p. 23; Oct. 3, 1925, p. 9; Oct. 10, 1925, p. 47.
91. On Jining, see *DFZZ* 1:10 (10/25/GX 30), 172; on Liaocheng, Linqing, and the area in between, see *SDZZ*, no. 9 (5/15/GX 34), 5a; on Dong'a, see *HWTK*, no. 4 (Jan. 1932), *mingling*, 37; generally, see Hou Renzhi, *Xu tianxia*, 49. For sale of the canal bed, see *SDZZ*, no. 9 (5/15/GX 34), 5a. For urban/rural differences, see Liu Yinhuai, "Jining de Yunhe," *Shandong wenxian* 5:1 (June 20, 1979), 84–85.

floods. Within a decade after the end of tribute, those priorities had been reversed, even near Jining, a major commercial city.[92]

Conflict among these interests sharpened once the central government would no longer pay to keep transport and local flood control in relative harmony by dredging the canal and strengthening its banks. Moreover, the end of government supervision shifted the balance of power among local interests. The 1915 report notes that yamen clerks made large sums of money by collaborating with private land reclamation near and even in the canal. Whether people had to pay rent or taxes for land they occupied became an important controversy between the occupants, yamen clerks, and village heads, on one side, and local assemblies and merchants on the other. In Jining, where commercial (and thus transport-oriented) interests should have been unusually strong, the County Assembly lost on this issue in the early Republic; urban members of the county elite brought it up in the 1930s, but lost again.[93]

This rural-urban rivalry is vital in understanding the net effects of South Huang-Yun's relatively strong elites. Urban elites in Jining—as we have seen with regard to railroads and the canal—had more success than those in North Huang-Yun in getting infrastructure built and maintained. They could not extend this success very far, however, because they were not strong enough outside Jining city (and a few county capitals) to impose their will on the rural elites and yamen underlings in their own hinterland. (These limits were evident, in a slightly different way, in cotton diffusion; see chapter 2.) Given this standoff between strong urban and rural elites, South Huang-Yun's relative success in getting state help produced only limited advantages.

Canal work had always been more dependent on the state in North Huang-Yun, since commercial interests were not as tightly organized there. Consequently, it declined very rapidly when grain tribute ended. Without tribute fleets, magistrates no longer had to answer to their superiors if the canal was impassable; thus, they had little reason to keep people from farming or otherwise impeding water flow in the canal. Furthermore, in 1903, control of the riverine *lijin* (internal customs) at Linqing was shifted from the magistrate to a commissioner

92. *NYHH*, pt. 1, p. 1; for an instance occurring after the end of the grain tribute, see Chen Yunlong, *Zhou Fu*, 197.
93. *NYHH*, Appendix, p. 9, on the area along the Beiyunhe; *JSYK* 1:2 (Feb. 1931) *mingling*, 10, on the south; 10–11, on the County Assembly.

dispatched from Jinan. With this shift, the magistrate lost whatever stake he might still have had in keeping river transport going.[94]

Magistrates could still make the canal work, if they wanted to. When Linqing was short of food in the winter of 1907–8, the magistrate had water diverted into the canal bed between Linqing and Liaocheng to help bring in supplies. However, he sought only to make the canal passable until the next dry season, not to address longer-term problems.[95] Except in such crises, local officials had little reason to do any canal work after 1902; the Linqing magistrate did not even interfere when private parties placed wooden "toll bridges" across a rain-filled canal in 1904, forcing grain to go by cart at several times the cost.[96]

A DOWNWARD SPIRAL

This shift in local priorities ensured that little would be done to promote the transportation that had been Beijing's first priority in Huang-Yun; it thus leads us to ask again why the central government not only withdrew, but stayed on the sidelines as adverse consequences mounted. Part of the explanation was clearly budgetary, but we have seen that small sums would have sufficed to continue basic canal maintenance. As chapter 5 will show, even the vastly larger sums needed for thorough repairs on the canal and the Yellow River would have been money extremely well spent. Magistrates, who served short terms, had little reason to maintain or improve the hydraulic system, but the failure of local and provincial interests to take effective action is striking. We will look at what action was taken, especially with local efforts, in the next chapter.

In the meantime, we can briefly examine why Huang-Yun interests were relatively weak. The reasons were linked to the relative economic decline of Huang-Yun—which they in turn accelerated—but stemmed more from a shift in the state's relative interest in inland and littoral areas.

94. *NCH*, April 16, 1903, p. 729. Though a magistrate with control of a customs barrier would probably have used some of the income to enrich himself, the situation is not quite as corrupt as "personal" income may suggest, since magistrates were expected to handle many local public tasks out of their "personal" budgets. See Zelin, *Magistrate's Tael*, 47–54, 181.
95. *NCH*, Jan. 1, 1908, p. 124.
96. *NCH*, Dec. 9, 1904, p. 1289.

First, the canal had begun to decay many years before it was finally abandoned. Trade along the Shandong portion probably peaked at least two decades before the Yellow River shift. Linqing suffered another blow near the time of that shift; it was sacked by the Taiping in 1853 and never fully recovered. On the eve of this event, Jining was bigger and more commercially important than Jinan; Linqing and Liaocheng were Jinan's equals. By 1900, Jinan had grown dramatically, Jining had held its own but grown relatively little, and Linqing and especially Liaocheng had contracted.[97]

Moreover, the merchants of Linqing or Liaocheng were never politically important, even during their heyday, except as part of larger groups based on their places of origin (Shanxi, Shaanxi, and Huizhou, Anhui). Jining merchants were better organized, but only two families included figures of national importance. Not only were Huang-Yun merchants not nationally powerful, but those in some especially hard hit towns, such as Liaocheng, were largely outsiders; rather than trying to revive Liaocheng after 1902, they moved to Jinan and other towns along the soon-to-be-built Tianjin-Pukou railway.[98]

In this respect, even South Huang-Yun lagged behind some very poor areas. For instance, although Huaibei (the northernmost part of Jiangsu and Anhui), was exceptionally poor, there were important merchants (particularly Xuzhou salt merchants) who needed its section of the canal, helped fund it, and brought in politically influential investors, including the sometime prime minister Duan Qirui.[99] And it appears that in Huaibei, unlike Shandong, transportation triumphed over cultivation when the two conflicted.[100]

However, Huang-Yun's loss of funds cannot be attributed simply to its having been "out-lobbied" by wealthier regions. As we shall see shortly, the defeat makes sense only in the context of the responses to international pressures of a state that enjoyed considerable autonomy from domestic interests.

Given the increasing concentration of political power in Jinan as

97. David Buck, *Urban Change*, 21–29; see also Yang Zhengtai, "Ming Qing Linqing," 115–20.

98. Interview notes, Liaocheng, November 1985. Many moved to Jinan, where even today one commercial district of the city is largely run by descendants of people who left Liaocheng in the early twentieth century.

99. *NSGB* 3:5 (Dec. 1916), *jinwen*, 26; Shi Nianhai, *Zhongguo de Yunhe* (n.d., probably 1934 or 1935), 175; *Jiaotong shi*, 1789–90.

100. Hou Renzhi, *Xu tianxia*, 48.

opposed to prefectural capitals in the last years of the Qing and growing economic ties between Jinan and the coast,[101] it is tempting to see
western Shandong's political losses as a straightforward result of relative economic decline. Shandong politics in the late Qing and early Republic did have an important east-west (or "Qi" versus "Lu") division,
but the west seems to have held the upper hand even after it lost
its economic edge.[102] Southwesterners dominated governorships and
assembly leadership posts for the first decade of the Republic and saw
to it that provincial money went to their projects in South Huang-Yun.
After Yuan Shikai's death, more people from eastern Shandong gained
power; nonetheless, the governorship stayed largely in western hands,
and western leaders had stronger ties to Beijing.[103] Only the 1924–25
invasion of Zhang Zongchang—a native of the Yantai area, backed by
the Fengtian clique—finally gave easterners political control of the
province.[104]

The question was less eastern versus western Shandong than the
state's approach to coastal versus inland China. The rise of ocean
shipping and Manchurian grain production meant that the Qing could
use a relatively modern, market-driven system to turn surplus extracted elsewhere into food for the capital.[105] At the same time, these
growing coastal areas featured other powerful political contenders.
The increased importance and vulnerability of the coast required a
concentration of resources there—military force in particular, but including all sorts of public services, since failures in almost any field

---

101. David Buck, *Urban Change*, 27–32, 44, 50, 53, 73.

102. On political divisions between parts of Shandong, see Wan Guangwei, "Shandong zheng Dang huodong," 32–42; Xia Lianju, "Shandong duli," 29.

103. Wan Guangwei, "Shandong zheng Dang huodong," 35–36; also Shao
Chuoran, "Tian Zhongyu," 43–50; see also *China Yearbook, 1926–1927*, 1190;
Zhongguo jindai ming ren tu jian (Taibei, 1977), 83, 227; Sonoda Ikki, *Xin Zhongguo
renwu zhi*, trans. Huang Huiquan (Shanghai, n.d.), 108–41; Howard L. Boorman, ed.,
Biographical Dictionary of Republican China (New York, 1967), 1:382a–383a, 429a–
430a; China Weekly Review, *Who's Who in China*, 3rd ed. (Shanghai, 1925), 41–42.

104. On Zhang Zongchang's reliance on people from eastern Shandong and Manchuria, see Wang Jiaoming, "Zhang Zongchang," 2:333, 346; Li Hengzhen, Xu Datong,
and Zhang Jinxiu, "Zhang Zongchang," 1–2, 12–19, 27, 36–39.

105. On the close economic ties between eastern Shandong and Manchuria, see
Gottschaung, "Migration," passim. Also see David Buck, *Urban Change*, p. 27. In 1910–
11, a crackdown on counterfeiting turned up huge numbers of real and fake Russian ru-
bles in eastern Shandong, where the Yexian and Huangxian (both near Yantai) banks
had become major clearinghouses for the foreign exchange obtained by Shandongese in
northern Manchuria (see also *Shina Shōbetsu Zenshi*, 4:1138). In the same year, the cotton trade between western Shandong (particularly Gaotang) and Yantai collapsed because the two sides could not agree on a mutually acceptable currency (see chapter 1).

could lead to further infringements on sovereignty.[106] The Lower Yangzi, for instance, had long been much richer than North China, but only in the changed atmosphere of the nineteenth century could this situation lead to an abandonment of grain tribute and the northern hydraulic system. Moreover—as we saw in the case of deforestation—the reorientation of the Chinese state benefited even poor coastal areas (such as Lijin, at the mouth of the Yellow River), at the expense of Huang-Yun.

Under the changed circumstances, it is unsurprising that an old, expensive, inland system for moving surplus seemed a logical place to cut back. The problem was that in abandoning the hydraulic system, the Qing ultimately gave up much more than a way of moving surplus. Put more abstractly, coastal market making both rewarded and required state making efforts. These opportunities and pressures made dismantling an expensive, command-based system of moving surplus very tempting. However, the result was a spiraling political disintegration in Huang-Yun, with great costs to both the region and the state.

By the Republic, the problems created by the central government's hydraulic neglect may have become the single biggest reason that the national government did not resume a leading role in water control. The system's technical problems had become quite daunting, at least if one hoped to "solve" rather than just ameliorate them. Meanwhile, as we shall see, the organizations responsible for water control were failing so completely that successful repairs required a large infusion not only of money, but of personnel as well—and not only riverworks specialists, but other officials, too. The rest of this chapter will examine the physical and sociopolitical state of the water control system in the early Republic.

STALKS AND STONES:
THE CYCLE OF TECHNICAL BACKWARDNESS

THE PHYSICAL PROBLEMS

Early Republican Huang-Yun faced both transport and flooding problems. Though our account focuses on their social and political dimensions, these cannot be understood without some physical description.

---

106. See, for instance, Charlotte Furth, *Ting Wen-chiang: Science and China's New Culture* (Cambridge, Mass., 1970), 177–82; Carl F. Nathan, *Plague Prevention and*

The Yellow River and other Huang-Yun rivers had a little shipping, but "transport problems" largely mean Grand Canal problems. These fall into three zones. From slightly north of Jining to the Jiangsu border (and all the way to the Yangzi) the canal was shallower and narrower than it was supposed to be. During droughts, only very small boats could pass.[107] Usually, however, it functioned fairly well; some of the most common complaints, such as delays at the locks, suggest a still busy waterway.[108] Shallowness caused problems for bulky cargoes, such as grain, but this section remained a viable commercial and passenger route: missionaries going to southwest Shandong, for instance, traveled from Shanghai on canal-borne houseboats.[109]

The northernmost section, from Linqing to Dezhou along the Zhili border (and on to Tianjin), was similar. Thanks to the Wei River, this section had enough water to compete as a conveyor of bulky cargoes (such as cotton) even after Dezhou and Tianjin were linked by rail.[110] Frequent complaints of crowding (especially near Tianjin) testify to the waterway's continued vitality.[111] Neither the five hundred–ton barges used on Western canals nor the large tribute boats could use the canal, but boats carrying eighty tons could still pass.[112]

Politics in Manchuria, 1910–1931 (Cambridge, Mass., 1967), v, 5, 42, 74. See also Spector, *Li Hung-chang*, 213–16, on the importance of government revenue derived from coastal trade; see Michael Hunt, *Frontier Defense and the Open Door* (New Haven, 1971), 8–9 and passim, on the relationship between the Chinese government's shift to encouraging Manchurian settlement and its fear of foreign intrusion; and generally, see the discussion of the relationships between state and market development through taxation in Rudolf Braun, "Taxation, Sociopolitical Structure, and State-Building: Great Britain and Brandenburg-Prussia," in *The Formation of National States in Western Europe*, ed. Charles Tilly (Princeton, 1973), 243–48, 310–27.

107. *NSGB* 3:6 (Jan. 1917), *jinwen*, 30; *NSGB* 8:2 (Aug. 1921), 56–58; *Jiaotong shi*, 1787; Freeman, *GCIC*, p. 3.

108. See, e.g., Chen Yunlong, *Zhou Fu*, 165–66.

109. See, e.g., H. C. Bartel, *The First Mennonite Mission in China* (Lawrence, Kans., 1913), 33.

110. *JSYK* 2:3 (March 1932), *jihua*, 1, 7; Freeman, *GCIC*, 3. Figures for the years 1920–29 in *Tianjin mianhua yun xiao gaikuang* (Tianjin, 1937) show junks carrying between 25 percent and 35 percent as much cotton into Tianjin from 1920 to 1923 as the railroad did, but then carrying in anywhere from 3 to 11 times as much per year from 1925 to 1929. For 1924, junks brought in about 20 percent more. Not all junks, of course, arrived by canal, but since western Shandong was Tianjin's biggest supplier and could obviously not have used ocean-going boats, it seems safe to say that most of the junk shipments represent canal traffic. We also have numerous anecdotal accounts saying that large amounts of cotton from Shandong and southwestern Hebei arrived by canal.

111. See, for instance, *NCH*, July 8, 1904, p. 82.

112. Freeman, *GCIC*, 35.

However, this section was particularly slow. Like the rest of the canal, it had not been thoroughly dredged for years, and sedimentation had raised its bed significantly. Consequently, it posed an acute flood threat. In the south, the floods were "allowed" to happen. In the north, people built a variety of ever higher barriers that jutted into the canal at odd angles, giving it an astonishing number of twists and turns. Linqing was forty-seven miles from Dezhou by straight line, sixty by road, and ninety-three by water;[113] furthermore, the curves made maneuvering large boats very slow. American surveyors taking houseboats from Dezhou to Linqing often found "we could [disembark,] cut across 3 or 400 yards [on foot] and wait half or 3/4 of an hour [for the boat] to come around to the same point." The trip took four and a half days.[114]

The middle seventy miles of the canal, from the Yellow River crossing (at Dong'a, slightly north of Jining) to Linqing was the worst. Except during very heavy rains or floods, this section was almost useless.[115] Peddlers in small boats sometimes used this stretch, but it could rarely float boats large enough for long-distance trade.[116] Much of this part of the canal became farmland.[117]

The canal also had serious flood problems. And although canal transport conditions stabilized by about 1910, the flood problem continued to get worse.

The peculiar problems of the Yellow River—the heaviest sedimentation of any river in the world, a river bed that for many miles runs above the surrounding land, a current that varies from a trickle to a torrent—are well known, and need not be reviewed here.[118] Grand Canal flooding has been overshadowed, but in early-twentieth-century Huang-Yun it was almost as serious. Generally its severity varied inversely with transit problems. The very dry central section rarely flooded; more often, other rivers flooded the farms that occupied the canal bed.[119] The northern section often had high waters, but

113. *JSYK* 2:3 (March 1932), *jihua*, 1, 2.
114. Carey, letter of Dec. 1, 1918.
115. Ibid., Dec. 5, 1918.
116. See, for instance, *Dong'a xianzhi*, 6:3b.
117. Carey, letter of Dec. 16, 1918; *JSYK* 1:2 (Feb. 1931), *yao wen*, 37.
118. For an easily readable overview see Freeman, "Flood Problems," 1113–67. See also *Xu tianxia*, 60.
119. See, for instance, *JSGB* 3:8 (Aug. 1933), *jihua*, 9; *Linqing xianzhi* (1934), 7:18a–30b on river transport options and problems in the area.

it also had an extensive series of dikes.[120] Along the provincial border, Zhili helped fund annual dredging, partly for fear that floods would sweep all the way to Tianjin (as they did in 1917).[121]

The southern section (and adjacent Huaibei) had the biggest problem.[122] Caught between the much stronger Yellow River to the north and the much stronger Huai River to the south, this section had no outlet to the sea. However, it collected water and debris from numerous rivers and streams, including, occasionally, the Huai and Yellow rivers. As a 1915 report put it, this area "used to be the pulse of the Grand Canal, but is now the anus."[123] The result was both frequent heavy flooding and the steady growth of the chain of shallow lakes that formed the canal's outlet.[124] Regular dredging kept canal traffic moving but was not enough to prevent floods. Like the Yellow River's, the Shandong Grand Canal's bed was too high; unlike the Yellow River, much of its shoreline had no dikes.[125] The situation on the lakes themselves was complicated by disagreement on their dimensions. Though "nature" was expanding them, local residents, beginning in the 1890s, launched numerous, often conflicting, attempts to reclaim lake land.[126] After examining the Shandong Grand Canal in 1919–20, John Ripley Freeman declared that it had the worst flood problem of any canal in the world.[127]

Eventually, these problems affected other waterways. Accumulating sediment on the canal and its lakes backed up the Wanfu and Zhushui rivers, which drained into them; this brought floods to areas seventy-five miles from the canal.[128] Other Huang-Yun river problems were also complicated by problems on the main waterways. The Wen River, for instance, dropped down to the lakes from the exceptionally bare hills of southern Shandong, whose deforestation was accelerated when the import of logs via the canal ceased. Like many such rivers, the Wen was prone to devastating flash floods: its 1917 flood discharged

---

120. *JSYK* 2:3 (March 1932), *jihua*, 7; *Linqing xianzhi* (1934), 7:23a–24b.
121. See, for instance, the *ci* of 2/1/XT 1 in file 394, document 2985, Nong shang gong bu.
122. Hou Renzhi, *Xu tianxia*, 48–49.
123. Freeman, *GCIM*, 93; idem, *GCIC*, 45; *NYHH*, pt. 1, p. 2.
124. Freeman, *GCIM*, 93; *Shandong gongbao* 1:34 (July 7, 1912), *wendu*, 1–2.
125. Shandong sheng jiansheting, *Junzhi Wanfu Zhushui He zhi* (hereafter, *Wanfu He*) (Jinan, 1934), 13, 14, 19, 28.
126. *Jining xianzhi* (1929), 2:47b–50b; *DFZZ* 1:10 (10/25/GX 30), 172–73.
127. Freeman, *GCIC*, 45.
128. Hou Renzhi, *Xu tianxia*, 48–50; *Wanfu He, yan ge*, 2–6, 10–19.

more water per second than the previous Yellow River flood at Dong'a—said to be the worst flood there in seventy years.[129]

POLITICAL ECONOMY AND THE CHOICE OF INFERIOR TECHNIQUES

The area's backward transportation, compounded by hydraulic neglect, in turn obstructed flood control. Most important, transport problems helped frustrate one of the most vital projects—replacing western Shandong's earth-and-stalk dikes with stone.

As we shall see shortly, the continued use of stalks where stone would have been both cheaper and more effective was heavily influenced by two problems discussed in earlier chapters: the currency and credit shortages in South Huang-Yun and the obstacles to bulky imports. A complete explanation, however, must also include crucial themes of this chapter: (1) differences between local and national priorities in water control, (2) the shift in the local balance of power on water control issues once the state withdrew, and (3) institutional problems created when responsibility for tasks once handled by the state became unclear. That these problems were allowed to continue illustrates a fourth and more general theme, which we saw foreshadowed by government reforestation efforts: the state's willingness to accept arrangements that were more costly and less effective in total welfare terms as long as the extra costs were not borne by the government and the extra floods occurred in areas marginal to the state's mercantilist and nationalist priorities. We have seen much of the first two themes already; we will see much more of the last two in the rest of this chapter and consider their implications for a general understanding of late imperial and Republican state making.

The government-operated quarry for the Shandong Yellow River was slightly east of Jinan at Wang Koushan, downstream from Huang-Yun. Since the river was wide and shallow in western Shandong—partly because the stone needed for training the river was lacking—shipping was very difficult, and the Grand Canal near the Yellow River had become too shallow to use. Both J. R. Freeman's Yellow River plan and the 1932 Yellow River Office plan called for building narrow-gauge railways just to bring in stone for river control. In the

129. Freeman, *GCIC*, 45, 46.

late 1920s shipping costs to a dike two hundred *li* (sixty-six miles) downstream from the quarry were more than four times the cost of the stone itself (¥1 per *fang*).[130]

Even this cost, however, pales next to the cost of moving stone upstream: official sources estimated that stone taken upstream two hundred *li* to western Shandong would cost nineteen times its price at the quarry.[131] Actual prices in the late 1920s and the 1930s were even higher.[132] Road-building projects in the 1920s were supposed to make it easier to supply flood control projects;[133] but even in the late 1930s, whatever stone was used came by water. No places in the Huang-Yun part of Shandong had built stone dikes by 1928, though over half the downstream locations east of Huang-Yun had done so; only Dong'a, one of the Huang-Yun counties closest to the main Yellow River quarry, was trying to do so.[134]

Lacking stone, brick, or often even wood, dike builders used various inferior materials. The most common was *gaoliang* (a type of sorghum) stalks. Foreign engineers commented that Chinese workers did the best job possible with this material.[135] However, the stalks weighed but one-twentieth as much as stone per unit volume. Moreover, even a stalk dike that was originally as effective as stone would not last nearly as long, since stalks gradually decompose in water. At best, they might last three years; one to two years was common, and improperly cut stalks, lacking the plant's roots, would decay in months.[136] Stone dikes would last twenty years without much care.[137]

130. *HWJB*, no. 4 (Spring 1921), 78, on the government quarry; no. 1 (Fall 1919), 10, on the difficulty of shipping; on shipping stone in particular, see no. 3 (Fall 1920), 134; regarding the Yellow River plans, no. 10 (Spring 1925), 28; regarding costs, *HWTK* no. 2 (Jan. 1930), *zhuan jian*, 5.

131. In 1920 *Hewu jibao* provided cost estimates that are consistent with the *HWTK* figures and our calculations. It gave rates of 2 *fen* per *li* for downstream traffic and ¥1 for the actual quarrying of the stone plus transport to riverside. It also stated that going upstream cost more than 8 *fen* per *li* and noted that near the quarry the upstream locations were supposed to use, stone would cost ¥3 at riverside. A distance of two hundred *li* upstream from the quarry roughly corresponds to the location of the crucial Likantun dike in Puzhou, near the provincial border; thus, some areas on the upper river would have paid less, but this particular distance is highly significant, since the Likantun dikes were necessary to making any of the upper river safe. *HWJB*, no. 3 (Fall 1920), 134; *HWTK*, no. 2 (Jan. 1930), *zhuan jian*, 5.

132. *HWTK*, no. 2 (Jan. 1930), *zhuan jian*, 15, 45.

133. Freeman, *GCIC*, 53.

134. *HWTK*, no. 1 (Oct. 1928), tables (no page number), and *mingling*, 10.

135. Ibid., 3–4.

136. Ibid., p. 4; Tyler, "Notes on the Hoang Ho," 2; *HWJB*, no. 1 (Fall 1919), 114.

137. *HWTK*, no. 4 (Jan. 1932), *jihua*, 3.

Consequently, good *gaoliang* dikes were ultimately very expensive. Resolving every doubt in favor of construction with stalks, it still appears that in either year for which we have price data (1920 and 1935) a stone dike at Likantun, Puzhou (a crucial location two hundred *li* upstream from the quarry, where numerous stalk dikes failed before a stone one was built in 1928), should have cost only 1.5 to 1.7 times as much to build as a stalk dike that would be equally effective for a much shorter period.[138]

Theoretically, the money saved by building cheap stalk dikes could be turned into an "endowment" to pay for restoring these dikes. For argument's sake, I have assumed that this money could have yielded 3 percent interest per month; many lenders in this area charged this rate but presumably netted less, since some loans were not repaid. Even if *gaoliang* dikes lasted two and a half years and the price of the stalks did not rise, stone would still have to cost 1.85 times the cost of an equally effective amount of stalk before the dike builders would break even on using stalks—more than the above estimates of the actual price difference. Adding the observed increase in stalk prices between 1920 and 1935 (5.5 percent per year) makes the break-even point 2.1:1. If stalk dikes lasted only two years, the break-even points become 2.2:1 without inflation and 2.5:1 with. These ratios are of course estimates, but every effort has been made to use assumptions favorable to stalk dikes; in all likelihood the true break-even points were much higher still.[139]

Moreover, our estimates of the quantity of stalks needed to maintain Huang-Yun people's dikes suggest that these locally "contributed" goods were an enormous burden for the peasantry: they would have been worth at least ¥1,100,000 per year and possibly as much as ¥4,200,000.[140] Even the lower figure is more than double all government spending on Shandong dikes; a middle figure approaches Shandong's annual share of the comprehensive 1932 Yellow River plan. Labor levies, of course, were also much larger with stalks, which needed frequent repairs, than they would have been with durable stone.[141] In other words, gross investment in Yellow River control

---

138. See dissertation, appendix H.
139. Ibid. A much fuller explanation is available in dissertation, 227–31, plus accompanying notes, and appendix H.
140. See dissertation, appendix G.
141. See, for instance, *HWTK*, no. 4 (Jan. 1932), *jihua*, 4.

(and thus the costs borne by peasants) remained very high; but it is high net investment (investment minus depreciation) that actually prevents floods and that is typically taken as a sign of a modern economy.[142] In short, making the Huang-Yun Yellow River a local responsibility meant that the state spent fewer resources, but the society spent more.

To consume fewer resources than those estimated above, a dike builder would have had to build dikes that were much less effective than either stone or brick; in fact, the savings would be relatively small unless the work was very shoddy. A supervisor who wanted simply to complete his job could use a very cheap combination of stalks and earth; one well-beaten *fang* of this mixture could have cost as little as ¥2.85 in 1920 and about ¥5 in 1935.[143] At such rates, the resources not used might well have yielded enough for dike maintenance as well as left a significant profit. However, building and repairing even such a minimal dike would have been only slightly cheaper than using brick (not including the initial cost of building a kiln).

More important, such a mixture would not have been very effective. Every contemporary writer argued that effective flood control required stone or brick dikes;[144] as we shall see later, effective flood control was unquestionably worth many times the cost of providing it. On the middle and downstream sections of the Shandong Yellow River (including its last few miles in Huang-Yun and everything east of Huang-Yun) and the Zhili section, the many stone dikes added after 1891 proved effective. On the upper section, however—from the provincial border to slightly west of Jinan, covering most of Huang-Yun—the Yellow River continued to be diked, ineffectively, with stalks.[145] Why?

The neglect of transport in Huang-Yun clearly played a major role, generating the high stone costs we have discussed above. But as we

142. Fernand Braudel, *The Wheels of Commerce*, trans. Sian Reynolds (New York, 1982), 244–45; Simon Kuznets, *Population, Capital, and Growth* (New York, 1973), 121–30; *HWJB*, no. 3 (Oct. 1919), 124, 134; no. 4 (Jan. 1920), 85; *HWTK*, no. 8 (Jan. 1936), *gong du*, 59; and dissertation, appendix H.

143. The principal price sources are *HWJB*, no. 4 (Jan. 1920), 85, and *HWTK*, no. 8 (Jan. 1936), *gongdu* 59; the information that a "well-packed" *fang* of stalks would be about 60 percent of its original height comes from *HWTK*, no. 2 (Jan. 1930), *zhuan jian*, 14. For more information, see dissertation, appendixes G and H.

144. For just a few of these, see Chen Yunlong, *Zhou Fu*, 247; Wu Tongju, *Zai xu*, 3821, 3835, 3880; memorial from Yuan Shikai of 11/1/GX 32, in *LFZZ*, GX 32, packet 37–38; memorial from Yuan Shuxun, 11/21/GX 34, in *Guangxu gong zhong dang*, 26: 482–484; *HWJB*, no. 1 (Fall 1919), 107; *HWTK*, no. 4 (Jan. 1932), 3–4.

145. *HWTK*, no. 1 (Oct. 1928), unpaginated table; no. 2 (Jan. 1930), *zhuan jian*, 3.

have just seen, stone was still more cost effective than stalks in the long run. To understand the continuing use of stalks, we must consider the administrative dimension of the state's abandonment of Huang-Yun.

The 1891 reforms designated some parts of the Shandong Yellow River—almost all on the middle and downstream sections—to be protected by official embankments. These dikes were to be maintained, as before, through a combination of civilian corvée labor and *he ying*, hereditary battalions that specialized in river conservancy; the work was supported out of the national budget.[146]

Elsewhere—mostly though not exclusively upstream—the river was to be controlled by people's dikes. No troops or national funds would be used.[147] Rather, dikes were to be maintained by local people with local resources under the supervision of a commissioner dispatched from the provincial capital.[148] Even when provinces gained more control over their budgets during the Republic, people's dikes were still expected to be self-sufficient, except for small sums given during great emergencies—Shandong budgeted only ¥4,800 per year for crises on people's dikes.[149] In the entire 1891–1937 period, no stone people's dikes were ever built, though many official embankments were stone. When key dikes at Likantun (as far upstream as one can go in Shandong) and in Puyang, Zhili, became official embankments again (in 1928 and 1915, respectively) they were immediately redone with stone.[150]

Because people's dikes organizations were temporary and informal, some costs were low; communities did not, for instance, have to support "river troops" during idle months. However, this system may have blocked the use of stone, since stone costs came in one large initial lump.[151] Without formal taxing power, it would have been difficult to levy these sums; without a permanent institution, it would have been impossible to borrow them. And since the finances of these

146. Ibid., no. 1 (Oct. 1928), tables; Wu Tongju, *Zai xu*, 3718, 3949, 3951–56; Chen Yunlong, *Zhou Fu*, 279.
147. Wu Tongju, *Zai xu*, 3731, 3939; *HH*, 357.
148. Wu Tongju, *Zai xu*, 3766; *HWJB*, no. 1 (Fall 1919), 109; no. 3 (Fall 1920), 130–32.
149. *HWTK*, no. 1 (Oct. 1928), *gongdu*, 13.
150. *HWTK*, no. 2 (Jan. 1930), *zhuanjian*, 15. Xu Shiguang, *Puyang heshang ji*, *ding*, 23a.
151. *HWJB*, no. 1 (Fall 1919), 109, emphasizes the problems of not having permanent organizations in place.

informal organizations were intertwined with the personal finances of the supervising commissioner—a point we will return to in the next section—there was a strong incentive to concentrate on short-term savings, since commissioners never knew how long they would remain in charge of a particular dike.

Moreover, payment for stone would have been in money and would have gone to the outsiders who quarried and shipped it. *Gaoliang* dikes were built of local products and by local labor. Thus, although the costs of good *gaoliang* dikes were exorbitant, it might nonetheless have been easier for very poor communities to raise those costs than the money for stone dikes. As chapter 1 showed, some counties in Huang-Yun suffered from frequent currency shortages, and there were many complaints that people's dikes were hampered by cash flow problems.[152] When the provincial Reconstruction Office did a major project in southwestern Shandong in the 1930s, it concluded that it would be much easier to levy labor and goods than to raise—or even use—cash;[153] financial transactions might have seemed still more formidable to people's dikes groups. Conceivably, villagers also had a moral preference for exactions that stayed in the area, even if they were heavier and less effective.

Shipping also presented logistical challenges. Even official dikes often had trouble getting stone during the brief interval after the river thawed and before farm work began;[154] in 1930, the Shandong Yellow River Office (Hewuju) wanted to use more stone but did not have enough boats for even its current shipping needs.[155] For small, informal, cash-poor people's dikes organizations, these bottlenecks must have been even more serious.

But stone was not the only alternative to stalks. Officials had been suggesting for years that brick be used where stone was too expensive.[156] Western Shandong exported brick in the heyday of the

152. *JSYK* 2:3 (March 1932), *baogao*, 45; *HWJB*, no. 1 (Fall 1919), 117; *HWTK*, no. 8 (Jan. 1936), *gongdu*, 86, 89; *HWTK*, no. 1 (Oct. 1928), *mingling*, 30–31.

153. *Wanfu He*, 37.

154. See, for instance, memorial of Zhou Fu, 11/28/GX 29 (from Shandong), and Zhang Renjun memorial (from Henan) of 6/22/GX 29, both in LFZZ, GX 29, packet 40; *HWTK*, no. 4 (Jan. 1932), *gongdu*, 7–8 (from Hebei); *HWJB*, no. 1 (Fall 1919), 117.

155. *HWTK*, no. 2 (Jan. 1930), *zhuan jian*, 5.

156. Wu Tongju, *Zai xu*, 3836, 3947; *SDZZ*, no. 18 (9/30/GX 34), 9a.

Grand Canal, and brick making is a significant sideline there today.[157] Li Hongzhang and others recommended setting up kilns every few *li* along the river; this would have avoided shipping problems and costs and would have allowed free time before the river thawed to be used for dike work. Such a system of kilns also would have required far less payment of money to outsiders than stonework, since bricks could have been made from the same local materials as stalk dikes: stalks or wood (for fuel) and earth. At a third the cost, on average, of stone, brick would have been much cheaper in the long run (and sometimes even in the short run) than effective *gaoliang* work.[158]

No doubt brick would have entailed its own organizational difficulties—financing and guarding kilns, for instance—but the benefits would have been enormous, and many private organizations handled equally complex projects. Multivillage "gate associations" managed irrigation and flood control in places as nearby and similar to Huang-Yun as south-central Hebei.[159]

The people's dikes system had another wrinkle, however. While it nominally made dikes "the people's" responsibility—thus placing the maintenance burden on those who would most need the work to be done well—it did not put control of dike work in local hands. Instead, it interposed commissioners from Jinan, most of them expectant magistrates or prefects; their role is the focus of the next section.

Thus, the use of stalks rather than stone or brick dikes illustrates a lack of "administrative integration." Reliance on local resources, instead of buying more suitable materials from elsewhere, and inability to move resources through time by borrowing for stonework or making bricks in winter reflect a government unable to do any better than to have each community face these problems alone, and almost from scratch, each year. Once we place a price on the local resources used, the stalk people's dikes emerge as far more expensive than stone dikes financed from above; moreover, they were clearly far less effective, both for the people themselves and for the state organs that had to control disorder after major floods.

To further clarify the idea of a failure of administrative integration,

---

157. Yang Zhengtai, "Ming Qing Linqing," 118; interviews and personal observation, Dongping and Linqing, November 1985.

158. Wu Tongju, *Zai xu*, 3822, 3836, 3947.

159. See, e.g., Duara, *Culture, Power, and the State*, 26–38. For examples from other parts of Shandong, see Hou Renzhi, *Xu tianxia*, 144.

it may be helpful to compare it to Prasenjit Duara's idea that early-twentieth-century China underwent "state involution."[160] As Duara explains it, state involution involved the proliferation of "entrepreneurial brokers," who made their living as intermediaries between the state and village society. China had always had such brokers, but it came to have more of them as the functions and revenues of local government grew in the twentieth century. Moreover, most of the older brokers were either real bureaucrats, restrained by the bureaucracy's internal discipline and Confucian code, or community leaders, who accumulated prestige and other nonmonetary benefits by getting the best arrangement possible for their village; the latter also refrained from being too predatory because the respect of other villagers and the village's sense of community were part of their power base. There was a third group of intermediaries in the traditional system—yamen clerks and runners—who fit neither of these descriptions and who were repeatedly denounced as parasites, but Duara minimizes their importance, saying that their low status and limited functions kept their predations small compared to those of twentieth-century entrepreneurial brokers.[161]

The twentieth century's entrepreneurial brokers were part of a state that was reaching further down into society and so sought local representatives not rooted in or responsive to the village; the power base of these new local officials was their office, not their local reputation. But the state could neither pay these new officials enough nor police them enough to make them truly responsive to its goals. The result was an abusive and useless new set of intermediaries and a state that extracted much more from the peasantry without having enough funds in the right hands to actually deliver more services. Consequently, state involution not only contrasts with the administrative breakthrough to the modern state elsewhere, in which more extraction did mean more resources devoted to implementing the wishes of the administrative center; it also gives us a way to look at the state's loss of legitimacy in the decades preceding the Chinese Revolution.

The picture presented here resembles Duara's in many ways. In particular, both emphasize an increase in the quantity of resources ex-

---

160. The following summary is drawn from Duara, *Culture, Power, and the State,* esp. 73–77, 217–43. Some of these points are also covered in the author's review of this book in *Agricultural History* 63:3 (Summer 1989), 108–10.
161. Duara, *Culture, Power, and the State,* 42–57.

tracted from peasants and the absorption of most of those resources by the lowest levels of the bureaucracy and subbureaucracy. However, this account also adds to and modifies his. First, the example of people's dikes administration shows that these problems need not have been the result of a self-consciously modernizing state involving itself in new tasks. In this case, the state deliberately chose—as it often had even at its height—to turn its former tasks over to local actors to save money, not to achieve greater penetration. The abandonment of Yellow River control during a period of rising state revenues was indeed novel and, as I will argue in the final section of this chapter, reflected a new mercantilist and nationalist statecraft forced on China by imperialism. However, the proliferation of exploitative local figures who carried out what were sometimes state functions without being subject to bureaucratic discipline was nothing new.

Second, the examples in this book of new local figures—such as dike commissioners on one hand and the OEI officials promoting cotton on the other—show that the sociology and behavior of twentieth-century brokers between state and society were more complex than Duara allows. Duara stresses that the new entrepreneurial brokers were not strongly rooted in either the village or the traditional bureaucracy.[162] The implicit assumption is that these two venerable institutions were the only ones whose organization and ethos could restrain power holders from excessive self-seeking; the other people who gained a share of political power in twentieth-century rural China were anomic riffraff. Yet in the case of people's dikes, as we shall see, much of the corruption was the work of expectant officials: people who held higher-level traditional degrees and whose position as magistrates-to-be meant that they did have a stake in the formal bureaucracy's assessment of their performance and perhaps some commitment to its norms. And after the commissioners were discontinued, these illicit profits were taken over by village leaders who show no signs of having been a new social group or having power bases outside the villages.

The county OEI leaders discussed in chapter 2 actually bear a stronger resemblance to Duara's institutional profile of the entrepreneurial broker. They operated below the county magistrate, but from the county seat, rather than the village; they were very poorly paid,

162. Ibid., 47, 152–53, 215.

but used their official appointment as a power base, and so on. However, most came from elite backgrounds. More important, these lower officials managed—at least in North Huang-Yun—to promote economic growth and increase government revenue while leaving most of the peasantry better off than before. Their impact was therefore exactly opposite that of both the dike commissioners and Duara's entrepreneurial brokers.

Thus a structural analysis of where various brokers stood in relation to the state and the village is not enough to explain their role in either a breakthrough in state making or its opposite. We also need to consider the state as donor, not just as extractor. In Huang-Yun dike maintenance, it was not merely that more resources were extracted without a breakthrough to a more efficient state: expected services actually disappeared. The nineteenth-century Yellow River Administration, which kept taking more resources and employees to do the same job, may have been a case of state involution; the Yellow River system in twentieth-century western Shandong combined large-scale waste with the consequences of deliberate regional triage.

All these problems suggest a need to consider state involution within at least two types of regional context. First, we need to locate places from the point of view of the state and with regard to centers of economic growth. There is a great deal of evidence that in areas that were accorded a high priority by early-twentieth-century state builders, increased taxes often were turned into increased services. Such was the case with many municipal governments and with many rural counties in economically growing areas, such as the "core counties" described in Keith Schoppa's study of Zhejiang.[163] The same was true, as we will see in the last part of this chapter, for at least one key service—flood control—in the newly emphasized areas of eastern Shandong. Those advances, however, came at a price, part of which was a central government withdrawal from areas like Huang-Yun. In such areas, local elites and quasi officials were freed from significant oversight and encouraged to take on more roles; they also increased extraction but were usually unable or unwilling to use these new resources effectively. And while such hinterland areas probably did not suffer the greatest increases in extraction, they appear to have been the ones in which the population became most alienated from the modern

163. Schoppa, *Elites*, 83–94.

state—a phenomenon that makes sense when we consider the decline of vital traditional services in places like Huang-Yun.

Duara's analysis, which aims for an overall assessment of whether North China experienced a breakthrough in political development, runs into a problem similar to one encountered by older works that tried to measure various places' degrees of modernization. By ignoring the possible links between the development of some countries and the underdevelopment of others, modernization theory missed the fact that both these phenomena are part of the modern world. Similarly, Duara's attempt to see in what ways North China as a whole did or did not become part of a modern state misses the fact that different subregions went in different directions, that successes in some areas were intimately related to failures in others, and that these different outcomes were all characteristic of early-twentieth-century China.

Second, we need to introduce local social structure as a variable in understanding the different results achieved by agents of the state in different areas. In certain places, new county- or subcounty-level operatives penetrated villages while remaining committed to the goals of networks centered elsewhere and mobilized enough people and resources to have a transformative effect. The diffusion of new cotton varieties in North Huang-Yun is a perfect example. In other times and places, as Duara suggests, such people may not have penetrated the village directly, but they were powerful and predatory enough to change the rural elite for the worse, forcing out old-style "protective brokers" by making their jobs impossible and hiring local toughs in their stead.[164] In still other places, such as South Huang-Yun, these new operatives seem to have had no effect at all. There it was traditional elites such as expectant officials and entrenched village heads who either became or always had been entrepreneurial brokers.

We shall return to the relationship between failed political integration and state involution later. Now, what is important is that the notion of state involution, although useful, needs revision to fit Huang-Yun. That revision involves fitting any particular case into the concerns discussed in this volume: a place's relationship to larger economic and administrative networks, its place in the goals of the central state (in turn affected by international politics), and the permeability of its social structure to outside agents. State involution is a model

164. See, e.g., Chen Yunlong, *Zhou Fu*, 165, 217.

of political change driven largely by political dynamics, the needs of the state, and (elsewhere in Duara's book) a general Chinese cultural setting: it seems to fit Huang-Yun better when we place it in the context of political and economic geography, local social variation, and this work's analysis of the state as donor and of administrative integration.

The continued use of stalks for people's dikes stemmed in part, as we have seen, from problems that all actors in Huang-Yun faced—poor transport and a deficient currency system—and that only higher levels of government could have remedied. However, people's dikes organizations also had special weaknesses that perpetuated the choice of inferior techniques. They had neither the usual advantages of formal government mobilization of people and resources nor those of reliance on the market's "invisible hand"; they did have unusual levels of corruption. The rest of this chapter examines this system in greater detail.

YELLOW RIVER CONTROL IN HUANG-YUN

The Grand Canal reforms officially abolished the battalions of troops (*ying*) who specialized in river work along that waterway; the 1891 reforms eliminated most of the *ying* on the Yellow River. While few people regretted this change at the time, many would regret it later; the new system that emerged had built-in tendencies toward inferior work and outright corruption.

Many reformers claimed that river troops were obsolete. Their ranks were steadily depleted by cutbacks and desertion.[165] By 1910, *Shandong zazhi* said that although that province's eighteen river battalions theoretically had five hundred men each, they could summon only one hundred each even in a crisis and normally had fewer than fifty members.[166] Like other old-style Qing troops, their rations were inadequate, and many had long since lost their theoretically inalienable land allotments. Many allegedly supported themselves by stealing supplies, by smuggling, and by banditry, while officers pocketed the pay of absent troops.[167]

---

165. Hoshi Ayao, *Dai Unga*, 178–85, 192–98; *Guangxu gong zhong dang*, 15:50; *HWJB*, no. 3 (Fall 1920), 126.

166. *SDZZ*, no. 59 (5/10/XT 2), 7b; *HWJB*, no. 1 (Fall 1919), 117–18.

167. *SDZZ*, no. 59 (5/10/XT 2), 9a; no. 76 (10/30/XT 3), 15a–b.

Equipment and training were also substandard. Confronted with bandit raids in 1900, Shandong river troops had only obsolete muskets; many had never learned to use firearms, anyway.[168] Throughout the Guangxu period, river troops were gradually cut back. Henan eliminated three river battalions.[169] *Shandong zazhi* recommended that Shandong do the same, arguing that costs could be cut 60 percent if the poor people along the river were hired seasonally to do the work.[170]

Elsewhere, however, officials successfully trimmed the number of river battalions while upgrading the remaining ones. A once notoriously useless battalion along the north Jiangsu Grand Canal was apparently turned into a model group, so proficient in river work and effective against bandits that when they were reassigned, "the gentry and people begged them to stay"; in Zhili, Yuan Shikai reduced Daming prefecture's three all-purpose battalions to one three-hundred-man *ying* specializing in Yellow River work.[171] The outside supervisor of Zhili's extensive 1915 Yellow River work said these troops were both experienced and particularly hardworking; O. J. Todd, who did Yellow River work in the 1920s, concurred; Freeman was impressed by the *ying* officers' knowledge of traditional techniques and of the river itself.[172] The few *ying* associated with the South Shandong Grand Canal and its locks who were not cashiered in 1902 were likewise given new training and better rations.[173]

The attrition of Shandong's Yellow River troops continued, however, especially in the west, and no resources were allocated to improve those who remained. Eventually, riverworks officials came to regret this loss. By 1920, the head of the Shandong Yellow River Office was sufficiently convinced that maintaining and upgrading the river troops was the way to nurture technically skilled Yellow River workers that he proposed taking funds away from the repair of earthen dikes to increase their salaries.[174] A 1931 account by the

---

168. *HWJB*, no. 1 (Fall 1919), 118; *Guangxu gong zhong dang*, 15:50.
169. Wu Tongju, *Zai xu*, 3717.
170. *SDZZ*, no. 59 (5/10/XT 2), 7b.
171. *Guangxu gong zhong dang*, 15:50, 408.
172. Xu Shiguang, *Puyang heshang ji, ding*, 17a, 21a, 22b; Oliver Todd, *Two Decades in China, Comprising Technical Papers, Magazine Articles, Newspaper Stories and Official Reports Connected with Work under His Own Observation* (Beijing, 1938), 93, 115–16; Freeman, "Flood Problems," 1142.
173. Chen Yunlong, *Zhou Fu*, 251–53.
174. *HWJB*, no. 3 (Fall 1920), 126.

Shandong Reconstruction Office blamed the Grand Canal's decay simply and unequivocally on the removal of "officials and troops" after 1902.[175]

Many observers noted that cashiering the river troops had involved losing the twenty to thirty years of riverworks experience many of them had accumulated. Many also noted inefficiencies that resulted from using short-term supervisors and laborers rather than having an organization in place at all times. In sum, numerous late Qing and especially Republican officials concluded that river work had to be placed under professional, technically skilled personnel (either river troops or modern engineers).[176] However, very few positions in the new provincial Yellow River offices created in the 1890s actually went to such people. Instead they were staffed by expectant magistrates or an occasional expectant prefect. The heads of the three zones into which the Shandong Yellow River was divided and each zone chief's principal assistants were also expectant officials.[177]

More important, such people also dominated field administration. The commissioners (*weiyuan*) sent to supervise official dikes, supervising both river troops and civilians, were also expectant officials (*houbu renyuan*). So were the two officials in charge of the north and south banks (about twenty-eight miles each) of the Zhili Yellow River. Most important of all, particularly in western Shandong, the people commissioned to supervise river work done "by the people" were all expectant civil officials.[178]

It is not clear exactly when expectant officials came to dominate Yellow River administration. Their participation began in the eighteenth century, but at least until 1853, they were still subordinate to the regular bureaucrats involved. They seem to have assumed leading roles after the 1853 shift;[179] it seems natural that, since many areas suddenly had to deal with river problems they had not had before, commissioners dispatched by the governors would quickly become important. Given the poor record of "people's dikes under official super-

175. *JSYK* 1:3 (March 1931), *gongdu*, 47.

176. *HWJB*, no. 1 (Fall 1919), 110, 118; no. 3 (Fall 1920), 109, 125–26, 133.

177. For a brief history, see *HWJB*, no. 4 (Spring 1921), 75; no. 1 (Fall 1919), 118, 9, 13.

178. Ibid., no. 4 (Spring 1921), 75, 12–13; Wu Tongju, *Zai xu*, 3951; *HWJB*, no. 1 (Fall 1919), 109.

179. On pre-1853 *weiyuan*, see Dodgen, "Hydraulic Evolution," 47–48; on post-1853 *weiyuan*, see *HWJB*, no. 1 (Fall 1919), 118.

vision" elsewhere—an 1833 report had concluded that this system was the most corrupt and ineffective of the three types in use on the Hubei section of the Yangzi[180]—it is hard to imagine a massive turn to these *weiyuan* except as a result of the multifaceted crisis of the middle and late nineteenth century.

Thereafter, expectant officials took over more river work as the size, number, and budgets of river battalions declined throughout the Guangxu period. A 1920 provincial study said that the key date was 1894, when Shandong set up offices for the upper, middle, and lower Yellow rivers and set aside the top thirteen positions for expectant officials—just three years after it had been decided to leave more river work to localities in the hope of increasing efficiency and saving money.[181]

The rules drafted in 1894 provided for "civil and military officials" to serve as supervisors, but civil officials were dominant. They had, for instance, sole control of procurement. In 1904, Shandong governor Zhou Fu ordered county magistrates to help mobilize corvée labor; however, they were to work under the commissioners, who would set the number of workers, their tasks, and their rations. Even the prefectural officials who were ordered to help with specific dikes were to work under the commissioners.[182]

The unchecked power of the commissioners in supervising people's dikes is dramatized in a *North China Herald* story from western Shandong, "illustrat[ing] the terrorizing practices by upper officials over subordinates." When Yellow River dikes in the area threatened to break, the commissioner in charge of the people's dikes of three counties in that area assembled the counties' magistrates at the most precarious dike and harangued them; throughout his lecture, which was accompanied by rain and hail, the magistrates were forced to kneel in the mud and were threatened with decapitation if they tried to rise.[183] While this story is undoubtedly exaggerated, it gives some sense of how unlikely county magistrates were to control the actions of the expectant officials. Significantly, the magistrates are called the commissioner's "subordinates," though most *weiyuan* were officially aspiring magistrates. A memorial about corruption on the north Jiangsu Grand

180. On the Hubei case, see Perdue, *Exhausting the Earth*, 194–95.
181. Wu Tongju, *Zai xu*, 3949–56.
182. Ibid., 3939, 3945–46, 3949; Chen Yunlong, *Zhou Fu*, 275, 283.
183. *NCH*, Oct. 5, 1906, 13–14.

Canal suggests a similar pattern. It says nothing about either local officials or river troops, who probably had little scope for graft, but emphasizes that the many poor expectant officials involved would "encroach on public funds" unless "scrupulousness" was "enforced."[184]

Not only were commissioners uncontrolled: as outsiders dispatched for a short time, they did not have the same stake in controlling future floods and repair costs that genuinely local organizations would have had. Even those who hoped that their performance would be well regarded and would lead to a magistracy could hardly be expected to introduce a new and initially onerous type of dike building during a short-term assignment; if they did not burden the people much more than other commissioners and there were no major floods during their term, that would probably be enough. As for those who were neither scrupulous nor determined to win plaudits, their positions made it very easy for them to "encroach on public funds." On official embankments, the commissioners controlled most of the procurement process, but at least there were river troops counting the inventory. In people's dikes areas, the commissioners had nobody at all to answer to.[185]

Commissioners were in a particularly advantageous position as purchasers of stalks. As we have seen, stalks were quite valuable, but most people gathered their own; stalks were rarely shipped very far or traded on a large scale.[186] Thus, commissioners not only had the power to demand stalk deliveries but had great latitude in setting and reporting the prices paid—advantages they would not have enjoyed had they purchased stone from official quarries or brick from kilns they did not control. There is no "smoking gun" showing that such advantages influenced the decisions of commissioners supervising Yellow River people's dikes. However, in 1917 the *North China Herald* reported a similar phenomenon on the north Jiangsu Grand Canal, saying that dike commissioners there preferred *gaoliang* dikes because a need for frequent work "is to the advantage of the contractor."[187] When Xu Shiguang led a large repair project on a Zhili Yellow River section that had previously been converted to people's dikes—and which, Xu noted, had then decayed rapidly—he estimated that 50–60

184. *Guangxu gong zhong dang*, 15:53.
185. Wu Tongju, *Zai xu*, 3945–46; *HWJB*, no. 1 (Fall 1919), 109; no. 2 (Spring 1920), 127.
186. Freeman, "Flood Problems," 1137; Wu Tongju, *Zai xu*, 3848.
187. *NCH*, April 21, 1917, p. 119.

percent of the money reportedly spent for materials for people's dikes had been embezzled. He set up various offices, led by river troops, to check on the people involved in purchasing, delivering, and stacking materials; his repairs, which were lasting, came in under budget.[188] There is, then, a strong circumstantial case that commissioners' small stake in lasting, effective dikes, and the opportunities for them and other middlemen to profit, had much to do with the continued use of stalks for people's dikes.

In 1902, Xiliang, then the governor of Henan, noted a pattern while cutting personnel on some riverworks managed jointly by Henan and Shandong. In Henan, positions such as the supervisor of a canal lock or stretch of dikes would generally be filled by expectant officials from Shandong; in Shandong, they would be filled by Henanese expectant officials.[189]

These river supervisors occupied an anomalous position in late Qing bureaucracy and society. They were not, like yamen runners, subcounty officials serving at home, whose power came from local connections that the magistrate, as an outsider, could not match. In fact, Xiliang's cuts caused large numbers of these people to return to their native places to wait for other appointments. Dismissed Grand Canal lock officers also went home. (In both cases, many of the returnees sought subcounty appointments at a level normally considered beneath expectant magistrates but that offered many opportunities for profit.) Nor were they like a magistrate's secretary, whose boss and patron was immediately present.[190] Like both secretaries and runners, however, their appointments were outside the orthodox civil service system, and native-place ties seem to have been important in getting these commissions.

Even without a local base comparable to yamen runners, commissioners were at least equally immune to control by magistrates. Meanwhile, their greater prestige and presumed connections in the provincial capital probably made them more immune than yamen runners to protests by gentry and other local elites. Zhou Fu said that the corruption of lock officials on the Shandong Grand Canal was well known,

188. Xu Shiguang, *Puyang heshang ji, ding,* 13a–b; *ding,* 11a; *hou xu,* 1b; *Xu tianxia,* 151.

189. Wu Tongju, *Zai xu,* 3721.

190. Ibid.; Chen Yunlong, *Zhou Fu,* 166–67. On magistrates' secretaries, see Ch'u T'ung-tsu, *Local Government in China under the Ch'ing* (Cambridge, Mass., 1962), 93–115.

but magistrates "did not dare to interfere"; dealing with the problem would require the governor's sending a personal representative (another *weiyuan*) to work with local notables and the boat owners suffering from extortion.[191]

Unfortunately, we know little about these officials or about how they were chosen. However, higher-level officials in the early Republic complained that expectant magistrates continued to get almost all river commissions; published personnel documents corroborate this impression. Since these commissioners were never assigned to their home counties, the new system of local responsibility placed the burden of riverworks on localities without creating local control.[192] The cuts in national and provincial river conservancy spending may have reduced the numbers of people living off river control, but it did not improve the type of people in charge. If anything, it made profiteering easier, at least for commissioners on people's dikes.

The informal system of stalk deliveries also provided opportunities for village heads and so-called local bullies (*tuhao*). In fact, the system's inadequacies left a lot of room for intermediaries to benefit themselves at the public expense, while still leaving people better off than they would have been if they had faced commissioners' exactions alone. (Markets provide a useful analogy to this poorly integrated administrative system: the more poorly they are integrated, the more a middleman can charge.)

The missionary Arthur Smith describes such a case from Caozhou in the 1890s. Villages had been assigned to deliver stalks for official dike repairs and were to be paid accordingly. Unfortunately, since the deliveries were to be made far away, the recipients could dictate any price by delaying the processing of these deliveries, forcing people to stay away from home at a ruinous cost. To avoid repetition of this problem, the county magistrate appointed a village headman to handle future stalk deliveries; he in turn appointed three of his protégés. Afterward, the villagers all believed that these people had been dishonest, but nobody wanted to return to in-person delivery. Since Shandong and Henan people were supposed to deliver straw to places as much as two days away—far further than stalks were ever shipped commercially—these people were indeed better off with dishonest

191. Chen Yunlong, *Zhou Fu*, 165.
192. See, e.g., *HWJB*, no. 1 (Fall 1919), 12–14, 19–22, 109, 118; no. 2 (Spring 1920), 13, 125.

mediators than no mediators at all.[193] Moreover, the illegal gains of fellow villagers—who might do their neighbors favors in the future—were quite likely diverted from nonresident commissioners and their minions, rather than from the dikes themselves.

Such abuses generated a consensus that different personnel were needed. In 1920, Lao Zhichang, head of the Shandong Yellow River Office, made clear his preference for either the old *ying* or modern engineers; he cited approvingly an earlier report's recommendations that expectant civil officials be replaced by people with modern technical training and that the use of short-term commissioners be ended as soon as possible.[194] But in spite of all such proposals, expectant civil officials dominated the Yellow River Office and "supervised" most local river work until the Northern Expedition. At that time, as chapter 5 will show, commissioners lost control of people's dikes to village heads and local bosses, not to either the reformed *ying* or modern engineers that the Yellow River Office had hoped would displace them.

Some expectant officials stayed in river conservancy work long enough to become quite knowledgeable. Some administrative improvements were made under their control, and the geological and meteorological studies undertaken in the early Republic proved very useful later.[195] But there were few substantial achievements in actual flood control.

Overall, Yellow River work after the 1891 reforms was probably better than in the 1880s. It was also much cheaper for the government than the 1880s work and the ineffectual work of the 1840s.[196] Any improvement, however, was only relative to these especially bad years. Moreover, in Huang-Yun, where the system was changed the most, flood control did not improve; it got much worse.

No evidence suggests that waste decreased after 1891. There were constant complaints that the commissioners were not only inexpert, but extremely corrupt. Lao Zhichang noted in 1920 that stone *fang* were almost always at least 30 percent underweight (the inside was

---

193. Arthur H. Smith, *Village Life*, 230–31; Freeman, "Flood Problems," 1137.

194. *HWJB*, no. 2 (Spring 1920), 125.

195. Ibid. no. 1 (Fall 1919), 12; no. 2 (Spring 1920), 13; no. 4 (Spring 1921), 85. For the description of surveying work, see Carey, "Michigan Engineers in China," *Michigan Technik* 33:3 (November 1920), 149–56; and on the use of this material by the Jiansheju in later years, see *JSYK* 1:2 (Feb. 1931), *yao wen*, 9; 1:3 (March 1931) *gongdu*, 5, 33–34.

196. Wu Tongju, *Zai xu*, 4178.

hollow); many *fang* were 50–60 percent underweight. On another occasion, he estimated that more than half of riverworks funds were wasted. Discussing the upriver people's dikes in particular, he stated that "squeeze" (extraction of illegal profits by supervising officials) had gotten worse since the "reforms." In the past, he concluded, the national government's liberality allowed waste and adequate river maintenance to coexist, but now it led to increased flooding.[197] *Shandong zazhi* blamed Yellow River problems mostly on officials' "quest for profit" and charged that the Grand Canal commissioner at Jining (the only part of the Shandong Canal still receiving government money) had embezzled 90 percent of the funds.[198] Waste and corruption took their greatest toll on Yellow River people's dikes, where there was nobody to check the commissioners and no government funds to steal and where the many other problems left no margin for error.

By the late 1920s, a further devolution had occurred, and sub-county power holders became a greater obstacle to river control than abuses by the Yellow River Office and the commissioners. We will look more closely at this situation in the next chapter. Here it is enough to note that the reign of the expectant officials over flood control contributed powerfully to the development of an underfunded, fragmented, technically backward, and corrupt flood control system that was both expensive and ineffective.

REDISTRIBUTING THE FLOOD PROBLEM

As we have seen, the switch to people's dikes was concentrated in certain areas. The available documents say little about how regional priorities were set and are not always consistent in what they do say. Given the importance of "benevolence" in Chinese political thought and the relative lack of emphasis on "efficiency," it is unlikely that one would ever find a document that frankly discussed sacrificing one area rather than another. Nevertheless, the results of official thinking here resemble those of the mercantilist and sovereignty-preserving logic we have already dubbed "the logic of self-strengthening": and once again, Huang-Yun suffered heavily from this logic. It is particularly striking

197. *HWJB*, no. 1 (Fall 1919), 107, 115; no. 3 (Fall 1920), 124.
198. *SDZZ*, no. 60 (5/20/XT 2), 6a; no. 76 (10/30/XT 2), 15a; *SDZZ*, no. 35 (6/15/XT 1), 22a–b.

that almost none of the discussion of cuts in the support of the Grand Canal even mentions the likely effects on the welfare of those living near it; one of the very few exceptions is a memorial from Chen Kuilong, the same official who later complained that inland areas like Henan were being bled to finance coastal modernization.[199] Some later provincial and national officials, particularly in the Republic, saw that the state's withdrawal from water control in Huang-Yun had gone too far, but they could not make the state reevaluate its regional priorities.

We have already seen the reasons behind the priorities assigned to different sections of the Grand Canal. The south Shandong Canal affected merchants who were bigger, better organized, and better connected than any in north Shandong. The north Jiangsu and Jhili sections, which also continued to get government funds, were of interest to still bigger and more influential merchants, including the Lianghuai and Changlu salt merchants, whose prosperity translated directly into government revenue.[200] Overall, these areas were more important to the state, had more access to private funds, and were technically less complex than the north Shandong Grand Canal; thus in these areas the state was likely to get a good return on a small investment.

The north Shandong Grand Canal had none of these advantages. As noted earlier, the Qing seem to have assumed that the north Shandong Grand Canal would remain open even after they ceased contributing to it in 1902, but they said nothing about how. The next year, when Beijing decided to relocate the Tianjin arsenal to Dezhou, the numerous high officials involved cited its position on the Grand Canal as an important advantage.[201] However, in allocating their own spending, they wound up behaving much as the central government later behaved regarding reforestation efforts. They concentrated on areas that most affected the government's economic concerns, which were also areas where the potential for private solutions was greatest. Thus they chose areas where money may have gone furthest in terms of

199. Memorial of 5/4/GX 28 from Chen Kuilong in *Guangxu gong zhong dang,* 16:204–5.
200. *Shuntian shibao,* 11/21/XT 3, p. 4; petition from Grand Canal intendant for southern Shandong (name illegible) to Governor of Shandong 4/12/Xianfeng 5 (1855), in archives of the Shandong governor (no file or packet numbers yet), First Historical Archives, Beijing; *NCH,* Dec. 8, 1917, p. 577.
201. Memorial from Zhu Enwen (at Board of War), 12/13/XT 2, in LFZZ, XT 2, packet 54–68.

mercantilist priorities but where it accomplished the least in terms of welfare.

In the Yellow River reforms, an ostensible criterion for allocating national funds was announced: the government would concentrate on the most difficult and dangerous parts of the river. In Shandong, the upper river (covering most of Huang-Yun), which was widest, was felt to be the least dangerous. It was overwhelmingly converted to people's dikes; only a few dikes, often ten miles from the river, remained official responsibilities.[202] Of 1,256 *li* (452 miles) of Shandong dikes that remained official responsibilities, only 213 were on the upper portion of the river, but the upper river included 285 of the 439 *li* that were to be maintained by "the people" under official supervision and all of the 92 *li* that were not even under official oversight.[203] While the upper section had had the fewest floods up to that point, it also had by far the least stonework and thus the highest percentage of dikes needing frequent repair.

The wider river bed there, which was dry much of the year, was particularly vulnerable to land reclamation. There had always been local pressures to allow farming closer and closer to the river. A significant minority of officials rationalized this by arguing that the river could best be controlled by narrowing its banks so its own waters would be forced to deepen its channel.[204] However, engineers who advocated crowding the river this way added the crucial proviso that this required stone inner dikes;[205] and neither the people's dikes nor the private (*si*) dikes built by people reclaiming river land used stone. Under these conditions, land reclamation and private dikes were often dysfunctional for overall flood control, but the reclaimers were hard to dislodge. In 1888, a frustrated central Shandong river commissioner deliberately engineered a flood to destroy private dikes that earlier officials had permitted;[206] even this, however, did not deter people for long.

---

202. *HWJB*, no. 1 (Fall 1919), 107; Wu Tongju, *Zai xu*, 3939; *NCH*, Oct. 27, 1917, p. 217.

203. *HWJB*, no. 3 (Fall 1920), 130.

204. See, for instance, the opinions of Liu E (Liu Tieyun) in Wu Tongju, *Zai xu*, 4142–46, and in *Lao Can youji*, chap. 1.

205. Freeman, "Flood Problems," 1154; Todd, *Two Decades in China*, 41.

206. Tyler, "Notes on the Hoang Ho," 6; Liu E, *Lao Can youji*, 167–69; according to this version of events, one expectant official involved advised buying out the people squatting too close to the river (much as Li Hongzhang and Zhou Fu wanted to do twelve years later), but others rejected such a buy-out as too expensive.

In general, the post-1891 decentralization meant that the people who were supposed to contribute goods and labor to maintain the dikes were often precisely those who had much to lose if efforts were focused on the outer dikes. After the state withdrew from the upper Shandong Yellow River, more people planted close to the river, thus eliminating the physical margin for error that had originally justified the central government's withdrawal.[207] Li Hongzhang and Zhou Fu advocated buying out these reclaimers, since the government could not evict them by force. However, the central government would not pay for the buy-out, and the one provincial effort to raise the needed funds that Beijing authorized failed, as we shall see in chapter 5.[208] The idea of moving people back from the Yellow River was dropped, and private dikes continued to interfere with larger-scale river control.

The upstream part of Shandong, which included such notorious bandit areas as Caozhou, also had particularly serious security problems. Every jurisdiction faced thefts of supplies, occasional interference with workers, and illegal cutting of trees that had been planted to strengthen the river banks, but these problems were most severe upstream. In 1919, the Yellow River Office tried to set up a quarry closer to the upper portion of the river, but banditry was so severe that the site was quickly abandoned.[209]

For all these reasons, it was obvious by the early Republic that the upper Shandong Yellow River could not be maintained through local efforts alone. In 1917, Yellow River Office head Lao Zhichang noted that while this had originally seemed the best area to turn into people's dikes, the squeeze problem had become steadily worse since the conversion to people's administration; as a result, the dikes had decayed seriously in this area, while the people had been worn out by exactions. He rated it as now more dangerous than the middle section. In his view (not borne out by statistics), it was still less dangerous than

207. See, e.g., Wu Tongju, *Zai xu*, 3939; Chen Yunlong, *Zhou Fu*, 153; *HWJB*, no. 3 (Fall 1920), 123.
208. Chen Yunlong, *Zhou Fu*, 154, 155, 688; Wu Tongju, *Zai xu*, 3756; also see below.
209. *SDZZ*, no. 59 (5/10/XT 2), 9a; *HWJB*, no. 1 (Fall 1919), 111, 118; *HWTK*, no. 1 (Oct. 1928), *mingling*, 25; no. 6 (Jan. 1934), *gongdu*, 7; *pian* from Yang Shixiang, 10/16/GX 32, in LFZZ, GX 32, packet 46–50; *HWTK*, no. 3 (Jan. 1931), *mingling*, 33, *gongdu*, 10; Freeman, *GCIM*, 21; also see chapter 3. *HWJB*, no. 4 (Spring 1921), 78.

the final section, but in that zone, the provincial government still accepted responsibility for most dikes.[210]

Henan and Zhili also turned many dikes that had been either official or joint official and people's responsibilities (*guan min gong shou*) into local burdens.[211] However, Henan and Zhili created fewer people's dikes than western Shandong did, and Zhili turned most of these dikes back into official ones as early as 1918.[212] All requests to convert any of Shandong's people's dikes to official embankments were rejected until after the Northern Expedition, and very few were granted even then.[213]

Henan and Zhili also maintained much more generous riverworks budgets than Shandong. At least in Henan, such budgets reflected a position for the Yellow River in the province's economic geography—and thus in the provincial government's mercantilist calculations—very different from that of the western Shandong Yellow River. Henan, an inland, relatively inaccessible, and largely poor province, had been hard hit by the central government's change of priorities in the late nineteenth century; as we saw earlier, at least one Henan governor complained about this change. Within the province, however, there were good reasons not to take money out of Yellow River control. The river ran very close to Kaifeng, the provincial capital, and through the center of one of the province's most economically developed areas; one of its most flood-prone points was near both the capital and the crossing of the province's only north-south railway. The east-west railway built in the province in 1925 ran along the river for many miles.[214] Moreover, the province had no treaty-port area that was a particularly promising or necessary place to modernize. Thus, while the central government deemphasized the Henan Yellow River, just as it did the western Shandong Yellow River, Henan's provincial government had no reason to do so. And for most of the Republican period, it was provincial decisions that counted. As for Zhili, its section of the Yellow River was quite short; and with provincial

210. *HWJB*, no. 1 (Fall 1919), 107, 108; no. 3 (Fall 1920), 130.

211. Wu Tongju, *Zai xu*, 3716–17; memorial from Yuan Shikai, 10/15/GX 30, in LFZZ, GX 30, packet 47–50; *Chongxiu Hua xianzhi* (1930), 11:29b–30a, 32a.

212. *Chongxiu Hua xianzhi*(1930), 11:31b; *HWJB*, no. 1 (Fall 1919), 10–11; *HH*, 366.

213. *HWTK*, no. 1 (Oct. 1928), *fa gui*, 6–8, *gongdu*, 13.

214. Perry, *Rebels and Revolutionaries*, 34, 276.

revenues soaring in the twentieth-century,[215] doing adequate Yellow River control was a very small burden for this province.

As a result of these differences, the Shandong Yellow River Office calculated in 1920 that it had ¥380 to spend for each *li* of dikes, versus a much higher figure for Henan and a figure six times the Shandong figure for Zhili.[216] While Shandong cut its already inadequate Yellow River budget even further after 1911, Zhili more than doubled its spending.[217]

Lower spending almost always meant more floods. Overall, there was vastly more flooding from the 1890s on than in the years between the 1855 river shift and 1890. Some commentators attributed this flooding to bad decisions made in the late 1860s, and, in fact, the twelve years before 1891 had seen serious annual flooding, as opposed to just three "major" floods in the previous twenty-five years.[218] However, the vast majority of these floods were on the middle and lower stretches of the Shandong Yellow River: those areas account for thirty-five of the incidents serious enough to be mentioned in the standard histories of river conservancy between 1879 and 1890, as against six in Zhili, one in Henan, and two for the upper zone of the Shandong Yellow River. After the 1891 changes, things improved greatly on the lower and middle stretches, where the Shandong government concentrated its remaining money and soldiers; that area dropped to eighteen floods in the 1891–1911 period and "only" six in the first twenty years of the Republic (eight in all for 1912–37). The number of serious floods in Zhili also dropped—from 1891 to 1937 it experienced the same number as from 1879–90—and the Henan Yellow River did not have another serious flood until 1933.[219]

However, the upper portion of the Shandong Yellow River, where most of the conversion to people's responsibility was carried out, suffered very badly. From just two major flooding incidents in 1879–90 and another two in 1855–79, it suffered three in the first decade after 1891 and nine more between 1902 and 1911. In the first twenty years

215. Duara, *Culture, Power, and the State*, 65–73.

216. *HWJB*, no. 3 (Fall 1920), 128. My own calculations suggest a ratio of slightly over 5 to 1: for Shandong, ¥520,000:1,787 *li* (*HWJB*, no. 3, p. 130) = ¥291 per *li*; for Zhili, ¥250,000:170 *li* = ¥1471 per *li*.

217. Compare the ¥250,000 with the late Qing budget of 73,500 *liang* (as cited in, e.g., Yuan Shikai's memorial of 11/23/GX 30 [LFZZ, GX 30, packet 47–50]), which would equal approximately ¥100,000.

218. Wu Tongju, *Zai xu*, 4143.

219. *HH*, 358–65, 379–81.

TABLE 3 A ROUGH GUIDE TO THE CHANGING REGIONAL DISTRIBUTION OF YELLOW RIVER FLOODS

	Henan	Zhili/Hebei	Shandong Upper	Shandong Middle and lower[a]
Approximate river-front length (each bank, in miles)	240[b]	30	90	160
Prereform				
1856–68	0	0	0	0 (0)
1869–78	1	1	2	0 (0)
1879–90	1	6	2	35 (4)
Postreform				
1891–1911	0	3	12[c]	18 (7)
1912–31	0	2	11	6 (6)
1932–37	3	1	2	2 (0)

NOTE: These figures count the number of times that counties within these areas are specifically mentioned in the lists of major floods in Zai xu and HH. They are neither the number of years in which there was flooding nor the number of dike breaks. Nor can they be regarded as a complete list, since we do not know the criteria for deciding which were "major" floods and since many of these lists of affected counties end in "and others." However, if we had complete lists of affected areas, the redistribution of flooding would probably stand out even more (see [a] below).

[a] Numbers in parentheses in the last column represent the number of "lower and middle" Shandong flooding incidents accounted for by Lijin county, the last county the river flows through before emptying into the sea. Floods that began this close to the river's mouth, while often very destructive, generally did not fan out over nearly as wide an area as those that occurred farther from the coast. Thus, the increasingly large percentage of "middle and lower" Shandong floods accounted for by this one location as time went on implies that the difference in the level of flood protection between this area and the "upstream Shandong" area widened even more than the numbers listed here might suggest.

[b] This figure overestimates flood risk, since most of the Henan Yellow River was above the point (near Kaifeng) where the river became most dangerous.

[c] Nine of these twelve floods occurred in the last eleven years of this twenty-year period.

of the Republic, it suffered eleven more (and two more between 1931 and the deliberately induced disaster of 1938).[220] These incidents of flooding cannot be blamed on overall decline, since the worst problems before 1891 occurred in areas downstream from western Shandong, where conditions improved considerably after 1891; the increase of flooding was specific to the area that was singled out for conversion to people's dikes.

In sum, the 1891 switch to people's dikes in western Shandong completely failed to create a more cost-effective flood control system. What did have some success, particularly compared to the 1880s, was the mixture of river troops, provincially organized corvée, and people's dikes on the middle and lower reaches of the river, in Henan and especially in Zhili. These improvements, however, and the overall transfer of funds from water conservancy to various modernizing projects elsewhere in North China, were made at the price of withdrawing national and provincial river funds from western Shandong, where the organizational changes that accompanied financial withdrawal aggravated its effects. The losses there more than outweighed gains elsewhere.

These priorities and results differed sharply from those prevalent before 1850, when liberal riverworks spending and emphasis on the Grand Canal ensured ample (if sometimes misspent) money for inland trouble spots.[221] Instead, the state now concentrated on mobilizing revenues and maintaining control in areas near the coast. In giving up on a now less important inland system for moving its surplus, the government also lost the ability to carry out other projects in that area— at great cost to its inhabitants.

The government did not have quite the same mercantilist reasons for overemphasizing coastal areas' flood control problems as it did for overemphasizing reforestation near the coast. Unlike fuel shortages or small floods, major floods threatened order and posed a humanitarian challenge that had to be dealt with wherever it occurred; Huang-Yun got a great deal of outside money (much of it private) for flood relief even when it could not get outside funds for flood control.[222] More-

220. Ibid., 358–65, 379–81.
221. See, for instance, Hu Ch'ang-t'u, "Yellow River Administration," 505–13; Greer, *Water Management*, 35; and above.
222. See the summary in Mantetsu, *Santō Chihō no Kōka Suisai Jōkyō*, 4, 25–26, 33–34, 48.

over, much of the area near where the Yellow River met the sea was as poor as most inland areas. There were, however, sovereignty-preserving reasons to emphasize flood control in the area between Jinan and the coast.

In the late nineteenth century, foreigners began taking over small water control tasks that affected them directly, such as dredging Shanghai harbor.[223] By the early Republic, foreign groups were seeking a role in the Liao, Huai, Grand Canal, and Yellow River conservancies, which together drained much of northern China. Generally rebuffed inland, they played an increasing role in many coastal areas.[224] As the next chapter will show, Chinese officials worried about the possible political results of permitting such involvement; more cynically, some of those who made money from river conservancy (or who used such posts as patronage) must have viewed the emergence of competition with alarm. Thus, just as the desire to give foreigners no excuses for further intrusions helped create the North Manchuria Plague Prevention Service and encouraged police reform in treaty ports,[225] some of the Shandong Yellow River Office's concentration on river control near the coast and the crossing of the Tianjin-Pukou railway seems attributable to fear of being supplanted by foreigners.

The 1923 dike breaks near the mouth of the Yellow River at Lijin provide a good example of these dynamics. Lijin itself was as poor as most of Huang-Yun, and hardly important to the state as a source of revenue. However, its position on the north Shandong coast made it a strategic point at a time when limiting Japanese influence in eastern Shandong was a high priority for the provincial and national governments, and this flood therefore got a great deal of attention. Because of the unusual severity of the 1923 flood, the national government did get involved, authorizing National Conservancy Board head Xiong Xiling (a Hunan warlord politician turned Tianjin businessman and philanthropist) to award a contract for repairs. (By contrast, virtually nothing was done about very large Yellow River floods in Huang-Yun

223. See, for instance, *NCH*, Aug. 14, 1896, p. 282, describing an expansion of foreign dredging activity to include Suzhou Creek as this became a more important trade artery.

224. Much of this is discussed in U.S. Department of State, *Records of the Department of State Relating to the Internal Affairs of China, 1910–1929*, Microcopy 329 (hereafter, Department of State), reels 214, 215, 216, and 218, which emphasize U.S. involvement but also refer to other countries.

225. See, e.g., Nathan, *Plague Prevention*, v, 5, 42, 74; Frederic Wakeman, Jr., "Policing Modern Shanghai," *China Quarterly*, no. 115 (Sept. 1988), 420.

in 1925 and 1926.) Both an American group and a Japanese group were reportedly interested; the Americans were assured that Japan would never be awarded a contract that would allow them to increase their influence in Shandong.[226] Meanwhile, the Shandong Yellow River Office estimated that it would need ¥6,000,000 to fix the break. Soon thereafter, the U.S. group made a bid of ¥1,500,000. The Yellow River Office then cut its bid to ¥3,000,000; reportedly this amount was still well above their costs, and one must assume they thought their political connections and the desire to avoid more foreign intrusion would make up the remaining difference in the bids. Though their guess was wrong in this case, the decision was controversial, even though the project entailed no permanent U.S. conservancy presence.[227] In 1920 a combined flood relief and road-building project proposed by the International Red Cross had been refused because of the mere possibility of Japanese involvement;[228] and as we shall see later, a Grand Canal restoration project was also dropped when it seemed that the Japanese would become involved.

In sum, nationalism, the emergence of competition, and the options created by the coastal economy combined to make various parts of the government stress flood control near the coast and in locations—such as near railroad bridges—that shared important features of the coastal situation. In Huang-Yun, however, these stimuli were absent; consequently, the government withdrew much of its support for flood control from this once-favored region and used those funds instead for improvements near the coast. With this shift in funds, hydraulic problems were also redistributed.

Rather than a pattern of state involution throughout North China, one finds two opposite patterns in different regions. There was reasonably successful state making in at least part of the new North China "core." State and market advanced in tandem, and the threat from other states and the possibilities for increased revenues pressured the state to pay attention to society's needs as well as its own. Meanwhile, market development and new technologies facilitated new ways of delivering services.

226. Department of State, reel 216, document 472, p. 671, from U.S. consul in Jinan (Gauss) to Ambassador (Schurman), Sept. 26, 1922.
227. *NCH*, Aug. 18, 1923, p. 448.
228. *NCH*, Nov. 20, 1920, p. 530. See also *NCH*, March 4, 1922, pp. 576, 585, for a case involving Yantai harbor.

To pay for this breakthrough, however, the state decreased its services elsewhere, leaving those regions to their own devices. Faced with huge new tasks, the local governments and quasi governments (such as people's dikes organizations) in neglected areas were in practice free to extract new revenues however they could, but they were usually unable to use markets to make the most of their resources the way core regions could. Consequently, they became more extractive while providing vastly less effective services than the traditional state had provided. A lack of political integration, therefore, meant that while some new core areas saw real state making, other areas suffered not merely involution, but devolution.

CHAPTER V

Dealing with Disaster

As we have just seen, Huang-Yun water control was hard hit by the reorientation of Chinese statecraft in response to imperialism. Our final chapter begins by estimating the economic magnitude of this blow. It then considers various attempts to cope with these problems and the social and political reasons for their failure. Thus, while much of chapter 4 looked "down" at Huang-Yun from the viewpoint of larger political units, this chapter focuses on problems and initiatives that emerged within Huang-Yun after the collapse of the centrally funded hydraulic system.

As we look at things from within Huang-Yun, a theme largely absent from our last two, state-centered, chapters will reemerge: the contrast between North Huang-Yun's permeable rural society and the resistance of entrenched rural elites in South Huang-Yun to initiatives they found threatening. It was these elites and their yamen-runner allies who generally determined where private dikes would go, what land would be reclaimed, and whether it would be on the tax rolls. The more outward-looking gentry that the state would have liked to work with—or even turn hydraulics over to, as it often did elsewhere—was very weak in southwest Shandong outside Jining. Attempts to treat the area's rural elites as if they were such a gentry failed, frustrating many repair projects. The one major project in this area that did succeed gave up on looking for gentry cooperation: it completely ignored local leaders' views on any matters requiring that one village's interests be balanced against another's (although acknowledging village heads' control of corvée and other matters within their villages).

The second part of this chapter looks at an early Republican attempt to restore the Grand Canal, the third at additional complications that emerged as the Republic descended into warlordism. Next comes a look at the formal governments' attempts to work with local leaders to maintain Yellow River dikes, from the late Qing to the Nanjing decade (1928–37), followed by a look at the one major hydraulic success of this time and place, a 1933–34 flood control project on two tributaries of the Grand Canal in southwestern Shandong. The chapter closes by considering the limited prospects for further application of that project's strategies.

THE ECONOMIC COSTS OF HYDRAULIC DECAY

The recurrent flooding in Huang-Yun is traceable to the intrusion of the Yellow River in 1852–55, but major floods along the river's new course did not begin until the 1880s. The national government responded by reducing river control spending in 1891, ensuring that these problems would not be solved. When the national government abandoned the Grand Canal, the initial effects on commerce were greater than those on agriculture, but before long, the canal and its tributaries also caused floods.

The annual cost of hydraulic decay in Huang-Yun from transport problems and flooding comes to at least ¥48,000,000, a figure almost five times Shandong province's revenue in 1920[1] and equal to almost 10 percent of Huang-Yun's agricultural output; the losses may have been more than ¥100,000,000 per year. Thus, repairing the hydraulic system would have been a far better investment than projects the government did undertake, such as railroad building. Since the abandonment of Huang-Yun's hydraulic system was tied to new obligations and priorities pressed upon the Chinese state by imperialism, it is also worth noting that these losses far exceed the gains of the Huang-Yun cotton farmers discussed in chapter 2, for whom the foreign presence created opportunities.

Hydraulic decay affected cultivation in at least four ways. Some

1. Duara, "State Involution," 140–41.

land was completely lost to cultivation because the Grand Canal was no longer able to help carry the waters of the Wenhe, Sihe, and other Shandong rivers toward the sea. Instead these waters formed a series of shallow lakes covering more than five hundred square miles in southwest Shandong and expanding Dongping Lake—near the junction of the canal and the Yellow River—by about fifty square miles. Second, some land near rivers, canals, and lakes that continued to be cultivated suffered more floods because of the state's withdrawal from its old commitments. Third, dike breaks led to massive floods, especially on the Yellow River. Finally, there was long-term soil damage from the deposit of salts on the soil during floods.[2] This last type of damage was little studied at the time; thus, there is little information about it, and it will be omitted here. The first three problems, however, are well enough documented to estimate their magnitudes. The calculations are explained in appendix B, and the results are summarized in table 4.

The commercial impact of hydraulic decline can be viewed in two ways. On the one hand, some trade was lost because the grain tribute ceased; much of this never would have existed without the subsidies built into the tribute system, and its loss should be seen as a one-time shock. In one sense, this might be the best measure of the blow that Huang-Yun commerce experienced in the late Qing. However, since merely maintaining the canal would not have kept these businesses going, these losses would distort an estimate of the costs of hydraulic decay per se. For that purpose, what matters are the recurring annual costs of having to use shipping methods that cost more than canal freight would have.

Many Shandong businesses provided services to the tribute fleet; others piggybacked on it, relying on the legal and illegal "private goods" carried by grain boatmen.[3] "Private goods" included many commodities used in local crafts, such as bamboo and various special woods. The end of this trade forced many producers of luxury goods to switch to making lower-grade products, but the extent of these losses is unclear. Carpenters in Liaocheng and Linqing apparently lost income and status when forced to make cheaper furniture out of local wood, but they did not have to leave their craft or native place.

2. Hou Renzhi, *Xu tianxia*, 48–49; Freeman, *GCIM*, 36, 93.
3. See Hoshi Ayao, *Dai Unga*, 202–5; *NYHH*, Appendix, 11–12.

TABLE 4   LOWER-BOUND ESTIMATES OF
AGRICULTURAL OUTPUT LOST FROM
HYDRAULIC DECAY IN AN AVERAGE YEAR,
HUANG-YUN, 1920S–30S

Category	Affected *mu*	Lost output (yuan)
From Grand Canal lake expansion	580,000	2,700,000
From Grand Canal–related floods on cultivated land	1,300,000	5,000,000
Land submerged by widening of Yellow River channel	3,000,000	12,000,000
Crop loss from Yellow River floods (major dike breaks only)	unknown	9,000,000
Crop loss from Wanfuhe floods	unknown	5,000,000
Total		33,700,000

NOTE: To avoid any danger of overestimating these losses, only productivity attribut-able to the land itself is counted. Thus these figures assume that all people who would have worked on submerged land had it been available had in the meantime found other full-time employment within Huang-Yun. The following are not included in the above estimates: damage from floods on the Wei River, Wen River, and various smaller rivers; noncrop property damage from floods (an absolute minimum of ¥7,000,000 per year from the Yellow River alone); deaths and noneconomic losses; long-term ecological damage; consequential damages (e.g., banditry). For more information on data, calcula-tion methods, and assumptions, see appendix B.

Northwest Shandong stopped importing or exporting a number of products after 1902, but few of these were staples.[4] However, the end of the lumber trade had a wider significance, as discussed in chapter 3.[5]

Even after 1902, a lot of canal traffic still went north from Linqing and south from Jining.[6] However, Liaocheng—the largest city be-tween Linqing and Jining and roughly the same size as they (and Jinan) in the 1840s[7]—lost its water transport in both directions. The guest merchants (mostly from Shanxi and Shaanxi) who dominated the city's trade had stayed on through the 1855 river shift and numer-ous other crises, always assuming that transportation would be re-

4. Interview notes, November 1985; also Yang Zhengtai, "Ming Qing Linqing," 118–19.
5. Hoshi Ayao, *Dai Unga*, 203, and chapter 3, above.
6. See discussion to follow in this section.
7. See the chart in Skinner, *The City in Late Imperial China*, 238.

stored sooner or later. But once grain tribute was abandoned in 1902 in principle, not just as a wartime expedient, the guest merchants concluded that the canal would never be restored. Consequently, many began to leave.[8]

A 1908 newspaper article noted that Liaocheng had been hit particularly hard by the decay of the canal since 1902 and by not being on the Tianjin-Pukou rail line that was replacing it as a north-south link; large numbers of houses were being pulled down.[9] Liaocheng had six or seven *hui guan* (clubs of residents, in this case merchants, from other areas) at the turn of the century, but was down to one by the 1930s.[10] In a 1920 essay, the Liaocheng-born scholar Fu Sinian argued that his hometown had been so dependent on the canal that it now had no chance of recovery; he recommended more emigration as the only answer to its current problems.[11] Although there were other reasons for Liaocheng's problems,[12] it is clear that in this case, the end of national canal maintenance was a devastating blow. However, as chapter 2 showed, agriculture in the area near Liaocheng continued to commercialize, even as the city shrank. In Jining, the urban sector seems to have recovered quickly from the end of the grain tribute; Linqing was hurt more than Jining, but less than Liaocheng.

Three thousand commercial boats a year visited Linqing from the south before 1901, but this number soon declined to almost zero.[13] Ever since the floods of 1824, when the Qing tried their first experiment with ocean shipping of tribute grain, local farmers had used any year without tribute fleets to reclaim part of the canal bed south of Linqing; now these actions were essentially unopposed.[14] The official customs duty collected at Linqing, already declining, now plummeted. Though the canal still functioned going north from Linqing, central government withdrawal was followed by the growth of a forest of local, private "customs" stations after 1902.[15] In the early 1930s,

8. Interview notes, November 1985.
9. *NCH*, Jan. 17, 1908, p. 124.
10. Interview notes, November 1985.
11. Kong Decheng, ed., *Fu Sinian quanji* (Taibei, 1980), 7:2513–28.
12. Wu Yunxian, "Liaocheng ke shu yu chubanye de xing shuai gaikuang," *Wenshi ziliao xuanji*, Jinan edition, no. 14 (1982), 109–28; Kong Decheng, *Fu Sinian*, 7:2528.
13. Unsigned draft manuscript of 1985, scheduled for inclusion in *Shandong shuili huikan*, no. 5.
14. Yang Zhengtai, "Ming Qing Linqing," 120.
15. The Linqing customs had dropped from 200,000 *liang* at its peak to 90,000 in 1896, shortly before the end of the grain tribute. In 1904–5, it was up to 130,000 *liang*

the Guomindang simultaneously took up the issue of the canal at a national level again and ordered the elimination of these irregular taxes;[16] however, they never got around to regaining control of the full canal bed.

While trade at Linqing had been declining for years before 1902—at least since the 1824 ocean tribute experiment—trade from the Yangzi Valley to Jining was still quite healthy. Hosea Morse, who in 1908 still referred to western Shandong as "the richer part of the province," noted the decline of the Grand Canal but said that "one small indication of the extent of traffic [on the canal] is found in the value of the transit pass trade with Shantung passing the Chinkiang [Jinjiang] Customs, traversing a distance along the Grand Canal of 250 miles, a part of it the worst portion of the route, to the nearest markets in Shantung, valued in 1904 at 3,646,000 taels and in 1905 at 3,331,000 taels."[17] This sum seems far too large for all of these passes to have been for goods bound for Shandong; but if even a small portion was, it would suggest an underlying trade that was still larger than that at many coastal ports.[18] *Shandong zazhi* estimated a 60–70 percent decline in traffic at Jining by weight over the few years after the end of grain tribute, but the decline in the value of goods traded was far

---

per year. The 1934 gazetteer records only ¥13,000 in "boat fees." However, using customs duties to estimate the actual volume of traffic through Linqing, which would be questionable in any period, is particularly complicated in this period. Beginning shortly after the end of grain tribute, various local actors created what by the 1920s was a "forest" of toll barriers in and near Linqing, reducing the original Linqing customs to just a "ticket stamping place"; in the 1930s, most of the barriers were eliminated, along with the official *lijin* collection. These changes in rates, and in rates of evasion, make it unclear how to interpret the decline in customs revenue. See *NYHH*, appendix, p. 12; Yang Zhengtai, "Ming Qing Linqing," 120; Gandar, *Le Canal Impériale*, 58. Memorial from Yang Shixiang, 2/12/GX 32, and two other memorials from Yang, both dated intercalary 4/7/GX 32, all in LFZZ, GX 32, packet 24A. *Linqing xianzhi* (1934) 9:8b. *NCH*, Jan. 27, 1903, p. 1120; Sept. 13, 1907, p. 605; Shandong guomin zhengfu mishuchu draft report (to national government) of July 10, 1928, in JD1:AH334; *Linqing xianzhi* 9:9a; Nong shang gongbao kanzai, "Mianhua ji mian sha, zhi, shengchan jishu de di gao can que," undated report (probably from early or mid 1920s), 12b-13a, in QZ1038:AH2034.

16. For the *shuili* efforts, see section "The Formal Government, Rural Bosses, and Local Resistance" at the end of this chapter; on the elimination of transit taxes, see *Linqing xianzhi* 9:9a; and *CZGB* 5:10 (July 1934), *mingling*, 16–57 (generally), and 5:12 (Sept. 1934), *mingling*, 14 (Linqing boat tax specifically).

17. Hosea B. Morse, *The Trade and Administration of the Chinese Empire* (London, 1913), p. 323.

18. For instance, the total receipts of the Donghaiguan (Shandong maritime customs) for GX 32 (1906) were 800,000 *liang*. See memorial of Yang Shixiang, 9/6/GX 33, in LFZZ, GX 33, packet 42B.

less.[19] Jining's waterborne trade to the south remained quite lively, at least in high value-added goods; the city's largest firm relied on the canal quite successfully as late as the 1930s. And after Jining got a railroad line, in 1912, its trade with points north and east recovered, too.[20]

Overall, it appears that the commerce of Jining—where trading interests were well organized and protected transportation—was not greatly hurt by the canal's decline. Linqing's trade was hurt more seriously, as local actions compounded government neglect. However, the commerce of towns between Jining and Linqing, such as Liaocheng, and of towns up the Wei River from Linqing (for example, Huaxian, in the Henan part of Huang-Yun) was devastated by the 1902 reforms.[21]

Since Chinese trade in general was expanding, however, the mere fact that waterborne commerce in Huang-Yun did not collapse completely could mask significant costs of canal decay. Using a combination of actual figures and estimates made by those planning the restoration of the canal, we arrive at a conservative estimate of ¥7,000,000 to ¥9,000,000 just from the extra transport costs borne by existing trade; adding estimates of lost benefits from trade that did not occur because of hydraulic decay would put losses much higher. The sources and calculations are discussed in appendix C; the results are summarized in table 5.

Adding transport and agricultural problems, plus a very minimal estimate of other property damage, ¥48,000,000–51,000,000 per year appears to be a very cautious estimate of the annual economic cost in Huang-Yun of hydraulic decay; one could generate a figure of ¥100,000,000 or even more.[22] How significant was such a sum in this region? Macroeconomic estimates for Republican China are invariably rough, but ¥500,000,000 per year seems plausible for Huang-Yun's agricultural output in the early Republic, and even ¥48,000,000 is 9.6

19. *Shandong zazhi*, no. 35 (6/15/XT 1), 22b. For market price-to-weight ratios from Republican Shanxi (which should not be radically different from those for Huang-Yun), see Sands, "Investigation," 64.

20. Regarding waterborne trade, *Santō Sainei*, 6–8; *JSGB* 3:7 (July 1933), *jihua*, 10; Hai Shan, "Yutang Chunqiu," pt. 1, pp. 56, 61, 62; see also pt. 2, pp. 91–92. On the railroad and Jining's trade, see *Santō Sainei*, 4–8.

21. On Huaxian, see Wou, "Development, Underdevelopment and Degeneration," 215–30. Huaxian is not treated in detail here, largely to avoid duplicating Professor Wou's research.

22. See dissertation, appendix I, esp. 448.

TABLE 5 LOWER-BOUND ESTIMATES OF ANNUAL LOSSES CAUSED BY DECAY OF CANAL TRANSPORT IN HUANG-YUN

	Ton-miles	Loss per ton-mile (yuan)	Total (yuan)
1. Through traffic diverted to railroad	11,000,000	.009	99,000
2. Short hauls total	30,000,000		
2a. Diverted to two-animal carts (if half of short hauls)	15,000,000	.089	1,335,000
Diverted to small carts (if half of short hauls)	15,000,000	.271	4,065,000
Short hauls total (if shared half and half)			5,400,000
2b. Diverted to two-animal carts (if one-fourth of short hauls)	7,500,000	.089	667,500
Diverted to small carts (if three-fourths of short hauls)	22,500,000	.271	6,097,500
Short hauls total (if shared one-fourth and three-fourths)			6,765,000
3. Adjustment for Wiggin's omission of Linqing-Dezhou section:			
3a. Diverted to two-animal carts (if half of traffic)	2,500,000	.089	222,500
Diverted to small carts (if half of traffic)	2,500,000	.271	677,500
Minimum total	5,000,000		900,000
3b. Diverted to two-animal carts (if one-fourth)	1,250,000	.089	111,250
Diverted to small carts (if three-fourths)	3,750,000	.271	1,016,250
Alternate Total	5,000,000		1,127,500
4. Extra distance traveled by boats on Linqing-Dezhou section	75,200,000	.009	676,800
Minimum estimate for all travel items (1 + 2a + 3a + 4)			7,075,800
More likely alternate estimate for all travel items (1 + 2b + 3b + 4)			8,668,300

NOTE: All estimates are limited to losses incurred because existing trade had higher freight costs; losses due to trade that failed to occur at all because of transport problems are excluded. For further details, see appendix C.

percent of this figure; ¥100,000,000 would be 20 percent. Since Huang-Yun's population was more than fifteen million, ¥48,000,000 comes to just over ¥3 per person; the area's per capita income, however, was probably well under ¥40.[23]

It is also instructive to compare these losses to crude estimates of the benefits Huang-Yun derived from its contact with the world economy. Various methods yield estimates ranging from less than ¥8,000,000 to about ¥15,000,000 for the increase in gross output attributable to the dissemination of U.S. cotton varieties—by far the most important foreign boost to Huang-Yun's income.[24] We can also make estimates based on consumption figures. A 1933 report estimated that thirty-five Shandong counties annually consumed ¥30,000,000 worth of goods that had crossed county lines. Those thirty-five counties had about 60 percent of Huang-Yun's population.[25] If these counties were typical, we would therefore project Huang-Yun's total consumption of such goods at about ¥50,000,000. Since it is goods consumed that make people better off, these figures represent an upper bound on the outside world's contribution to Huang-Yun's welfare, unless imperialism somehow led to increased consumption of local goods. (This is extremely unlikely, given limited increases in total output, more land being devoted to export crops, and the focus of agricultural improvement efforts on industrial crops.) Moreover, the majority of the goods crossing county lines in this survey came from other counties in the sample or represented long-established trade with other parts of China.[26] Therefore, even if imports were seriously undercounted, Huang-Yun's gains from

23. Estimate of output is based on figures from *SSYZ* and Second Historical Archives for the Shandong section of Huang-Yun, adjusting for an estimate of output in the rest of Huang-Yun; these figures, in turn, match very well estimates derived by multiplying the amount of cultivated land by Pan Fu's estimate of ¥8 per *mu* output and anecdotal accounts as well. For more details on the loss calculations, see appendix B. See also John L. Buck, "Statistical View," 33–47. On population of the Huang-Yun counties in Hebei and Henan, see *China Yearbook, 1926–1927*, 4–9. Using the most expansive boundaries of Huang-Yun that are plausible, the Henan and Hebei sections together would have had close to seven million people, but this includes all of certain counties of which at most a part should be included, or perhaps no part at all.

24. See Doi Akira and Tonō Fumino, *Hokushi Jijō Soran* (Dalian, 1936), 261, for a yield-per-*mu* figure to be multiplied by the total number of *mu* in U.S. cotton (available in dissertation, appendix D). Other per *mu* output figures in *XCJSXK* 3:18–19 (Feb. 1934), 14–15; *Santō no Mensaku*, 47–54; and Lin Maoquan, *Wenji*, 65a–b.

25. *SSYZ* 2:151–201.

26. See especially the southwest Shandong and Jining figures in *SSYZ* 2:165–89 (esp. 167) and the discussion of Jining as a "reexporting center" in *Santō Sainei*, 4–5.

joining the world economy must have been considerably smaller than even our most conservative estimate of the harm done when a hard-pressed state abandoned Huang-Yun water control.

These losses, of course, fell unevenly. They were presumably highest in heavily flooded South Huang-Yun, which also gained least from new trade opportunities. For the most unfortunate areas, hydraulic losses toward the high end of the range calculated above would have been combined with a decline of 7.5 percent in income resulting from the shortage of self-gathered fuel described in chapter 3 and from stalk requisitions for flood control that I have estimated at anywhere from 3 percent to 7 percent of average income for the people in the counties along the Yellow River (8 percent to 20 percent if the entire burden fell on those within three miles of the river).[27] For such people, the costs of the new political economy were truly staggering.

Another point is also noteworthy. The costs of neglecting the hydraulic system clearly dwarfed the costs of fixing it. If we take the lowest estimates of repair costs from chapter 4 and elsewhere, thorough hydraulic repairs would have more than paid for themselves in "social savings" within a year; even using the highest cost figures, such an investment would have returned almost 45 percent a year.[28] These rates of return far exceed those on projects the state or foreigners actually did finance. For instance, building China's railroads returned, by a generous estimate, about 20 percent per year in social savings and carried the heavy political cost of increased foreign leverage on China.[29] Thus, even without humanitarian concerns, restoring Huang-Yun's water conservancy should have been a high priority. Even if the government had levied new taxes so it could pay for modernizing projects and old ones both, Huang-Yun residents would have been far better off than with hydraulic neglect: the social savings would have more than made up for the rest of the public-sector costs for all of Shandong, let alone Huang-Yun. Why, then, were so few repairs made?

27. For estimates of income lost when people could no longer meet their own fuel supply needs outside the market, see chapter 3, "Isolation, Fuel Shortages, and Deforestation"; for estimates of the burden imposed by stalk requisitions for Yellow River dikes, see also dissertation, appendix G, 438–40.

28. Calculations based on dissertation, 203, 342, 527.

29. For figures that can be used to derive social savings, and thus a rate of return to the entire society on railway investment, see Heunemann, *Iron Horse*, 127, 225–27. If one takes his total social savings of ¥372,000,000 as a return on total railway investment (domestic and foreign) of ¥1,570,000, one gets a return of 23.7 percent.

THE GENTRY AND THE FOREIGNERS

The difficulty of repairing the hydraulic system made government help necessary, but it also discouraged the government from taking back the reins. The rest of this chapter will look at Republican-era attempts to reverse the decline of the hydraulic system without massive central government aid. These efforts began in 1914, with an attempt to restore the Grand Canal.

The project's sponsors and administrators were overwhelmingly from the city of Jining. The general director of the Shandong Grand Canal Project, the four "advisers" (*ci yi yuan*), and twelve of the top twenty-four officers came from Jining (four were from elsewhere in Shandong, including one who had once been the Jining magistrate; eight were from other provinces). The Jining participants were the city's elite, and they were heavily involved in other modernizing activities. Three had been among the four leaders of the effort to bring railroads to Jining; three had worked in the Shandong industrial department; one had headed the provincial mining bureau; one was a former director of Shandong's largest mining company; at least two were involved in spinning mills; one was the director of a cigarette factory in Jining; one had worked on two major railroads; one had been a provincial assemblyman; one was the former head of the Jining consultative assembly; one headed the Jining Chamber of Commerce; two had worked in modern schools, and so forth. The most important figure was the group's director, Pan Fu.[30]

Pan Fu belonged to one of Jining's two most prominent families. His family had been in the county for more than five hundred years and had produced its first official in the sixteenth century.[31] Pan Fu himself earned a *juren* degree at age twenty; he soon began combining commerce, industry, and office holding as industrial intendant (*daotai*) of Shandong province.[32] During a period out of office, he led the group of Jining gentry who protested the planned route of the Tianjin-Pukou railroad, persuading gentry and officials from all four provinces the railroad would pass through to join them. (See chapter 3.) Though these efforts were only partially successful, they demonstrated Pan Fu's

---

30. *NYHH*, 14–19. See also *NSGB* 2:6 (Jan. 1916), *zhengshi*, 24; 3:6 (Jan. 1917), *jinnian*, 30; *SDZZ*, no. 41 (9/15/XT 1), 24b–25a. For Pan Fu's importance, see Carey, letter of April 9, 1919.

31. *Jining zhilizhou xuzhi* 4:9b–22a.

32. *China Yearbook 1926–1927*, 1190; *Zhongguo jindai ming ren tu jian*, 227.

knack for organizing other members of the elite.[33] After a brief period in Jiangsu in 1911, where he made a smooth transition from the Qing governor's staff to the revolutionary government, Pan returned to his old position as Shandong industrial *daotai* in 1913.[34] In 1915, he organized investors to create one of Jinan's first spinning mills; this company later built Linqing's first mill. He later became governor of Shandong, China's deputy finance minister and finance minister, head of the national salt administration, and director of the national conservancy bureau. In 1927, he was the prime minister of the last northern warlord government.[35]

Pan worked closely with several other southwest Shandong politicians, including Zhou Ziji of Shanxian (Shandong's first Republican military governor and later finance minister) and Jin Yunpeng of Jining (an associate of Yuan Shikai and Duan Qirui, military governor of Shandong after Zhou Ziji, and later prime minister); together, this regional clique (*bang*) controlled most key Shandong offices until Zhang Zongchang conquered the province in the mid-1920s.[36] In a city in which commerce and officialdom were very closely linked, Pan Fu stood atop both spheres.

Pan Fu's father was sufficiently prominent to be "in charge of" the 1919 celebration of the last day of the seventh lunar month at Jining's largest temple, at which "most all the Chinese officials of Jining were present."[37] In his own generation, Pan's blood relatives included a brigade leader (*lu zhang*), whose troops were often in Jining, and a local assemblyman, who was a director of most of the city's major charities.[38]

However, the family lacked a strong presence in the Jining countryside. At no point, it seems, did they own more than a thousand *mu* of land. While this was a considerable amount, it was not a great deal for such a wealthy family. The charities in which Pan Fu's brother was influential had 80 percent of their endowments on deposit with urban

33. See, e.g., *SDZZ*, no. 2 (1/30/GX 34), 12, and no. 5 (3/15/GX 34), 1–5. See also Yuan Jingbo, "Jining huochezhan," 4–7.

34. *China Yearbook 1926–1927*, 1190; *Zhongguo jindai ming ren tu jian*, 227.

35. Ibid.; Boorman, *Biographical Dictionary*, 2:440a; Sonoda Ikki, *Xin Zhongguo renwu zhi*, 134.

36. Wan Guangwei, "Shandong zheng Dang huodong," 32–42; Shao Chuoran, "Tian Zhongyu," 43–50.

37. Carey, letter of Sept. 28, 1919.

38. *Jining zhilizhou xuzhi* (1927), 4:65b; express telegram from Zhang Shuyuan and others, received May 13, 1918, and marked "#36" in JD00:AH1164.

firms, rather than in land. The Pan family itself did not designate any charity land until 1922, when they put their thousand *mu* in a trust. Moreover, the family could not hold on to this rather modest tax-exempt estate when the national political winds shifted; in 1929 (with Pan Fu's government defeated), an investigation of unknown instigation determined that this land was not being used for charitable purposes and should be "liquidated" by the county magistrate.[39]

This defeat not only stands out against the family's many successes, but against the success of those in Jining who resisted more than twenty years of efforts by the local government and civic leaders (including at least two Pans) to get them to make payments for land they had reclaimed from lake beds. None of Jining's "urban reformist elite"[40] appear to have had the rural presence that elites involved in land reclamation and water control in eastern and southern China generally had.[41]

This set of political strengths and weaknesses was important, for there were two major political prerequisites to reviving the canal. The first was to get the national government involved, thereby facilitating the use of foreign capital and contractors. The close ties between merchants and officials in Jining made this city's elite well suited to this task; the large number of southwest Shandong politicians in Jinan and Beijing helped, too. Thus, the pattern observed in our discussions of the struggle over railroad routes and the struggle to maintain minimal canal functions amidst the 1902 budget cuts shows up again in this case: South Hung-Yun urban elites were richer, better organized, and better able to influence higher levels of government than anyone in North Huang-Yun.

However, the state was no longer interested in donating water control services to Huang-Yun; at best, it might help secure loans. Thus the second task, for which Pan Fu and friends were less well suited, was to tap the production of the land that would be reclaimed or benefited so that the project could pay for itself. Here, as the story of the

---

39. For the Pan holdings, *Jining zhilizhou xuzhi* (1927), 4:9b–22a, 4:64b, 5:10b–11a, 13b, 21b. For the investigation, Report of the Shandong Provincial Government to Nanjing on Work of September 1929, p. 2, in JD2:AH110.

40. This term was coined by Joseph M. Esherick in *Reform and Revolution in China: The 1911 Revolution in Hunan and Hubei* (Berkeley, 1976).

41. See, for instance, Frederic Wakeman, *Strangers at the Gate: Social Disorder in South China, 1839–1861* (Berkeley, 1966), 153–55; Peter Perdue, "Water Control in the Dongting Lake Region during the Ming and Qing Periods," *Journal of Asian Studies* 41:4 (August 1982), 747–65.

Pans' clan land suggests, the relevant pattern resembles the one we saw in the study of new cotton varieties: elites from Jining and South Huang-Yun's county capitals could not overcome the opposition of the area's rural bosses, who were also much stronger than their North Huang-Yun counterparts.

The project's sponsors originally emphasized transportation, but that was not what interested rural people. When the Grand Canal Board solicited written opinions (*yijianshu*) from people not on their committee, they received twenty-eight replies from various southwestern counties. Unlike the project's original sponsors, these people generally did not live in county capitals, much less in a regional center like Jining, and were of far lower status. Seventeen of the twenty-eight are described simply as "citizens" (*gongmin*). Of the remaining eleven, four are listed as village leaders. Another was the head of a local militia. One represented the fourth district of Dongping in the Dongping county assembly. One, referred to as "gentry" (*shenmin*), was probably lower gentry, since no past or expected office is given. Two were modern school graduates—one from a middle school and one from a lower-level normal school. Only one, a former assistant in an office of the *shiyeting* (industrial office) in Jining, may have moved in the same circles as the project's sponsors.[42]

These people were not necessarily representative of rural leaders. That they submitted suggestions, however, may make them a reasonable sample of those influential rural people who might help promote the project in the countryside. Of the summaries of these twenty-eight documents, only one specifically advocated improving navigation. Twenty-six of the other twenty-seven focused on flood control, reclamation of lake land, or both; fifteen at least mentioned reclaiming land from the lakes. If Pan Fu's committee took seriously its stated goal of building broad support for canal work, it would have to stress land reclamation.[43]

Moreover, the committee soon had to abandon its initial idea that transport alone could finance the project. T. H. Wiggin's report to potential American financiers concluded that tolls would cover only the interest on slightly more than ¥2,000,000, while ¥5,000,000 was needed for even the simplest version of the project. Even those who

42. *NYHH*, 25–26, 54.
43. Ibid.; for the committee's goal, 5.

thought Wiggin too pessimistic admitted that tolls were too uncertain to be the basis of the project.[44]

Nor was it necessary to finance the Grand Canal project that way. The most pessimistic estimate of land that could be reclaimed by reviving the canal was 580,000 *mu*. Wiggin estimated that 1,920,000 *mu* south of Jining would either be made arable or made safe from flooding for the first time in decades; a later estimate exceeded 2,000,000 *mu*. Freeman suggested a modification of the plan that would add more than 300,000 *mu* near Dongping.[45] The value of this land far exceeded any estimates of the project's costs; the challenge was to tap that wealth in advance to finance the work.

Part of the problem was that there were claims on much of the land to be "created." Most of the lake land to be reclaimed had been dry until 1855, or even 1902. Before that, people had farmed the same land that was now to be reopened. The Grand Canal Board was not prepared to completely ignore the customary claims of their descendants, even though the former owners had abandoned their legal claims by having the submerged land removed from the tax rolls.[46]

In part, the board's attitude probably stemmed from a realistic assessment that the government could not exclude people from the land. The government had failed completely ten years before when it claimed ownership of "camp land" (*tun tian*) in western Shandong.[47] A 1904 reclamation project near Jining had also been ruined by conflicts over land claims. The provincial government had chartered a Jining city company that had enough capital to undertake extensive reclamation. However, the higher, and thus more easily drained, public lands had already been reclaimed illicitly by local people, apparently in cooperation with rural elites, village heads, and yamen clerks. In the end, the company had been unable to assert control over the higher land, which could yield quick profits; as a result, they could not finance up-river conservancy, and everyone's land wound up being flooded again.[48] Moreover, the planners seem to have assumed that old ownership claims should be respected; they even planned to pay

44. Freeman, *GCIC*, 67; see also *GCIM*, 129–35, 37.
45. For these estimates, *NYHH*, Appendix, 9; Freeman, *GCIC* 68; Hou Renzhi, *Xu tianxia*, 48; and Freeman, *GCIM*, 122, respectively.
46. Freeman, *GCIM*, 28; *NYHH, shuili guifu diaocha*, 11.
47. See below, "The Formal Government, Rural Bosses, and Local Resistance."
48. *DFZZ* 1:10 (10/25/GX 30), 172–73; see also *Jining zhilizhou xuzhi* 2:48a.

some compensation for 78,000 *mu* submerged since 1855 that would now be officially added to the Dongping reservoir.[49]

Pan Fu claimed that the well-watered land to be reclaimed would be especially valuable, but thought it unwise to try to sell it. Instead, he argued for respecting documented claims to the land and assessing a ¥1 per year "betterment tax" on it for a period of twenty years. This fee would be the same for private land that was currently completely submerged and marginal land that was arable in some years but would benefit from improved flood protection. The planners knew that even these fees would be hard to collect; but if they could collect on just a quarter of the land to be drained south of Jining, this would yield ¥480,000 of revenue per year, versus ¥400,000 for 8 percent interest on the ¥5,000,000 needed for that part of the canal. Moreover, some land would not be successfully claimed by anyone, since many families had died out or left the area. In those cases, a series of chartered companies would rent out the land, operating through village heads, and a portion of the rent would automatically go into a fund to maintain water control works.[50]

The Shandong Grand Canal Board, located in Jining, spent most of the years 1915 through 1918 sorting through land claims.[51] Some of the relevant documents must have already been in government hands. Most, however, were responses to notices and announcements the board had ordered, inviting people to make their claims. People with stamped proofs of ownership were to present them to their village head, who would bring them to the county government for further consideration and would guarantee their validity; investigation by torture was specifically provided for if fake documents were found mixed in with legitimate ones. People who had unstamped written documents were required to get the guarantee of their village head and of two heads of nearby villages. Nothing was said about those who had no written documents; however, a written statement by the village head attested to by two others would probably have sufficed. The board made no provisions for claims not guaranteed by a village head, except by threatening to punish any village head who intimidated or coerced claimants. The board also drew up rules to govern land that would be rented; it gave most of the power to choose and discipline tenants to

49. Freeman, *GCIM*, 118.
50. Ibid., 28, 35, 37–37A; idem, *GCIC*, 68; *NYHH, shuili guifu diaocha*, 12.
51. Department of State, reel 215, document 313, p. 293.

village heads. The Grand Canal Board had its own investigators, but its charter explicitly provided that when investigating matters "among the people" it was to rely on village heads or village council members.[52] Moreover, the most common form of stamped proof would probably be tax receipts—meaning that next to village heads, yamen runners would have the most to say about land claims.

A village head who certified somebody's claims was performing a very valuable service, and perhaps also taking some risk. He probably also had to arrange for a second village head to guarantee his village's unstamped documents, since most people probably had no personal connections with the heads of other villages. Thus the village heads not only had a vital role in allocating enormous amounts of property; the provisions for their exercise of this role required them to act collectively. Most descriptions of the headman in the late Qing and Republic treat him either as the last link in the vertical chain of command leading down from the magistrate or as a broker (honest or otherwise) standing between his particular village and this vertical chain of command.[53] In this case, however, higher authorities in southwestern Shandong were treating village heads in much the same way as they had during the disputes over *tun tian* a decade earlier (about which more later): as people who could not only each deal with the formal government on behalf of their own villages, but who could work together across village lines and collectively represent a large rural constituency in dealings with officialdom. In the Guomindang period, as we shall see, the Shandong government took this practice still further, creating a formal association composed of the village heads along a certain stretch of the Yellow River.[54]

Accepting customary land claims but insisting on a benefits tax gave the Canal Board a plausible way of repaying the loans it needed. By acknowledging that village heads would have the major role in assigning reclaimed land and getting them on record about who owned it, the board improved the odds of eventually collecting the tax. Even

52. *NYHH, shuili guifu diaocha*, 11–14; *gui zhang*, 13.
53. See, for instance, Duara, *Culture, Power, and the State*, 219–23, 237–39. There is also debate about to what extent village heads were on their own or were spokesmen for a more collegial village elite; see, for instance, Huang, *Peasant Economy*, 242–43. It seems likely to me that in South Huang-Yun (more so than in the areas described by Huang and Duara), village heads were often the most powerful figures in their villages, not just one member of a fairly equal oligarchy; but the evidence either way is scant, and for current purposes this issue is unimportant.
54. See *HWTK*, no. 1 (Oct. 1928) *fagui*, 5–10.

so, this compromise did not by itself raise the capital needed for the project. Originally, Pan Fu tried to raise private domestic money: one large government-chartered company would do the basic engineering projects, and smaller local companies would take on discrete, clearly profitable bits of reclamation. However, he soon concluded that without secure long-term financing in place, local gentry investors would lose their enthusiasm for even the small-scale, quick-return projects. He then appealed to the provincial and the national governments, and finally to foreigners.[55]

After the horrendous Huai River floods of 1911, Beijing became more willing to let foreigners move into the river conservancy vacuum. Seeing no chance of taming the Huai on their own, the Qing allowed the American Red Cross to study the river and submit a new conservancy plan. Negotiations continued after the 1911 Revolution, and a feasibility study was completed in 1914. The study concluded that it would be extremely difficult to fix the Huai without also working on the Grand Canal.[56] While the Jiangsu Grand Canal was most immediately relevant, it was agreed that it would be best to coordinate these efforts with Pan Fu's Shandong Grand Canal restoration. As he had done in advocating a rail line for Jining, Pan Fu also used China's foreign policy woes as an argument for aiding his usually neglected home region; he argued that western Shandong's economy should be developed so that eastern Shandong, increasingly controlled by Japan, did not become the "dominant" part of the province.[57]

Negotiations on the Shandong Grand Canal, with Pan Fu representing Shandong, were separate from those for a loan to the central government for Jiangsu canal work. However, all parties agreed that if possible a single contractor should do the Shandong canal, the Jiangsu canal, and the Huai River.[58]

The U.S. ambassador had suggested to the contractors, American International Corporation (AIC) and Siems and Carey Railway and Canal, that they close the Jiangsu deal before reaching an agreement with Shandong. However, they were so impressed with Pan Fu, and with the determination that he and Shandong civil governor Cai Rugai

---

55. *NYHH, shuili guifu diaocha*, 13–14; pt. 1, pp. 5–6; *gongcheng jihua*, 1–2; *gong kuan gailue*, 1–2; Department of State, reel 214, document 210, p. 286.

56. Department of State, reel 214, document 232, p. 459; document 210, p. 279; document 223, p. 342.

57. *NYHH*, Appendix, 23–24.

58. Department of State, reel 214, document 219, p. 293.

showed to get on with the work, that they reversed this order. In April 1916, Shandong agreed to borrow US$3,000,000—approximately ¥6,000,000—from AIC, which hired Siems and Carey.[59]

The foreigners saw this contract as a major advance: the U.S. ambassador called it "the most favorable ever obtained by any foreign firm for a loan in China" and said the terms were "almost too severe for China." For one thing, the agreement called for the foreigners to supervise the work directly. In the past, Ambassador Reinsch said, the Chinese had always wanted to supervise the work themselves "partly because the introduction of a foreign supervising firm greatly reduced the opportunities for gain [by the officials]." In fact, the foreign contractors would not only manage the construction itself; they had the right to recommend managers for the canal and any reclaimed public land until the twenty-year loan was repaid; AIC could also examine all relevant accounts of the Canal Board and the provincial government and could veto proposed supervising engineers.[60]

AIC also got very good financial terms. Reinsch emphasized that this was the first construction loan contract to provide for a 10 percent commission: in other words, 10 percent of the loan would go directly to AIC as its fee for choosing contractors, floating the loan, and the like. At first the loan was secured only by canal tolls, but a series of amendments added other security: income from the reclaimed land, a provincial pledge to make up any deficiencies, and a lien on ¥300,000 per year of national revenues raised in Shandong, which could not be forwarded to Beijing unless loan payments were up to date. Essentially AIC had secured both national and provincial guarantees, though they had never dealt directly with the national government. The 7 percent yield, Reinsch said, was extremely good for a loan that was "completely secure."[61]

A similar agreement was soon concluded for Jiangsu, along with an understanding that AIC would get the first chance to bid on controlling the Huai. Later, the two loans were consolidated into one loan of US$6,000,000.[62] The Shandong provincial assembly and military

59. Ibid., reel 214, document 221, p. 333; document 213, p. 293.

60. Ibid., document 214, p. 296; document 216, p. 300; document 221, p. 334; document 223, pp. 343–44, 353, 362.

61. Ibid., document 221, p. 333; document 224, p. 376; document 223, pp. 344–63; document 225, p. 384; document 224, p. 469; document 215, p. 299; document 222, p. 336.

62. *Far Eastern Review* 15:4 (April 1919), 356.

governor Sun Faxu briefly objected to parts of the agreement. When this opposition arose, Pan Fu and the Shandong members of the national parliament hurried to Jinan to argue with the provincial assembly; meanwhile, the national government offered the portion of the stamp tax collected within Shandong as a substitute for the ¥300,000 worth of land taxes the provincial assembly did not want used as security. Sun Faxu was transferred out of Shandong and replaced by Zhang Huaizhi of Dong'a, a friend of Pan Fu's who favored the canal.[63] AIC could hardly have received stronger assurances that the project had influential protectors in both Jinan and Beijing.

Nevertheless, the deal soon began to fall apart. The problem, simply put, was Japan. When renovation of the Shandong Canal had been discussed in 1914, the Chinese were bound by an 1898 treaty to offer Germany a piece of the project; the Germans declined and said they had no objections to Americans undertaking the project. By 1917, when a contract was actually signed, Japan had claimed Germany's privileges in Shandong, though neither China nor the United States recognized this claim. In fact AIC—whose directors and officers included a Rockefeller, a Morgan, a DuPont, and Willard Straight—had been organized on Reinsch's initiative to finance projects that would help the United States maintain the "open door" and limit Japanese influence.[64]

A year after the contract was signed, Japan lodged a formal protest. At first, Reinsch reported that this protest was not serious but just an attempt to set a precedent for other cases. Just days later, however, AIC informed him that even a purely formal Japanese protest would scare off potential bondholders; consequently, they would offer the Industrial Bank of Japan (IBJ) five-twelfths of the project.[65]

Reinsch was aghast. Such an agreement appeared to endorse Japan's "special position" in Shandong, and AIC was closely linked to the U.S. government. If the United States tried to stop the project now, it might provoke a test of Japan's privileges, which the United States

63. Department of State, reel 214, document 234, pp. 464–69; document 235, p. 490; on Zhang Huaizhi, see China Weekly Review, *Who's Who in China*, 3rd ed. (1925), 41–42.
64. Department of State, reel 214, document 213, p. 293; document 231, pp. 447, 449; document 256, pp. 837–39; on AIC's board members see its 1917 *Bulletins* 1:1 and 1:2 and its 1919 *Annual Report*.
65. Department of State, reel 214, document 231, pp. 447–49; document 234, p. 469; document 236, p. 493.

wished to avoid until the war in Europe was over. Worse yet, since the Shandong Canal project was supposed to lead to a larger Grand Canal–Huai River project, it would extend Japanese influence into huge new areas. Meanwhile, Reinsch emphasized, the Chinese would be justifiably enraged at the United States; the United States had overcome initial Chinese resistance to foreign participation in inland riverworks by portraying the Huai River project as a purely humanitarian effort, led by the Red Cross and undertaken by a country with no territorial ambitions. However, AIC insisted that without Japanese participation, political uncertainties would make financing impossible.[66]

The Chinese government was indeed angry that AIC not only brought in a Japanese bank, but planned to share the enormous management prerogatives contained in the contract.[67] The only change in the contracts with the Chinese was an added clause allowing AIC to float up to five-twelfths of the loan "in a place other than the United States." The arrangements for Japanese subcontractors were made through agreements between AIC and IBJ, agreements that did not require a Chinese signature. On March 31, 1917, Reinsch reported that Pan Fu and other Chinese felt the AIC-IBJ agreement was a "betrayal"; however, by April 14, he reported that they had been "forced by circumstances to swallow their disgust."[68]

In May, the Anhui provincial assembly voted to oppose all transprovincial plans for the Huai and all foreign participation in conservancy. Beijing remained committed to this project and tried to get the Anhui vote reversed.[69] However, the AIC-IBJ deal had created just the sort of political uncertainty that AIC had hoped to avoid. Under such conditions AIC wanted more guarantees and insisted that the modified agreement be submitted to the Chinese parliament; Pan Fu and other Chinese officials preferred simply approving the modifications by exchanging letters. Although the Chinese parliament was insignificant, AIC continued to insist; the company did, however, release some funds to finance more surveying by American engineers.[70]

66. Ibid., document 236, pp. 493, 497; document 237, pp. 500, 502; document 238, pp. 504–5.

67. Reprints of *Peking Daily News* for Feb. 6 and 13, 1917, in ibid., document 249, pp. 785, 787, 790; document 252, p. 800 (Reinsch to Secretary of State Lansing, March 31, 1917), in ibid.

68. Ibid., document 254, pp. 809, 812; document 256, p. 824.

69. Ibid., document 261, p. 869.

70. Ibid., document 256, p. 827; reel 215, document 277, p. 0004; document 294, p. 148.

The plan these surveyors drew up was even more optimistic and ambitious than the one commissioned by Pan Fu. For ¥13,318,000, the favored option promised navigability for barges of up to five hundred tons, reclamation of more than 1,000,000 *mu* of land, another 1,100,000 *mu* made safe from flooding, a beginning on Yellow River training in the area near where it met the canal (including new dikes, a drainage tunnel, and a new way to get materials to the river for future work), irrigation water for 180,000 *mu*, a telephone line along the canal, and new dredging boats and other equipment. These benefits would pay for the project within a single year.[71]

None of this, however, spoke to the political qualms of American financiers, and the start of work continued to be delayed. Had AIC been ready to begin work by February 1921, famine victims could have been hired to do much of the work and paid with Red Cross relief grain, but it was not. The Chinese and the U.S. ambassador blamed AIC; Freeman, the project's chief engineer, cited precautions against bandits; and AIC continued to insist that the "contract" issue be resolved first. In May 1921, Pan Fu complained that it had been more than three years since letters had been exchanged incorporating all the changes AIC had sought; almost US$900,000 had been spent, but no construction had been done. AIC replied that since the Chinese parliament had not yet "enacted" the contract, bonds could not be sold, and the time limit on AIC's option had not yet begun to run.[72]

Meanwhile, the dollar cost of the project had approximately doubled since 1914.[73] However, the planning group's final report, dated August 1920, was still very favorable, and AIC's Japanese partners remained enthusiastic. (Had the extent of Japanese enthusiasm been known, it might not have reassured the Chinese. IBJ had already been approached by Japanese mills seeking assurances that the reclaimed land in Shandong would be planted in cotton for export to Japan.)[74]

Meanwhile, the project lost political support. Pan Fu went into temporary retirement in November 1921; Xiong Xiling became involved in other projects; Pan Fu's friend and Jining compatriot Jin Yunpeng ended three years of intermittent premiership in late 1921; Zhou Ziji,

71. Freeman, *GCIM, GCIC*, passim.
72. Ibid., p. 21; Department of State, reel 215, document 328, p. 381; reel 216, document 424, pp. 201–2, 204.
73. Department of State, reel 215, document 351, p. 596; *HWJB*, no. 10 (Spring 1925), 27.
74. Department of State, reel 216, document 424, p. 199.

also a western Shandong native and early backer of the project, left the national stage after the defeat of the Anfu clique in early 1922.[75]

Jiangsu province, meanwhile, obtained Beijing's permission to withhold ¥3,000,000 in land taxes over three years for its own Grand Canal project; this ended thoughts of a unified Grand Canal–Huai River project.[76] By 1919, the privileges that Japan had seized in eastern Shandong during World War I had become one of the most explosive issues in Chinese politics; a project that would bring the Japanese into western Shandong would have been wildly unpopular, no matter what its local benefits.[77] In 1922, a large Yellow River break in Lijin, near the mouth of the river, created a more urgent claim on Shandong's conservancy funds, as well as a new focus for American diplomats and engineers seeking a role in Chinese riverworks.[78] In 1916, foreigners had thought that Shandong was the province most dedicated to canal restoration, but by 1922 it was the only province where no canal work was going on; the Canal Board itself soon closed for lack of funds.[79] The board's demise ended any hope of getting foreign expertise and 8 percent loans for a project likely to yield much more.[80]

Thus, the ability of South Huang-Yun's urban elites to reach higher levels of government—which had helped meet at least Jining's minimal infrastructural needs in 1902 and 1911—was not enough this time. The planners' uncertain access to the proceeds of land reclamation had made foreign loans and national guarantees essential and meant that getting the needed resources would hinge on larger political events. However, the appeal to nationalism that had moved extraprovincial gentry and officials on the railroad issue cut the other way this time. Once AIC brought in Japanese partners, those who were primarily concerned with preserving China's autonomy soured on canal restoration.

From this point on the outlook for all Huang-Yun conservancy

75. Ibid., reel 215, document 351, p. 604; *China Yearbook 1926–1927*, 1190; Boorman, *Biographical Dictionary*, 1:382; *Zhongguo jindai ming ren tu jian*, 83.
76. Department of State, reel 216, document 380, p. 0019; *Jiaotong shi*, 1790–1810.
77. See, for instance, Chow Tse-tung, *The May Fourth Movement* (Cambridge, Mass., 1960), 85–92. Curiously, no summary account has been written of anti-Japanese feelings and actions in Shandong itself, but numerous sources testify to strong anti-Japanese feelings among every group in Shandong society.
78. Department of State, reel 216, document 450, p. 457; document 472, pp. 671–72.
79. *China Yearbook 1923*, 547.
80. Freeman, *GCIC*, 67.

efforts only got worse. Numerous warlord battles were fought in Huang-Yun over the next four years. Zhang Zongchang, who wound up master of Shandong, had no ties whatsoever to western Shandong. He himself came from the far east of the province, and his original power base was people from his home county who worked as security guards in Manchurian mines; throughout his career, he surrounded himself with people from that area.[81] The western Shandong elite had almost all backed the losing, pro-Zhili side in the Zhili-Fengtian war (though Pan Fu and Zhang Zongchang were later reconciled).[82] In fact, Zhang was so suspicious of western Shandong that he ordered that the Dezhou arsenal be dismantled and reassembled near Jinan, where he felt more confident of controlling it.[83]

Zhang Zongchang's rule was probably the worst Shandong experienced in our period; Henan's situation was little better. Major construction projects were out of the question. The 1925 Yellow River floods were Shandong's worst since 1855. The next serious attempts to repair Huang-Yun's hydraulic system came after the Northern Expedition.

NATIONAL DISUNITY AND HYDRAULIC CONTROL: THE WARLORD YEARS

While water control suffered from even greater neglect during the 1920s, national disunity was less a handicap than one might suspect. Provincial governments' internal policies were much more significant than conflicts between provinces, except insofar as military spending might otherwise have gone to riverworks. Problems at the grass-roots level were the most important; and these, as we will see later, span the years from the late Qing to World War II.

Some research that later proved valuable for water control was done during the 1920s.[84] Various roads completed in the mid-1920s as relief projects, mostly under Red Cross supervision, were designed

81. Li Hengzhen, Xu Datong, and Zhang Jinxiu, "Zhang Zongchang," 1–2, 17, 36–37, 39.
82. Ibid., 46–47; and *NCH*, Nov. 14, 1925, p. 277 (noting that Jin Yunpeng's brother was a high aide to Wu Peifu); on Pan Fu's later work with Zhang Zongchang, see *NCH*, July 2, 1927, p. 4.
83. Chen Ruilin, "Dezhou 'Beiyang jiqi zhizaoju' yu lujunbu Dexian bing gongchang shi mo," *Dezhou shi zhi tongxun*, no. 2 (1986), 29–30.
84. Greer, *Water Management*, 40–42, on the training of Chinese in Western hydraulic techniques in these years (though larger gains were made in the 1930s); on Yellow River research, see Shen Yi, *Huang He taolun ji*.

to facilitate future canal and river work in western Shandong.[85] Some new techniques were successfully tested on Pu county dikes in 1925–26, though they could not be more widely applied at the time.[86]

The standard mainland history of Yellow River control emphasizes the lack of coordination among provinces during the Republican period.[87] Provincial rivalries did indeed interfere with conservancy. It was not until the 1930s that Henan, Hebei, and Shandong developed a joint plan for lower Yellow River repairs.[88] However, this problem was far less important than more local political failures.

The most serious Grand Canal problems were almost all within one province, Shandong. Other provinces, like Jiangsu, did not do the best canal work possible, but they did keep its entire length open; AIC's plans for the Shandong Canal were designed to be compatible with various approaches to the Jiangsu section.[89] Moreover, as late as 1906 Shandong governor Yang Shixiang had thought Shandong could maintain the Grand Canal on its own if it could contribute slightly less for a few years to provisioning troops in Beijing, Tianjin, and Manchuria;[90] what he sought from Beijing resembled the permission that Jiangsu secured in 1920 to temporarily use some of the national taxes it collected for canal work. In this sense the weaker central governments of the 1920s represented an opportunity. Shandong could easily have withheld enough money to make a difference; missing was the determination to address water control problems.[91]

Moreover, a surprising amount of cooperation on water control continued. In the 1930s Shandong regularly sent money and labor to help with the Hebei section of the Yellow River, just as it had sent people to help with the Henan section of the river in the 1700s. Jiangsu and Anhui contributed to Shandong riverworks that benefited them. Jiangsu contributed ¥200,000 to the repair of several crucial Yellow River dikes in Puxian, Shandong, after the 1925 floods, while

85. Freeman, *GCIC*, 53; on later road building by relief agencies in Shandong, see *China Yearbook 1928*, 328.

86. See the account in Lin Maoquan, *Wenji*, 1:6a–16b, 184a–187a; on the experimental value of this limited work, see *HWTK*, no. 2 (Jan. 1930), *zhuanjian*, 13–15.

87. *HH*, 366.

88. *HWTK*, no. 4 (Jan. 1932), *jihua*, 4.

89. *JSYK* 1:3 (March 1931), *gongdu*; *HH*, 33, 366–67; Department of State, reel 214, document 221, pp. 332–33.

90. Memorial from Yang Shixiang, 2/23/GX 32, in LFZZ, GX 32, packet 37–38; Wu Tongju, *Zai xu*, 3806–09.

91. Freeman, *GCIC*, 17–18.

Shandong province spent only ¥520,000 per year for routine Yellow River work in the entire province.[92] In 1915, eleven Shandong river battalions worked on a major flood control project in Zhili.[93] In the mid-1920s, Daming county in Hebei convinced the Henan Yellow River Office to force Huaxian to make some long-neglected repairs. This pressure worked even at the peak of warlordism, and even though Daming, being further downstream, could not really threaten Huaxian directly.[94] Huaxian, in turn, managed to get partial reimbursements from Shandong counties that benefited from this work.[95] Shandong and Henan agreed in 1910 to block any local projects that interfered with the larger needs of the Wei River, and both sides kept to this agreement for more than twenty years; freakishly heavy rains led to the construction of illegal private dikes on both sides of the border in 1931, but the agreement was renewed in 1932.[96] This was much greater success than the Shandong authorities usually had in eliminating private dikes that affected only their own province.

Cross-provincial cooperation was, of course, limited. Neighboring provinces might contribute for a particular repair, but long-term projects could not count on steady assistance or use revenues from remote provinces to secure loans. But, as shown above, Shandong and Henan had not obtained outside funds for major hydraulic repairs during the last twenty years of the Qing, either. The national government and other provinces contributed large sums for hydraulic repairs and relief after major floods, but little to prevent the floods from occurring in the first place. However, Shandong's own government did even less after some major western Shandong floods, providing only relief funds.[97]

92. *HWTK*, no. 3 (Jan. 1931), *gongdu* 51, 97, 98; no. 4 (Jan. 1932), *gongdu*, 7; no. 1 (Oct. 1928), *gongdu*, 21.

93. Xu Shiguang, *Puyang Heshang ji, ding*, 15a–b.

94. *Chongxiu Hua xianzhi* (1930), 11:31b–32b.

95. *HWTK* no. 8 (Jan. 1936), *mingling*, 16.

96. Hou Renzhi, *Xu tianxia*, 146.

97. In the case of Lijin, the provincial government ignored frequent warnings of disaster but did provide both reconstruction and relief aid afterward. In the 1925, 1933, and 1935 floods, which were concentrated in western Shandong, the government provided large amounts of relief afterward (less in 1925, more in 1933 and 1935), but only very limited funds for repairs. On Lijin, see Asia Development Co., *Repairing the Yellow River Break—Kung Chia Ko, Shantung* (1923); on the western Shandong breaks, see Shandong Huang He shuizai jiuji weiyuanhui, *Shandong Huang He shuizai he shuizai jiuji baogao shu* (Jinan, 1935 and 1936); Lin Maoquan, *Wenji*, 1:6a–16b; on relief generally, see Mantetsu, *Santō Chihō no Kōka Suisai*, 4, 25–26; on warnings that were ignored, see, for instance, Department of State, reel 215, document 412, p. 167; document 419, pp. 188–90; *NCH*, Aug. 16, 1924, p. 248.

The most serious failures of cooperation were between and within counties in the same province. Problems between two counties on opposite sides of a provincial border could threaten political stability; provincial riverworks authorities got involved, and the resources required were often small relative to provincial capacities. When two counties within the same province clashed, however, the projects in question were often quite large relative to their total resources and so could be carried out only if each county government had an effective system for planning and levying contributions for riverworks within its own county. As we shall see, however, most county governments in Huang-Yun had no such control; the critical decision making, taxing, and levying of labor was generally done by bosses entrenched at much lower levels.

THE FORMAL GOVERNMENT, RURAL BOSSES, AND LOCAL RESISTANCE

After the Northern Expedition reached Beijing, North China became relatively stable; the new provincial regimes were never fully subordinated to the new central government, but at least they did not fight each other. Renewed efforts were made to control Huang-Yun's waterways, and the unsatisfactory system of dispatching river commissioners to people's dikes areas was ended.[98]

However, the Shandong government's attempts to devise a new system were frustrated by the control rural bosses and yamen runners had over land reclamation and private dike building. This control, and general rural opposition to involvement by the formal government, hobbled attempts to coordinate large-scale riverworks. Since both the provincial and national governments insisted that immediate beneficiaries fund Huang-Yun water control—as they had since the 1891 reforms—such opposition was financially crippling.

Although village-state clashes became more direct after the eclipse

---

98. It is unclear exactly when and how the river commissioners were abolished. However, they figure in accounts of 1923 and 1925 floods and then are never mentioned again; the post-1928 Shandong Yellow River system, as we shall see later, depended on village heads and "dike heads." Lin Maoquan, *Wenji*, 1:6a–16b, 184a–187a, makes it appear that the 1925 crisis was so serious that local elites on the one hand and he and Pan Fu on the other simply cut out the middlemen and dealt with each other directly, but there is no other source to confirm this version of events.

of the river commissioners, they were a continuation of Qing and early Republican conflicts. Once again, these clashes were most common in South Huang-Yun, where the opportunities for private reclamation were greatest, rural elites most able to resist the state, and the absence of coordinated water control most dangerous.

Most land reclamation went on unofficially, through the connivance of village heads, yamen clerks, and the claimants themselves, and often against the will of county officials and assemblies.[99] We have already seen some examples of village heads and yamen runners protecting small projects that frustrated larger schemes. The Jining assembly battled yamen runners for more than twenty years to tax reclaimed lake land (*hu tian*) to finance water conservancy, without success.[100] And, in contrast to the case of agricultural extension in North Huang-Yun, county-and higher-level authorities never developed a reliable set of local agents for land reclamation and water control matters.

The most forceful attempt to tax untaxed land to finance water control did not involve reclaimed land, but the land involved was closely related to conservancy. In 1902, when Zhou Fu asked to retain some of the Shandong land tax for hydraulic repairs, he was told that he could use instead whatever revenue was gained by converting *tun tian*—land once granted tax-free to those who worked on the Grand Canal—into regular, tax-paying land.[101]

Many provinces had *tun tian*, but Shandong had the most: more than 1,700,000 *mu* in thirty western counties. With the end of grain tribute, the Qing planned to convert this to ordinary land, charging a "sale price" to its cultivators as a commutation of service obligations and removing barriers to pawning, selling, and taxing it. Originally, they planned to charge 5 *liang* per *mu*; this would have yielded a one-time windfall of 8,500,000 *liang* (¥11,900,000) in Shandong alone, a sum almost equal to the rest of the province's revenue.[102] It is not clear how much annual income the government hoped to realize thereafter from putting this land on the books. However, if even an unusually low rate—perhaps $\frac{2}{10}$ *liang* per *mu*—had actually been collected and shared equally by Beijing and Jinan, these lands could

99. *NYHH*, Appendix, 9; *Jining xianzhi* 4:47a–51b; *Dongfang zazhi* 1:10 (10/25/ GX 30), 173; *Shandong gongbao* 1:34 (July 7, 1912), *wendu*, 1.

100. *JSYK* 1:3 (March 1931), *mingling*, 10–11.

101. Chen Yunlong, *Zhou Fu*, 163, 211.

102. Ibid., 155, 156.

have again fulfilled their erstwhile function: paying for routine upkeep on the Grand Canal.

However, it was clear from the start that nowhere near 8,500,000 *liang* could be collected. Most of the land was very poor, so that 5 *liang* per *mu* would have been a heavy burden. Moreover, though this land was theoretically inalienable, much had been pawned or sold, often several times; many cultivators were unaware of any unusual obligations. Making them "buy" this land was bound to strain both budgets and tempers. By late 1902, pessimistic reports from officials and petitions from the countryside led the Qing to create a new price schedule: 3,000 *zhi qian* (between 2 and 3 *liang*) per *mu* for the best land, 1,000 for poorer land, and no charge for the most sandy or alkaline land.[103] Changing the prices into copper eliminated one way in which it was feared that yamen underlings would cheat people and cause unrest—manipulating the silver-copper rate.[104] Zhou Fu also proposed allowing purchasers to pay over three years.[105]

Even these payments proved uncollectible, however. The multitude of old and lost records and of landholders unaware of their land's special status created a situation bound to lead to fraud, extortion, and unrest.[106] Almost ten months after collection began, only four of the thirty counties affected had collected even half the amount due. Many had collected no money at all. Groups of *tun zhang* (village heads in *tun tian* areas) had led protests in South Huang-Yun's Juye county; in northern Liaocheng, several hundred *tun min* (the people on this land) protested in the county capital and attacked and wounded a yamen runner before being scattered by troops with guns.[107] The Liaocheng magistrate was removed; but when his successor tried to collect the tax, more than five thousand people invaded the yamen itself, smashed property and "the head of an unfortunate underling," and left only when he promised to give up on these imposts. Unrest was reported in several other counties, along with a few compromises.[108]

The biggest protests occurred further south, in and near Jining.

103. Ibid., 156.
104. *Jining zhilizhou xuzhi* 4:14a; see also *NCH*, March 18, 1904, 575.
105. Chen Yunlong, *Zhou Fu*, 156.
106. *Jining zhilizhou xuzhi* 4:14b.
107. *Zhou Fu*, 227–28.
108. *NCH*, Nov. 27, 1903, p. 1120; Kato Chokushi, "Shingai Kakumei no Santō Shō ni okeru Minshu Undō," *Shiron*, no. 34 (1981), 47–49.

When the plan to "sell" *tun tian* was announced in February 1902, Jining's *tun min* were among the first to petition against it; some *tun zhang* and at least one local constable (*dibao*) also collected money to finance lawsuits.[109] Nonetheless, magistrate Yao Liankui decided to collect the money, perhaps for the treasury, perhaps for himself.[110]

Yao's first attempt yielded no money. In January 1904 he tried again, persuading a pawnbroker named Li Mou to pay for some *tun tian* and then citing this as a precedent. During the Lantern Festival of 1904, *tun zhang* from all over Jining met at a temple near the city gate to discuss the situation. Afterward, thirty-two of them entered the city to petition the magistrate again and to "talk" with Li Mou. Before long, one was arrested. As word spread through the large Lantern Festival crowd in the streets, people became increasingly angry; some broke into the yamen, freed the prisoner, and ceremonially burned some of the magistrate's private property. Granaries and other official structures were not damaged, and when the fires burned out the crowd dispersed. Still, the magistrate felt sufficiently threatened to request troops.[111]

Similar events soon occurred in Yuncheng, Jiaxiang, Puzhou, Fanxian, Wenshang, Shouzhang, and Dongping. In Yuncheng, the magistrate had summoned a group of *tun zhang* to discuss the land purchases and claimed that only one, Ren Qinghe, had objected. Ren Qinghe was soon arrested, but a crowd of more than two thousand people surrounded the magistrate's yamen and obtained his release.[112] Back in Jining, bandit groups had used the situation to recruit people for their own activities.[113]

A worried governor dispatched two battalions to the affected areas and ordered the circuit's intendant to take control. The arrival of troops did not bring compliance, however. In Jining, some bandits fled and peace returned; however, the *tun min* still refused to pay.[114] In Yuncheng, troops were attacked. Rather than risk a major clash be-

109. *Jining zhilizhou xuzhi* 4:14a.
110. "Tunmin kang jiao dijia de douzheng," *Jining shi shiliao*, no. 2 (1983), 73.
111. Ibid., 73–74; *Jining zhilizhou xuzhi* 4:14a.
112. Zhongguo diyi lishi danganguan and Beijing Shifan Daxue lishixi, eds., *Xinhai geming qian shi nianjian minbian dangan shiliao* (Beijing, 1985) (hereafter, *Xinhai geming qian shi nian*), 1:150, 153.
113. *Jining zhilizhou xuzhi* 9:14a.
114. Ibid., 4:14b, 4:15a.

tween troops and people in Jining, the intendant consulted a group of Jining gentry and merchants and asked one of them to mediate at another meeting with *tun zhang*.[115]

Eventually, an agreement was reached in which people would pay for their land in copper at rates half the prices Zhou Fu had proposed and between one-fifth and one-twelfth the court's original prices. Payments were to be spread over seven years.[116] Even these sums were never paid; Shandong's *tun tian* receipts were less than 1 percent of the original goal, and only a small fraction of the land was ever placed on the tax rolls.[117]

Several aspects of this incident are noteworthy, beyond the frustration of Zhou Fu's Yellow River plans. First, it was expected. Censors, other officials, petitioners, and resident foreigners all predicted that trying to collect money for *tun tian* would yield violence, not revenue. Even the plan's chief sponsor admitted that unless yamen underlings were carefully controlled, they would provoke resistance. *North China Herald* correspondents in Jining and in northwest Shandong reported that those who had to collect these unpopular payments sought to distance themselves by calling this "the foreigners' tax" and claiming it was for the Boxer Indemnity. Zhou Fu also reported that people thought this money would go to the indemnity. If it was indeed yamen workers who spread this rumor—in the heartland of the recent Boxer uprising, and while most of the area's troops were elsewhere—this would strongly confirm the view of many memorialists that the government had no agents it could trust with an assignment as delicate as collecting these payments.[118]

More generally, this story shows remarkable government weakness in the countryside. Not only is the effort's total failure striking, but the way the authorities proceeded suggests the urban nature of their world. After an initial rebuff, the Jining magistrate turned to a city-based pawnbroker to set a precedent of payment; while he may have been easy to reach, he was unlikely to inspire rural compliance. When the circuit intendant wanted to compromise, he met with "gentry and

115. "Tunmin," 74–78.
116. *Jining zhilizhou xuzhi* 4:15b, 16a.
117. *Shandong quansheng caizheng shuomingshu*, sect. 2, p. 10; Duara, "Power in Rural Society," 344.
118. *Jining zhilizhou xuzhi* 4:13b–14a; Chen Yunlong, *Zhou Fu*, 155–56; *NCH*, Jan. 27, 1903, p. 160; Feb. 11, 1903, pp. 236, 267; Feb. 25, 1903, p. 372; Nov. 27, 1903, p. 1120; Sept. 30, 1904, p. 740; *Xinhai geming qian shi nian*, 150–52.

big merchants" in Jining city, and chose Chen Shouhe as chief negotiator.[119] Since 1875, Chen had been the manager of the Yutang soy sauce factory, Jining's oldest and largest manufacturing enterprise, owned by a family that included a recent grand councillor. Part of Chen's job was to attract investment from gentry families, their clan endowments, and public charities; he was extremely well connected among retired officials in Jining. However, there is nothing to suggest that he had much influence in the countryside; it does not even appear that the company owned much land, though it had diversified into money shops, salt shops, and Jinan flour mills.[120] When these representatives of the Jining government and elite sat down with the *tun zhang*, they met across a rural-urban divide.

On the other side, the protestors had strong rural networks, based on leadership by village heads. The collective actions of the Jining *tun zhang*—organizing for lawsuits, planning protest strategies, and meeting as a group with Jining and Yuncheng officials—suggest that they were more than just individuals who implemented orders from above in their villages.[121] They also had many ties to heterodox networks; in fact, as had been the case among the Boxers of southwest (but not northwest) Shandong, secret society leaders and "orthodox" village leaders were often the same people. Ren Qinghe, a Yuncheng *tun zhang* who led local opposition to payments, was one of many participants who had been involved in the Big Sword Society (the southwestern "Boxers").[122] The government's postmortem on this case said that Ren collected money from twenty-four villages on the "pretext" of resisting the payments and was able to levy soldiers and weapons according to the amounts of land in each.[123] These village-by-village levies of money, people, and weapons suggest an organization in many ways superior to what the government and urban elite had in the countryside.

The government and county capital elites were not helpless, of course; they had numerous ways of profiting from the rural population. They collected rural produce for consumption or resale, collected

119. "Tunmin," 74.
120. Hai Shan, "Yutang chunqiu," pt. 1, pp. 55–56; pt. 2, pp. 99–102.
121. See *Jining zhilizhou xuzhi*, 14a–15a; *Xinhai geming qian shi nian*, 153–54, 156.
122. Esherick, *Boxer Uprising*, 104, 107–8, 126, 153; Kato Chokushi, "Shingai Kakumei no Santō Shō ni okeru Minshu Undō," 48–49.
123. *Xinhai geming qian shi nian*, 154.

routine taxes, made profits by lending money or controlling its exchange, and so forth. In fact, as our study of credit showed, South Huang-Yun's urban elites controlled the flow of goods and money in ways that generated especially large profits in some sectors. Moreover, although Jining ran a large trade deficit with the surrounding counties, it does not appear that Jining residents were selling off rural assets; this information too suggests that South Huang-Yun's major city received more real resources from villages than it returned to them, without paying for the difference.

Ordinarily, the urban elites of both Jining and South Huang-Yun's county capitals made these profits with the cooperation of the very groups—yamen runners and village heads—who frustrated them this time. Even on this occasion, when those groups turned against and defeated them, urban elites could at least meet with people capable of ending the conflict. Further north, in Liaocheng, the magistrate had conceded defeat by making a promise to a crowd invading his yamen; contemporaneous accounts mention no leaders. In fact, given the general weakness of both urban and rural elites in North Huang-Yun, it is hard to imagine who could have meaningfully held negotiations like those in Jining.

Still, this incident made it clear that relations between Jining's urban elite and the countryside would not sustain major initiatives (like land surveys or the adoption of American cotton) that threatened village and subcounty powerholders. As we saw, the Pan family put little of its wealth into rural land. The Jining gazetteer mentions no other family trusts holding land for the education, old age, or other needs of lineage members, but several such trusts did invest in the Yutang enterprises. At one point, the Sun (Yutang) family did own quite a bit of land, though it is unclear where it was; the family also had interests in Zhejiang, and in the mid-1920s they moved as much money as possible out of Jining to the safety of Shanghai. While merchants and officials had long been very closely entwined in Jining, there seems to have been little urban wealth invested in the surrounding countryside.[124]

The *tun tian* debacle ensued when officials tried, against their better judgment, to do more than their influence in the countryside would allow: that is, to act against the interests of rural elites. Most of the

<hr>

124. Hai Shan, "Yutang chunqiu," pt. 1, pp. 64–65, pt. 2, pp. 101–2; see also Jing Su and Luo Lun, *Landlord and Labor* 27, 109–10; *Santō Sainei*, passim.

time government and urban elites gave up before violence broke out. However, they continued to make occasional attempts, such as the gentry-sponsored land reclamation companies mentioned above and the Jining Assembly's attempts to collect payments from people farming public "lake land."[125] Without exception, the urban elite's forays into conservancy, reclamation, and land registration failed.

By the 1930s, Shandong's Yellow River Office (Hewuju; hereafter YRO) and Reconstruction Office (Jiansheju; hereafter RO), backed by a revived central government, planned numerous river projects. However, these plans depended on co-opting or overpowering village heads and local bosses. The RO eventually completed one huge dredging and diking project, covering the Wanfu He, Zhushui He, and various smaller rivers that fed into the Grand Canal and associated lakes. However, its second major river project—restoration of the canal itself—never got far, and the YRO's plans for better Yellow River control went nowhere at all. The sometimes violent opposition of subcounty powerholders accounted for many of these failures. Such opposition often frustrated projects much larger than the area in which it emerged. In one case, ten uncooperative *li zhang* in Shouzhang county stopped dike repair along a five-county stretch of the upper Shandong Yellow River.[126]

One continuing problem with both the people's dikes and provincial mobilizations of corvée labor was that burdens fell entirely on those closest to the river; villages more than three miles away rarely helped unless a very large flood seemed imminent.[127] This imbalance caused some serious delays. In Dexian, the entire burden of both Madun He and Grand Canal work fell on one district (*qu*), making it impossible to work on both in one season; this problem often meant leaving a half-finished project to face the autumn floods.[128] Concentrating burdens on especially small groups sometimes prompted refusals to work; however, attempts to levy labor from the whole county were rare and usually failed.[129] Both the YRO and county magistrates acknowledged that those closest to the river were often overtaxed and agreed that other beneficiaries of flood control had to contribute;

125. *JSYK* 1:4 (April 1931), *mingling*, 10–11.
126. *HWTK*, no. 3 (Jan. 1931), *gongdu*, 21–24.
127. *SDZZ*, no. 59 (5/10/XT 2), 8b.
128. *JSGB*, no. 267 (Nov. 24, 1935), *gongdu*, 5–6; no. 270 (Dec. 15, 1935), *mingling*, 24; no. 283 (Mar. 15, 1936), *mingling*, 39.
129. *JSYK* 2:3 (Mar. 1932), *gongdu*, 1.

however, neither could make them do so. When a Dong'a dike officer (*nian zhang*) complained about the money cost of needed stone, the YRO's only suggestion was that he levy additional labor from people along the river to pack and ship stone.[130] Since moving laborers involves more complications (housing, food, and so forth) than moving money, falling back on corvée administered by local bosses reinforced the tendency for riverside communities to bear the costs alone.[131] And if the bosses saw no reason to mobilize people for a project, usually neither the YRO nor even the more aggressive RO could force them.[132]

Provincial agencies also had trouble preventing local administrators from provoking resistance to labor levies. For example, two separate groups of people repairing the Madun He in northwest Shandong and southwest Hebei in 1934 struck because county authorities embezzled the money the province sent to pay wages and conscripted workers instead.[133] Characteristically, one of the North Huang-Yun strikes was organized with the help of outsiders (from the Communist Party), and neither was organized by village elites. Both were eventually crushed by troops; though their dissociation from local powerholders may have made these protests more socially radical than South Huang-Yun protests, neither left any lasting concessions or institutionalized legacy.[134] By contrast, the only case I have found of a South Huang-Yun protest by corvée laborers over embezzlement—which occurred in 1911—was led by village heads and made no demands for structural change; however, a private association of Jining gentry and merchants in Beijing was approached to make up for the missing funds. Village heads also seem to have played a major role in the eighteenth-century resistance to corvée in South Huang-Yun.[135]

130. *HWTK*, no. 1 (Oct. 1928), *mingling*, 10, 30–31. It should be noted that this particular substitution of labor for money was possible in Dong'a, which was not far from the official quarries and produced some stone itself; it would not have been practical for most of Huang-Yun.

131. On village heads' control of corvée assignments, see Duara, "Power in Rural Society," 159; and Shandong sheng jiansheting, 40, 48.

132. *JSGB*, no. 280 (Feb. 23, 1936), *gong du*, 10.

133. "Du Buzhou," 17–18.

134. Ibid., 18.

135. *SDZZ*, no. 92 (undated; probably 6/15/XT 3), 40b–41a. (The text is unclear about exactly which *tongxianghui* was asked for money; it may have been a Jining group, but it was probably the *tongxianghui* of Shandong people in Beijing, who published *SDZZ*.)

Zhongguo Renmin Daxue, Qing shi yanjiu suo, *Kang Yong Qian shiqi cheng xiang renmin fankang douzheng ziliao* (Beijing, 1979), 335–37.

Some conflicts, however, were even more intractable than those involving unwilling workers; these arose when villagers opposed having
anybody do certain projects. These incidents occurred mainly in South
Huang-Yun and involved three closely linked phenomena: illicit land
reclamation, unregistered land, and private dikes built to divert floods
away from waterfront land. In particular, control of the upper Yellow
River in Shandong was crippled by rampant private dike building in
Pu, Yanggu, Heze, Shouzhang, Fan, Yuncheng, and Yincheng counties. These dikes protected the large amounts of land inside the outer
dikes that had been reclaimed, often illegally; there were more than a
million such *mu* in Fan county alone. These dikes hindered overall
Yellow River control, but those who built them did not want to give
them up.[136]

The YRO repeatedly ordered private dikes destroyed, but enforcement depended on village heads, who, the office admitted, almost
unanimously ignored the orders.[137] In the 1890s Li Hongzhang, Zhou
Fu, and others had recommended buying out private reclaimers.[138]
This buy-out never happened, partly because the *tun tian* payments—
money from other occupiers of legally public, water conservancy-
related, land—could not be collected. In 1933, the provincial YRO
told Governor Han Fuju that a new method was needed to eliminate
such dikes, because reliance on village heads had failed completely.[139]
Once again, nothing happened.

With private dikes, as with work stoppages, the RO intervened
much more than the YRO. However, it usually stepped in only after
land-use conflicts had stalemated projects for years; governments used
force only after serious flooding or violence against workers on RO
projects.[140]

In several instances, either a village head or somebody whom the
government described as a "local bully" (*tuhao*) rallied enough people
to halt work. Many of the documented cases involved the RO's Wanfu
He project, which we will consider shortly. Another revealing case

136. *HWTK*, no. 6 (Jan. 1934), *gongdu*, 25–26, 39; no. 4 (Jan. 1932), *gongdu*,
29–30.
137. Ibid., no. 6 (Jan. 1934), *gongdu*, 39–40.
138. Chen Yunlong, *Zhou Fu*, 216–17.
139. *HWTK*, no. 6 (Jan. 1934), *gongdu*, 39–40.
140. *JSYK* 2:8 (Aug. 1932), *gongdu*, 5–6; *mingling*, 22, 24–25; 2:6 (June 1932),
gongdu, 3; *JSGB* 3:6 (June 1933), *gongdu*, 5–8; 3:8 (Aug. 1933), *gongdu*, 10; *mingling*, 6.

comes from Chiping, an unusually soggy county just north of the Yellow River in northwest Shandong.

In Chiping, private dikes had long been keeping a 1,500-*mu* area very wet; part was cultivated, and part used by people who made clay tiles. In 1932 RO surveyors planning a project to control the nearby Mei River were attacked. Nevertheless, in 1933 the RO unveiled a plan that would have ruined the tile makers' livelihood, as well as what the RO claimed was the "monopoly on land and water" of the project's leading opponent, Du Mingzhe. The county government sent workers, suggesting that they knew a local levy wasn't feasible. The workers were obstructed by local women "making a racket" and then attacked by five armed men, all surnamed Du. Later that year, the area suffered heavy flooding. The following spring, the county sent more workers, this time accompanied by county troops; they were again harassed by women and children "egged on" by Du's "lies." When stalemate persisted, new troops were brought in, this time from outside the county, and a meeting of nearby district (*xiang*, a subcounty unit) leaders was convened. Only at this point did the planners learn about the tile makers who provided Du's community base, although the RO's retrospective report said half the households in the district made tiles. Eventually, troops forced Du and others to flee, and the county and RO drafted a new plan that supposedly protected the tile makers and promised better river control. A final odd touch is added by the report's comment that prior to 1932, the Mei River had been handled locally, without serious friction, for more than six hundred years.[141]

What is most striking here is the government's ignorance of local society; the county and RO seem not to have consulted any local figures until there had been violence, work delays, and unnecessary floods. Moreover, the idea of compensating those who were "in the way" seems not to have been discussed; perhaps it was understood that no money was available. Though the protestors gave every sign of being a settled community, the authorities took two years to find out why they opposed the plan; instead, officials focused exclusively on dealing with a few male "toughs," who they assumed had coerced or deceived the others. It is also noteworthy that this small piece of

141. *JSGB*, no. 269 (Dec. 8, 1935), *mingling*, 21–24. It is unclear from the text whether the heavy flooding occurred in 1934 or whether it was by then 1935, another flood season having passed with nothing accomplished.

North Huang-Yun, which resembled South Huang-Yun in economic geography and social structure—lots of water, private dikes, unregistered land, and a powerful rural "boss"—clashed with the state in a similar way. Nonetheless, the state here turned to district leaders, who were part of the formal government chain of command, to link them to local society, rather than meeting with the village elites who were essential partners in settling disputes further south.

One way or the other, the RO and YRO were usually unable to overcome local bosses' opposition to their plans. The resulting stalemates left riverwork undone while placing huge burdens on a few communities. Early 1930s petitions from riverside communities in Pu and Fan counties on the upper Yellow River said that the residents would prefer official dikes and corvée labor to the existing combination of people's dikes and the six-county common fund (described below); they felt that requisitions could get no worse and that stepped-up coercion would at least get the work done.[142]

Moreover, local control of riverworks exacerbated a familiar problem in Chinese history—tax evasion leading to a greater burden on those still taxed, leading to more tax evasion. The less land taxed at the start of this cycle, the faster it gets out of control; since under the "people's repair" (*min xiu*) system in effect along most of Huang-Yun's waterways only land very close to the rivers was assessed, the situation quickly became desperate.

The post–Northern Expedition YRO's problems with the upper zone of the Shandong Yellow River furnish a perfect example. After the huge floods of the mid-1920s, the YRO was determined to coordinate the local, often haphazard, maintenance of people's dikes. However, returning these dikes to official status was too expensive to be politically feasible. Instead, a commission was formed of officials from the five (later six) up-river counties: the county magistrates, the head of each county riverworks office, and three supervisors from the YRO.[143] Meanwhile, on-the-spot control of people's dikes work had passed from the expectant officials to village-level figures, generally referred to as *li zhang*. They were sometimes invited to confer with this board, but were not members of it.[144]

142. *HWTK*, no. 4 (Jan. 1932), *mingling*, 9–10.
143. Ibid., no. 3 (Sept. 1931), *gongdu*, 21–24.
144. Ibid., no. 1 (Oct. 1928), *gongdu*, 18; no. 3 (Sept. 1931), *gongdu*, 16, 22–23; no. 6 (Jan. 1934), *gongdu*, 2.

Besides discussing ways to coordinate work on people's dikes, the commission was also supposed to collect a strictly limited land surtax from those affected by its work. This money was to be used for essential Yellow River work in these counties and to aid localities facing excessive maintenance burdens. In connection with this, a limit was set on the amount that any dike leader could levy for work on his particular dike.[145]

Land in these counties was said to be affected by the commission's work if the Yellow River had flooded it in 1925; each county was assigned a quota based on how much of this land it reported having.[146] This arrangement did not, even in theory, spread the cost of these dikes over all the beneficiaries, many of whom lived in other counties. Still, had it been carried out, it would have given the work a broader base than the people's dikes system had provided.

However, the plan failed completely. Though it introduced a new criterion for flood control payments, no new survey was made; and since the burdens on assessed land could still be heavy, it still made sense to hide land. There was no incentive for any county to get its villages to report accurately; to do so would just raise that county's contribution to the common fund, not distribute a fixed county contribution more fairly or improve flood control in that county. For villages and their leaders, who would have the same people's dikes obligations regardless of the fate of the common fund, there was even less reason to cooperate. Much of the flooded land that had not been reported in 1925 was not reported because it did not need the tax remissions being granted; it was already tax free because it was unregistered. Much of it was probably also recently reclaimed, often reflooded, and hard to trace. Finally, knowing that other counties were cheating made each county even less likely to cooperate fully.[147]

Consequently, the commission—and the YRO—were nearly helpless. A check by the YRO in Shouzhang, for instance, turned up 97,500 *mu* of "hidden land" that should have been assessed for this fund; just 20,500 was recorded. Yuncheng originally reported 226,000, but then "found" 123,000 more; a petition from Yuncheng

145. Ibid., no. 3 (Jan. 1931), *gongdu*, 21; no. 6 (Jan. 1934), *gongdu*, 2–3; no. 1 (Oct. 1928), *fagui*, 5–8; no. 6 (Jan. 1934), *gongdu*, 3.
146. Ibid., no. 7 (Jan. 1935), *gongdu*, 7.
147. Ibid., no. 4 (Jan. 1932), *mingling*, 10; no. 7 (Jan. 1935), *gongdu*, 8.

said that neighboring Yincheng had more than 800,000 *mu* that should have been assessed, but only 228,650 was on the books.[148]

Some frustrated local officials turned to exposing hidden land in other counties. Only Yincheng county, however, was forced to increase its payments significantly. In a settlement the next year, Yincheng added 121,748 *mu* to its rolls (though about 600,000 were allegedly being hidden there); Yuncheng added 7,454 (though 123,000 were found there); Shouzhang added 9,783 (compared to the more than 90,000 *mu* of hidden land the YRO found there). In at least three counties unregistered land still exceeded registered.[149]

While the levy for the cooperative dike maintenance efforts was only ¥0.2 per *mu* registered in the flood zone, that represented as large a burden as the annual charges on *tun tian* that had led to the 1904 riots. As in that case, much of the land involved was poor and, of course, flood prone.[150]

Moreover, common fund cash charges were just a small part of the burden that those who admitted holding land in the flood zone would bear. The burdens that moved the YRO to inaugurate limits on sums collected by dike leaders in 1929 must have been heavy indeed, since the dikes needed all the help they could get.[151] However, these limits were no more effective than the five-county common fund itself.

A plea from Dongping suggests how heavy river control burdens could be. In 1931, the magistrate reported that each *mu* in the part of Dongping along the Grand Canal had to be assessed for 2.3 *fang* of dike work, which was partly stone and partly earth. However, even if all of it were the cheapest type of earthwork, this would amount to ¥1.2 per *mu*, or more than four times the county's basic land tax rate; since stonework in Dongping cost ten or more times as much as earthwork, the actual burden must have been much heavier still.[152] The final cost of this project exceeded the entire county's land tax.[153]

Exactions for people's dikes were not recorded the way those for officially run projects like the one in Dongping were. Thus, we take a

148. Ibid., *mingling*, 23; *gongdu*, 33–34, 6.
149. Ibid., *gongdu*, 34–35, 4, 7.
150. Ibid., no. 6 (Jan. 1934), *gongdu*, 3; no. 7 (Jan. 1935), *mingling*, 21–22.
151. Ibid., no. 6 (Jan. 1934), *gongdu*, 2–3.
152. *JSYK* 1:2 (Feb. 1931), *mingling*, 2; 1:4 (April 1931), *baogao*, 20; 2:3 (March 1932), *lunzhe*, 18; *Dongping xianzhi* (1936), 7:10b. Based on its distance from the quarry the actual price should have been ¥6–7.
153. *JSYK* 1:4 (April 1931), *baogao*, 22.

different approach to estimating those exactions: estimating the amount of stalks needed for people's dikes, assuming they were actually collected, and valuing them at the lowest plausible market price. The results are rough, but nonetheless striking: if those living within three miles of the river had borne this burden alone, it would have equaled anywhere from 8 percent to 20 percent of their income; even if the cost had been spread over all residents of the riverfront counties, it would have ranged from 4 percent to 7 percent of income.[154]

Within two years, people in the affected counties were calling for the abolition of the common fund system. By 1931, people's dikes levies in the relevant parts of Pu and Fan counties were several times the basic land tax, but flood control had not improved. The YRO acknowledged the accuracy of complaints that Pu county had a great deal of unregistered land but did not try to increase its payments, probably reflecting a realization that those who were being assessed could bear no more.[155]

When people discovered that other counties were not doing their part in water control projects, they often stopped work. Reciprocal accusations by upper Yellow River counties led to several work stoppages and kept several projects from being started.[156] In 1929, after major floods on the Wanfu He, a tributary of the Grand Canal in southwest Shandong, the RO ordered each county to do something about its section of the river. Work began quickly in Jinxiang, which had tried to arrange a Wanfu He project before. After several months, though, no work had been done in neighboring Yutai; the Jinxiang magistrate reported that people there feared that a half-finished project would make things still worse, and stopped their work. As it turned out, the project did not move until 1933, though the RO had counted on it as a prerequisite for canal work planned for 1931.[157]

The Guomindang's Grand Canal efforts showed how much further things had deteriorated since the late Qing, particularly in southwest Shandong. Their 1931 plan envisioned less than earlier ones, and the state committed less money; only ¥3,500,000 was budgeted for the south Shandong section, or less than half of what had been proposed

154. For estimating methods, see dissertation, appendix G, 435–40. The ranges above result from varying estimates of how large people's dikes were.
155. *HWTK*, no. 3 (Sept. 1931), *gongdu*, 15, 74; no. 6 (Jan. 1934), *gongdu*, 3, 25–26; no. 7 (Jan. 1935), *mingling*, 39, *gongdu*, 7.
156. *HWTK*, no. 7 (Jan. 1935), *mingling*, 8.
157. *JSYK* 2:1 (Jan. 1932), *lunzhe*, 8, 9; also *Wanfu He*, 2.

in 1916. The first stage was to cost ¥800,000, which was all the RO was confident of raising; this was soon reduced to ¥600,000. That amount was met; half of it represented relief wheat donated by the Red Cross to feed the project's workers. As before, the canal builders were initially counting on borrowing most of the rest of the money and repaying it with revenues from reclaimed land.[158] However, in the midst of the Great Depression, and with some of China's foreign loans nearing default, any borrowing would have had to be domestic. And, as we have seen, no government had yet succeeded in obtaining such revenues.

Another plan called for selling almost 300,000 *mu* of publicly owned wasteland that had been created from the lakes of southwest Shandong since the end of the grain tribute. However, the RO did not explain how it would collect this money when nobody else had been able to collect rents or taxes on such land. The Pan family continued to lead unsuccessful efforts to do so; meanwhile, at least one affected county announced plans to use any money collected for local schools rather than for the canal project.[159]

A plan submitted the following year for the north Shandong Grand Canal cost ¥3,660,000, without saying where this money would come from. The plan was less ambitious than those of 1916, but the cost of those earlier plans had since tripled, to more than ¥6,000,000.[160] In 1933, the RO placed the total cost of restoring the canal, including dredging its tributaries, at ¥10,293,889. It estimated that this would create ¥23,760,000 worth of flood-free land.[161] However, prospects for ever collecting money from this land—much less borrowing against those revenues—were bleak. Determined to at least reduce the canal's flood danger, the Reconstruction Office took a simpler, more coercive approach to two of its tributaries—and achieved the RO's only significant hydraulic success.

THE ENGINEERS AND THE SOLDIERS

Although the Wanfu He and its tributaries are less famous than the Yellow River or the Grand Canal, they posed a problem of almost

158. *JSYK* 2:3 (March 1932), *lunzhe*, 21; 2:4 (April 1932), *baogao*, 67–68 (also report for April 1932, p. 9a, in JD2:AH117); 2:5 (May 1932), *yaowen*, 4.
159. Ibid., 1:3 (March 1931), *gongdu*, 39–40; 1:4 (April 1931), *gongdu*, 8, 10.
160. Ibid., 2:4 (April 1932), *lunzhe*, 1–28; see esp. 2–3.
161. *JSGB* 3:8 (Aug. 1933), *jihua*, 11, 15.

equal gravity. By the late 1920s, they were flooding more than 3,000,000 *mu* in years with average rainfall.[162] The total length of riverbank was 947 *li* (557 km), much of it without any dikes;[163] the Yellow River and the Grand Canal each had about 1,700 *li* of banks in Shandong. The Wanfu He had an acute sedimentation problem, and after decades of neglect, it was arguably in worse shape than the more famous waterways. By the 1930s the annual fall preparation for floods on these rivers and the lakes they fed was Shandong's largest water control project. The repairs planned by the RO required more than twenty-six million *fang* (more than four billion cubic feet) of earth;[164] the 210 *li* of the Grand Canal between Linqing and Zhangqiu required less than one and a half million.[165]

The project also posed serious social challenges. It required cooperation from people in nine southwest Shandong counties. One of them, Heze, was one of the counties where Yellow River cooperation was failing disastrously; many of the others had comparable reputations for disorder. This area had also recently frustrated such reformist outsiders as the promoters of U.S. cotton. Violent local disputes over these rivers had been raging for decades.

However, in some ways the project was very straightforward. Almost all the work consisted of moving earth, which took up 95 percent of the project's ¥6,900,000 budget:[166] first dredging mud out of the river or digging a new channel, then using this same mud plus other dirt to form the river's new wall. Very little brick or stone work was planned.[167] If the RO could use corvée labor and get either local governments or the workers themselves to provide food and housing, it could do this project largely outside its own budget. If the levied laborers were being diverted from other useful activities, then the economic cost of this project might have been as high as in a project using more purchased goods and skilled wage workers; however, the RO would never feel these costs.

Using corvée labor and making the laborers feed themselves were hardly new ideas. Placing these burdens on the laborers was easiest

162. *Wanfu He*, preface, p. 1.
163. Ibid., 37.
164. Ibid., preface, p. 3.
165. *NYHH*, Appendix, 12–13.
166. *Wanfu He*, 63.
167. Ibid., 64.

with small projects on which workers stayed close to home; this was a major reason for the central government's partiality toward people's dikes.[168] The Wanfu He project combined these features with one major advantage of larger, official projects. While it placed the burden of the project almost entirely on localities, higher levels of government provided the centralized coordination and coercion that the upper Shandong Yellow River, for instance, sorely lacked.

RO engineers effectively set corvée quotas, since they determined the specifications—depth and width to be dredged to, height and width of levees—for each stretch of riverfront.[169] In each county a committee of the magistrate, the head of the county Jiansheting (local Reconstruction Offices; hereafter, county RO), and an engineer dispatched by the RO was established, which, in consultation with the county's ward heads, decided how to levy labor. In some counties every village was subjected to corvée (usually at a rate of five to six workers per day per 100 *mu* of land), including some 80 *li* from the river; in some, only certain wards were affected. However, the RO brushed aside the issues of fair burden sharing that had caused so many disputes among the upper Yellow River counties. There were to be very few transfers of money and none of workers between counties to address imbalances. Juye, for instance, provided more than a quarter of the project's total labor, though it had only a seventh of the affected population and had suffered far less from the river than Jining and Yutai.[170]

Once the work began, the engineer the RO sent to each county had the final say on all matters. The magistrate was to assist this engineer, helping him get the necessary workers and punishing anyone who obstructed the project. Below the level of the chief engineer, the magistrate, and the head of the county RO, the chain of command stretched through the ward head, district head, and down to the village heads (*zhuang zhang, cun zhang,* or *shou shi*). The village heads were responsible for selecting laborers for the work assigned to their village and making sure they brought their own food and tools; arranging shelter, if necessary; and acting as foremen to make sure their village's work was completed. District and ward heads supervised larger areas and reported to the chief engineer; he served as a roving inspector (as

168. Ibid., 40, 48.
169. *HWTK,* no. 4 (Jan. 1932), *mingling,* 10.
170. *Wanfu He,* 37–38, 41–44.

did the magistrate and the county RO head), and overall manager.[171] In sharp contrast to the various Yellow River organizations, then, this project had a formal, clearly delineated hierarchy, which reached from the village head through the chief engineer and finally to the provincial government.

The village heads had considerable power, since they could choose who would work on the project;[172] the copious rules and procedures appended to the RO report mention no way of appealing these decisions. However, village heads had a much more circumscribed role than in routine people's dikes maintenance, in illicit private reclamation, or in the early Republican Grand Canal project, largely because their role in verifying land ownership was limited. Moreover, the Wanfu He project gave the village heads no opportunities for acting collegially: they were simply part of a vertical chain of command.

Higher up the ladder, the engineers dispatched to each county may at first seem similar to the earlier river commissioners (*weiyuan*). However, there were crucial differences. First of all, as engineers, they were chosen for their technical skills. Second, they were responsible to designated superiors for implementing a plan largely drafted in Jinan, rather than being able to decide themselves how much flood protection to provide, and how. Third, since this project involved few materials besides earth, the opportunities for graft were limited. Finally, they had authority to use troops to gain local cooperation, though only as a last resort.[173]

The RO report on this project emphasizes that its most difficult aspects were social and political, not technical.[174] However, the report pays little attention to problems of determining land ownership, which take up so much space in accounts of Grand Canal and Yellow River projects. The ownership of land that was to be occupied by the new riverworks was to be determined jointly by people from the RO and an "experienced" district head; the county was to devise and collect a surtax on the land the project benefited after it was completed and then use the funds collected to compensate those who lost land. The RO also announced that any currently cultivated land occupied by the project should be paid for regardless of whether the land was legally

171. Ibid., 62, 41, 39, 40, 42.
172. Ibid., 41–42, 121–22.
173. Ibid., 122.
174. Ibid., 39–40, 121–23.

registered. This stipulation avoided the sort of petitions that had swamped the Grand Canal Board's Jining office; and the extra land costs were borne by the county, not the RO. Since the RO was not borrowing for the project, it could simply announce that collecting and making land payments were local affairs, and however they might be resolved, they need not delay the actual work.[175]

The RO also sidestepped the problem of allotting reclaimed land. In the short term, the project would not significantly reduce the amount of submerged land; the principal benefit would be flood protection for land already in use.[176] Some "new" land would be created as the rivers were diverted from one bed to another. However, since the project was not financially dependent on collecting a share of this land's output, the RO could avoid the issue, leaving the counties to fend for themselves after the work was done. The RO acknowledged that many people whose land was occupied were upset at the procedures the counties followed, but this unhappiness made little difference to the RO.[177]

Nonetheless, the RO still needed to resolve numerous conflicts over land and water rights; its retrospective account reported that before the Wanfu He project could proceed, it had had to resolve more than a hundred long-standing disputes (*que fen*) between villages (or occasionally counties) that interfered with river control. Their causes were mundane—usually disputes over dike placement, irrigation water, or who should maintain facilities used by more than one village. However, southwest Shandong is infamous for feuding, and many of these disputes were long-lived and ferocious. Some had begun when the 1855 Yellow River shift altered the Wanfu He; a few had gone on for centuries. These feuds often began with lawsuits, but later turned violent; several led to violence every autumn, so that no coordinated flood control work had been done since the 1850s. Not only villagers, but investigators from the county yamen and above had been killed; this ferocity had led county governments to simply give up on policing these disputes.[178]

The flooding, disputes, and government inaction continued for the

175. Ibid., 46, 57, 70, 76.
176. Ibid., 113–14.
177. Ibid., 57–58.
178. Ibid., 39, 67, 71, 81, 91, 123. This last assessment is supported by the late Guangxu Board of Punishment records at the First Historical Archives in Beijing;

first twenty years of the Republic.[179] Increasingly serious flooding in the mid-1920s and increased political stability after the Northern Expedition led some counties, encouraged by the new RO, to try to dredge the Wanfu He in 1929 and 1930. The limited records available include seven cases in which these attempts were stopped by violence and others in which some villages refused to work until they knew other villages were cooperating, causing stalemates like those that plagued Yellow River work.[180] However, unlike the YRO, which tried to get the disputants to agree among themselves, the RO intervened more directly.

In most cases, the RO began by having its engineer inspect the area himself and then call a meeting with the heads of the villages involved, the relevant magistrate or magistrates, the county RO heads, and occasionally some local gentry. Several of these meetings are described as being very contentious and lasting several days.[181]

The "agreements" reached reflected the technical needs of the project, not a compromise between the parties, suggesting that the meetings were primarily occasions to put pressure on the parties, rather than chances for them to negotiate. Of the eleven cases described in the RO's final report, six were resolved in a winner-take-all fashion: the solution held to be the best for the project overall was adopted, and no compensation of any sort was given to the losers. In two others, the RO imposed a technical solution that it claimed benefited both sides. Only three cases were decided by a recognizable compromise.[182] In the two cases recorded elsewhere, the RO simply overruled local objections to the project without making any adjustments.[183] In one case both the county magistrate and the county RO head favored a compromise, with some water going into each of two possible river beds. Even in this case the agreement reached under the aegis of the RO called for dredging and diking only the bed that the RO preferred;

---

although the counties along the Wanfu He are well represented in the hundreds of Shandong cases included there, I found no mention of any of the killings associated with these feuds.

179. Ibid., 92.

180. *JSYK* 2:1 (Jan. 1932), *lunzhe*, 7–10, 67, 77, 80, 81, 86, 91, 94; *JSGB* 3:8 (August 1933), *gongdu*, 10.

181. *Wanfu He*, 70, 71, 79, 88, 92.

182. Ibid., 76, 92.

183. *JSGB* 3:8 (Aug. 1933), *gongdu*, 10; *mingling*, 6; *JSYK* 2:6 (June 1932), *gongdu*, 8–12.

the county government was merely given permission to work on the second bed later at its own expense.[184]

If these meetings did not much resemble negotiations, they were not adjudications, either. Just as the RO had not bothered distinguishing between registered and unregistered land occupied by the project, none of the accounts of these disputes mentions the legal bases of claims. The decisions are never explained based on the relative antiquity of two courses, which village had first attacked the other, or previous agreements; instead the solution that best satisfied engineering concerns was chosen.

Not surprisingly, these agreements did not always end the disputes. When conflict continued, the RO ordered the county government to arrest the leaders of the opposition (usually the village heads) and disperse those obstructing the work. Where even this failed to halt violent opposition, the RO asked for provincial troops. In one case along the Jining-Yutai border, troops were sent in in April 1931, more than a year after an RO inspector had "settled" the issue. Even this tactic did not work, as more than a hundred armed Jining villagers drove out the troops and the work party, killing four people and several animals. After massive flooding in the fall of 1931, however, the heads of these villages agreed to begin work on the dike. In this one case, the RO sweetened defeat a bit, providing ¥7,000 to help the flooded area bear construction costs. Arrangements were also made for the county militia to attend the work party and for very strict punishments for any future interference.[185] Many other cases ended with arrests; in one of them, people arrested in Shanxian were sent to Jinan to be punished.[186]

The RO did not rely exclusively on force, however. In a section combining an account of the Wanfu He project with recommendations for future work, the project report repeatedly emphasized the need to sway local opinion. Its recommended tactics for doing so show how the RO saw its relation to local society.

The engineer is told not to expect a rousing welcome. The general populace, the report says, are like "infants" who will be slow to see the project's benefits and are easily led astray. The district, township, and village leaders are moved solely by self-interest. The gentry (*shen-*

---

184. *Wanfu He*, 67, 70.
185. Ibid., 81–82, 87–88, 90, 94.
186. *JSGB* 3:8 (Aug. 1933), *mingling*, 6.

shi) can be convinced to support the project, but gaining their support will not be easy. The main goal in dealing with gentry is "avoiding slander"—keeping them from being active opponents.[187]

The engineer is advised to work from the top down. The people consider the magistrate their "father and mother official," so an early, enthusiastic endorsement from him is essential. Where this occurred, the report says, gaining the support of others went smoothly; where it did not the whole project proved very difficult.[188] After gaining the magistrate's support, the engineer is advised to hold meetings with as many low-level leaders as possible to make sure they understand and support the project. Though nothing is said here about what the explanation should include, elsewhere the report emphasizes that the chain of command must be made very clear and each participant's tasks laid out very precisely to avoid shirking. Only in discussing meetings with local notables does the report suggest explaining the project's benefits.[189] Such explanations were presumably also given to others, but it is interesting that so little is said about them.

Moreover, though the RO report advocates winning over influential civilians, such people were not co-opted into the administration of the project. As noted above, the chain of command for this project below the county level was the regular set of subcounty officeholders and village heads. Though the project's rules allowed for "enthusiastic" nonofficeholders to take part in management and supervision, this participation did not happen.[190] In those counties where lists of supervisors and their occupations are available, all of them were concurrently officeholders of some sort. Where we know their ages, more than two-thirds were under 40. While hardly conclusive, this information also suggests that offices were not bestowed in order to co-opt, for instance, the patriarchs of important families. In Jining, we have extensive lists of important gentry and merchants, but nobody with any of their surnames appears on the project rolls.[191] The contrast to Pan Fu's Grand Canal project—with its numerous gentry and merchant officers, suggestions solicited from rural school teachers, and so forth—could hardly be sharper.

187. *Wanfu He*, 121–22.
188. Ibid., 120–21.
189. Ibid., 39–40, 120.
190. Ibid., 41.
191. Ibid., Appendix, 81–89.

The report said little about motivating the actual peasant laborers. It stressed that each person's and group's tasks should be clear; for peasants, this explanation was to be provided by their village head, who would serve as team leader. In particular, the report said, peasants should be shown exactly what work their village had to finish to avoid having their corvée drag on into the next agricultural season; supervisors are even advised to consider an explicit division of tasks within the village, with each family being assigned a discrete section. The only other specific idea is that there should be several "beginning work rituals," featuring the county, ward, and village heads and as many spectators as possible;[192] there were no provisions for the hired performers, games, prizes, and so forth that were used to keep up morale on large projects in Zhili (1915) and eastern Shandong (1923).[193] Above all, the engineer is advised that he must continually encourage the workers and threaten the subcounty officials if he expects to finish his section of the project.[194]

What can we conclude from the unusual success of this project? First of all, it shows again that sufficient resources did exist to take on large riverworks projects. If the labor costs figured into the Wanfu He project accurately reflect the workers' opportunity costs, the project cost as much as dredging and diking the worst parts of the Yellow River would have; the burden per county of the Wanfu He project was almost certainly more than it would have been for a Yellow River project.[195] It is likely that some of the labor cost for the Wanfu He was artificial, because there was seasonal "surplus labor": that is, the workers levied were not forgoing any alternate activity. However, this could not have been true of most of the almost seventeen million person-days of work levied over a nine-month period.[196] At any rate,

192. Ibid., 40, 47–48, 50–51.

193. Xu Shiguang, *Puyang Heshang Ji*, *bing*, 12a. Asia Development Co., *Repairing the Yellow River Break*, 6.

194. *Wanfu He*, 39–40, 48–51, 119–22.

195. At almost ¥7,000,000 for 9 *xian*, the cost per *xian* was about ¥770,000 (not, of course, evenly distributed). By contrast, the projects that the Hewuju dreamed of having the six *xian* on the upper section of the Shandong Yellow River do without outside help would have cost "only" ¥2,000,000. See *HWTK*, no. 7 (Jan. 1935), *mingling*, 62.

196. *Wanfu He*, 37, 63, 119; on the concept of "surplus labor," see Arthur Lewis, "Economic Development with Unlimited Supplies of Labor," *Manchester School of Economics and Social Studies* 22:2 (May 1954), 139–91. The idle season for male workers in this area averaged fewer than two months per year. See John L. Buck, *Land Utilization*, 307.

winter labor could have been used at many other crucial river sites by building with brick.

Second, this success story tells us something about the social bases of politics in South Huang-Yun. The county governments' inability to do this work is not surprising, but the RO's success is. And even this one successful intrusion into an often recalcitrant local society suggests how little basis there was for more lasting cooperation. There are no signs that a traditional local gentry defined by exam degrees or any other extralocal attainments played a role in managing rural water control here. Not only do no such people appear in the project as it materialized in the 1930s; they do not even figure prominently in the accounts of long-running land and water disputes. Where key disputants are identified, they are almost always village heads or "local bosses" rather than degree holders or former officials or their relatives. To the extent that county governments had stopped intervening in these disputes, the gentry, however defined, were deprived of one of the strongest cards they had to play in rural disputes—influence with their social equals in the bureaucracy. And the RO's technocratic methods of dispute resolution, as we saw, would do little to restore such influence.

In some parts of China—usually richer ones—water control had long been managed by elite consensus. This system may have been less efficient than turning decisions over to engineers, but it did an adequate technical job while placating as many interests as possible. But along the Wanfu He, land and water rights depended on village heads and yamen runners, the lowest-ranking but most permanent and locally rooted figures in county government. The formal state and elites with broader interests were largely excluded. Meanwhile, the more narrowly focused rural leaders could not resolve their disputes over water control, despite the mounting costs of such disputes. In this they were no different from their counterparts along the shores of the upper Yellow River.

Thus it was up to officials above the county level to break the local deadlock. Earlier, Pan Fu and other South Huang-Yun elites had hoped to bring the state in as a source of outside funds. Failing that, they hoped to use it as a guarantor to protect the gains of future beneficiaries (reclaimers, owners of flood-prone land) in return for having these beneficiaries pay for the project. In other words, the area's urban elites saw that they could not manage water control in the "liturgical" fashion common in other Chinese times and places; thus, they hoped that the government could be used to overcome the "free-rider" and "holdout" problems that make it hard to finance infrastructure.[197] If the government would not finance the projects itself, they hoped it could generate some of the needed funds by selling clear and secure title to the land improved by these projects. From the government's perspective, the area seemed to lack and to need such secure titles; moreover, unlike flood protection, they could be sold to or withheld from individuals.

As it turned out, however, those on the land—and the village heads, yamen clerks, and others who provided the effective guarantees of their land rights—were uninterested in the deal the government was offering. Thus, those able to offer flood protection were unwilling to simply donate it out of general revenue and unable to sell a divisible good like land rights to pay for it; meanwhile, those who were outcompeting the state as guarantors of land rights were unable to provide flood protection. In such a situation, the RO's solution—using force to make local people and local leaders accept the coordination that flood control required—seems a natural one. What is surprising is that they successfully forced such coordination, mobilizing peasants to a degree that was quite unusual for North China in this period.

However, the structure of the project still left village heads firmly in control of at least one important matter: assignment of labor within the village. No attempt was made to reach peasants without going through the village heads, as North Huang-Yun cotton societies had done. Force was used to make South Huang-Yun's village heads step in line, but not step aside; there is no sign of a serious challenge to them before World War II.

Although the RO did find an approach to flood control that did not require basic social or political change or large cash expenses, this approach had inherent limitations. First, corvée labor often could not be substituted for other inputs, as it was here, without a great loss of efficiency, and the ability to extract labor did not necessarily imply the ability to extract a theoretically equal amount of money. Even if

---

197. The concept of "liturgy" comes originally from Max Weber; see Max Weber, *Economy and Society*, ed. Guenther Roth and Claus Wittich (Berkeley, 1978), 194–99, 1023–25, 1097–99. For an application to China, see Mann, *Local Merchants*, esp. 12–21, 30–35. On "free riders," see Mancur Olson, *The Logic of Collective Action* (Cambridge, Mass., 1965), pp. 9–16, 60–65.

enough cash could be found for a project of this size, using it might not be simple; officials along the Wanfu He apparently feared that just putting that much money into circulation could have caused economic "convulsions."[198] In part, this fear was a result of currency manipulations and restrictions that benefited not only rural tax farmers, but some of the same county capital elites that were interested in improving southwest Shandong water control (see chapter 1).

Second, coercion also costs money. For various reasons, the provincial government was willing to pay these costs even when it was unwilling to pay directly for water control.[199] Moreover, in the case of Wanfu He, the provincial government got off lightly, using a few battalions for a relatively short time. Had the YRO simultaneously sought military support, or the RO for its north Grand Canal project, these costs might have upset Jinan more. During the Wanfu He project, the RO received reports of illegal dike building by landlords in another part of Jining and in Ciyang. The RO agreed that these dikes could cause floods but did not think floods were imminent; it advised these counties not to "provoke a clash," but simply to report again if more dikes were built.[200] This advice, in contrast to its aggressive approach on the Wanfu He, suggests that the RO felt its coercive power was already stretched thin. Such a feeling would help explain why the RO often waited until after floods had occurred to intervene and would suggest that bigger projects were still beyond its political resources.

Moreover, earthen riverworks like those built on the Wanfu He require frequent maintenance. Each county along the Wanfu He was ordered to establish a maintenance committee including the magistrate; the county RO head; and all the ward, township, district, and village heads along the river. In addition to annual dredging and dike maintenance, this committee was to see to it that trees were planted along the river banks and protected from farmers, fuel gatherers, and livestock. Again, the actual work was to be divided up and assigned to

198. *Wanfu He*, 119.
199. On Han Fuju's initiative in this project and willingness to use troops, see *Wanfu He*, p. 2. Han backed a number of reform initiatives in southwest Shandong by sending in personnel, but not money. For a participant's view that these initiatives were nothing but an attempt to bring this area under Han's control, see Xu Shuren, "Wo zai xiang jianshe pai de huodong yu jian wen," 50–68. This is surely too simple, but Han was certainly aware that "quieting" the southwest had often been seen as the key to securing control over Shandong.
200. *JSYK* 2:7 (July 1932), *gongdu*, 10.

villages working under their village head; he in turn would answer to a chain of people leading up to the magistrate. Expenses were to be met by the counties.[201] If the counties fulfilled this plan themselves and "settled" disputes stayed settled, the province's plan would be a great success; but if the province had to continually supervise, threaten, or occupy the counties, the Wanfu He approach might accomplish little. As for using this approach elsewhere, the suppression of cotton rushing in north Huang-Yun suggests that there might have been a social base for organizations to maintain imposed riverworks if the RO could convince a critical mass of people that they would benefit directly. Otherwise, maintenance might have been even harder there than in the southwest, since there was not only no rural gentry to work with, but not even much village leadership. The repeated incursions on the north Shandong Grand Canal suggest that the latter scenario was more likely.

The Wanfu He itself needed further work soon after this project. In 1933 a major Yellow River flood in Lanfeng, Henan, caused some of the river's water to flow through an old bed and into the Wanfu He. The fall harvest on almost 2,000,000 *mu* was affected, and the Wanfu He dikes were badly damaged; however, the flood waters drained in less than a month, the winter wheat was sown on time, and the RO considered its work to have passed this test.[202] That such a large flood could strike a "successfully" fortified area raises a final point, particularly important in view of limits on how large an area the Wanfu He approach could be applied to: "local solutions"—even those covering nine counties—could not really substitute for larger-scale hydraulic work. The Yellow River floods two years later drove this point home. Water swept down the Grand Canal and into the Wanfu He—and counties along that river had the highest casualties and most refugees.[203]

201. *Wanfu He*, 115–18.
202. Ibid., 106, 107, 113.
203. *HH*, 381; Mantetsu, *Santō Chihō Kōka Suisai Jōkyō*, 6–7, 10–24, 35–36.

Conclusion:

Huang-Yun, China, and the World

The preceding pages have tried to give a guided tour of Huang-Yun's society and political economy. The specific commodities, activities, and networks studied were chosen because they were important, reasonably well documented, and illuminated different aspects of two crucial themes: the significance of local social variations within Huang-Yun and the consequences of Huang-Yun's changing place in a larger Chinese political economy.

I have tried to use this story to shed light both on theoretical concerns and on the experience of the residents of a poorly documented region; doing so involved using as large a mix of qualitative and quantitative sources as possible. It also required experimenting with ways of analyzing space that were true to Huang-Yun's experience in this period—one in which geography changed rapidly rather than providing a fixed setting—while trying to retain as much as possible of the rigor of more conventional schemes based on physiography. It remains for this chapter to tie together what we have learned about Huang-Yun, what Huang-Yun's history tells us about more general questions, and what the analysis employed here suggests about ways to frame other regional studies.

First, the book provides case studies of the spread and limits of late Qing and Republican markets. The actions of the supposedly very weak Chinese state in the early twentieth century actually had a great

267

impact on market making, whether the state promoted this process (as with cotton) or deliberately limited it (as with credit). Local government, however, was particularly important in these processes, and as local elites increasingly captured county and subcounty government in the post-Taiping period,[1] local social structures ultimately shaped and limited the participation of hinterland people in larger markets. Just as provincial or even central governments often saw questions about coinage, exchange rates, and infrastructure in light of their struggles against control by other levels of government or foreigners, local elites and officials saw that such "economic" questions as whether to help promote American cotton and how to organize silver-copper exchange also raised questions about how to maintain control of their domains. Thus, the different configurations of rural, county-level, and urban elites gave us the very different responses of North and South Huang-Yun to similar pressures and opportunities.

I would therefore argue more broadly that while both the "breakthrough" and "involutionary" models contain important advances, neither is fully adequate for understanding the nature and limits of rural development in prerevolutionary China. Both reject dualism and consider the peasant economy in the context of China's overall development;[2] neither, to my mind, goes far enough. Myers, Brandt, and Rawski rightly challenge the notion that China's modern-sector growth came at the expense of, or in isolation from, traditional economic activity, but suggest instead a straightforward stimulatory effect, limited only by the extent of railroads, telegraphs, and steamships and by the amount of time Chinese entrepreneurs had before the onslaught of World War II. I have tried to suggest here that the relations between the modern and traditional sectors were political as well as economic and differed for different activities in ways that were decisively shaped by state strategies. These interactions also appear less one-sidedly positive once we look at indirect effects and at nonmarket activities such as fuel gathering and flood control. Finally, they may have also been self-limiting, both through elite and local government reactions to pressures from the coast (as in the case of South Huang-Yun credit) and through more general responses to the massive dis-

1. See, for instance, Kuhn, *Rebellion*, esp. 211–15.
2. For economic dualism generally, the classic source is Lewis, "Economic Development," 139–91. An influential though somewhat different version of "dualism" for China is Murphey, *Treaty Ports*.

locations that occurred as the political economy generated more "natural" disasters in places like Huang-Yun.

Huang, on the other hand, posits an involutionary dynamic built into "the peasant economy" that could not be significantly altered by the modern sector or by state and elite interventions. Whatever change did occur in the late nineteenth and early twentieth century is contrasted to the more fundamental changes in early modern England without much attention to how important Chinese changes might nonetheless have been. At least for the case of Huang-Yun, I think I have shown that the strategies of state builders, foreigners, local elites, and other nonpeasant actors did produce important changes (both positive and negative) in the political economy of Huang-Yun and in the daily lives of its people.

Furthermore, as important as the commercialized parts of the rural economy were—especially cotton and handicrafts—it is dangerous to ignore changes in noncommercialized economic activities. At least in "less advanced" areas like Huang-Yun, noncommercial activities remained a huge part of the economy, and by no means an unchanging one. It is often difficult to estimate the magnitude of changes in such nonmarketized activities as rural fuel gathering and flood control, but these changes are nonetheless an important part of overall rural living standards; in the case of Huang-Yun, their sharp decline outweighed modest but real gains from commercial and technological developments. Our direct measurements of these changes, though crude, are a necessary step toward understanding the vast in-kind portions of rural economic life, which have usually been approached either through anecdotes or very remote proxies.

I have also emphasized that although these changes occurred outside the market, they can be linked to the same factors that drove the political economy of cotton, credit, and other commercialized activities. This work has tried to broaden our picture of the rural economy to include both monetized and nonmonetized components and to begin treating nonmonetized activities with at least some of the system and rigor attained by recent studies of the cash economy. Such a composite picture, I think, offers our best chance to advance ongoing debates about trends in rural living standards, about relations between the modern and traditional sectors (and thus prerevolutionary China's prospects for a "breakthrough" to sustained growth), and about the three subjects I will close with: the role of the state, the significance of imperialism, and the relationships between regions (and spatial units generally) in China.

Huang-Yun's story requires and suggests new ways to put together our contrary images of the late Qing and Republican state. First, we have the familiar picture of the decay of the Chinese state in the nineteenth and early twentieth centuries. This decay is reflected in a lack of central control over the country and poor performance of basic functions: maintenance of order, avoidance of natural disasters, and defense of Chinese sovereignty against outsiders.[3] Events in Huang-Yun provide ample documentation of these trends and some preliminary ways of measuring their impact on ordinary people. However, more recent literature has given us a picture of state making in early-twentieth-century China, linking certain late Qing and Republican developments to the emergence of China's strongest state ever after 1949. This scholarship notes the complementarity of social developments—particularly in major cities—and the needs of a modern state and points out parallels to state making in Europe and elsewhere.[4]

Both of these trends were real. Together, they require us to go beyond either simple linear or simple cyclical schemes, which suggest that political and economic variables all move in the same direction at any one time and do so throughout a whole country (or at least a whole macroregion). We also needed new schemes for understanding such local phenomena as villages' permeability to outsiders and the willingness of villagers to seek opportunities in broader networks. These are usually assumed to change together and to track either a linear (Wolf) or cyclical (Skinner) pattern of macrolevel change. In this case, however, permeability and openness turned out to be quite distinct and to reflect trends in the wider world only as those changes were refracted through local differences in social structure.[5]

---

3. See, for instance, Sheridan, *China in Disintegration*, 18–26; Fairbank, "Introduction," vol. 10, pt. 1, pp. 3–6, 34.

4. See generally Duara, *Culture, Power, and the State*; Vermeer, *Economic Development*; Greer, *Water Management*; Joseph Fewsmith, *Party, State, and Local Elites in Republican China: Merchant Organizations and Politics in Shanghai, 1890–1930* (Honolulu, 1985); MacKinnon, *Power and Politics*. Mann takes a position closer to the one suggested here, arguing for "state making" in China's "cores" during the late nineteenth and twentieth centuries while reserving judgment on what happened in the "peripheries" (*Local Merchants*, 6, 10).

5. For Skinner's argument, see "Closed Community," 270–81. For Wolf, see

One could try to reconcile the existence of two well-documented but contrary stories by saying that the particularities of a fragmented China defy useful generalization; one could even argue that there was nothing worth calling "the state" in that period of Chinese history. However, such an approach is unsatisfying. It offers no organizing framework for our findings; it also ignores the existence of governments in Beijing and Nanjing that did have substantial influence over wide territories, the persistence of cross-provincial cooperation on certain important matters (such as river control), and the continuity across the Qing-Republican divide in methods of mobilizing people and resources for these tasks. Most of all, it ignores the existence of broadly similar provincial regimes that each governed a population larger than most European countries and that sometimes showed impressive ability to reach grass-roots society.

Instead of giving up on generalizing about the Chinese state in this period, this study has tried to analyze systematically the simultaneous occurrence of state making and unmaking. It argues that certain regularities in where we find each tendency point to connections between these trends, which in turn display an understandable historical logic.

A first distinction is between the state in its capacity as extractor of resources and the state in its capacity as donor of services (and thus deployer of resources). There is no question that the extractive capacities of the Chinese state increased significantly in the late 1800s and the 1900s, as those who see a process of state making have emphasized.[6] Although—as Prasenjit Duara and others have noted—this extraction was quite inefficient, with much of what the peasantry gave up remaining in the hands of local collectors, the revenue reaching counties and provinces soared as well. Even if we reserve the designation "state" for the central governments in Beijing and Nanjing, we would still find its revenues increasing. What weakened, however, was the exclusive character of the state's revenue extraction, as sub-county officials, bandits, provincial politicians, secret societies, warlords, and others also extracted greater resources from the population.[7]

"Closed Corporate Peasant Communities in Meso-America and Central Java," *Southwestern Journal of Anthropology* 13:1 (Spring 1957), pp. 1–18.

6. See, e.g., Duara, *Culture, Power, and the State*, 65–85.

7. See, for instance, Elizabeth Perry, "Tax Revolt in Late Qing China: The Small Swords of Shanghai and Liu Depei of Shandong," *Late Imperial China* 6:1 (June 1985), pp. 110–11.

Connected to this multiplication of uncoordinated extractors was enormous inefficiency in the deployment of resources; and it is largely this inefficiency and the consequent failure of the state to be an effective donor of public order, flood control, and so forth that have attracted the attention of those arguing that the Chinese state collapsed in this era. The exactions of rival warlords provide the clearest case of increased burdens on the peasantry without improved services, although these predations cover only part of our period. But even after the end of significant fighting in Huang-Yun, we still find heavy exactions by local powerholders with little coordination in their use; water control in South Huang-Yun, in which huge in-kind contributions managed by subcounty potentates produced less flood control than older, cheaper systems, provides a long-standing, everyday example.

Distinguishing between extraction and delivery of services also leads us to a geographical disaggregation of the mixture of state making and state collapse; this regional variation, however, has thus far been passed over by the major analyses of the period. In strategically important and heavily commercialized areas—the Yangzi delta, the Beijing-Tianjin area, and so forth—the state redoubled its presence rather than allowing other contenders to capture the new machinery being created. Moreover, the strong commercial economies of these areas allowed revenue not only to be collected locally, but to be circulated and deployed with relative ease. Consequently, one finds the simultaneous strengthening of state and society in core areas noted by Keith Schoppa, Elizabeth Perry, Stephen MacKinnon, and others.[8] One also finds that in these areas government became a more successful donor as well as a more successful extractor—police, public health, and other key services do seem to have improved. Thus it makes sense that analyses of these areas see a process of state making that, on the local level, looks not too different from early modern Europe. It is not that these areas lacked the avaricious subcounty personnel that Philip Kuhn, Prasenjit Duara, and others have focused on, but that in these areas civilian elites and an increasingly active state placed limits on their behavior.

However, as this book's accounts of transportation, flood control,

---

8. Elizabeth Perry, "Collective Violence in China, 1880–1980," *Theory and Society* (May 1984), pp. 427–54, esp. 449; MacKinnon, *Power and Politics*, 6–11, 219–24; Schoppa, *Elites*, 5–8, 186–87.

and reforestation emphasize, the vigor that the late Qing and Republican state showed in these coastal areas was achieved at a great price. Part of that price was the state's withdrawal from areas to which it had once paid greater attention but which now had neither enough wealth nor a sufficient foreign threat to hold the interest of hard-pressed regimes. The Tongzhi Restoration (1862–70), with its tax cuts for the Yangzi Valley made possible by a huge decrease in canal-borne grain tribute, would appear to be the turning point;[9] it took thirty more years, however, before the state institutionalized the neglect of canal maintenance and inland Yellow River control implicit in these policies.

Focusing too narrowly on the influence that wealth gave to coastal areas might imply that the Chinese state of our period was the captive of wealthy classes in these areas. While these groups obviously were powerful and account for some of the attention the state paid to areas such as Jiangnan, there is ample evidence that the Chinese state still retained a good deal of autonomy from any particular class.[10] Moreover, wealth alone cannot explain the shift we observed in Yellow River funding, to cite just one example. Many of the counties near the river's mouth—Lijin, Binxian, and so on—were just as poor as those on the upper section of the Shandong Yellow River. The huge shift of funds from the upper to the lower section had more to do with the state's own interest in defending its sovereignty near the coast, where it was most threatened, than with the influence of any particular group in those coastal counties.

This geographical analysis of changes in the Chinese state leads in turn to another perspective that this book has tried to emphasize. Though we have learned a great deal in recent years about the Chinese state in the high Qing, few analyses of the post-1850 state have looked at the implications of this reassessment. Some have noted that our emerging picture of a fairly efficient eighteenth-century state highlights the state's later decline; however, relatively little has been done with our improved understanding of what the traditional Ming-Qing state sought to do. Even work that argues for a new type of state making

9. Polachek, "Gentry Hegemony," 223–27; Wright, *Last Stand*, 163–67.
10. E.g., Parks Coble, *The Shanghai Capitalists and the Nationalist Government, 1927–1937* (Cambridge, Mass., 1986); Lloyd Eastman, *The Abortive Revolution* (Cambridge, Mass., 1974); Esherick, *Reform and Revolution.* Fewsmith, 4–7, provides an overview of literature arguing for the autonomy of the state from Shanghai capitalists and other Yangzi Valley elites even during the Nanjing decade.

in early-twentieth-century China often points to the absence of a "self-consciously modernizing" orientation in early-twentieth-century Chinese regimes.[11]

Undoubtedly, these regimes were less wholeheartedly committed to modernization than some, such as Meiji Japan; in some ways, however, a fundamental break had already occurred in Chinese statecraft. From an emphasis on "reproduction," in which all areas mattered and those that seemed to have the greatest troubles sustaining subsistence on their own often received particular attention, the state moved to a focus on defending key areas, competing with other states, and—as more recent Chinese leaders have put it—encouraging some areas to "get rich first." In doing so, they took on a number of the tasks often considered characteristic of modernizing states: reforming banking and currency, standardizing weights and measures to encourage trade, increasing government extraction, creating professional urban police forces, and even building modern infrastructure such as telegraphs.[12]

Moreover, these efforts were reasonably successful in the regions they targeted. This success is indicated both by case studies of core areas and by recent work suggesting that early-twentieth-century China actually did achieve the most often cited benchmark of "success" for twentieth-century states: a relatively high rate of real GNP growth and very rapid growth in industry.[13] Looking back from today, we can see in early-twentieth-century Chinese state building many features of a now common type of "Third World" state: heavy dependence on customs revenue, commercial taxes, and foreign loans; a strong orientation toward its modern cities and international competition; and many new capabilities despite a weak grass-roots presence in the countryside. And compared to many states that have followed this course after it, late Qing and Republican China did not do badly. Even in the sphere of preserving national autonomy, in which the Chinese state was much less successful than in promoting modern-sector growth, it fared better than most of pre-1945 Asia.

11. Duara, *Culture, Power, and the State,* 4, 248.
12. On weights and measures, see, e.g., *Shandong zheng su shicha ji;* on banking and currency, Rawski, *Economic Growth,* 120–80; on police, MacKinnon, *Power and Politics,* 151–63, and idem, *A Late Qing-GMD-PRC Connection: Police as an Arm of the Modern State* (Tempe, Ariz., 1983); on revenue, Duara, *Culture, Power, and the State,* 58–73.
13. Rawski, *Economic Growth,* 268–333, esp. 331–32.

At the same time, though, the state abandoned at least some traditional roles of the Ming-Qing state. For our purposes, the most important task it abandoned was underwriting the ecological stability of inland North China through the Grand Canal and Yellow River conservancies. Other examples, however, could be advanced. For instance, there was a redirection of military expenditures, which in the Ming and early Qing had flowed toward China's inner Asian frontiers and were accompanied by attempts to promote the grain trade and otherwise stabilize subsistence in the northwest. In the new era, in which the threat to China came from the coast, military expenditures were concentrated on the creation of a few modern divisions and arsenals in Jiangnan, coastal Fujian, the Beijing-Tianjin area, and other eastern cores.[14] A third example involves the budgetary shift from extending the irrigation network in newly settled parts of the southwest and other frontiers to deepening coastal harbors, linking major cities by rail, and building pilot factories in major cities.[15]

Here, too, the Tongzhi Restoration stands as an early watershed. Though it may have been "the last stand of Chinese conservatism" in its emphasis on Confucian education, disinterest in popular mobilization, and tax cuts to revive an agricultural economy,[16] the restoration marked an early instance of the Qing government's responding to the new opportunities and threats of the mid-nineteenth century by freeing Jiangnan (and other wealthy regions) from the obligation to subsidize poorer areas. By the early twentieth century, the Chinese state had adopted a de facto policy of "picking winners"—here defined as much in terms of regions as of industries. This strategy bears a much closer resemblance to the strategies of twentieth-century states for international competition than to Ming-Qing efforts to stabilize an autarchic empire and preserve the state's autonomy from Yangzi Valley elites.[17]

---

14. On grain trade in the northwest, see Terada Takanobu, *Sansei Shōnin no Kenkyū: Mindai ni okeru Shōnin oyobi Shōgyo Shihon* (Kyoto, 1972), esp. 17–80, 101–6, 120–57; Peter Perdue is currently exploring relationships between the grain supply and defense in the northwest during the Qing.

15. On water control on the frontiers, see James Z. Lee, *State and Economy in Southwest China, 1250–1850* (Cambridge, Eng., forthcoming).

16. For the classic statement of this view, see Mary C. Wright, *The Last Stand of Chinese Conservatism: The T'ung-chih Restoration, 1862–74* (Stanford, 1957), esp. 1–10, 300–12.

17. Both the Ming and early Qing emperors quite consciously sought to keep the Jiangnan elite from getting too strong. On the Ming, see, e.g., L. Carrington Goodrich and Fang Chaoying, eds., *Dictionary of Ming Biography* (New York, 1976), 385, 387–

(It is also worth noting that the increasing recruitment, after 1850, of officials who had not passed the exams, though clearly a separate phenomenon, made obsolete the regional quotas that had helped the Ming-Qing state limit the national power of Jiangnan elites.[18])

Furthermore, in redeploying its own resources, the state sent powerful signals to regional elites about how to deploy theirs. The tax cuts and other incentives that the state offered in the Yangzi Valley succeeded in getting elites who had lost or removed their wealth during the Taiping Rebellion to resume investing in land and in water control and other improvements. And despite the claims of some scholars that Yangzi Valley elites were drawn away to the treaty ports in the twentieth century, there is ample evidence that many retained a rural presence, either returning in person after a sojourn in Shanghai or investing some of their urban earnings in rural projects.[19]

Meanwhile, South Huang-Yun families like Pan Fu's lost much of their land during the contemporaneous Nian Rebellion. (North Huang-Yun had no comparable families.) However, they received very different signals about the future of their region; and, as we have seen, they rebuilt their fortunes after 1870 through activities concentrated in Jining, Jinan, Beijing, and Tianjin. The twentieth-century countryside was left to rural bosses with much less capital and much narrower horizons.

The mid-nineteenth-century shift in state priorities—and its echoes in elite strategies—had staggering welfare costs for Huang-Yun. Although the area did gain some benefits from Manchurian development, the growth of foreign trade, and the rise of a modern sector in coastal cities, the costs of the new statecraft—in isolation, ecological decay, and floods—overwhelmed these gains. And it was primarily in areas marginalized by this shift that large numbers of peasants embraced the Communist alternative to this style of state making: an alternative that, at least at first, promised people in the hinterlands

---

88; on the high Qing, see Philip Kuhn, *Soulstealers: The Chinese Sorcery Scare of 1768* (Cambridge, Mass., 1990), esp. 70–72.

18. On the rise of nonexam recruitment, see Ho, *Ladder of Success*, 47–50. On regional quotas, see Benjamin Elman, "Political, Social and Cultural Reproduction via Civil Service Examinations in Late Imperial China," *Journal of Asian Studies* 50:1 (Feb. 1991), 14–15.

19. See Fei Xiaotong, *China's Gentry*, for the most famous statement of the "social erosion" hypothesis; Schoppa, *Elites*, is a good example of the literature showing that many Yangzi Valley elites continued to follow the mobility strategies described by Skinner, which involve an eventual return of both human and economic resources to their native places.

that they could improve their lives without waiting for waves of progress from core areas to spread to them.

These conclusions also have methodological implications. One is that we need to think about space dynamically. While the notion of physiographic macroregions with essentially unchanging boundaries has been enormously productive,[20] it becomes increasingly strained in the twentieth century. The treatment of space here, with attention to its vague and shifting boundaries, provides no substitute for that framework, even for the twentieth century, but it does suggest a supplement that calls our attention to the political dynamics that help create market boundaries, cores and peripheries, and ecological variables themselves. Moreover, it suggests a possible distinction between those characteristics of "core-ness" that refer to centrality in spatial networks and those that refer to centrality in a spatial hierarchy.

In an essay written almost twenty years ago for China specialists, the Islamicist Ira Lapidus pointed out that the dominant metaphor for the links holding China together was that of hierarchy—vertical links between localities and larger units—while the key institutions of the Islamic world were generally thought of as networks (horizontal connections among groups, with none able to command the other). Nonetheless, he suggested, it might be equally possible to conceptualize Chinese cohesion in terms of networks and that of the Islamic world in terms of hierarchy.[21] Since then, we have indeed seen a great deal of attention paid to Chinese networks—religious sects, interregional trade networks, native-place associations, and private groups of literati—which, while not perfectly horizontal, were certainly more so than the official Chinese polity.

Some of these networks—particularly those, such as literati networks, that could thrive only where there were concentrations of wealth—map quite well onto the regional hierarchies familiar to us from the political map of China and the macroregional maps devised by G. William Skinner.[22] Some, however, do not. The centrality of

---

20. Skinner, "Marketing and Social Structure," is the original source for this model and quite likely the most influential piece of writing in modern Chinese studies.

21. Ira M. Lapidus, "Hierarchies and Networks: A Comparison of Chinese and Islamic Societies," in *Conflict and Control in Late Imperial China*, ed. Frederic Wakeman, Jr., and Carolyn Grant (Berkeley, 1975), pp. 26–42.

22. See, for instance, Benjamin Elman, *From Philosophy to Philology: Social and Intellectual Aspects of Change in Late Imperial China* (Cambridge, Mass., 1984), on the rise of networks of *kao zheng* scholars.

Shanxian, a poor rural county in South Huang-Yun, to the sprawling White Lotus networks of North China is but one striking example.[23] The contrasts between North and South Huang-Yun outlined in this book suggest that we might be able to group the various attributes of core areas as either network or hierarchy core-ness; without some such distinction, it is extremely difficult to assess the core or peripheral status of some areas studied here.

According to some of the crucial variables, South Huang-Yun seems far more core-like than North Huang-Yun. Cropping indices (number of crops per year per acre) were higher, indicating more intensive use of land; not surprisingly, such usage was accompanied by greater use of irrigation, more output, and more people per acre. Land ownership was more concentrated. There were far more degree holders, and in the Republic, far more politicians with influence beyond the region. State revenues were also higher in this area. In the eighteenth century, resistance to tax reform in this area resembled that of Jiangnan rather than that of most of the rest of North China. In fact, it conformed to the classic pattern for core areas discussed by Skinner: resistance to the state came from entrenched local powerholders rather than from the heterodox and the dispossessed, who are the state's principal antagonists in poor and underruled peripheries.[24]

But by other criteria—per capita income, participation in larger markets, consumption of specialized goods, and the general permeability to outside organizers (including those seeking to change tax-collection practices, cropping patterns, or other operations) discussed in chapter 2—North Huang-Yun clearly had more of the attributes of a core. Other criteria could be added, such as being relatively safe from ordinary banditry in stable periods but including cities (particularly Linqing) that were favorite targets of rebel armies in unstable times.[25]

Some scholars have suggested that if various aspects of core-ness do

23. On Shanxian, see, for instance, Susan Naquin, "Connections between Rebellions: Sect Family Networks in Qing China," *Modern China* 8:3 (July 1982), pp. 337–60.

24. See, e.g., Zelin, *Magistrate's Tael*, 149–52; a more detailed discussion of "core" characteristics in North and South Huang-Yun can be found in dissertation, 379–81. See Skinner, "Cities and the Hierarchy," 308, for the analysis of what types of resistance to the state characterize cores and peripheries.

25. See dissertation, appendix E, on per capita income; on Linqing rather than Jining as a target for insurgents and raiders of various sorts, see Naquin, *Shantung Rebellion*, 88; Yang Zhengtai, "Ming Qing Linqing," 119–20; and dissertation, 367–70.

not co-vary strongly enough, we should jettison the core-periphery framework.[26] Instead, I prefer to group the above phenomena under two types of core-ness. Vertical, or hierarchical, centrality refers to those criteria of special interest to a generally conservative but revenue-hungry state. These include total wealth, the ability to meet increased tax quotas, and producing elites who were able to make themselves heard on the national or provincial level and/or to resist demands that threatened their positions. At least in our case, these characteristics all appear to co-vary and to be far more pronounced in southern than northern Huang-Yun.

Network, or horizontal, core-ness refers to position in another set of connections having less to do with bureaucratic channels of command; this type of core-ness is stronger in North Huang-Yun. One crucial example would be participation in long-distance trade. While the Grand Canal flourished, Liaocheng and especially Linqing were the major depots for Shandong's long-distance trade, not Jining; North Huang-Yun even depended on long-distance trade for part of its food supply.[27] Linqing and Liaocheng also had large communities of guest merchants and trade fairs in specialized products that brought people from Manchuria, Mongolia, and all over North China and the northwest.[28] Jining's trade, though considerable, was mostly regional, less specialized, and controlled by resident merchants and officials.[29] In our own period, North Huang-Yun grew cotton for coastal mills and had more ties to far-flung credit and currency markets; this area also grew more of other export crops, such as peanuts and tobacco, and imported far more kerosene, machine-spun yarn, and other modern goods.[30]

As emphasized in chapter 2, outsiders found it far easier to change structures and procedures in North Huang-Yun than in South. This was true even for representatives of the state, as long as they focused on penetrating local society (a task for which entrenched brokers and tax farmers were an obstacle) rather than maximizing extraction (for which such people were often an asset). Though North Huang-Yun was never as large or reliable a source of taxes as South Huang-Yun

26. Myers and Sands, "Spatial Approach."
27. Xu Tan, "Ming Qing shiqi de Linqing shangye," 135–57, esp. 148–49.
28. Ibid.; Yang Zhengtai, "Ming Qing Linqing," 115–20; *Linqing xianzhi* (1934), *shihuo* section.
29. Jing Su and Luo Lun, *Landlord and Labor*, 27.
30. *SSYZ* 2:151–201 on imports.

(as witness lower land and salt tax quotas and the frequent complaints about evasion of the Linqing customs), the state found it easier to influence the way revenue was collected there. The 1728 tax reforms did not encounter the same resistance from local elites that they did in southwest Shandong; two centuries later, the Guomindang's campaign against irregular local surcharges also fared much better in North than South Huang-Yun.[31]

In short, the very lack of concentrated wealth and strong elites that made North Huang-Yun less central in vertical terms facilitated its inclusion in more horizontal networks. In the late nineteenth century, as the Chinese state became less interested in any part of Huang-Yun, South Huang-Yun's somewhat greater ability to attract attention from the bureaucracy continued: its portion of the canal still got some funding, it got a branch line of the railroad, and a few of its sons continued to play significant roles on a larger political stage. However, vertical centrality was less an advantage than it had once been. Here North Huang-Yun had the edge; its greater participation in horizontal networks allowed it to adapt more successfully, though not painlessly, to a new role in the wider world.

Huang-Yun's story should also influence how we think about the impact of imperialism. Throughout this book, I have emphasized the importance of imperialism as a shock to Huang-Yun, even though the actual foreign presence there was tiny. Moreover, though most of the actual contacts with foreigners described here were relatively benign, I argue that China's encounter with the West had very negative effects on life in Huang-Yun.

To see this we must go beyond looking at the more easily measured first-order effects of imperialism—such as Huang-Yun farmers' new opportunities to trade peanut oil for kerosene and have better lighting than before or Huang-Yun's share of the costs of wars, indemnities, and the New Army—as some purely economic studies have done.[32] Instead, we must treat the transformation of the Chinese state as part of the political-economic impact of imperialism, not as separate from, and exogenous to, a model of economic impact. Regime changes in-

---

31. On the eighteenth-century case see Zelin, *Magistrate's Tael*, 149–52, and dissertation, 376–77; on the twentieth-century parallel, see *CZGB* 5:3 (Dec. 1933), *gongdu*, 3, 10–12; 6:7 (April 1935), *zhuanzai*, 11.

32. Heunemann, *Iron Horse*, 2–13, 240–48; Rawski, *Economic Growth*, 5–10, 106–16.

volve many contingencies and so fit poorly into general models; but when concrete cases show how inseparable they are from economic change, we should revise models, not ignore phenomena.

To the extent that this work emphasizes the impact of imperialism even on an inland area, it shares the perspective of work in the "dependency" and "world systems" traditions.[33] It also takes a crucial claim of those two literatures—that instead of seeing the emergence of "developed" and "underdeveloped" areas as the presence of "modernization" in one case and its absence in another, we should explore the ways in which these outcomes are parts of a single process[34]—and applies this insight to the domestic politics of a huge country suddenly thrust into the world economy and state system.

Beyond this point, however, the argument here diverges from either a dependency or world systems perspective. First, the emphasis here is not on the deleterious effects of Huang-Yun's incorporation into the world system; it stresses the rending of old networks rather than the damage done by new ones. To the extent that actual incorporation occurred in Huang-Yun, it was probably better than the alternative of the destruction of old networks without integration into new ones. Nor were all of Huang-Yun's ties to the new economy the dendritic sort—in which localities have no choice in what higher-level central place they trade with—which dependency and world systems theory usually assume link peripheries to their cores; China's old nested hierarchy of central places, which ensured some competition and choice at each level, was never thoroughly destroyed.[35]

Moreover, rather than viewing the manner of incorporation—whether, for instance, an area became a supplier of cash crops, low-wage factory labor, or migrants—as determining an area's social structure and politics, the emphasis here has been on how local social structure and Chinese domestic politics shaped the manner in which different subregions were or were not incorporated. The West's assault on China was not determined by local variables, and insofar as the

33. Wallerstein, *Modern World-System*; Henrique Cardoso and Ernesto Faletto, *Dependency and Underdevelopment in Latin America* (Berkeley, 1979); Moulder, *Modern World Economy*.

34. See, e.g., Wallerstein, *Modern World-System*, 3, 10, 232; Cardoso and Faletto, *Dependency*, pp. 8–28.

35. See Carol A. Smith, "Regional Economic Systems: Linking Geographic Models and Socioeconomic Problems," in *Regional Analysis*, ed. Carol A. Smith (New York, 1976), pp. 34–36, 51–58, for a discussion of dendritic versus Skinnerian marketing hierarchies in the context of imperialism.

reorientation of the Chinese state followed necessarily from imperialism, the destruction of Huang-Yun's old networks might be a purely
dependent phenomenon. But as we have seen in discussing water control and railroad building, numerous ways remained to shore up the
old system, even within the context of an overall shift to emphasis on
more accessible areas. It took a combination of at least three developments to produce such a wrenching transition: relentless foreign
aggression, the rising costs of managing ecological decay, and a temporary decline in the economic surplus generated in the Yangzi Valley.
And even then, if we can imagine a different modus vivendi being
worked out between China and the foreign powers, perhaps Huang-
Yun could have been let down more easily—particularly since the
post-Taiping Yangzi Valley was soon generating a greater absolute
surplus than ever before.[36] Third, even if we grant that the state had to
abandon Huang-Yun, our stories of credit and cotton markets show
that various local responses were possible, with very different consequences for both long-term outcomes (for example, changes in income
levels, political structure, and so on) and contemporary experience.

Finally, the book aims to make specific the ways in which large processes such as state making and market integration, as shaped by local
differences, in turn shaped the lives of ordinary people in this zone. In
looking at local credit markets, tax payment, cash-cropping opportunities, changing labor demand in agriculture, threats to gleaning rights,
the increasing scarcity of fuel, growing flood problems, and mounting
demands for corvée labor, in-kind requisitions (in South Huang-Yun),
and service in unpleasant and socially divisive cotton patrols (in North
Huang-Yun), I have tried to break down the effects on everyday life as
specifically as possible by subregion, type of community, class, and so
on. Other dimensions could be added, if sources permitted. For instance, though I have said little here about gender, one might make
a case that many of the most severe problems discussed here affected
women more than men. Women made up a large portion of the gleaners and fuel gatherers, not to mention the cooks who had to manage
with very little fuel; there is some evidence that females also suffered

---

36. This is not the place to enter the debate over whether rural per capita output in
the middle and lower Yangzi was soaring (Brandt) or essentially stagnant (Huang) from
1870 to 1937. But given urban growth, the resumption of population growth, and even
a very modest estimate of rural growth, the area's absolute surplus must have increased
significantly.

disproportionately from postflood famines in Shandong.[37] Conversely, the modern goods that did begin to reach some homes in the region—mostly in North Huang-Yun—included two (kerosene and machine-spun yarn) that particularly reduced the burdens on women. Though the evidence I have found is very scant, it suggests that in the 1930s, peasant women in southwest Shandong, where these goods were scarce, worked much longer days than their North Huang-Yun counterparts.[38]

Much more would need to be done before such an argument could be sustained and even more before we had a thorough "peasant's eye view" of the processes described here; the definitions of classes used here, for instance, remain quite rough. Nonetheless, the distinctions—and connections—drawn here are a beginning. Analyses like these can help us see how large structural processes were played out, how they changed a variety of important (though often everyday) activities, and how the experience of those changes varied systematically with type of community, one's place in that community, the community's place in the preimperialist order, and changes in the dominant notions of political economy. In that way, they can help us seek a history that is informed by social science, but retains its humanistic virtues as well.

37. On gleaning and fuel gathering, see chapters 2 and 3; on mortality after Yellow River floods, see Lillian Li, "Life and Death in a Chinese Famine: Infanticide as a Demographic Consequence of the Yellow River Flood of 1935," *Comparative Studies in Society and History* 33:1 (July 1991), 466–510.

38. On the exceptionally long workday and poor conditions of southwest Shandong women, see Tian Hong, "Luxi nongfu shenghuo de yibian," *Dagong bao*, July 8, 1934, p. 11; the article explicitly links these problems to the fuel shortage, lack of kerosene and machine yarn, and so forth. By comparison, the workday for women in northwest Shandong appears to have usually been shorter, even for those involved in weaving: see, e.g., "Lubei shi xian nongye diaocha baogao," 8, 21, 33.

List of Counties in Northwest and Southwest Shandong

As discussed in the Introduction, the boundaries of Huang-Yun cannot always be fixed precisely. The same is true of the internal division between North and South Huang-Yun, which for purposes of chapter 2 (which relies on Shandong data) is the same as that between northwest and southwest Shandong. Thus, in making the calculations for that chapter, I tried in every case to classify any ambiguous counties to make my claims as difficult as possible to prove. For instance, four particularly poor counties at the northern edge of southwest Shandong—Puzhou, Fanxian, Shouzhang, and Yanggu—were first left out of the southwest and then experimentally included in the northwest when calculating per capita incomes, since I wished to make my demonstration that per capita income in the northwest was greater than in the southwest as robust as possible. What follows is a list of the counties defined as northwest and southwest for purposes of chapter 2. A fuller explanation of the decisions made for individual counties, the sources used in doing so, the relatively minor differences between my boundaries and those found in Esherick's *Origins of the Boxer Uprising*, plus the calculations of per capita income, acreage under cotton, and so forth, may be found in dissertation, appendixes D and E.

Northwest: Liaocheng, Tangyi, Chiping, Qingping, Xinxian, Guan-xian, Guantao, Gaotang, Enxian, Linqing, Wucheng, Xiajin, Qiuxian, Dezhou, Pingyuan, Yucheng, Chaocheng, Guancheng.

Southwest: Ciyang, Wenshang, Jining, Jinxiang, Jiaxiang, Yutai, Heze, Caoxian, Shanxian, Chengwu, Dingtao, Juye, Yuncheng, Yin-cheng, Dong'a, Pingyin.

Counties at least part of which belong in southwest, but omitted from these calculations: Puzhou, Fanxian, Yanggu, Shouzhang, Deng-xian, Yixian, Couxian, Qufu, Taian.

Northwestern county omitted from this calculation (because of in-adequate data): Boping.

Agricultural Losses
from Hydraulic Decay

EXPLANATION OF BASIC ESTIMATES

The amount of land "lost" through the expansion of the southwestern Shandong lakes is inherently imprecise. At any given time, people were trying to farm some part of these shallow lakes; they often succeeded for a while, but only large-scale projects could permanently reclaim most of the land.

The minimum assessment of lake land that could be reclaimed by repairing the Grand Canal was 580,000 *mu*, most of it in Jining and Yutai.[1] The plan from which this estimate derives involved restoring a minimal version of the old canal, not improving it; thus the lowest estimate of land to be reclaimed from this project should be a conservative estimate of the amount of crop land lost through canal decay. (More liberal estimates ranged as high as 1,920,000 *mu* from this project, and a 1919 plan for a lower canal also promised to reclaim 400,000 *mu* further north, from under Dongping Lake.)[2] Eight yuan per *mu* seems a cautious estimate of this land's productivity;[3] thus, the minimum value of crops not produced because land had turned into

1. *NYHH, zhuan lie,* 9; *JSYK* 1:4 (April 1931), *lunzhe,* 17–18.
2. *GCIM,* 35–36, 135.
3. *NYHH, zhuan lie,* 11–12, 19–20, for this estimate. Dissertation, appendix E, using output figures from the 1930s, calculates a per *mu* product for the Shandong part of Huang-Yun of ¥8.6. Since much of the land in question here was in the Jining-Yutai area, its yield would probably have been higher; the same appendix estimates per *mu* output in southwest Shandong at ¥10.2 per *mu*.

lake exceeded ¥4,500,000 per year. If all the laborers who would have worked on this land in fact found equally productive work—a dubious assumption, but one that builds in added caution—we should cut the estimate of additional output to include only the output attributable to the land itself; a good proxy for this is rent, which was usually 60 percent in this area. (Losses from floods, to be considered below, need no such adjustment, because labor had already been put into the crop at the time it was lost.) Thus, we will use an estimate of ¥2,700,000 lost.[4] Were we to use later figures, derived after further lake growth, losses would run as high as ¥9,600,000.[5]

Canal flooding was even more costly. The worst effects of these floods were actually felt in northern Jiangsu,[6] and so lie outside our purview. However, even the losses in Shandong were massive. In the last years of the Qing an average of 1,311,693 *mu* per year in seven southwest Shandong counties (Jining, Yutai, Wenshang, Couxian, Yixian, Dongping, and Dong'a) were granted tax remissions because of flooding caused by canal decay.[7] Losses were probably greater after 1911, since the condition of the canal worsened steadily, but figures for those years were never compiled.[8]

Moreover, tax remissions provide a very conservative estimate of flooded land. Not all such land got tax remissions, since the government was not eager to give up revenue. Besides, much flooded land was not on the tax rolls at all. Perhaps as much as 40 percent of all farmland in China was unregistered by the late Qing.[9] Hydraulic decay probably made Huang-Yun's tax rolls particularly inaccurate; some land that had been removed as "submerged" was still farmed, and new land created by reclamation or the shifting of river beds was rarely registered. Huang-Yun also had most of Shandong's 1,700,000 *mu* of *tun tian*, land originally given tax free in return for Grand Canal or tribute fleet labor; this land generally stayed off the tax rolls even once these duties lapsed.

Aside from the figure on tax remissions we have only one vague figure: a 1914 report said that "over the years" the canal had flooded

4. For examples of rents in this area, see Huang, *Peasant Economy*, 205, 210, 212.
5. Hou Renzhi, *Xu tianxia*, 48.
6. Ibid.
7. *NYHH, shuili guifu diaocha,* 1–2; *zhuan lie,* 21.
8. *JSYK* 1:3 (March 1931), *gongdu,* 40; 1:4 (April 1931), *lunzhe,* 17–18.
9. Wang Yeh-chien, *The Land Tax in Imperial China, 1753–1908* (Cambridge, Mass., 1973), 7, 24, 27.

more than 70,000,000 *mu* in these same seven counties.[10] If "over the years" referred to the entire period since the Yellow River shift, this figure would match the tax remission figure of about 1,300,000 *mu* per year; otherwise the annual losses would be much larger. Thus the assertion that using 1,300,000 *mu* errs on the side of caution is confirmed.

Using the same ¥8 per *mu* output estimate used above, we see that Grand Canal flooding cost southwest Shandong more than ¥10,000,000 per year.[11] However, since land could qualify for a tax exemption while still yielding some crop, we will halve this in the interest of further caution. The resulting ¥5,000,000 per year still gives us a total crop loss from the canal alone of at least ¥7,700,000 per year.

Yellow River decay took a much larger toll, but estimating potential reclamation from Yellow River repairs is very difficult. Experts disagreed about how wide the river's channel should be, and nobody had solid information about how much of the land inside any given set of dikes was fully submerged and how much was farmed but subject to frequent flooding. However, Freeman (who seems to have been borne out by post-1949 river control work) estimated that from just east of Kaifeng to the intersection of the Yellow River and the Grand Canal—approximately two hundred miles, all of it in Huang-Yun—a strip varying from three and a half to seven and three-quarter miles wide, all of it inside the official embarkments, could be turned from either submerged or very frequently flooded land to secure and fertile land.[12] If the smallest width applied everywhere, this strip would contain 2,688,000 affected *mu* within Huang-Yun. Freeman thought a

10. *NSGB* 1:5 (Dec. 1914), *zhengshi*, 2.
11. Multiplying 1,300,000 *mu* times ¥8 per *mu* gives ¥10,400,000. While land that could yield only one crop per year would produce only about ¥5 per *mu*, land that yielded three crops in two years—which was far more normal in southwest Shandong; some of the land even yielded two crops every year—would produce about ¥8 per *mu*. Pan Fu hypothesized that this land, since it would be exceptionally well watered, might yield much more, but I ignored this possibility for caution's sake. As with the earlier estimates, I then halved this number to make a generous allowance for the possibility that some land that was considered so flooded as to be freed of tax liability might still have yielded something; since crops usually had to be less than half of normal to get tax remissions, this calculation is almost certainly more cautious than necessary. On output estimates, see *NYHH, zhuan lie*, 11–12, 19–20.
12. Freeman, "Flood Problems," 1123, calculated that at the time a strip from four to eight miles wide was submerged, but the river should be only a quarter-mile wide at most times and only a half-mile even at peak times.

much wider strip could be reclaimed in many places; moreover, the river was also somewhat wider than necessary in parts of Huang-Yun east of the canal. Thus, rounding off losses from a too-wide Yellow River at 3,000,000 *mu* is still very conservative. Even if we assume that all this land was only "frequently flooded" rather than "always submerged," we should add ¥12,000,000 per year more of lost crops, for a running total of ¥19,700,000.[13]

Much more land was flooded, of course, in years when the outer dikes gave way. To avoid counting any flood damage twice, we will consider here only the six floods between 1900 and 1937 in which a dike clearly outside the reclaimable strip described by Freeman gave way.[14] O. J. Todd estimated that the 1933 Yellow River floods—either the second or third worst between 1890 and 1937—did more than ¥240,000,000 of damage.[15] Since that figure alone would add ¥6,000,000 per year if spread over the 1900–37 period—some of it, admittedly, outside Huang-Yun—it is hard to see how the six (at least) floods involving dike breaks outside Freeman's strip could add less than ¥9,000,000 per year, bringing Huang-Yun's agricultural losses to ¥28,700,000 per year.[16]

Moreover, hydraulic problems were cumulative. For instance, Grand Canal problems aggravated the ills of the Wanfu and Zhushui rivers and their tributaries; these less famous waterways carried the waters of far southwestern Shandong (Caoxian, Heze, Shanxian, and so forth) into the chain of lakes near Jining, which in turn led to the southbound canal, the Huai River, and the ocean. It took years for the canal's decay to noticeably affect these rivers: the 1915 Grand Canal study did not yet see any problems.[17] But as the canal became unable to receive the waters and silt of these rivers, they became uncontrollable, bringing the southwest its worst floods since 1855.[18]

13. This figure is obtained simply by multiplying the number of *mu* moved from one category to another times the difference in our estimate of average crop lost per year for each category.

14. Wu Tongju, *Zai xu*, vol. 10, *fulu*, 1–4.

15. Todd, *Two Decades in China*, 91.

16. The two floods for which we have figures together come to ¥284,000,000, or ¥7,000,000 "per year." If we add the 1925 flood, generally agreed to be as bad as or worse than the better documented 1933 flood and assign it the same figure as the 1933 flood, the figure jumps to about ¥13,000,000, with three floods still unaccounted for. Thus, even though the above figures include some land outside Huang-Yun (in southeast Zhili in 1917 and southeast Shandong and north Jiangsu in 1933), a figure of ¥9,000,000 per year average still seems quite cautious.

17. *NYHH, zhuan lie*, 2.

18. *Wanfu He*, 113.

A 1930 study estimated the annual crop loss resulting from these rivers' post-1900 deterioration at ¥3,000,000–¥8,000,000 just in the area near their mouths (in Jining and Yutai); the variation depended on whether the floods only ruined the fall crop or also prevented planting the spring crop.[19] By the mid 1920s, silt build-up was causing upstream floods as well; the crops lost in 1929–30 (the first two years for which we have reliable data) alone came to more than Y30,000,000.[20] Thus, for the 1920s and 1930s, the crop loss estimate should be raised by at least ¥5,000,000 per year, a figure that still underestimates the damage being done annually.

Thus, our most conservative annual crop loss estimate now runs to almost ¥35,000,000. This figure still excludes losses caused by the Wei River and by many smaller but volatile rivers as well as damage that had its origins in Huang-Yun but was felt elsewhere. It also omits losses of things other than crops. The houses, livestock, and other possessions lost in southwest Shandong in the 1935 Yellow River flood alone came to more than ¥100,000,000;[21] adding noncrop property damage just from this flood and the two other comparably bad Yellow River floods would add another ¥7,000,000 per year, for a total of more than ¥41,000,000. Adding the transport losses discussed in appendix C, the total becomes ¥48,000,000 to ¥51,000,000. And, of course, such figures still do not include losses in numerous lesser floods or deaths or other noneconomic losses.[22]

GENERATING HIGHER FIGURES

The materials that could be the basis for higher estimates of flood damage are mentioned above: other estimates of land flooded, inclusion of noncrop damage, and so on. To arrive at a figure of more than ¥100,000,000 we need only modify a few conservative assumptions. Eliminating the practice of halving the estimated annual Grand Canal and Yellow River flooding losses could be justified by arguing that although this land might well have yielded some crop while being re-

19. Ibid., 83–84.
20. Ibid., 108, 113.
21. Mantetsu, *Santō Chihō no Kōka Suisai Jōkyō*, 52.
22. Ibid. summarizes these losses. A fuller account is available in Shandong Huang He shuizai jiuji weiyuanhui, *Shandong Huang He shuizai jiuji baogao shu* (Report of the Shandong Yellow River flood and relief efforts), vols. 1 and 2 (Jinan, 1935 and 1936), which appears to have also been the basis for most of the shorter, more accessible report cited here.

corded as flooded, this situation would be more than balanced by flooded land that failed to apply for tax remissions because it was unregistered or that sought remissions but did not get them or that was submerged but continued to pay taxes because its owners lacked influence in the yamen. Dropping that practice would add ¥17,000,000 per year to the losses; one could even argue for multiplying the tax remissions figure, which would add much more. Using higher estimates of canal-submerged "lake land" would add up to ¥7,000,000 per year; higher estimates of land submerged unnecessarily along the Yellow River would add about 3,000,000 *mu*, yielding ¥14,400,000 more. If instead of counting noncrop property losses from just the three worst floods we were to add the three other floods that were almost as bad, plus dozens of lesser floods, we could easily increase the annualized estimate of this damage from ¥7,000,000 to ¥15,000,000, adding a further ¥8,000,000 to our total. By a similar principle, the estimates of crop damage done by the six worst Yellow River floods could easily be double or an even higher multiple of the estimate used here, which took a figure 1.5 times the damage in one of the worst of these floods to represent a forty-year total. Certainly an additional ¥10,000,000 from this source would be plausible. Together these revisions would add more than ¥56,000,000 to the estimate of ¥48,000,000–¥51,000,000 made above. Such steps would put our total estimate over ¥100,000,000. Even that number would still not include floods on various other waterways or the cost of dike repair itself or the ¥5,000,000 by which the transport estimate could be increased even without relying on the higher figures implied by the lost 1935 report (see appendix C). We have also maintained the questionable assumption that if hydraulic control had made any additional farmland available, farming that land would have required diverting labor that was already fully employed elsewhere; dropping that assumption would add several million additional yuan to our figures. Nor have we adjusted per *mu* yield estimates for the prime location of much of this land.

Thus a figure of well over ¥100,000,000 would not be implausible; our ¥48,000,000–¥51,000,000 figure is almost certainly an underestimate. Even so, it is certainly high enough to show that the state's withdrawal had a devastating impact on Huang-Yun; and it is the figure used in the rest of this book.

Extra Transport Costs Incurred Because of Hydraulic Decay in Huang-Yun

T. H. Wiggin's estimate that 41,000,000 ton-miles per year would switch from other modes of transport to the Shandong Grand Canal if it were restored was based on a 750-page study; unfortunately, I have found no sign of the original and have only the conclusions and a few paraphrases in other sources (chiefly *GCIM* and *GCIC*). Of this shipping 11,000,000 ton-miles were through traffic and 30,000,000 ton-miles were local traffic within Shandong. (Wiggin actually broke this down further by sections of the canal, but this refinement need not concern us here.)

Freeman estimated the cost of canal shipping at ¥.009 per ton-mile. Railroads cost ¥.0172 per ton-mile over a parallel route (*GCIC*, 66); I have assumed that they were the alternate mode of shipping for through traffic. *Shina Shōbetsu* (4:234) gives rates for various local forms of land transport in the form of day rates for a porter with a particular type of conveyance, how many *jin* he can haul, and how far he can go; since these are day rates, they do not include any costs for overnight accommodations; hence, they may actually underestimate the rates one would have to pay for local hauls of more than thirty miles. For the cheapest per-ton-mile conveyance, a two-animal yoked cart, the rate works out to ¥.098 per ton-mile (assuming that two strings of *jing qian* equaled ¥1). For the more common "small" cart (that is, a wheelbarrow), the rate works out to ¥.280 per ton-mile. Thus the difference between canal transport and the two-animal cart works out to ¥.089 per ton-mile; between the canal and the small cart, ¥.271 per ton-mile; the ratios are slightly under 2 to 1 for the railroad, slightly under 11 to 1 for the two-animal cart, and more than 31 to 1 for the small cart. A 1935 report on the feasibility of restoring the canal (quoted in *Xu tianxia*, 32) gives similar proportions.

Conveyance	Multiple of Canal Boat Costs per Ton-Mile
Railroad	1.7
Light railroad	2.0
Mule cart	10.8
Wheelbarrow	16.0
Truck	25.0
Carrying on poles	28.3

These rates presumably reflect the cost of each method over the distances that it was actually used; for long hauls, for instance, wheelbarrows would not remain cheaper than trucks.

If we split the 30,000,000 ton-miles of local traffic evenly between the two-animal cart and the small cart, this gives us

$$15,000,000 \times .089 = 1,335,000$$
$$15,000,000 \times .271 = 4,065,000$$
$$\overline{\hspace{3cm}}$$
$$¥5,400,000$$

If we change the division to a more likely three-fourths by small cart and one-fourth by two-animal cart we get

$$7,500,000 \times .089 = 667,500$$
$$22,500,000 \times .271 = 6,097,500$$
$$\overline{\hspace{3cm}}$$
$$¥6,765,000$$

This is the figure adopted here. If we added Wiggin's claim that total trade would increase 50 percent because of improved agricultural conditions and the like, these figures would be much higher.

For the extra expenses incurred along the Linqing to Dezhou section, not discussed by Wiggin, similar methods were used. First, I assumed that this section would accrue additional traffic after repairs at the lowest rate per mile of route that Wiggin assigns to any of the sections he does discuss: 100,000 ton-miles per mile of route. (This is extremely conservative, since Linqing was one of the largest ports on the northern Grand Canal and the place where the Wei River—a major artery for shipping from Henan and Shaanxi—met the canal, while Dezhou was an important place for traffic to switch from canal to railroad and vice versa.) Next, I used a length of fifty miles between these places, which is what this section would have been if it had been straightened out (see below). This yields a figure of 5,000,000 ton-miles; diverting half of it from two-animal carts and half from small carts would save ¥900,000. If the proportions were one-fourth and three-fourths, the savings would be ¥1,127,500.

However, various flood control measures, as discussed in the text, had lengthened this section by forty-seven miles. It is unlikely that the five thousand boats that continued to ply the Linqing to Tianjin run of which this was a part made fewer than two round trips each per year, since they would then be losing money. If they made exactly two round trips per year each and carried an average load of eighty tons, this would equal 75,200,000 extra ton-miles of shipping; at the ¥.009 per ton-mile cost of canal shipping, this involved unnecessary expenditures of ¥676,800 (see *JSGB* 3:8 [Aug. 1933], *jihua*, 9–10; *GCIC*, 35, 66; *Shina Shōbetsu* 4:229, 543–44, 547; Gandar, *La Canal Impériale* 56n).

Adding these components together, we find a minimum loss in extra short-haul transportation costs from canal decay of ¥6,976,800; adding the ¥99,000 lost by long-distance shippers puts the total over ¥7,000,000. If we assume that three-fourths rather than one-half of local traffic moved by small cart, the losses are ¥8,668,300; if we accept Wiggin's claim that canal traffic would have picked up further from a general expansion of commerce after repairs, the total cost of decay becomes much higher.

Bibliography

Adachi Keiji. "Daizuhaku Ryūtsū to Shindai no Shōgyo Teki Nōgyo" (The soybean trade and commercial agriculture in the Qing dynasty). *Tōyōshi Kenkyū* 33:3 (1974), 360–89.

Alitto, Guy. *The Last Confucian.* Berkeley: University of California Press, 1979.

Amano Motonosuke. *Santō Nōgyo Keizairon* (Essays on the economics of agriculture in Shandong). Dalian: Minami Manshu Tetsudo, 1936.

American International Corporation. *Annual Report, 1919.* New York, 1920.

———. *Bulletin* 1:1, 1:2. New York, 1917.

Armstrong, Alexander. *Shantung.* Shanghai: Shanghai Mercury, 1891.

Asia Development Co. *Repairing the Yellow River Break—Kung Chia Ko, Shantung.* N.p., 1923.

Asian Development Bank. *Asian Energy Problems.* New York: Frederick A. Praeger, 1982.

Aston, T. H., and Philpin, C. H. E., eds. *The Brenner Debate: Agrarian Class Structure and Economic Development in Pre-industrial Europe.* Cambridge, Eng.: Cambridge University Press, 1985.

Averill, Stephen. "Party, Society, and Local Elite in the Jiangxi Communist Movement." *Journal of Asian Studies* 46:2 (May 1987), 279–303.

Baker, John Earl. *Explaining China.* London: A. M. Philpot, 1927.

Balazs, Etienne. *Chinese Civilization and Bureaucracy.* Trans. H. M. Wright. New Haven: Yale University Press, 1964.

"Banking and Currency in Tsinan." *Chinese Economic Monthly* 2:2 (November 1924), 5–10.

Bartel, H. C. *The First Mennonite Mission in China.* Lawrence, Kans. (?), 1913.

Bayly, C. A. *Rulers, Townsmen and Bazaars: North India in the Age of Brit-

ish Expansion, 1770–1870. Cambridge, Eng.: Cambridge University Press, 1983.

Bedeski, Robert L. *State-Building in Modern China: The Kuomintang in the Prewar Period.* China Research Monograph no. 18. Berkeley: University of California, Institute of East Asian Studies, 1981.

Bergère, Marie-Claire. "The Role of the Bourgeoisie." In *China in Revolution: The First Phase, 1900–1913,* ed. Mary C. Wright, 229–95. New Haven: Yale University Press, 1968.

"Biangeng Jinan ge xian xiao di tu rang" (Altering the salt land of southern Hebei through irrigation). *Nongye zhoubao* 4:3 (January 25, 1935), 98–99.

Billingsley, Philip. *Banditry in Republican China.* Stanford: Stanford University Press, 1988.

Boorman, Howard L., ed. *Biographical Dictionary of Republican China.* New York: Columbia University Press, 1967.

Brandt, Loren. "Chinese Agriculture and the International Economy, 1870s–1930s: A Reassessment." *Explorations in Economic History* 22:2 (April 1985), 168–93.

———. *Commercialization and Agricultural Development: Central and Eastern China, 1870–1937.* Cambridge, Eng.: Cambridge University Press, 1989.

Braudel, Fernand. *The Wheels of Commerce.* Trans. Sian Reynolds. New York: Harper and Row, 1982.

Braun, Rudolf. "Taxation, Sociopolitical Structure, and State-Building: Great Britain and Brandenburg-Prussia." In *The Formation of National States in Western Europe,* ed. Charles Tilly, 243–327. Princeton: Princeton University Press, 1975.

Bray, Francesca, ed. *Agriculture.* Vol. 6, pt. 2, of *Science and Civilization in China,* ed. Joseph Needham. Cambridge, Eng.: Cambridge University Press, 1984.

Bressler, Raymond G., and King, Richard A. *Markets, Prices, and Interregional Trade.* New York: John Wiley and Sons, 1970.

Buck, David. *Urban Change in China: Politics and Development in Tsinan, Shantung, 1890–1949.* Madison: University of Wisconsin Press, 1978.

Buck, John L. *Chinese Farm Economy: A Study of 2866 Farms in Seventeen Localities and Seven Provinces in China.* Chicago: University of Chicago Press, 1930.

———. "Cost of Growing and Marketing Peanuts in China." *Chinese Economic Journal* 5:3 (September 1929), 767–88.

———. *Land Utilization in China: Statistical Volume.* Chicago: University of Chicago Press, 1937; reprint ed., New York: Garland Press, 1982.

———. "A Statistical View of Shantung." *Chinese Economic Journal* 1:1 (January 1927), 33–47.

Canaday, Frank. Papers of Frank H. Canaday. Harvard-Yenching Library, Harvard University.

Cardoso, Henrique, and Faletto, Ernesto. *Dependency and Underdevelopment in Latin America*. Berkeley: University of California Press, 1979.

Carey, Clifton O'Neal. "Michigan Engineers in China." *Michigan Technik* 33:3 (November 1920), 149–56.

———. Papers of Clifton O'Neal Carey. Bentley Historical Library, University of Michigan, Ann Arbor.

Carlson, Ellsworth. *The Kaiping Mines, 1877–1912*. Cambridge, Mass.: Harvard University Press, 1957.

Chen Bozhuang. *Xiaomai ji mianfen* (Wheat and wheat flour). Shanghai: Jiaotong Daxue yanjiusuo, 1936.

Chen Hanseng. *Landlord and Peasant in China*. New York: International Publishers, 1936.

Ch'en, Jerome. "Local Government Finance in Republican China." *Republican China* 10:2 (April 1985), 42–54.

Chen Ruilin. "Dezhou 'Beiyang jiqi zhizaoju' yu lujunbu Dexian bing gong-chang shi mo" (The 'Beiyang Arsenal' of Dezhou and the army's military factory in De county from beginning to end). *Dezhou shi zhi tongxun*, no. 2 (1986), 27–30.

Chen Yunlong, ed. *Qiu pu Zhou shang shu (yu shan) quanji, Zhou Fu* (The collected memorials of Zhou Fu). Taibei: Wenhai chubanshe, 1967.

Cheng Shouzhong, ed. *Shandong kaocha baogaoshu* (Report of Shandong investigations). Jinan, 1934(?).

China Weekly Review. *Who's Who in China*. 3rd ed. Shanghai: China Weekly Review, 1925.

China Yearbook, 1926–1927 and 1928. New York: E. P. Dutton, 1927 and 1928.

"China's First Agricultural Institute." *China Weekly Recorder*, May 12, 1923, p. 382.

Chinese Economic Bulletin. 1921–33.

Chinese Economic Journal. 1927–35.

Chintao Minseibu Tetsudōbu. *Chōsa Shiryō* (Investigative materials), no. 3. Qingdao: Minseibu Tetsudōbu, 1918.

Chintao Shubigun Minseibu Tetsudōbu. *Tōhoku Santō (Bokkai Santō Engan Shokō Iken Chīfū Kan Toshi)* (Northeast Shandong [all ports on Shandong's Bohai coast, and cities between Weixian and Yantai]). Chōsa Hōkoku Sho (Chōsa Shiryō no. 17) (Research report [research materials no. 17]). Qingdao: Chintao Shubigun Minseibu Tetsudōbu, 1919.

Chongxiu Hua xianzhi (The further revised gazetteer of Hua county). 1932.

Chongxiu Taian xianzhi (A further revision of the gazetteer of Taian county). 1925.

Chow Tse-tung. *The May Fourth Movement*. Cambridge, Mass.: Harvard University Press, 1960.

Chu, Samuel. *Reformer in Modern China*. New York: Columbia University Press, 1965.

Ch'u T'ung-tsu. *Local Government in China under the Ch'ing*. Cambridge, Mass: Harvard University Press, 1962.

Chūgoku Nōson Kanko Chōsa Kai. *Chūgoku Nōson Kanko Chōsa* (An investigation of customs and practices in Chinese villages). 6 vols. Tokyo: Iwanami Shoten, 1953–58.

Coble, Parks. *The Shanghai Capitalists and the Nationalist Government, 1927–37*. Cambridge, Mass.: Harvard University Press, 1986.

Cochran, Sherman G. *Big Business in China: Sino-Foreign Rivalry in the Cigarette Industry, 1890–1930*. Cambridge, Mass.: Harvard University Press, 1980.

The Concise Columbia Encyclopedia. New York: Columbia University Press, 1983.

Cronon, William. *Changes in the Land: Indians, Colonists, and the Ecology of New England*. New York: Hill and Wang, 1983.

Da Qing li chao shilu (Veritable records of the Qing dynasty) Gaozong, Dezong (Qianlong, Guangxu reigns). Reprinted Taibei: Hualien chubanshe, 1964.

"Dang zai Dezhou diqu zaoqi huodong de jijian da shi" (A few big events from the early period of Party activities in the Dezhou area). *Dezhou shi zhi tongxun*, no. 2 (1986), 24–26.

Darling, M. L. *The Punjab Peasant in Prosperity and Debt*. Oxford: Oxford University Press, 1947.

Dengxian xiangtu zhi (Gazetteer of local places of Dengxian). 1907.

Deping xianzhi (Gazetteer of Deping county). 1935.

Deutschland Reichsmarineamt. *Denkschrift Betreffend die Entwicklung des Kiautschou-Gebiets*. Annual. 1902–8.

Dodgen, Randall. "Hydraulic Evolution and Dynastic Decline: The Yellow River Conservancy, 1796–1855." *Late Imperial China* 12:2 (December 1991), 36–63.

Doi Akira and Tonō Fumino. *Hokushi Jijō Soran* (Comprehensive survey of conditions in North China). Dalian: Minami Manshū Tetsudō Kabushiki Kaisha, 1936.

Dong Taisheng, ed. *Shandong ge yao ji* (A collection of Shandong ballads). Jinan: Shandong shengli minqun jiaoyuguan, 1933.

Dong'a xianzhi (Gazetteer of Dong'a county). 1934.

Dongfang zazhi. 1901–37.

Dongping xianzhi (Gazetteer of Dongping county). 1936.

"Du Buzhou tongzhi yi zhong gong Jin Nan tewei de jijian da shi" (Comrade Du Buzhou remembers some big events concerning the Chinese Communist Party special committee for the area south of Tianjin). *Dezhou shi zhi tongxun*, no. 1 (1984), 17–19.

Duara, Prasenjit. *Culture, Power, and the State: Rural North China, 1900–1942*. Stanford: Stanford University Press, 1988.

———. "The Political Structure of a North China Village in Late Imperial and Republican Times." *Stone Lion Review*, no. 5 (Spring 1980), 49–54.

———. "Power in Rural Society: North China Villages, 1900–1940." Ph.D. dissertation, Harvard University, 1983.

———. "State Involution: A Study of Local Finances in Rural North China,

1911–1935." *Comparative Studies in Society and History* 29:1 (January 1987), 132–61.

Eastman, Byron. *Interpreting Mathematical Economics and Econometrics.* New York: St. Martin's Press, 1984.

Eastman, Lloyd. *The Abortive Revolution: China under Nationalist Rule, 1927–37.* Cambridge, Mass.: Harvard University Press, 1974.

Elman, Benjamin. *From Philosophy to Philology: Social and Intellectual Aspects of Change in Late Imperial China.* Cambridge, Mass.: Harvard University Council on East Asian Studies, 1984.

———. "Political, Social and Cultural Reproduction via Civil Service Examinations in Late Imperial China." *Journal of Asian Studies* 50:1 (February 1991), 7–28.

Elvin, Mark. *The Pattern of the Chinese Past.* Palo Alto: Stanford University Press, 1972.

En xianzhi (Gazetteer of En county). 1909.

Esherick, Joseph M. "Number Games: A Note on Land Distribution in Pre-Revolutionary China." *Modern China* 7:4 (October 1981), 387–411.

———. *The Origins of the Boxer Uprising.* Berkeley: University of California Press, 1987.

———. *Reform and Revolution in Hunan and Hubei.* Berkeley: University of California Press, 1976.

Esman, Milton, and Uphoff, Norman. *Local Organizations: Intermediaries in Rural Development.* Ithaca: Cornell University Press, 1984.

Fairbank, John K. "Introduction: The Old Order." In *The Cambridge History of China,* vol. 10, pt. 1, ed. John K. Fairbank, 1–34. Cambridge, Eng.: Cambridge University Press, 1978.

Fairbank, John K.; Reischauer, Edwin, O.; and Craig, Albert M. *East Asia: Tradition and Transformation.* Boston: Houghton Mifflin, 1973.

Fan Qianyun. "Luxi zai hou ji ying banli nong zhen yu banfa yaodian" (Important points regarding managing urgently needed agricultural relief after the west Shandong floods, and how to manage it). *Xiangcun jianshe ban yuekan* 5:3 (September 1935), 1–9.

Far Eastern Review. 1914–21.

Fauvel, A. A. *La Province Chinoise du Chan-toung: Géographie et Histoire Naturelle.* Brussels, 1892.

Fei Xiaotong (Fei Hsiao-t'ung). *China's Gentry: Essays on Rural-Urban Relations.* Chicago: University of Chicago Press, 1968.

Feng Huade. "Hebei sheng xian caizheng zhi chu fenxi" (An analysis of income and expenses in the county finance of Hebei province). In *Zhongguo jingji yanjiu* (Research on the Chinese economy), ed. Fang Xianting (H. D. Fong), 2: 1039–55. Changsha: Shangwu yin shu guan, 1938.

———. "Hebei sheng yashui xingzhi zhi yanbian." (Changes in the nature of the brokerage tax in Hebei province). In *Zhongguo jingji yanjiu* (Research on the Chinese economy), ed. Fang Xianting (H. D. Fong), vol. 2, pp. 1067–79. Changsha: Shangwu yin shu guan, 1938.

Feuerwerker, Albert. *China's Early Industrialization: Sheng Hsuan-huai*

(1844–1916) and Mandarin Enterprise. Cambridge, Mass.: Harvard University Press, 1958.

Fewsmith, Joseph. *Party, State and Local Elites in Republican China: Merchant Organizations and Politics in Shanghai, 1890–1930*. Honolulu: University of Hawaii Press, 1985.

First Historical Archives of China, Beijing.

"Foreign Funds for Railways." *Beijing Review* 29:21 (May 26, 1986), 28.

Franck, Harry A. *Wandering in Northern China*. New York and London: Century, 1923.

Frankel, Francine. *India's Green Revolution: Economic Gains and Political Costs*. Princeton: Princeton University Press, 1971.

Freeman, John Ripley. "Flood Problems in China." *Proceedings of the American Society of Civil Engineers*, May 1922, pp. 1113–67.

———. "Grand Canal Investigations." Typescript copy of final report to the Grand Canal Board and the American International Corporation, 1921. At least two slightly different versions of this report exist, one held at Cornell University, one at the University of Michigan; they are referred to here as *GCIC* and *GCIM* respectively.

Fu Sinian. See Kong Decheng, ed.

Furth, Charlotte. *Ting Wen-chiang: Science and China's New Culture*. Cambridge, Mass.: Harvard University Press, 1970.

Gamble, Sidney D. *North China Villages*. Berkeley: University of California Press, 1963.

———. *Ting Hsien: A North China Rural Community*. Stanford: Stanford University Press, 1968.

Gandar, Dominique. *Le Canal Impériale: Étude Historique et Descriptive*. Shanghai: Imprimerie de la Mission Catholique, 1903.

Geertz, Clifford. *Agricultural Involution*. Berkeley: University of California Press, 1963.

Gillin, Donald. "'Peasant Nationalism' in the History of Chinese Communism." *Journal of Asian Studies* 23:2 (February 1964), 269–89.

Gong shang banyuekan. 1934.

Gongzhong dang. See Guoli Gu Gong Bowuyuan wenxian bianji weiyuanhui.

Goodrich, L. Carrington, and Fang Chaoying, eds. *Dictionary of Ming Biography*. New York: Columbia University Press, 1976.

Gottschang, Thomas. "Migration from North China to Manchuria, 1891–1942: An Economic History." Ph.D. thesis, University of Michigan, 1982.

Greer, Charles. *Water Management in the Yellow River Basin of China*. Austin: University of Texas Press, 1979.

Guo Shijie, ed. *Jiu Zhongguo Kailan meikuang de gongzi zhidu he bao gong zhidu* (The wage system and the contract labor system at the Kailan Coal Mine of old China). Tianjin: Xinhua shudian, 1985.

Guo Yizhi. "Pochan shengzhong de yige Jinan nongcun" (A south Hebei village in the throes of bankruptcy). In *Zhongguo nongcun jingji lunwen ji* (Collected essays on the economy of China's agricultural villages), ed. Qian Jiaju, pp. 514–20. Shanghai: Zhonghua shuju, 1935.

Guoli Gu Gong Bowuyuan wenxian bianji weiyuanhui, eds. *Gongzhong dang Guangxu chao zouzhe* (Secret palace memorials of the Guangxu period). Taibei: Guoli Gu Gong Bowuyuan, 1973–75.

———. *Gongzhong dang Yongzheng chao zouzhe* (Secret palace memorials of the Yongzheng period). Taibei: Guoli Gu Gong Bowuyuan, 1977–79.

Hai Shan. "Kuangfeng juanqi liehuoran—ji huochaichang gongren de sanci ba gong" (A storm wind sweeps up a great blaze—remembering the three strikes of the workers at the Jining Match Factory). *Jining shi shiliao*, no. 1 (1983), 78–88.

———. "Yutang chunqiu—Jining shi Yutang jiangyuan jian shi" (Chronicles of Yutang—a short history of Jining municipality's Yutang soy sauce factory). Parts 1 and 2, *Jining shi shiliao*, no. 1 (1983), 48–78, and no. 2 (1983), 90–106.

Harriss, Barbara R. "There Is Method in My Madness: Or Is It Vice-versa?" *Food Research Institute Studies* (sometimes listed as Stanford Food Research Institute. *Studies.*), 17:2 (1979), 197–218.

Hartwell, Robert M. "Demographic, Political, and Social Transformations of China, 750–1550." *Harvard Journal of Asiatic Studies* 42:2 (1982), 365–442.

Hatada Takashi. *Chūgoku Sonraku to Kyōdotai Riron* (Chinese villages and theories of cooperative systems). Tokyo: Iwanami Shoten, 1973.

Hayami, Yujiro. *A Century of Agricultural Growth in Japan.* Minneapolis: University of Minnesota Press, 1975.

He Benshui. "Yucheng cheng Nan de nongcun" (Rural villages south of the county capital of Yucheng). *Minjian ban yuekan* 3:19 (February 10, 1937), 10–11.

He Yunlong. "Heze nongcun de shishi" (The actual situation in Heze rural villages). *Nongye zhoubao* 4:14 (April 12, 1935), 488–89.

Hebei mianchan lu bao. 1935–38.

"Henan nongcun jinrong zhi diaocha" (An investigation of rural credit in Henan). *Shehui jingji yuebao* 2:11–12 (double issue, November–December 1935), 52–67.

Heunemann, Ralph. The *Dragon and the Iron Horse.* Cambridge, Mass.: Harvard University Press, 1984.

Hewu jibao. 1919–22.

Hinton, Harold C. *Grain Transport via the Grand Canal, 1845–1901.* Harvard Papers on China, no. 4. Cambridge, Mass.: Harvard University, East Asian Research Center, 1950.

Ho Ping-ti. *The Ladder of Success in Imperial China.* New York: Columbia University Press, 1962.

———. *Studies on the Population of China, 1368–1953.* Cambridge, Mass.: Harvard University Press, 1959.

Hoshi Ayao. *Dai Unga* (The Grand Canal). Tokyo: Kinfu Shuppansha, 1971.

Hou Renzhi, ed. *Xu tianxia qun guo li bing shu, Shandong zhi bu* (A continuation of the book of strengths and weaknesses of the areas and commanderies of China, Shandong section). Beijing: Yanjing Daxue yanjiuyuan, 1940.

Hsiao, Kung-ch'uan. *Rural China: Imperial Control in the Nineteenth Century.* Seattle: University of Washington Press, 1960.

Hsu, Immanuel C. Y. *The Rise of Modern China.* New York: Oxford University Press, 1975.

Hsu, Leonard S. *Silver and Prices in China.* Shanghai: Commercial Press, 1935.

Hsu, Ying-sui. "Tobacco Marketing in Eastern Shandong." In *Agrarian China: Source Materials from Chinese Authors,* ed. and trans. Research Staff of the Institute of Pacific Relations, 171–72. London: George Allen and Unwin, 1939.

Hu Ch'ang-t'u, "The Yellow River Administration in the Ch'ing Dynasty." *Journal of Asian Studies* 14:4 (August 1955), 505–13.

Hu Zhangzhun. "Shandong zhi mianye" (The cotton of Shandong). *Shandong wenxian* 1:3 (December 1975), 20–24.

Huang, Philip C. C. "Analyzing the Twentieth-Century Chinese Countryside: Revolutionaries versus Western Scholarship." *Modern China* 1:2 (April 1975), 132–60.

———. *The Peasant Economy and Social Change in North China.* Stanford: Stanford University Press, 1985.

———. *The Peasant Family and Rural Development in the Yangzi River Delta, 1350–1988.* Stanford: Stanford University Press, 1990.

Hucker, Charles O. *The Ming Dynasty: Its Origins and Evolving Institutions.* Ann Arbor: University of Michigan, Michigan Center for Chinese Studies, 1978.

Hummel, Arthur. *Eminent Chinese of the Ch'ing Period.* 2 vols. Washington, D.C.: Government Printing Office, 1943–44.

Hunt, Michael. *Frontier Defense and the Open Door.* New Haven: Yale University Press, 1971.

HWJB. See *Hewu jibao.*

HWTK. See *Shandong hewu tekan.*

I Songgip. "Shantung in the Shun-chih Reign: The Establishment of Local Control and the Gentry Response, Part 1." Trans. Joshua Fogel, Yamane Yukio, and Inada Hideko. *Ch'ing Shih Wen-t'i* 4:4 (December 1980), 1–34.

Ichiko, Chuzo. "The Role of the Gentry: An Hypothesis." In *China in Revolution: The First Phase, 1900–1913,* ed. Mary C. Wright, 297–317. New Haven: Yale University Press, 1968.

Imai Shuin. "Kōnichi Konkyochi no Keisei Katei ni tsuite nochi Kōsatsu" (An investigation of the formation process of an anti-Japanese base area). *Shichō,* no. 108 (June 1971), 22–60.

Imperial Maritime Customs. See Zhongguo Haiguan Zong Shuiwusi.

"Improving Inland Waterways." *China Reconstructs* 34:8 (August 1985), 8–10.

Isaacs, Harold. *The Tragedy of the Chinese Revolution*. Stanford: Stanford University Press, 1951, reprinted 1961.

Ji Bin. "Nongcun pochan sheng zhong Jinan yige fanrong de cunzhuang" (A prosperous south Hebei village in the throes of bankruptcy). In *Zhongguo nongcun jingji lunwen ji* (Collected essays on the Chinese rural economy), ed. Qian Jiaju, 502–13. Shanghai: Zhonghua shuju, 1935.

Jiao-Ao xianzhi (Gazetteer of Jiao-Ao counties). 1928.

Jihe xianzhi (Gazetteer of Jihe county). 1933.

"Jindai Lu Xibei diqu nongmin douzheng shilue" (A historical sketch of the struggles of peasants in modern northwest Shandong). *Liaocheng difang shizhi*, no. 2 (July 1983), 11–15.

Jing Qi. "Dong'a luxing jian wen ji" (Record of things seen and heard on a trip to Dong'a). *Shandong wenxian* 2:3 (December 1976), 150–53.

Jing Su and Luo Lun. *Qing dai Shandong jingying dizhu jingji yanjiu* (Economic research on managerial landlords in Shandong in the Qing dynasty). Proofs for revised edition (original edition abridged and translated by Endymion Wilkinson as *Landlord and Labor in Late Imperial China*). Jinan: Qilu shushe, forthcoming.

Jining shi shiliao, no. 1–2 (1983).

Jining xianzhi (Gazetteer of Jining county). 1929.

Jining zhilizhou xuzhi (A continuation of the gazetteer of Jining independent district). 1927.

Jining zhilizhou zhi (Gazetteer of Jining independent district). 1859.

Johnson, Chalmers. *Peasant Nationalism and Chinese Communist Power*. Stanford: Stanford University Press, 1962.

Johnson, David; Nathan, Andrew J.; and Rawski, Evelyn S. *Popular Culture in Late Imperial China*. Berkeley: University of California Press, 1985.

Jones, Susan Mann. "The Organization of Trade at the County Level: Brokerage and Tax-Farming in the Republican Period." In *Select Papers from the Center for Far Eastern Studies, No. 3, 1978–1979*, ed. Susan Mann Jones, 70–99. Chicago: University of Chicago, Center for Far Eastern Studies, 1980.

Kambe Masao, ed. *Dō A Keizai Kenkyū* (Research on Far Eastern economies). Vol. 1. Tokyo, 1942.

Kann, Eduard. "Copper Banknotes in China." *Chinese Economic Journal* 5:1 (July 1929), 551–61.

———. *The Currencies of China*. Shanghai: Kelly and Walsh, 1926.

Kato Chokushi. "Shingai Kakumei no Santō Shō ni okeru Minshu Undō" (Popular movements in Shandong province in the period of the 1911 Revolution). *Shiron*, no. 34 (1981), 43–63.

Kelley, David. "Temples and Tribute Fleets." *Modern China* 8:3 (July 1982), 361–91.

Kita Shina Hattatsu Kabushiki Kaisha Chōsaka. *Rosai Mensaku Chitai no Ichi Nōson ni Okeru Rōdoryoku Chōsa Hōkoku* (Report on the investigation of labor power in the West Shandong cotton-growing area). Beijing: No publisher, 1943.

Kōain Kijitsubu. *Hokushi ni okeru Rinsan Shigen Chōsa* (Investigation of forest resources of north China). Tokyo, 1940.

Kokuritsu Pekin Daigaku Fusetsu Nōson Keizaisho. *Santō Sainei Kenjō o Chushin Toseru Nosam Ryūtsū ni Kanchiru Ichi Kōsatsu* (An investigation of matters relevant to Shandong, Jining county and city as center and controller of the circulation of agricultural commodities). Beijing: Pekin Daigaku, 1942.

Kong Decheng, ed. *Fu Sinian quanji* (Complete works of Fu Sinian). 10 vols. Vol. 7. Taibei: Lianjing chuban shiye gongsi, 1980.

Krishna, Raj. "Farm Supply Response in the Punjab (India-Pakistan): A Case Study of Cotton." Ph.D. dissertation, University of Chicago, 1961.

Kuhn, Philip A. "Local Taxation and Finance in Republican China." In *Select Papers from the Center for Far Eastern Studies, no. 3, 1978–1979,* ed. Susan Mann Jones, 100–36. Chicago: University of Chicago, Center for Far Eastern Studies, 1980.

———. *Rebellion and Its Enemies in Late Imperial China.* Cambridge, Mass.: Harvard University Press, 1970.

———. *Soulstealers: The Chinese Sorcery Scare of 1768.* Cambridge, Mass.: Harvard University Press, 1990.

Kuznets, Simon. *Population, Capital, and Growth.* New York: W. W. Norton, 1973.

Lapidus, Ira M. "Hierarchies and Networks: A Comparison of Chinese and Islamic Civilizations." In *Conflict and Control in Late Imperial China,* ed. Frederic Wakeman, Jr., and Carolyn Grant, 26–42. Berkeley: University of California Press, 1975.

Lary, Diana. "Violence, Fear and Insecurity: The Mood of Republican China." *Republican China* 10:2 (April 1985), 55–63.

Lee, En-han. *China's Quest for Railroad Autonomy, 1904–1911.* Singapore: Singapore University Press, 1977.

Lee, Frederic. *Currency, Banking, and Finance in China.* Washington, D.C.: Government Printing Office, 1926.

Lee, James Z. *State and Society in Southwest China, 1250–1850.* Cambridge, Eng.: Cambridge University Press, forthcoming.

Lee, Robert H. G. *The Manchurian Frontier in Ch'ing History.* Cambridge, Mass.: Harvard University Press, 1970.

Leonard, Jane Kate. "Grand Canal Grain Transport Management." *Modern Asian Studies* 22:4 (1988), 665–99.

Levenson, Joseph R. *Liang Ch'i-ch'ao and the Mind of Modern China.* Cambridge, Mass.: Harvard University Press, 1953.

Lewis, Arthur. "Economic Development with Unlimited Supplies of Labor." *Manchester School of Economics and Social Studies* 22:2 (May 1954), 139–91.

Li Guijin. "Qing mo bizhi gaige ji qi shibai yuanyin de qiantan" (A preliminary discussion of late Qing monetary reform and the reasons for its failure). *Hebei cai mao xueyuan xuebao,* no. 4 (1983). Reprinted in *Jingji shi,* no. 2 (1984), 129–37.

Li Hengzhen, Xu Datong, and Zhang Jinxiu. "Women suo zhidao de Zhang Zongchang" (The Zhang Zongchang we knew). *Wenshi ziliao xuanji,* Jinan edition, no. 3 (1982), 1–75.

Li, Lillian. "Life and Death in a Chinese Famine: Infanticide as a Demographic Consequence of the 1935 Yellow River Flood." *Comparative Studies in Society and History* 33:3 (July 1991), 466–510.

Li Shilu. *Xiu fang suo zhi* (Records of repairing embankments and barriers). Original edition, 1936. Reprinted by Zhongguo shuili gongcheng xuehui, 1937.

Li Shizhao. "Ji Gaotang Guguantun baodong de lingdao ren" (Remembering the leaders of the uprising in Guguantun, Gaotang). *Wenshi ziliao xuanji,* Jinan edition, no. 10 (1981), 43–60.

———. "Jie Zhanbo tongzhi shilue" (A historical sketch of Comrade Jie Zhanbo). *Liaocheng diqu dangshi ziliao,* no. 10 (1984), 61–65.

———. "Zhao Yizheng lieshi zhuanlue" (A biographical sketch of the martyr Zhao Yizheng). *Shandong dangshi ziliao,* no. 2 (1981), 167–77.

Li Yushu, ed. *Zhong Ri guanxi shiliao* (Historical materials on relations between China and Japan). Vol. 6. Li Liupeng, series ed. Taibei: Zhongyang yanjiuyuan jindai shi yanjiusuo, 1976.

Lin Maoquan. *Wenji* (Collected works). N.p.; preface dated 1926.

Lin Xiuzhu (also known as Lin Maoquan), ed. *Lidai zhi Huang He shi* (A history of Yellow River control). Jinan: Shandong Hewu Zongju, 1926.

Linqing xianzhi (Gazetteer of Linqing). 1934.

Lippitt, Victor D. "The Development of Underdevelopment in China." *Modern China* 4:3 (July 1978), 251–328.

Liu E (Liu Tieyun). *Lao Can youji* (The travels of Lao Can). Jinan: Qilu shushe, 1985.

Liu Jinyi. *Zhongguo tielu chuangjian bai nian shi* (A hundred years of Chinese railroad building). Taibei: Taiwan tielu guanliqu, 1981.

Liu Nanyun. "Yi Dang zai Jining shi de zaoqi huodong" (Remembering the activities of the Party in its early days in Jining municipality). *Jining shi shiliao,* no. 1 (1983), 5–17.

Liu Yunhuai. "Jining de Yunhe" (The Grand Canal of Jining). *Shandong wenxian* 5:1 (June 20, 1979), 84–86.

Love, H. H. Papers of H. H. Love. Olin Library, Cornell University.

Lu Weijun. *Han Fuju.* Jinan: Shandong renmin chubanshe, 1985.

———. "Han Fuju tongzhi xia de Shandong jinrong" (The money market in Shandong during the rule of Han Fuju). *Shandong shi zhi ziliao,* no. 8 (1985), 57–70.

———. "Han Fuju tongzhi xia de Shandong shui shou" (Tax collection in Shandong during the rule of Han Fuju). *Shandong shi zhi ziliao,* no. 1 (1984), 147–74.

"Lubei shi xian nongye diaocha baogao" (A report on an investigation of agriculture in ten north Shandong counties). *Shandong nong kuang baogao,* no. 13 (January 1930), 1–45.

Luo Ziwei. "Zouping si chao mian guan" (A look at private currency in Zouping). *Xiangcun jianshe xunkan* 4:29 (July 1935), 26–31.

"Luxi ge xian nongcun jingji xianzhuang" (The current economic situation in the rural villages of each county of western Shandong). *Nongcun jingji* 1:11 (September 1, 1934), 75–77.

McCloskey, Donald N. *The Applied Theory of Price.* New York: Macmillan, 1985.

McCloskey, Donald N., and Nash, John. "Corn at Interest: The Extent and Cost of Grain Storage in Medieval England." *American Economic Review* 74:1 (March 1984), 174–87.

MacKinnon, Stephen. *A Late Qing-GMD-PRC Connection: Police as an Arm of the Modern Chinese State.* Selected Papers in Asian Studies, n. s., no. 14. Tempe, Ariz.: Western Conference of the Association for Asian Studies, 1983.

———. *Power and Politics in Late Imperial China: Yuan Shi-kai in Beijing and Tianjin, 1901–1908.* Berkeley: University of California Press, 1980.

Mai Shudu. "Hebei sheng xiaomai zhi banyun" (The circulation of wheat in Hebei province). *Shehui kexue zazhi* 1:1 (March 1930), 73–107.

Mallory, Walter. *China: Land of Famine.* New York: American Geographical Society, 1926.

Mann, Susan. *Local Merchants and the Chinese Bureaucracy, 1750–1950.* Stanford: Stanford University Press, 1987.

Mantetsu. See Minami Manshū Tetsūdo Kabushiki Kaisha.

Mao Zedong. "Analysis of the Classes in Chinese Society." 1926. Reprinted in *Selected Readings from the Works of Mao Tse-tung,* 11–22. Beijing: Foreign Languages Press, 1971.

Matsuzaki Yujiro. *Santō Shō no Sai Nishiki* (More knowledge about Shandong). Qingdao, 1941.

Meng Da. "Zhang gu shang jiang Zichong jia shi ji Linqing fengguang" (The Family of General Zhang Zichong and the Linqing Scene). *Shandong wenxian* 1:1 (June 1975), 74–76.

Merriman, John M. "The Demoiselles of the Ariège, 1829–1831." In *1830 in France,* ed. John M. Merriman, 87–118. New York: Franklin Watts, 1975.

Minami Manshū Tetsūdo Kabushiki Kaisha Chōsa Kenkyūjo. *Hokushi Nōson Gaikyō Chōsa Hōkoku* (A report of an examination of the situation of North China villages). Tokyo: Minami Manshu Tetsudo Kabushiki Kaisha, 1940.

———, Tenshin Jimusho Chōka. *Santō Chihō no Kōka Suisai Jōkyō* (The situation of the Shandong area Yellow River flood). Tianjin: Mantetsu, 1936.

———. *Santō no Chikugyu* (The livestock of Shandong). Tianjin: Mantetsu, 1936.

———. *Santō no Mensaku* (The cotton production of Shandong). Tianjin: Mantetsu, 1942.

Minguo ribao. Jinan edition. Weekly supplement. 1929–30.

Morse, Hosea B. *The Trade and Administration of the Chinese Empire.* London: Longmans, Green, 1913.

Mote, Frederic. "The Growth of Chinese Despotism." *Oriens Extremis* 8:1 (August 1961), 1–41.

Moulder, Frances. *Japan, China, and the Modern World Economy.* Cambridge, Eng.: Cambridge University Press, 1977.

Murphey, Rhoads. *The Treaty Ports and China's Modernization: What Went Wrong?* Ann Arbor: University of Michigan, Center for Chinese Studies, 1970.

Myers, Ramon H. *The Chinese Peasant Economy: Agricultural Development in Hopei and Shantung, 1890–1949.* Cambridge, Mass.: Harvard University Press, 1970.

Myers, Ramon H., and Sands, Barbara N. "The Spatial Approach to Chinese History." *Journal of Asian Studies* 45:4 (August 1986), 721–44.

Nadaud, Martin. *Mémoires de Leonard, Ancien Garçon Maçon.* Paris: Voix Ouvrières, 1948.

Nanjing University, College of Agriculture and Forestry. *Bulletin.*

Naquin, Susan. "Connections between Rebellions: Sect Family Networks in Qing China." *Modern China* 8:3 (July 1982), 337–60.

———. *Shantung Rebellion.* New Haven: Yale University Press, 1981.

Naquin, Susan, and Rawski, Evelyn S. *Eighteenth-Century China.* New Haven: Yale University Press, 1987.

Nathan, Carl F. *Plague Prevention and Politics in Manchuria, 1910–1931.* Cambridge, Mass.: Harvard University Press, 1967.

Nee, Victor. "Toward a Social Anthropology of the Chinese Revolution." *Bulletin of Concerned Asian Scholars* 11:3 (July–September 1979), 40–50.

Needham, Joseph, general ed., Wang Ling and Lu Gwei-Djen, associate eds. *Civil Engineering and Nautics.* Vol. 4, pt. 3 of *Science and Civilization in China,* ed. Joseph Needham. Cambridge, Eng.: Cambridge University Press, 1971.

Nevius, Helen S. Coan. *The Life of John Livingston Nevius.* New York: Fleming H. Revell, 1895.

Nong shang gongbao. 1914–26.

Nongye zhoubao. 1929–37.

North China Herald. 1900–37.

Olson, Mancur. *The Logic of Collective Action.* Cambridge, Mass.: Harvard University Press, 1965.

Owen, Norman. "Abaca in Kabikolan: Prosperity without Progress." In *Philippine Social History: Global Trade and Local Transformation,* ed. Alfred McCoy and Eduard de Jesus, 191–216. Honolulu: University of Hawaii Press, 1982.

———. *Prosperity without Progress: Manila Hemp and Material Life in the Colonial Philippines.* Berkeley: University of California Press, 1984.

Pan Mingde. "Zhongguo jindai diandangye zhi yanjiu, 1644–1937" (Research on the pawnshop industry of modern China). Master's thesis, Guoli Taiwan Shifan Daxue, 1983.

Paulson, David. "War and Revolution in North China: The Shandong Base Area." Ph.D. dissertation, Stanford University, 1982.

"Peanut Trade of Shantung." *Chinese Economic Journal* 16:16 (April 19, 1930), 199–200.

"The Peanut Trade of Tsingtao." *Chinese Economic Bulletin* 11:348 (October 22, 1927), 213–14.

Peng Zeyi. "Qingdai qianqi shougongye de fazhan" (The development of handicrafts in the Early Qing). *Zhongguo shi yanjiu*, no. 1 (1981), 43–60.

———, ed. *Zhongguo jindai shougongye shi ziliao* (Sources on the modern history of Chinese handicraft industries). Beijing: Zhonghua shuju, 1962.

Perdue, Peter C. *Exhausting the Earth: State and Peasant in Hunan. 1500–1850*. Cambridge, Mass.: Harvard University Press, 1987.

———. "Water Control in the Dongting Lake Region during the Ming and Qing Periods." *Journal of Asian Studies* 41:4 (August 1982), 747–65.

Perkins, Dwight H. *Agricultural Development in China, 1368–1968*. Chicago: Aldine, 1969.

———. "Government as an Obstacle to Industrialization: The Case of Nineteenth-Century China." *Journal of Economic History* 27:4 (December 1967), 478–92.

Perry, Elizabeth J. "Collective Violence in China, 1880–1980." *Theory and Society* (May 1984), 427–54.

———. *Rebels and Revolutionaries in North China, 1845–1945*. Stanford: Stanford University Press, 1980.

———. "Tax Revolt in Late Qing China: The Small Swords of Shanghai and Liu Depei of Shandong." *Late Imperial China* 6:1 (June 1985), 83–111.

Polachek, James. "Gentry Hegemony in Soochow." In *Conflict and Control in Late Imperial China*, ed. Frederic Wakeman and Carolyn Grant, 211–56. Berkeley: University of California Press, 1975.

Pomeranz, Kenneth. "The Making of a Hinterland: State, Society, and Economy in Inland North China, 1900–1937." Ph.D. dissertation, Yale University, 1988.

———. Review of Prasenjit Duara, *Culture, Power, and the State: Rural North China, 1900–1942*. *Agricultural History* 63:3 (Summer 1989), 108–10.

Qingping xianzhi (Gazetteer of Qingping county). 1936.

Quan guo jingji weiyuanhui, mianye tong zhi weiyuanhui. *Henan sheng mianchan gaijinsuo gongzuo zong baogao* (General report of the office for the improvement of cotton production in Henan province). N.p., 1936.

Rankin, Mary. *Elite Activism and Political Transformation in China: Zhejiang Province, 1865–1911*. Stanford: Stanford University Press, 1986.

Rawski, Thomas G. *China's Republican Economy: An Introduction*. Toronto: University of Toronto-York, Joint Center for Modern East Asia, 1978.

———. *Economic Growth in Prewar China*. Berkeley: University of California Press, 1989.

Records of Former German and Japanese Embassies and Consulates. Microfilm RG 242, T-179. Washington, D.C.: National Archives, 1962.

Ren Jimin. "Heze xian tuikuang Mei mian yi yu minsheng yi" (An account of attempts to expand American cotton in Heze and make the people's livelihood more prosperous). *Xiangcun jianshe xunkan* 3:18–19 (double issue, February 1934), 13–16.

Rosenblith, R. "Forests and Timber Trade of the Chinese Empire." *Forestry Quarterly* 10:4 (December 1912), 647–72.

Ross, Lester. *Environmental Policy in China*. Bloomington: University of Indiana Press, 1988.

Rowe, William T. *Hankow: Commerce and Society in a Chinese City*. Stanford: Stanford University Press, 1984.

Rozman, Gilbert N., ed. *The Modernization of China*. New York: Free Press, 1981.

———. *Urban Networks in Ch'ing China and Tokugawa Japan*. Princeton: Princeton University Press, 1973.

Sands, Barbara N. "An Investigation of the Nature and Extent of Market Integration in Shanxi Province, China, 1928–1945." Ph.D. dissertation, University of Washington, 1985.

Santō Kōshogun Chitai no Chiiki Chōsa. See Tōa Kenkyūsho.

Santō no Mensaku. See Minami Manshū Tetsūdo.

Santō Sainei. See Kokuritsu Pekin Daigaku.

Schmidt, Vera. *Die Deutsche Eisenbahnpolitik in Shantung*. Wiesbaden: Otto Harrassowitz Verlag, 1976.

Schoppa, R. Keith. *Chinese Elites and Political Change: Zhejiang Province in the Early Twentieth Century*. Cambridge, Mass.: Harvard University Press, 1982.

Schrecker, John. *Imperialism and Chinese Nationalism: Germany in Shantung*. Cambridge, Mass.: Harvard University Press, 1971.

Schultz, Theodore. *Transforming Traditional Agriculture*. New Haven: Yale University Press, 1964.

Schwartz, Benjamin. *In Search of Wealth and Power: Yen Fu and the West*. Cambridge, Mass.: Harvard University Press, 1964.

Scott, James C. *Weapons of the Weak*. New Haven: Yale University Press, 1985.

Second Historical Archives of China, Nanjing. Following is a list of the names of files from the Second Historical Archives that are cited by number in the notes:

JD00:AH1164. Lu Jing Shandong tongxianghui chengwei Lu jing dong dao ri shen yuken jiao you guan wenjian (Documents related to the appeal of the association of Shandong residents in Beijing, saying that banditry is growing worse daily in Shandong and pleading for its suppression). July 1918.

JD00:AH1166. Shandong sheng baogao liding shengnei "jiaofei" banfa ji tuixing qingxing you guan wenjian (Documents related to the publication of plans for "suppressing banditry" in Shandong province and their implementation). September to October 1923.

JD1:AH334. Shandong sheng baogao zai qing zhang (Shandong government reports of disasters and accounts). July 1927–October 1928.

JD2:AH110. Shandong sheng zhengfu 1929 nian 4–12 yue gongzuo baogao (Work reports of the Shandong provincial government, April–December 1929).

JD2:AH117–119. Shandong sheng zhengfu 1932 nian 1–12 yue xing zheng baogao (Reports of the Shandong provincial government on administration, January–December 1932).

JD2:AH124. Henan sheng zhengfu 1931 nian 7,8,11,12 yue xingzheng baogao (Reports of the Henan provincial government on administration, July, August, November, and December 1931).

JD2:AH1832. Shandong sheng zhang weiyuanhui qing jiu gaisheng shou zai ge xian de 1931 nian de tianfu juanchu (The accounting commission of Shandong province's request that in order to provide relief for the counties affected by disasters, their 1931 land taxes be excused). May–June 1932.

JD2:AH3082, 3083, 3084. Henan kezheng mianhua shuijuan (The harsh levying of taxes and contributions on cotton in Henan). April 1931–January 1935. (File also includes some earlier documents.)

QZ1038:AH2034. Nong shang gong bu kanzai mianhua ji miansha zhi shengchan jishu de di gao (can que) (Records of the Ministry of Agriculture, Commerce, and Industry on highs and lows in the production and production techniques for cotton, cotton thread, and cotton cloth—incomplete file). Undated, but probably compiled in early to mid 1920s.

"Sha yanxun" (Killing the Salt Intendant). In *Shandong minjian xiaoshuo* (Popular stories from Shandong), 258–68. Jinan: Shandong renmin chubanshe, 1984.

Shandong caizheng gongbao. 1933–35.

Shandong Caozhoufu Heze xian xiangtu zhi (Gazetteer of local places in Heze county, Caozhou prefecture, Shandong). 1888.

"Shandong Gaomi, Wei xian zhi nongcun jiehuo" (Village borrowing in Gaomi and Wei counties, Shandong). *Gong shang banyuekan* 6:4 (February 15, 1934), 49–52.

Shandong gongbao. 1912–13.

Shandong gongyun shi ziliao.

Shandong hewu tekan. 1928–36.

Shandong Huang He shuizai jiuji weiyuanhui. *Shandong Huang He shuizai jiuji baogao shu* (Shandong Yellow River flood relief report). Jinan, 1935–36.

Shandong jianshe gongbao. 1933–36.

Shandong Minzhong jiaoyu yuekan. 1930–37.

Shandong Nan Yun Hu He su jun shiyi zhoubanchu. *Diyijie baogao* (Shandong Canal and Lake Dredging and Restoration Board, first report). Jinan(?), 1915.

Shandong quan sheng caizheng shuomingshu (A book explaining the finances of Shandong province). Jinan, 1913.

Shandong quanye huikan. 1921–24.

"Shandong sheng diyi xingzhengqu xian zheng gaijin an shuomingshu" (An explanation of cases of county administrative reform in the first administrative district of Shandong). *Xiangcun jianshe xunkan* 4:28 (July 1935), *te zai*, 15–20.

Shandong sheng gongzhe jiaoyuke. *Shandong sheng ge xian xiangtu diaocha* (An investigation of local circumstances in each county of Shandong province). Jinan, 1920.

Shandong sheng jianshe yuekan. 1931–32.

Shandong sheng jiansheting. *Junzhi Wanfu Zhushui He zhi* (Report on dredging and repairing the Wanfu and Zhushui rivers). Jinan, 1934.

Shandong sheng jiaotong tu (A map of communications in Shandong province). Jinan: Shandong sheng ditu chubanshe, 1985.

Shandong sheng nongye qu hua weiyuanhui. *Shandong sheng zonghe nongye qu hua* (A comprehensive view of the agriculture of Shandong province as divided into districts). Jinan: Shandong kexue jishu chubanshe, 1982.

Shandong sheng xian zheng jianshe shiyan qu gongbao. 1935–36.

Shandong sheng zhengfu shiyeting. *Shandong gong shang baogao* (Report on industry and commerce in Shandong). Jinan, 1931.

Shandong shengli minzhong jiaoyuguan. *Shandong minjian yule* (Popular games of Shandong). Jinan, 1933.

Shandong shiye gongbao. 1931.

Shandong tongzhi (Comprehensive gazetteer of Shandong). 1915 and 1934 editions. Jinan.

Shandong zazhi. 1908–12.

Shandong zheng su shicha ji (A report of an investigation of government and customs in Shandong). Jinan: n.p., preface dated 1934.

"Shantung Groundnut Trade." *Chinese Economic Bulletin* 9:29 (September 11, 1926), 157.

Shao Chuoran. "Tian Zhongyu bachi Shandong sheng yihui xuanju de chouwen" (The scandal of Tian Zhongyu controlling the elections in the Shandong provincial assembly). *Wenshi ziliao xuanji*, Jinan edition, no. 5 (1978), 43–50.

Shaw, Norman. *Chinese Forest Trees and Timber Supply.* London: T. Fisher Unwin, 1914.

Shen Yi, ed. *Huang He taolun ji* (Collected discussions of the Yellow River). Taibei: Commercial Press, 1971.

Sheridan, James. *China in Disintegration: The Republican Era in Chinese History, 1912–49.* New York: Free Press, 1975.

———. "Chinese Warlords: Tigers or Pussycats?" *Republican China* 10:2 (April 1985), 35–41.

Shi Nianhai. *Zhongguo de Yunhe* (The Grand Canal of China). N.p.: Shixue shuju, n.d.

Shina Shōbetsu. See Tōa Dobunkai.

Shouguang xianzhi (Gazetteer of Shouguang county). 1934.

Shue, Vivienne. *Peasant China in Transition.* New Haven: Yale University Press, 1980.

Shuilibu, Huang He Shuili Weiyuanhui (Bureau of Water Conservancy, Commission on Yellow River Water Conservancy). *Huang He shuili shi shuyao* (Outline of the history of Yellow River water conservancy). Beijing: Shuili dianli chubanshe, 1984.

Shuntian shibao. 1911.

Skinner, G. William. "Chinese Peasants and the Closed Community: An Open and Shut Case." *Comparative Studies in Society and History* 13:3 (1971), 270–81.

———. "Cities and the Hierarchy of Local Systems." In *The City in Late Imperial China*, ed. G. William Skinner, 275–351. Stanford: Stanford University Press, 1977.

———. "Marketing and Social Structure in Rural China," parts 1, 2, and 3. *Journal of Asian Studies* 24:1 (November 1964), 3–44; 24:2 (February 1965), 195–228; 24:3 (May 1965), 363–99.

———. "Regional Urbanization in Nineteenth-century China." In *The City in Late Imperial China*, ed. G. William Skinner, 211–49. Stanford: Stanford University Press, 1977.

———, ed. *The City in Late Imperial China*. Stanford: Stanford University Press, 1977.

Smil, Vaclav. *The Bad Earth: Environmental Degradation in China*. Armonk, N.Y.: M. E. Sharpe, 1983.

———. *Biomass Energies*. New York: Plenum Press, 1983.

———. *Energy in China's Modernization*. Armonk, N.Y.: M. E. Sharpe, 1988.

Smil, Vaclav, and Knowland, William. *Energy in the Developing World: The Real Energy Crisis*. Oxford: Oxford University Press, 1980.

Smith, Arthur H. *Chinese Characteristics*. London: Oliphant, Anderson, and Ferrier, 1900.

———. *Village Life in China*. New York: Fleming, Revell, 1899.

Smith, Carol A. "Regional Economic Systems: Linking Geographical Models and Socioeconomic Problems." In *Regional Analysis*, ed. Carol A. Smith, 3–67. New York: Academic Press, 1976.

Smith, George H. "Improving China's Cotton." *China Weekly Recorder*, December 12, 1923, p. 128.

Sonoda Ikki. *Xin Zhongguo renwu zhi* (Personages of New China). Trans. Huang Huiquan. Shanghai: Liangyou tushu gongsi, 1930. Reprint. Kowloon: Shiyong shuju, 1969.

Spector, Stanley. *Li Hung-chang and the Huai Army*. Seattle: University of Washington Press, 1964.

SSYZ. See Zhongguo shiyebu, guoji maoyiju.

Stross, Randall. "Number Games Rejected: The Misleading Allure of Tenancy Estimates." *Republican China* 10:3 (June 1985), 1–17.

———. *The Stubborn Earth: American Agriculturalists on Chinese Soil, 1898–1937*. Berkeley: University of California Press, 1986.

Sun Jingzhi. *Huabei de jingji dili* (Economic geography of North China). Beijing: Kexueyuan chubanshe, 1958.

Tang Chengtao. "Huo guo yang min de 'Li Ji qianpiao'" (The "Benefit Jining Copper Notes" which brought calamity to the nation and disaster to the people). *Jining shi shiliao*, no. 1 (1983), 89–91.

Tawney, Richard Henry. *Land and Labor in China*. Orig. ed., 1932. Reprint. Armonk, N.Y.: M. E. Sharpe, 1966.

Terada Takanobu. *Sansei Shōnin no Kenkyū: Mindai ni okeru Shōnin oyobi Shōgyo Shihon* (Studies of Shaanxi merchants: merchants and commercial capital in the Ming dynasty). Kyoto: Toyoshi Kenkyusha, 1972.

Thaxton, Ralph. *China Turned Rightside Up*. New Haven: Yale University Press, 1983.

Thorp, James. *Geography of the Soils of China*. Nanjing: National Geological Survey of China, 1936.

Tian Hong. "Luxi nongfu shenghuo de yibian" (An account of the lives of women in western Shandong). *Dagong bao*, July 8, 1934, p. 11.

Tianjin mianhua yun xiao gaikuang (An outline of the shipping and distribution of cotton in Tianjin). Tianjin: Jin cheng yinhang Tianjin fenhang, 1937.

Tiedemann, Rolf. "The Persistence of Banditry: Incidents in Border Districts of the North China Plain." *Modern China* 8:4 (October 1982), 395–433.

Tilly, Charles. "Food Supply and Public Order in Modern Europe." In *The Formation of National States in Western Europe*, ed. Charles Tilly, 380–455. Princeton: Princeton University Press, 1975.

———. "Reflections on the History of European State-Making." In *The Formation of National States in Western Europe*, ed. Charles Tilly, pp. 3–83. Princeton: Princeton University Press, 1975.

Ting, Leonard G. *Recent Developments in China's Cotton Industry*. Shanghai: China Institute of Pacific Relations, 1936.

Tōa Dobunkai. *Shina Shōbetsu Zenshi* (The complete book of the provinces of China). Vol. 4: *Shandong*. Tokyo: Tōa Dobunkai, 1918.

Tōa Kenkyūsho. *Santō Koshōgun Chitai no Chiiki Chōsa* (Areal report on lake region of Shandong province). Report no. 14, class C, no. 158-D. Jinan(?): Tōa Kenkyusho, 1940.

Todd, Oliver J. *Two Decades in China, Comprising Technical Papers, Magazine Articles, Newspaper Stories and Official Reports Connected with Work under His Own Observation*. Beijing: Association of Chinese and American Engineers, 1938.

Tongji yuebao. 1929–30.

Tsao, Lien-en. "The Currency System in Manchuria." *Chinese Economic Journal and Bulletin* 6:4 (April 1930), 375–91.

"Tunmin kang jiao dijia de douzheng" (The struggle of the camp people against paying for the Land). *Jining shi shiliao*, no. 2 (1983), 73–76.

Tyler, William Ferdinand. *Notes on the Hoang Ho or Yellow River*. Special Series no. 29. Shanghai: Imperial Maritime Customs, 1906.

Vermeer, E. B. *Economic Development in Provincial China: The Central Shaanxi since 1930*. Cambridge, Eng.: Cambridge University Press, 1988.

———. "Income Inequality in Rural China." *China Quarterly*, no. 89 (March 1982), 1–33.

Wakeman, Frederic, Jr. "Policing Modern Shanghai." *China Quarterly*, no. 115 (September 1988), 408–40.

———. *Strangers at the Gate: Social Disorder in South China, 1839–1861.* Berkeley: University of California Press, 1966.

Wallerstein, Immanuel. *The Modern World-System.* 2 vols. New York: Academic Press, 1976.

Wan Guangwei. "Minguo chunian Shandong zheng Dang huodong de neimou yu sheng yihui de chouwen" (The plots involved in government and Party activities in Shandong in the early Republic and the scandals of the provincial assembly). *Wenshi ziliao xuanji,* Jinan edition, no. 5 (1978), 32–42.

Wang Jiaoming. "Zhang Zongchang xing bai jilue" (A recollection of Zhang Zongchang's rise and fall). In *Beiyang junfa shiliao xuanji* (A collection of selected historical materials on the northern warlords), ed. Du Chunhe, Li Binsheng, and Qiu Quan, vol. 2. Beijing: Shehui kexue chubanshe, 1981.

Wang Mengshang. "Zhuyi jiejue nongcun nengyuan wenti" (Pay attention to solving the energy problems of rural villages). *Guangming ribao,* July 19, 1980, p. 4.

Wang Ruizheng and Zhu Bi. "Wei Chi, Xiu Zhi, tongzhi zai Linqing de geming huodong huiyi" (Recollections of the revolutionary activities of Comrades Wei Chi and Xiu Zhi in Linqing). *Liaocheng diqu dangshi ziliao,* no. 10 (1984), 3–10.

Wang Shouzhong. "Qing mo Shandong shouhui lu kuang li quan yundong" (The movement for recovery of rights over railways and mines in late Qing Shandong). In *Zhongguo difang shi zhi luncong* (Collection of essays on Chinese local history), ed. Zhongguo difang zhi xiehui, 247–65. Beijing: Zhonghua shuju, 1984.

Wang Xiangcen. "Heze shiyan xian baozhen xiang xiang nong xuexiao" (The rural school in Baozhen district of Heze experimental county), pts. 1 and 2. *Xiangcun jianshe xunkan* 4:14 (December 1934), 10–25 and 4:18 (February 1935), 10–18.

Wang, Yeh-chien. *The Land Tax in Imperial China, 1753–1908.* Cambridge, Mass.: Harvard University Press, 1973.

Weber, Max. *Economy and Society.* Ed. Guenther Roth and Claus Wittich. Berkeley: University of California Press, 1977.

Wiens, Thomas. *The Micro-Economics of Peasant Economy: China, 1920–1940.* New York: Garland, 1982.

Will, Pierre Etienne. *Bureaucracy and Famine in Eighteenth-Century China.* Stanford: Stanford University Press, 1990.

Winkler, Robert, and Hays, William. *Statistics: Probability, Inference, and Decision.* 2d ed. New York: Holt, Rinehart, and Winston, 1975.

Wittfogel, Karl A. *Oriental Despotism.* New Haven: Yale University Press, 1957.

Wolf, Eric. "Closed Corporate Peasant Communities in Meso-America and Java." *Southwestern Journal of Anthropology* 13:1 (Spring 1957), 1–18.

Wong, R. Bin, and Will, Pierre Etienne. *Nourish the People: China's State Civilian Granary System, 1650–1850.* Ann Arbor: University of Michigan Press, 1991.

Wou, Odoric Y. K. "Development, Underdevelopment and Degeneration: The Introduction of Rail Transport into Honan." *Asian Profile* 12:3 (June 1984), 215–30.

Wright, Mary C. *The Last Stand of Chinese Conservatism: The T'ung-chih Restoration, 1862–74.* Stanford: Stanford University Press, 1957.

Wu Chengming. "Wo Guo ban zhimindi ban fengjian guonei shichang" (The internal market of our country in the half-colonial, half-feudal period). *Lishi yanjiu*, no. 168 (April 1984), 110–21.

———. *Zhongguo zibenzhuyi de mengya* (The sprouts of capitalism in China). Beijing: Renmin chubanshe, 1985.

Wu Guogui. "Yutang xinghuo—Jining shi Yutang jiangyuan gongyun gai" (Yutang sparks—an outline of the labor movement at the Jining soy sauce factory). *Shandong gongyun shi ziliao* (Materials on the history of the Shandong labor movement), no. 16 (February 10, 1985), 12–17.

Wu Jianyong. "Qingdai Beijing de liangshi gongying" (The grain supply of Qing dynasty Beijing). In *Beijing lishi yu xianshi yanjiu* (Research on the history and present condition of Beijing), 167–86. Beijing: Zhonghua shuju, 1989.

Wu Jinzan. "Zhonghua Minguo linye fazhi zhi yanjiu—Minguo yuan nian zhi Minguo sanshiwu nian." (Research on the forestry rules of the Republic of China—from the first year of the Republic to the thirty-fifth). Ph.D. dissertation, Zhongguo Wenhua Daxue, Taibei, 1982.

Wu Tongju, ed. *Zai xu xing shui jin jian* (A further continuation of the mirror of water works). Vol. 10. Taibei: Wenhai chubanshe, 1966.

Wu Xiangxiang, ed. *Lu an shan hou yuebao tekan—tielu* (Special report on the Shandong question—railroads). Minguo shiliao congkan (Series of Republican history materials), no. 17. Original ed., 1923. Reprint. Taibei: Chuanji wenxue chubanshe, 1971.

Wu Yunxian. "Liaocheng ke shu yu chubanye de xing shuai gaikuang" (An outline of the rise and decline of the book engraving and publishing industries of Liaocheng). *Wenshi ziliao xuanji*, Jinan edition, no. 14 (1982), 109–28.

Wucheng xian zhi xu bian (A further edition of the gazetteer of Wucheng county). 1912.

Xia Lianju. "Shandong duli qianhou" (Before and after Shandong's independence). *Wenshi ziliao xuanji*, Jinan edition, no. 12 (1981), 20–55.

Xiangcun jianshe banyuekan. 1933.

Xiangcun jianshe xunkan. 1934–36.

Xiao Dichen, ed. *Shandong minjian chuanshuo* (Traditional popular stories of Shandong). Jinan: Shandong shengli minzhong jiaoyuguan, 1933.

Xie Xinhou. "Liaocheng Shifan xuesheng de geming fengchao" (The revolutionary agitation of students at Liaocheng Normal School). In *Guang you chunqiu: Shandong geming douzheng huiyi congshu* (Glorious peaks: a collection of recollections of Shandong revolutionary struggles), ed. Liaocheng diqu xingzheng gongzhe chuban bangongshi, 36–49. Jinan: Shandong renmin chubanshe, 1981.

Xu Puqi and Zhang Shouqian. "Daming Xingtai liang xian shicha gaiyao" (Outline of an inquiry in the two counties of Daming and Xingtai). *Hebei yuekan* 1:3 (March 1933), 1–12.

Xu Shiguang. *Puyang heshang ji* (A record of [Work] on the river in Puyang). N.p., 1915.

Xu Shuren. "Wo zai xiang jianshe pai de huodong yu jian wen" (My activities and what I saw and heard in the rural reconstruction group). *Wenshi ziliao xuanji*, Jinan edition, no. 2 (1982), 50–68.

Xu Tan. "Ming Qing shiqi de Linqing shangye" (The commerce of Linqing in the Ming and Qing periods). *Zhongguo jingji shi yanjiu*, no. 2 (1986), 135–57.

Xu Yunbei. "Lu Xibei dang de jianshe pian duan huiyi" (A short recollection of the building of the Party in northwestern Shandong). In *Guang you chunqiu: Shandong geming douzheng huiyi congshu* (Glorious peaks: a collection of recollections of Shandong revolutionary struggles), ed. Liaocheng diqu xingzheng gongzhe chuban bangongshi, 1–15. Jinan: Shandong renmin chubanshe, 1981.

———. "Xuzhuang dang zhibu de zaoqi huodong" (The activities of the Xuzhuang Party branch in its early period). In *Guang you chunqiu: Shandong geming douzheng huiyi congshu* (Glorious peaks: a collection of recollections of Shandong revolutionary struggles), ed. Liaocheng diqu xingzheng gongzhe chuban bangongshi, 54–64. Jinan: Shandong renmin chubanshe, 1981.

Yan Guangyao, Sun Bocai, and Zhou Chengpeng. "Diaocha Shandong zhi nongye zhuangkuang" (Investigating the agricultural situation in Shandong). *Kexue* 4:5 (January 1919), 460–72.

Yan Zhongping. *Zhongguo mian fangzhi shi gao 1289–1937* (Draft history of cotton and textiles in China 1289–1937). Beijing: Kexue chubanshe, 1963.

Yang Junan, ed. *Nong yan he nong ge* (Rural sayings and rural songs). Beijing: Beijing University Press, 1932.

Yang Zhengtai. "Ming Qing Linqing de sheng shuai yu dili tiaojian de bianhua" (The glory and decline of Linqing in the Ming and Qing periods and changes in geographic conditions). *Lishi dili*, no. 3 (1983), 115–20.

Yongzheng zhupi yuzhi (Vermilion endorsements and palace memorials of the Yongzheng period). 10 vols. Taibei: Wenyuan, 1965.

Yuan Jingbo. " 'Yan Ji zhixian' yu 'Jining huochezhan' xiujian xiao shi kao-lue" (A short history and look at the sources on 'The Yanzhou Jining Line,' and 'Jining Railway Station'). *Jining wenshi ziliao*, no. 1 (March 1986), 3–9.

"Yucheng xian shehui diaocha" (An investigation of society in Yucheng county). *Nongye zhoubao* 4:19 (May 17, 1935), 668–69.

Zelin, Madeleine. "Huo-hao Kuei-kung." Ph.D. dissertation, University of California, Berkeley, 1979.

———. *The Magistrate's Tael.* Berkeley: University of California Press, 1984.

Zhang Yufa. *Zhongguo xiandaihua de ququ yanjiu: Shandong sheng, 1860–1916.* (Regional studies of Chinese modernization: Shandong province, 1860–1916). Taibei: Zhongyang yanjiuyuan, jindai shi yanjiusuo, 1982.

"Zhang Zongchang zhi xia de Shandong" (Shandong under Zhang Zongchang). *Xiangdao zhoubao*, no. 131 (September 25, 1925), 1205–6.

Zhengfu gongbao. 1916.

Zhong Gong Jining Shi wei dangshi ziliao zhengli xiao zu bangongshi. "Jining xinghuo" (Jining sparks). *Jining shi shiliao*, no. 1 (1983), 40–51.

Zhong Zhongming. "Yanggu Poli baodong huiyi" (Recollections of the uprising at Poli, Yanggu). In *Guang you chunqiu: Shandong geming douzheng huiyi congshu* (Glorious peaks: a collection of recollections of Shandong revolutionary struggles), ed. Liaocheng diqu xingzheng gongzhe chuban bangongshi, 27–35. Jinan: Shandong renmin chubanshe, 1981.

Zhongguo dier lishi danganguan. See also Second Historical Archives of China, Nanjing.

Zhongguo dier lishi danganguan, eds. *Zhi An zhanzheng* (The war between the Zhili and Anfu cliques). Part of *Zhonghua Minguo shi dangan ziliao congkan* (Series of archival materials on the history of the Chinese Republic). Ed. Wang Shijun. Nanjing: Jiangsu renmin chubanshe, 1980.

Zhongguo diyi lishi danganguan. See also First Historical Archives of China, Beijing.

Zhongguo diyi lishi danganguan and Beijing Shifan Daxue lishixi, eds. *Xinhai geming qian shi nianjian minbian dangan shiliao* (Historical material from archival sources on popular disturbances in the ten-year period before the 1911 Revolution). Beijing: Zhonghua shuju, 1985.

Zhongguo haiguan zong shuiwusi (Chinese Maritime Customs Administration). *Decennial Report, 1912–1921.* Shanghai, 1923.

Zhongguo jiaotongbu, jiaotong shi weiyuanhui. *Jiaotong shi* (History of communications). Nanjing: Jiaotongbu, 1937.

Zhongguo jiaotongbu youzheng zongju. *Postal Atlas of China.* Nanjing: General Directorate of Posts, 1933.

Zhongguo jindai huobi shi weiyuanhui, eds. (Sometimes also listed under Wei Jianyu, ed.). *Zhongguo jindai huobi shi ziliao* (Historical materials on the modern history of Chinese currency). Vol 2. Shanghai: Chunlian chubanshe, 1965.

Zhongguo jindai ming ren tu jian (Famous people of modern China). Taibei: Tian yi chubanshe, 1977.

Zhongguo jindai shi yanjiushe and Shandong Shifan Daxue lishixi, eds. *Qing Shilu Shandong shiliao xuan* (A selection of material from the veritable records of the Qing dynasty pertaining to Shandong history). Jinan: Qilu shushe, 1984.

Zhongguo Renmin Daxue, Qing shi yanjiu suo, *Kang Yong Qian shiqi cheng xiang renmin fankang douzheng ziliao* (Materials on the antitax struggles of city and county people in the Kangxi, Yongzheng, and Qianlong reigns). Beijing: Zhonghua shuju, 1979.

Zhongguo shiyebu, guoji maoyiju. *Zhongguo shiye zhi, Shandong sheng* (Industrial gazetteer of Shandong province). Nanjing: Guoji maoyiju, 1934.

Zhou Fu. See Chen Yunlong.

Zhu Bingnan. "Zhongguo zhi yingye shui" (China's business tax). *Shehuixue zazhi* 6:3 (September 1935), 343–463.

Index